THE BEST PLAYS OF 1958-1959

*Illustrated with photographs, and
with drawings by* HIRSCHFELD

THE
BURNS MANTLE
YEARBOOK

from "A Touch
of the Poet"

THE BEST PLAYS OF 1958-1959

EDITED BY LOUIS KRONENBERGER

DODD, MEAD & COMPANY

NEW YORK · 1959 · TORONTO

"A Touch of the Poet": By Eugene O'Neill. Unpublished dramatic composition copyrighted 1946 by Eugene O'Neill. First published in 1957 by Yale University Press and © reserved by Carlotta Monterey O'Neill. All rights reserved. All inquiries regarding this play should be addressed to the Richard J. Madden Play Co., Inc., 522 Fifth Avenue, New York, N. Y.

"The Pleasure of His Company": By Samuel Taylor with Cornelia Otis Skinner. © Copyright 1958, as an unpublished work, by Samuel Taylor and Cornelia Otis Skinner and © Copyright 1959 by Samuel Taylor and Cornelia Otis Skinner. Reprinted by permission of Random House, Inc. See CAUTION notice below. All inquiries should be addressed to the authors' agent: MCA Artists, Ltd., 598 Madison Avenue, New York 22, N. Y.

"Epitaph for George Dillon": By John Osborne and Anthony Creighton. Reprinted by permission of the publisher, Criterion Books, Inc., 257 Fourth Avenue, New York 10, N. Y. Copyright © 1958 by John Osborne and Anthony Creighton. See CAUTION notice below. All inquiries should be addressed to Harold Freedman, Brandt and Brandt Dramatic Department, 101 Park Avenue, New York, N. Y.

"The Disenchanted": By Budd Schulberg and Harvey Breit. © Copyright 1959 by Budd Schulberg and Harvey Breit. Based on the novel of the same name, Copyright 1950 by Budd Schulberg. Reprinted by permission of Random House, Inc. See CAUTION notice below. All inquiries should be addressed to the authors' agent: Ad Schulberg, 277 Park Avenue, New York 17, N. Y.

"The Cold Wind and the Warm": By S. N. Behrman. Suggested by his *New Yorker* series and book, "The Worcester Account." © Copyright 1958, as an unpublished work, by S. N. Behrman. © Copyright 1959 by S. N. Behrman. Reprinted by permission of Random House, Inc. "The Cold Wind and the Warm" is the sole property of the author and is fully protected by copyright. It may not be acted by professionals or amateurs without formal permission and the payment of a royalty. See CAUTION notice below. All inquiries should be addressed to the author's agent: Harold Freedman, Brandt and Brandt Dramatic Department, Inc., 101 Park Avenue, New York, N. Y.

"J. B.": By Archibald MacLeish. Copyright © 1956, 1957, 1958 by Archibald MacLeish. Selections reprinted by permission of and arrangement with Houghton Mifflin Company, the authorized publishers. See CAUTION notice below. All inquiries should be addressed to Houghton Mifflin Company, 2 Park Street, Boston 7, Mass.

"Requiem for a Nun": By William Faulkner and Ruth Ford. From the novel by William Faulkner, adapted to the stage by Ruth Ford. Copyright 1950, 1951 by William Faulkner and © Copyright 1959 by William Faulkner and Ruth Ford. Reprinted by permission of Random House, Inc. See CAUTION notice below. All inquiries should be addressed to the authors' agent: Harold Ober Associates, Inc., 40 East 49th Street, New York 17, N. Y.

"Sweet Bird of Youth": By Tennessee Williams. Copyright © 1959 by Two Rivers Enterprises, Inc. All rights reserved. Reprinted by permission of New Directions. See CAUTION notice below. All inquiries should be addressed to the author's agent: Audrey Wood, MCA Artists, Ltd., 598 Madison Avenue, New York 22, N. Y.

"A Raisin in the Sun": By Lorraine Hansberry. © Copyright 1958, as an unpublished work, by Lorraine Hansberry and © Copyright 1959 by Lorraine Hansberry. Reprinted by permission of Random House, Inc. See CAUTION notice below. All inquiries should be addressed to the publisher: Random House, Inc., 457 Madison Avenue, New York 22, N. Y.

"Kataki": By Shimon Wincelberg. Copyright © 1959 by Shimon Wincelberg. Included by permission of the author. Stock and amateur rights controlled by the author: c/o Paul Kohner, Inc., 9169 Sunset Boulevard, Hollywood 46, Calif.; and c/o Jay Garon-Brooke Associates, Inc., 224 East 33rd Street, New York 16, N. Y.

© BY DODD, MEAD & COMPANY, INC., 1959

Library of Congress Catalog Card Number: 20-21432

CAUTION: Professionals and amateurs are hereby warned that the above-mentioned plays, being fully protected under the Copyright Laws of the United States of America, the British Empire, including the Dominion of Canada, and all other countries of the Copyright Union, the Berne Convention, and the Universal Copyright Convention, are subject to royalty. All rights, including professional, amateur, motion picture, recitation, lecturing, public reading, radio and television broadcasting, and the rights of translation into foreign languages, are strictly reserved. Particular emphasis is laid on the question of readings, permission for which must be secured from the author's agent or publisher in writing. All inquiries should be addressed to the author's agent or publisher. In their present form these plays are dedicated to the reading public only.

PRINTED IN THE UNITED STATES OF AMERICA

EDITOR'S NOTE

IN editing this forty-second volume in the *Best Plays* series, I continue to find myself under very pleasant obligations. Once more my wife, Emmy Plaut, has provided help that is more fairly called collaboration. For general editorial assistance I am immensely indebted to Barbara Kamb. I must also thank, for the use of photographs, the Editors of *Life* Magazine and Doris O'Neill; for the use of its tabulation of Hits and Flops, *Variety* and Mr. Abel Green; and for editorial help, Garrison Sherwood. Particular thanks are due, for their reports, to Miss Cassidy, Mr. Hobson and Mr. Hewes, and for very kindly granting the use of their sketches, to Boris Aronson, Oliver Smith, Ben Edwards, Rouben Ter-Arutunian, Irene Sharaff and Alvin Colt.

And it remains, as always, a great pleasure to be associated in this project with Mr. Hirschfeld.

LOUIS KRONENBERGER

CONTENTS

Editor's Note v

Summaries of the Seasons
   The Season on Broadway 3
   The Season in Chicago 39
   The Season in London 43
   Off Broadway 49

The Ten Best Plays
   A Touch of the Poet 59
   The Pleasure of His Company 78
   Epitaph for George Dillon 101
   The Disenchanted 121
   The Cold Wind and the Warm 144
   J. B. 168
   Requiem for a Nun 189
   Sweet Bird of Youth 209
   A Raisin in the Sun 232
   Kataki 255

A Graphic Glance by Hirschfeld 275

Plays Produced in New York 289

Facts and Figures
   Variety's Tabulation of Financial Hits and Flops . . 341
   Statistical Summary 343
   Long Runs on Broadway 344
   New York Drama Critics Circle Awards 346
   Pulitzer Prize Winners 347
   Books on the Theatre 349
   Previous Volumes of Best Plays 354
   Where and When They Were Born 369
   Necrology 377
   The Decades' Toll 389

CONTENTS

INDICES
- Index of Authors and Playwrights 391
- Index of Plays and Casts 394
- Index of Producers, Directors, Designers, Stage Managers, Composers, Lyricists and Choreographers 401

THE SEASON IN PICTURES
(Photographs follow page 86)

"Freres Jacques" scene from the revue "La Plume de Ma Tante"

Outstanding Broadway Performances 1958-1959

Juanita Hall, Conrad Yama and Miyoshi Umeki in "Flower Drum Song"

Sidney Poitier and Claudia McNeil in "A Raisin in the Sun"

Dolores Hart, Cyril Ritchard and Cornelia Otis Skinner in "The Pleasure of His Company"

Roddy McDowall, Tammy Grimes and Jack Gilford in "Look After Lulu"

Robert Stephens, Alison Leggatt and Avril Elgar in "Epitaph for George Dillon"

Sig Arno and Maureen Stapleton in "The Cold Wind and the Warm"

Backdrop for "Juno" designed by Oliver Smith

Ben Edwards' set design for "A Touch of the Poet"

Costume sketches for "Redhead" by Rouben Ter-Arutunian

Design by Rouben Ter-Arutunian for a drop in "Redhead"

Costume designs: "A Touch of the Poet" by Ben Edwards, and "Juno" by Irene Sharaff

Boris Aronson's set design for "J. B."

Costume designs by Alvin Colt for "Destry Rides Again" and "First Impressions"

Set design by Oliver Smith for "Destry Rides Again"

Costume designs by Irene Sharaff for "Flower Drum Song"

Backdrop design by Oliver Smith for "Flower Drum Song"

THE SEASON IN PICTURES

Scene from "A Majority of One," with Gertrude Berg and Cedric Hardwicke

Rosemary Harris and Jason Robards, Jr., in "The Disenchanted"

Gwen Verdon in "Redhead"

Eric Portman and Helen Hayes in "A Touch of the Poet"

SUMMARIES OF THE SEASONS

THE SEASON ON BROADWAY

BROADWAY'S roll call of names during 1958-59 was resounding enough: Eugene O'Neill, Tennessee Williams, Elmer Rice, S. N. Behrman, Noel Coward, John Osborne, Paul Osborn, Samuel Taylor, Sean O'Casey, Marc Blitzstein, Harold Rome, Norman Corwin, Abe Burrows, Richard Rodgers and Oscar Hammerstein, Walter and Jean Kerr, Betty Comden and Adolph Green, Budd Schulberg and Harvey Breit and—from farther afield—William Faulkner, Archibald MacLeish and Pearl Buck. It had certainly a bracing sound to it, and it made a brave statistic. But when the trumpets had died away, there remained the business of how great an occasion they were blown for; and when the statistics were broken down, somehow the season itself seemed to have broken down with them. There had been much to talk about, even to argue about and raise one's voice over; but rarely had there been the theatrical shock, the dramatic high voltage of something new, fresh, vibrant—and all the better for turning up unheralded. Not really often, for that matter, was there the sense of sustained talent moving along a straight track, or even of something powerful and exciting if not quite well ordered and controlled.

In addition there were some amiable trifles and upsy-downsy bits of carpentering, some honorable failures and colorful messes, or the shows with a good profile but a bad full face, with a good first act but a collapsing second, or the shows redeemed by their acting or enhanced by their sets—all sorts of things in which the part was better than the whole, or the production better than the play, so that, should anyone be speaking at their funerals, there would be suitable and saving things to be said. But all too often the occasions themselves resembled funerals, with far more to suppress about the dear departed than to extol.

Just what had happened to create a season less disappointing because of something untidy about the result than because of something unworthy about the intentions is perhaps not too hard to discover. It derived in part from the ever more derivative nature of show business which, when it should be seeking a real grip on its own artistic problems, cannot keep its clumsy or grasping or impious hands off the other arts. It partly derived from the showy nature of the theatre which too often regards theatricality as an end in itself rather than a means to something larger. It derived finally from Broadway's catch-as-catch-cannibal methods, whereby "flexibility"—which means any sort of last-gasp or last-minute rewrite—is had at the cost of probity, significance or good sense. Because of this final weakness, too often what fails has no more character than what succeeds has merit. Thus Elmer Rice's *Cue for Passion* is simply a modern *Hamlet* à la Freud; Paul Osborn wastes his time and talent slumming in the world of Suzie Wong; Abe Burrows clumps into the vicarage world of *Pride and Prejudice* and promptly does away with the vicar; Rodgers and Hammerstein, in *Flower Drum Song*, demonstrate that East is East and West is West and never the twain shall differ; and Mr. and Mrs. Kanin, in *Rashomon*, do over a celebrated movie in kindergarten psychological colors and matching clichés. All these people, it will be noted, are busy adapting other people's work, and often adulterating it into the bargain.

Now it can be pleaded that every age has re-created certain great and archetypal figures of history and legend in its own image; and that those who last season turned to Shakespeare and the Bible, or Lincoln and Jane Austen, could cite Oedipus, Faust, Don Juan and Hamlet himself for their purpose. But the nub lies just there, in how exalted is the usual purpose of adaptation on Broadway. Whether or not the endless adapting on Broadway last season was a dire portent, it was clearly not a chance phenomenon. No one will question that Broadway's better producers want good *plays*, or that Broadway's more creative-minded playwrights want to write them. And when Broadway gets something as richly promising as *A Raisin in the Sun* or as amply fulfilled as *Long Day's Journey into Night* it exults in a sense of its own vitality no less than its own virtuousness. But it sometimes seems to me that Broadway is almost happier with adaptations and rewrites and arrangements for four hands; with starting off with someone else's story, since there it is, tangibly, in book form rather than mistily in brain form, and since *from the very first moment* it asks for rewrite, it necessitates tinkering and tampering, it literally sets carpentry above creation and gimmickry above form. Such a method has its points no doubt, and can even point to its undoubted successes; but on a Broadway that over the last fifty years has produced hardly more than half a dozen playwrights of any real stature and stamina, are we not entitled to ask: Have we today many more than half a dozen producing firms who care about stature and stamina, or do very much to help them along?

Fortunately, though the season on a creative basis was distinctly disappointing, it had its very redeeming special occasions, its unlooked-for treats, its satisfying evenings with the classics. Fortu-

"Angels" in various guises descending upon a new Broadway offering

nately, too, scene and costume designers did for the eye what playwrights failed to do for the mind; and actors often enhanced, and occasionally transformed, what they were performing in. All these things left Broadway itself, at the end of the season, better off than they leave *The Best Plays*. *The Best Plays* cannot bring you the scenery that brightened *Rashomon*, the acting that transformed *A Majority of One*, or the top dances in *Destry Rides Again*. It was another of those seasons when choosing the Best Plays turned out to be troublesome, all the more so if they were to *be* plays and not simply stage novelties or theatre pieces. Thus, whatever the claims of a *Rivalry*, in which Lincoln and Douglas locked horns, clearly—and very renownedly—it possessed the form of a debate, it took its eloquence from the debaters, and owed any additional effectiveness to the way it was staged and spoken. It is perhaps easier to justify what was often eliminated from the Best Ten than what was sometimes included. Still, the point there is simple enough: in a pinch, the misuse of talent has taken precedence of the absence of any. In a happier season, Mr. Faulkner and Mr. Williams would perhaps, whatever their prestige, not have qualified. But in such a season as this, a Faulkner whose trigger sometimes catches, or a Williams whose aim is wild, still outrank those who know nothing of how to handle a gun, or who bag what is hardly worth bringing down.

As is usual and, all in all, logical, the season proved more rewarding for drama than for comedy. In two or three of the best plays—*Epitaph for George Dillon, A Raisin in the Sun*—there was a blending of both. Comedy, again, was certainly the successful side of Mr. Behrman's play and the better part of Mr. Williams's. (In a certain sense, indeed, the comedy interludes of "serious" plays represent almost the best comic work being done these days, for such interludes spring spontaneously out of character or situation, and offer genuine comment on human relationships or commentary on social attitudes. By doing this relevantly and naturally, they often come to be real theatrical ozone, where in all but the best of our avowed comedies, a basic situation is attenuated, adulterated and finally done to death by gags and gimmicks that are more like carbon monoxide. What there seems to be least hope for on Broadway today is genuine vital comedy, since wherever it might be usefully savage, it winds up less tiger than tabby cat; and wherever it treats of manners and attitudes, it shows almost no elegance or tone. Wackiness is where Broadway's comedy oftenest shines; but even its wackiness is largely machine-made now.)

The season got off to an early serious start with Eugene O'Neill's *A Touch of the Poet*, one of the two plays in his never-completed eleven-play cycle that O'Neill did not tear up. In this play, which—taking place near Boston in 1828—was originally intended to open the long family chronicle, O'Neill, as in *Long Day's Journey into Night*, dramatized in the course of one agitated day the downward movement of a lifetime. In this play again, as in *The Iceman Cometh*, O'Neill told of one whose life would crumble except for his dreams, and whose dreams themselves fall apart at last. And in this play, as again and again in his other work, O'Neill mingled centripetal force with centrifugal wastefulness, the sense of giant strength with the effect of giant sprawl, and sure theatrical instincts with a wavering dramatic imagination.

O'Neill's hero, Con Melody, was an Irish officer of peasant birth who has become a hard-up, hard-drinking innkeeper, but who under the influence of booze and Byronism nurses a gilded dream of being a fine-born gentleman. Sneering at the Yankees as vulgar traders while enjoying none of their trade, he finds that his fiery daughter Sara has in tow a young American whose family want no truck with the peatbog Melodys. Con rides forth swaggeringly to avenge such an insult, only to stumble blankly home, all the posturing and pride crushed out of him, to kill that last remnant of his dream, his blooded mare.

Con stands apart from O'Neill's other tosspot dream-addicts in having a family about him: a lowborn wife who loves him, a daughter increasingly roused to hate. In the effect of his braggart ways on his family, in his costly game of lies-and-consequences, he smacks of Sean O'Casey's Paycock. Though the consequences are not the same—Con, having been broken, is reborn and Americanized—in both plays the character much surpasses the action. In *A Touch of the Poet* there is too much lurking farce for first-rate drama. Its best scenes have a tense, grandly flaring quality of theatre that is heroic without being hollow; but beyond constant letdowns of both flatness and verbosity, there is never the squared, cubed, nth-powered intensity of cumulative drama. And the final broken-but-reborn note is too last-minute a symbol—actually points too much toward a sequel ahead. But though overlong and very uneven, the play has impact in a theatre whose playwrights generally stand much closer to Con Melody than to O'Neill in trying to pass for what they are not.

There followed several plays with a touch of the neurotic about them. N. Richard Nash's *Handful of Fire* had the vividly vague Latin-American look of Tennessee Williams' *Camino Real*. In the shadow of a bordello and a gambling joint, love's fire goes in for chain-smoking—madam loves racketeer, racketeer loves girl with smudged morals but pure heart, girl loves peasant who, hurt by corruption, would fain turn corrupt. In a swirl of bought love and vended lust, everyone gets a bit tarnished and defeated. The cutlery of gangsterdom flashes but nowhere stabs, the henchmen of gangsterdom stand waiting but never close in; and over a horse trough, at length, girl and peasant are purified and made one.

As in his *See the Jaguar* and *Girls of Summer,* Mr. Nash favored agony and symbolism. But *Handful of Fire* was all agitated Love and Life, with scant evidence of loving and living. Too often characters, cast in roles that smelled of camphor, indulged in rhetoric that smacked of corn. Despite effective moments, the play seldom distinguished symbols from stencils, or vibrancy from mere tremolo. Mr. Nash was far more rewarding when humorously indulging in the outright corn of the first half of *The Rainmaker*.

In *Comes a Day*, Speed Lamkin provided another example of the current Somewhere-South-of-Natchez school of writing that substitutes knife blades for nosegays and sadist's whips for planter's punch. If it yet includes mention of a bird and a bottle, the bird, here, has its head cut off through maniac rage and the bottle is never out of its fuddled owner's hands. The befuddled owner is also an impoverished paterfamilias whose implacable wife wants a rich husband for their daughter, without caring a straw that he is an upstart or more than two straws that he may be a monster. Even when his inhumanly cruel nature becomes plain, Mother still wants him; it takes psychopathic violence plus an epileptic fit to rule him out.

George C. Scott acted the monster with striking bravura—all abrupt key changes, thumped pedals and jangling discords—and helped make the play, at times, theatrically strong meat. But *Comes the Day* was horrifying at the expense of being very little else. There was much plain speaking but little reality, much hard hitting but not much intensity—the Freud and the fury were only gooseflesh deep.

Vesuvian drama poured forth, too, in Michael V. Gazzo's *The Night Circus*. Here, as in his *Hatful of Rain*, Mr. Gazzo proved garishly grim; his scene—shifting between a crummy bar and a sleazy apartment—fitted the play's inwardly lonely, outwardly violent, anarchically dreaming characters. In pre-nuptial revolt against a stodgy suburban future, a beautiful girl ran off on her wedding day with a hardboiled, memory-tortured sailor. What followed involved the unborn child of the fiancé she had walked out on, the father she drives to suicide, and her tempestuous life with the sailor who at length walks out on her.

For picturing a rootless tangled world, for portraying a Jazz-Age no less than Beat-Generation heroine—a self-dramatizing, greedily restless girl who destroys others on the way to destroying herself—Mr. Gazzo had an ear for what is harsh, an eye for what is tarnished. But his chronicle of lives near precipices and gutters was overdone and hence lurid, his talk was florid and even embarrassing. In time so much violence quite outlawed intensity; so much blatant naturalistic detail seemed not real life but mere stage stuff.

Neurosis quieted down somewhat in Albert Beich and William H.

Jessica Tandy and Hume Cronyn in "The Man in the Dog Suit"

Wright's *The Man in the Dog Suit*, which told of a mousy fellow who worked in his wife's family's bank and quailed before her snobbish, stuffy, Babbitty relatives. Suddenly he took to going about in a dog suit he had worn to a costume party, and to enacting his untidy daydreams. Now he bit a lady and now a banker; now he scandalized the town, now horrified his in-laws, till the bank bellowed at him: "The desk or the dog suit!"

Not without small virtues as a stage piece, the play as a whole had no fresh or sustained effect. The man in the dog suit was the same who in a dozen previous works had wooed conformity to achieve security, who first shook with fright and then shook himself free. The in-laws were cut to a pattern, the satire was too close to a formula—or to farce; and the end was too glib. The authors should themselves have constantly chanted "The desk *and* the dog suit!"—the satiric pen without the too cautious hand.

Such were the characteristics of John Osborne's *Epitaph for George Dillon*, it could easily have been the offspring of his *Look Back in Anger* and his *The Entertainer*. Having actually been written earlier than either, it was more like a parent to both. Into a lower-middle-class family home, not haggard with poverty but flabby and limp with failure, comes George Dillon, a youngish down-and-outer, a flop as both actor and playwright. Toward the sentimental woman who has taken him in he shows no gratitude; and sneering as he cadges, he stays on without good will. Another woman, a disillusioned Leftist, who alone in the family is capable of intellectual sympathy for George, is quickly roused by his snide dismissive ways to intellectual contempt. Given to doubt and self-mockery, he yet puts a bleat for George into every snarl at others, and when success comes to him it proves the worst failure of all: by sleazily vulgarizing one of George's plays, a cheapjack producer makes a provincial hit of it.

Osborne and his collaborator Anthony Creighton made of George Dillon someone raspingly real—someone given to the kind of intellectual self-poisoning that encourages moral apathy; someone with just so much of Hamlet in him as mopes about, baits Polonius and upbraids Ophelia. He has, very vividly, a toad's venom in a world of worms. That world is often made vivid too: in their earlier encounters with George and one another, its members are full of Osborne bite. On the whole, however, that world becomes less moving and dramatically less fused than the family world of *The Entertainer;* nor has George himself the vituperative brilliance of Jimmie Porter in *Look Back in Anger*. The play itself indeed flattens out toward the end, tends to repeat its effects rather than develop new ones. For all its sharpness of characterization and truthfulness of effect, and despite a notably good cast, the authors had largely written everyone's epitaph a full act before concluding their story.

The Manley Halliday whom Budd Schulberg and Harvey Breit wrote of in *The Disenchanted* was, under really no disguise at all, Scott Fitzgerald. They wrote of him, in a running narrative, in defeat; they also showed him, by way of flashbacks, in decline. The razzle-dazzle days of the twenties, the champagne-bath marriage of an irresistible playboy and an irresponsible wife, the dropping of banknotes like confetti, produced a writer as drained as his bank account. To get money to go on with a book, he agreed to write a popular Hollywood movie. Collaborating—it is 1939—with a Depression-Age young writer, he finds he lacks not only the stomach for short-order hackwork but equally the resources. Weeks pass as he fishes for ideas in water that has gone over the dam, as he tosses crumpled typewriter paper after crumpled memories, as he fights against a deadline that becomes an obituary.

With Jason Robards, Jr. and George Grizzard impressive as the two writers, the main story was full of vibrantly nostalgic moments, as it had others that were tense and moving. At other times it seemed underdramatized, while the flashbacks did more to convey an oversymbolic Jazz Age than to explain a disintegrating writer. What destroyed any such man must go beyond mere high-stepping idiocies to the broad lure of affluent high life; must go beneath the killing froth of a marriage to its dark neurotic lees. Involved also, perhaps, was a gifted writer's imagining that memory could afterwards recoup with words what had been squandered on embarkations for Cythara. But if the crucial twists and turns of Halliday's road down remained uncharted, nothing was adulterated or glossed over. The play treated writers like writers, Hollywood like Hollywood, truth like truth; it knew that for the bedeviled writer good intentions can be paved with hell. Whatever its weaknesses as playwriting, it dealt feelingly with authorship.

The World of Suzie Wong, which Paul Osborn adapted from a novel by Richard Mason, though it proved a stampede to the box-office, seemed a shambling step backward for the stage. It told of a young Hong Kong prostitute debauched at thirteen but in essence still fine and pure, and of an even finer and purer young Canadian painter who, though achingly tempted, resisted a loving and willing Suzie, in scene after scene, till near the end—and at the very end, after her baby was killed, presumably married her.

The first in a quite unmeaningful series of stage works with an Oriental flavor—there followed *Flower Drum Song, Rashomon, A Majority of One* and *Kataki*—*Suzie Wong* was, in story terms, a period-piece reproduction that could almost pass for the real thing. It came in the original raspberry plush, every dusty looped inanity, every faded tasseled cliché in place. Though the swarming street and café scenes had hurly, and sometimes burly too, the more intimate boudoir passages were all played *largo,* with silences like swelling organ notes and pauses aquiver with heartbreak. As Suzie, French-Chinese France Nuyen captivated with her looks and personality. Otherwise, *The World of Suzie Wong* proved a more slushy than sexy blend of sex and slush, a special treat for matinee ladies munching tear-splashed caramels.

Elmer Rice, in *Cue for Passion,* went to *Hamlet* not only for his title but quite openly for his basic characters and plot. And with any such retelling comes the added fascination of comparison: it is like returning to a former home to see how someone else has furnished it. In *Cue for Passion* the furnishings were sparser and very modern, with a picture window to let in strong, clear, psychoanalytical light. Hamlet, called Tony Burgess, came home—sulky, sneering, perverse—after two years in Asia, certain that his new stepfather had been his mother's paramour, suspecting he was also his father's murderer. This was an Oedipus-uncomplex Hamlet, so drawn to his mother that he hated his father, so identified with the lover's role that to kill his stepfather would be to kill himself. Truth tumbled out in a climactic modern Closet Scene, but consequences took a therapeutic rather than tragic turn.

Cue for Passion proved interesting in its way, which was too purely intelligent a way. The trouble was rather less how much it left out of Shakespeare than how much it put in of Freud. To put all its neuroses in one bedstead was to rob a great character of his tangled richness, a story of its resonant depths, was to turn what T. S. Eliot called "the Mona Lisa of literature" into a simple blueprint, to convert *Hamlet* into *The Importance of Being Ernest Jones.* And yet, by adhering to things like soliloquies and ghosts, *Cue for Passion* never quite went its own way either. It proved most striking where, near the end, it shifted the moral limelight from the son to the mother, with Diana Wynyard performing these late scenes brilliantly. And indeed, as a theatre piece, *Cue for Passion* held attention throughout; it was as creative drama that it seemed too explicit and unlarge, and—in its manner of writing—too literary.

Milton Geiger's *Edwin Booth* was a farrago of many scenes that never resembled a play. Something had been borrowed from the legend of the Mad Booths, and something from the lives; there were puns and pomposities, speeches from Shakespeare and a José Ferrer who for all his costume changes could not evoke a once-great actor. But it perhaps mattered less that *Edwin Booth* was never valid stage biography than that it proved so resolute a bore. Had it, however foolish, recaptured something splendidly gaudy; had John Wilkes Booth provoked hisses or Edwin Booth huzzas, a bad play might have come off a pleasant romp. But there was not even much make-believe: on an all-purpose stage where anything could happen, almost nothing did.

J.B. was Archibald MacLeish's re-enactment, in a contemporary

THE SEASON ON BROADWAY

setting, of the Book of Job. It was also, in a double sense, a theatre piece: the action took place inside a night-lit circus tent where a sideshow *Job* had been performing. Two out-of-work actors, Zuss and Nickels, toying with the Biblical masks of God and Satan they find lying around, are suddenly aware of a Voice from outside them and are caught up in a story near at hand. In the story, J.B. is a rich, admired American industrialist with a devoted wife and five children. Then disaster looms and mounts: his children are senselessly killed or brutally murdered; his possessions are lost, his house is destroyed, his wife goes away, his body festers. All this happens against a crossfire, Biblical and profane, between Zuss and Nickels; then J.B. wrestles with his soul, with his comforters, with his God, till at the end his health is restored and his wife returns.

Judged as a theatre piece, *J.B.*—at least in the first half—had a striking theatricality. In addition to the circus setting and Boris Aronson's graphically sombre set, the spoken verse was often expressive; while the bearers of ill tidings to J.B.—liquored-up soldiers, flashbulb photographers, raincoated police—were peculiarly scarifying. The story, moreover, was varied and salted by the lively exchanges between Zuss and Nickels. Judged as philosophic drama, though an effort of a sort and size unusual in today's American theatre, *J.B.* was not altogether satisfying. Mr. MacLeish has said that for him Job's ordeal alone matches the mass sufferings of the modern world; and his J.B. is a more relevant figure when seen less as an individual than as a symbol of the victims of totalitarianism (even the "happy" ending could speak for thousands of reclaimed D.P.s). In any case, a suffering J.B. raised an agonized Why, seeking to root out his sins. His modern-day comforters, with their pat clerical, Communist and psychiatric cures, brought not light but added darkness; and J.B. found his suffering ultimately explained not so much in any Will of God as in the buffetings of life; not, again, in God's wisdom but in human love.

This final note of affirmation seems unsatisfying, not just on philosophic grounds but for lacking dramatic truth, for not having the pulse of the play itself behind it. Indeed, the second half of the play, with J.B. lying on the ground begging to know why, can scarcely have any pulse; it resembles the situation, in which everything must be endured and nothing can be done, that Matthew Arnold held ill-fitted for dramatic narrative. Zuss and Nickels, to be sure, proved helpful here, and in some degree Elia Kazan's staging gave mere utterance the effect of action. But Kazan gave life to the second act in too rhetorical, too loud-speakered, too high-pressured a way. Despite its ingenuity and its frequent authority, *J.B.*

never overcame certain difficulties that philosophic drama is heir to.

W. S. Gilbert made a widely applicable point when he spoke of a "much too French French bean"; certainly *Sweet Bird of Youth* was altogether too Tennessee-Williamsy Tennessee Williams. So, for some time, has been almost everything Mr. Williams has written. It indicates great individuality if a man's work bears his unmistakable signature; but when we get that signature in the brightest conceivable ink, with flamboyant loops and flourishes, and some blood-red blots to boot, something further has entered in. In *Sweet Bird of Youth* Mr. Williams continued faithful, if that is the best word, to the South. He wrote this time of a young man of no morals and much lure who was the gigolo of a decayed, frowsy, tempestuous former movie queen and who had got her to stop over in his old home town so that he could see his old-home-town girl. The girl, it turns out, has been diseased by him, and her enraged, racist, Big-Daddyish father is determined to have the young man castrated. Out of this situation, with half a play left to go, Mr. Williams contrives a number of frantic scenes and banged crescendoes, and a finale in the vein of mutilation of *Orpheus Descending* and *Garden District*.

In the first act, when Mr. Williams is concentrating on the young man and the movie queen, he blends something richly sordid with something raffishly amusing, and his best-drawn character is given superb vitality by Geraldine Page. Here Mr. Williams' great natural sense of theatre is rewarding, and his writing gifts do not overflow their banks. But soon, when the beslimed past action of the play flows into the muddy present, the whole thing overflows indeed and, amid theatrical eddies and swirls, everything plausible drowns. Since, in his own work, Mr. Williams goes on repeating himself, critics can hardly do otherwise. And the sense of repetition can only increase their dissatisfaction, only strengthen their indictment. Whether a world of loathing and disgust, of sex violence and race violence, of lurid and bestial revenges, constitutes Mr. Williams' personal reaction to life or simply his philosophic vision of it, it has come to seem compulsive in him rather than convincing in his people. And with a growing loss of perspective, of all feeling for contrasts, of all power of control, even his enraged symbols have lost their force, have ceased really to be symbols and become mere props, have passed even beyond props into parodies. It is not that Mr. Williams takes so grisly a view of life, it is that he also takes so lurid a one; not that he sings such frenzied arias, but that he sings them two octaves higher than they are written. At its best, *Sweet Bird of Youth* has both force and fascination. But far too often everything seems ex-

THE SEASON ON BROADWAY

Tennessee Williams

cessive, with a fuming and rioting depravity. There is an art to cursing life no less than to conveying it.

Right on the heels of *Sweet Bird of Youth* came the best new play of the season, Lorraine Hansberry's *A Raisin in the Sun*. Concerned with a Negro family's personal kinks and racial difficulties, and with its struggles to find a place in the world, it was in its general pattern fairly familiar. There were the small commotions of family life, the gulfs separating generations, the now prosaic, now picturesque aspects of a particular minority culture, the stress of minority problems. There was the family's varying attitudes toward all this and toward themselves, their ambitions to escape from a confining and often humiliating life, and to achieve an independence, whether of income or of outlook, that would constitute self-fulfillment. Something close to this has been the stuff of many novels and plays about Negro or Jewish, Irish or Italian families, which is simply to stress how central, how almost inevitable, a theme and subject matter it is. That being so, what is familiar about the design will be all to the good so long as there is something fresh and vital about the detail; and in *A Raisin in the Sun* there was something very fresh—and often humorous and dramatic and touching—indeed. There was actually that sense of something that wholly fits the theatre and yet looks full-faced out toward life that could be one definition of a sound play.

What gave a certain scope to the family dreams, and leverage to the dramatic action, was the insurance money that the matriarch of the family had inherited from her husband. In the very degree that this money can alter their lives, it complicates it, makes for friction rather than fulfillment. In particular, the house in a white neighborhood that the mother buys, which precipitates white opposition, also leads to family conflict. But the plot pauses constantly to etch or enliven character, to define or satirize attitudes, to release that self-mocking humor that is so rich and saving a characteristic of have-not peoples. The arty, callow daughter of the house, with her two delightfully different suitors, can be as funny as, with his enraged frustrations, the chauffeur son can be disturbing. Moreover, there was an almost perfect cast to catch all the play's nuances and inflections. Very minor matters aside, what alone for me seemed amiss in the play was the ending: it was a "right" ending, perhaps, but not a real one. Whether the mother—who is carefully shown to represent a cautious and "respectful" generation of Negroes—would have bought in a white neighborhood is, I think, doubtful, but would be unimportant did not so much derive from it. In any case, the son—who is really the chief character, though the mother comes to overshadow him—should, in the state he was in, have gone through with selling the house back to the white community for all he could get. For here was a *real* Angry Young Man. In a novel, there could have been time for him to quiet down, to have a change of heart; as things stood in the theatre, at that moment his anger had to be vented, his resentments revenged: the right ending, for me, would lie in how guilty and ashamed he would feel afterwards. But this moot point aside, *A Raisin in the Sun* is both valid and vigorous.

In *Requiem for a Nun,* William Faulkner carried on, from his novel *Sanctuary,* the story of Temple Drake—a painfully sordid story in the novel that, in its aftermath on the stage, is grim, gloomy, haunted with a sense of guilt. In *Requiem for a Nun* the once whorish Temple is now respectfully married, while her once whorish Negro servant is under sentence of death for murdering Temple's child. The play roots out the events leading up to the murder and the motives for it—a desperate act on the servant's part to prevent Temple's running away with another man and abandoning her husband and child. But of more importance than the events themselves, which are told retrospectively with almost no stage action, are the feelings of the characters involved. Set against the sense of guilt with which Temple and her husband are infected, set against their inability to find relief within themselves or salvation without, is the sense of religious peace in the simple Negro woman.

If in some ways there is much about the play that is characteristic of Faulkner, there is a good deal less of his particular characterizing force. Plainly, the medium of the stage has bothered and at times beggared him. He has told of what happened instead of showing it; and combining unwonted plainness of language with a certain flatness of effect, he has fallen, as it were, between a novelist's ability to stir the depths and a playwright's to raise the dust. The result, though often well told simply as narrative, though generally interesting and at times telling, yet seems remote and without Faulkner's dark urgent power. And there is something un-Faulknerishly black and white in the contrast between the guilt-ridden Temple and the God-flooded servant: one almost wonders whether the point of the servant's finding of faith is not how sardonically it stresses Temple's sense of lostness.

Rashomon, which Michael and Fay Kanin adapted from the famous Japanese film, would seem to require a film for any real success. In this woodland tale of rape and murder, this triangle story of the long ago, each in turn—a bandit, a wife, the spirit of a husband—gave a contradictory account of what had happened, only for a woodcutter who had witnessed the event to give an account that contradicts all three. Indeed, the woodcutter's version is a farcically debunking one, wholly at variance with the romantic and melodramatic self-dramatizings of those involved. They, *Rashomon* suggests, told only what they wanted to tell—and not always to seem innocent, sometimes just to seem interesting.

All this was laced with exotic faraway atmosphere, with picturesque characters and costumes, and with peasant humor—and much enhanced by good acting, Oliver Messel's set, and Jo Mielziner's lighting. But despite pleasant moments that suggested a primitive legend, and theatrical moments that involved a psychological guessing game, *Rashomon* had no real outward charm (here the cinema can be twenty times more rewarding than the stage) and no great psychological lure (here the stage has itself been a dozen times more rewarding in the past). On this latter score, *Rashomon* rather

Claire Bloom, Rod Steiger and Noel Willman in "Rashomon"

seemed like Pirandello for the retarded; and indeed one had to be a bit retarded not to anticipate—while assuming it would not turn up—a great amount of Mr. and Mrs. Kanin's dialogue. Their gift for sentence-long cliché, their mastery of the obvious and undistinguished, made somewhat secondary their late-in-the-play lapse (with Director Peter Glenville's concurrence) into primitive slapstick, where what had seemed called for was a kind of sardonic savagery.

Shimon Wincelberg's *Kataki* was a two-character play that took place on a bare South Pacific island late in World War II. Only one character, a stupid young GI, spoke English; the other, as befit his nationality, spoke Japanese. This tale of two stranded enemy soldiers forced into a life together and at length into saving each other from death raised difficulties for playwright and audience alike. As though two-character plays were not hard enough, Mr. Wincelberg had to work, as it were, with one character tied behind his back. As the GI bumbled clichés and blundered at human relations, the far decenter Jap had literally to make actions speak louder than words, and Sessue Hayakawa often touchingly made them do so. The relationship between the two men, for what it revealed of human and national psychology, for what it augured of drama or provided as comedy, above all for its aspects of practical primitive adjustment, was interesting even when monotonous and had moments of real force. It was a relationship easier to complicate than resolve, and Mr. Wincelberg was driven to introduce a god (or devil) from a flying machine.

Since so much of it depended on acting, and since it achieved its theatricality by the device of sacrificing routine theatrical advantages, *Kataki* was in a sense more theatre piece than play. For much these reasons, it had more fascination than interest, and showed a sense of diminishing returns. But by its very spareness it was capable on occasion of resonant moments.

John Synge, in *God and Kate Murphy,* told of a strong-willed, mendacious Irish mother who spoils the happiness of both her sons. One wanted to be a priest, but Kate refused him an education, needing her money to buy a pub; the other son—when the pub was a going concern—she tricked out of marriage and forced into the priesthood. There was nothing scandalously incompetent about the story, there was just nothing individual or freshly felt: it had a flat, hand-me-down quality, whether Kate stood for Ireland or just for herself.

Pearl Buck's *A Desert Incident* was written in a good cause—to warn us against the fight for secret weapons that can end in a war that destroys mankind. It was never, however, much good as theatre.

A garrulous play, with that other dangerous weapon—sex—used to thicken the plot, it moved from scene to scene with slow, dogged, now grimly playful, now reasonedly earnest steps, the sort of thing that, in a good cause or not, must lack value from a lack of effectiveness.

The season, where comedy was concerned, once again saw the gag and the wisecrack, the benevolently comic and the broadly farcical, enthroned. That is to say that what was aimed at, by and large, was popular taste, what was sought after was box-office success. The fast farce, when well done, is one of America's chief contributions to theatrical laughter; but even it too often seems yoked to the fast buck. Among last season's comedies, there were sound satiric and topical themes and funny ideas, and certainly good actors to illustrate or enliven them. But again and again, playwrights—in developing them—took the line of least resistance, sought the level of quick rewards or, wearied or hurried, threw bad jokes after good ones, or used wadding instead of wit. The idea that comedy is criticism, that it can rouse the mind as well as jab the funnybone, and while jabbing the funnybone perhaps bring the blush to one's face—this, somehow, is not much favored. The idea, again, that there are higher forms of wit than the wisecrack, such things as elegance and style, as the pregnant pause and the urbane look—this too is seldom sought. The only new comedy last season with any feeling for tone was *The Pleasure of His Company;* the only other—and it was but half a comedy, really—with any human concern for what underlay it was *The Cold Wind and the Warm.* For the rest, the playwrights —however clever—were listening for their laughs, were indeed playing for them; and often not seeming to care much from whom, or for what reason, they came.

Phoebe Ephron's *Howie,* which opened the season, will be remembered, if at all, for just that. Another of those farce-comedies, of which *The Show Off* still seems the best, about a jobless jawing know-it-all quartered on his wife's long-suffering family, *Howie* held up to view a kind of double horror: he was not only always correcting people, he was actually always correct. Even in his proper niche, a TV quiz program, he couldn't mind his tongue. But despite amusing moments and lively thrusts, *Howie,* as a whole, lacked voltage. The theme seemed too familiar, the plot too makeshift, the wackiness too wooden. Howie should have been much more magnetically repellent when holding the floor; the family more explosively aroused when hitting the ceiling.

Drink to Me Only, by Abram S. Ginnes and Ira Wallach, proved no offset; it featured farce in an anything-goes sort of script, all too much of which went awry. Concerned with a rich playboy—on trial for shooting his wife in the backside—who insists that before the gun went off he had drunk two bottles of Scotch, the play—and the defense—turns on whether a man can drink that much and not pass out. In the ensuing demonstration Tom Poston, particularly at the second-bottle stage, showed a real gift for exuberant pantomime, as George Abbott, in his staging, did for moderate pandemonium. But no play can keep from falling on its face just by having the hero continue to do so, and even at its fitful best, as a jolly intemperance lecture, *Drink to Me Only* tended to pall.

In *The Girls in 509* Howard Teichmann wrote of a violently Republican battle-ax and her niece who, for the twenty-five years since F.D.R. went to the White House, have been hiding under assumed names in a decaying family hotel. When somebody finally intrudes, the gals seem less like Republicans than Know-Nothings. They are amazed that the banks have reopened and that there is a different Man in the White House; they are even more pleasantly amazed when it turns out that an eccentric brother's habit of investing in screwball inventions has reaped them millions in air-conditioning, Cellophane and nylon. Unhappily Mr. Teichmann's inventions paid off a good deal less well. His play had truly funny moments, when a gag cut sharp as a razor or a prop turned into a vise; but his situations never developed any story and had to be relentlessly kept going with comic-strip characters and hit-or-miss gags. The main trouble, however, was that with just enough bright gags for a topnotch revue sketch, Mr. Teichmann insisted on stretching his lone bright idea into a play.

If only by contrast with such shenanigans, *The Pleasure of His Company* seemed to shine quite bright; indeed, it was Broadway's first suavely managed drawing-room comedy in several seasons. With Cornelia Otis Skinner's help, Samuel Taylor—on whose shoulders, if on anyone's, the opera cape of Philip Barry seems to have fallen—had whipped up a bright tale of the prodigal father who, turning up for his daughter's wedding, turns everything about him upside down. And in the theatre Cyril Ritchard, on whose shoulders had fallen both acting the prodigal and directing the play, much enhanced the gloss.

An international charmer and flirt, the prodigal soon has his daughter more interested in him than in her serious young ranchman fiancé: father's ideal of enjoying every real or sham pleasure goes to her head like champagne. Simultaneously the blood rushes to the ranchman's, who denounces Father in ringing tones. The play, thereafter, gets a bit shaky—and talky—what with having to side with either irreproachable dullness or irresponsible dash. Earlier, however, it has its genuine rewards. Drawing-room comedies, like drawing-room furniture, tend to be fragile and spindly, and with heavy handling this one might have easily crashed to bits. Happily, the authors showed a feeling for tone, and made the dialogue—half insulting, half elegant—a nice blend of spit and polish.

In *Once More, with Feeling*—a farcical assault on the world of music—Harry Kurnitz might have been thought to tincture insight with elegance also. But Mr. Kurnitz's way of treating an egomaniac orchestra conductor who as quickly shatters his musicians' fiddles as his trustees' feelings, was to let fly now at chicanery and now at sham, and in between to go in for shenanigans. Mr. Kurnitz has a talent for funny gags, and his play was sprinkled with them. It had on occasion a funny situation as well, and in the conductor's shameless manager a first-rate farce character. The manager's rich low-down nature was right up Kurnitz's alley—which is Schubert with a touch of Tin Pan. But with the world of music, as with that of art in *Reclining Figure*, Mr. Kurnitz remains incorrigibly Broadway. All brass and no silk, *Once More, with Feeling* has none of the stealthy purr-and-scratch of music-world wit; its rascals are roughnecks, its megalomaniacs commit mayhem, its bull-fiddles see red. There is not a touch of urbane caricature, only a sense of plebeian cartooning.

Leslie Stevens' *The Marriage-Go-Round* had three strings to its bow: Claudette Colbert, Charles Boyer and Julie Newmar. They were enough to convert one of the season's crudest commodities into one of its solidest hits. Miss Colbert and Mr. Boyer played a happily married academic couple who at opposite ends of the stage gave cutey-cute lectures on marriage which (on a midstage merry-go-round-like set) they themselves helped to illustrate. As the play's third or G string, Miss Newmar played an amply built Swedish blonde who had chosen Mr. Boyer to give her a child. While an aware Miss Colbert waited, wondered, and tried to act wise, Mr. Boyer first laughed off, then warned off, then fought off his Viking admirer, and then all but succumbed.

Never was a play less given to digression: *The Marriage-Go-Round* was sex and marriage, marriage and sex, with never a servant to interrupt, or a caller to intrude, or a child to compete. Such consistent single-mindedness, such endless double meanings had a way—despite funny lines now and then, and finished performances by Miss Colbert and Mr. Boyer—of seeming no less tedious than tawdry.

Patate, which Irwin Shaw adapted from Marcel Achard's Paris hit,

THE SEASON ON BROADWAY

Charles Boyer and Claudette Colbert in "The Marriage-Go-Round"

was a comedy about a heel who has grown rich, and his down-at-heel *patate*, or fall guy. But France and America, on Broadway, rubbed elbows with a spectacular avoidance of funnybones. Jokes congealed, situations evaporated, Tom Ewell as Patate gamely struggled and sank. More perhaps was involved than national brands of humor: the speed at which light comedy travels, for example, or the split second in which a fleeting notion can be trapped. In any case, the fun of *Patate* remained incommunicado throughout.

In *The Cold Wind and the Warm,* with its stage memories of Jewish neighborhood life in Worcester, Mass., S. N. Behrman wived farce with feeling. Where the characters in Behrman's earlier urbane comedies seemed not so much human beings as assorted points of view, often here they seemed not so much human beings as pieces on a racial chessboard. And wherever Behrman commemorated traditional Jewish characters enacting set routines and pat refrains, his play was both warmhearted and entertaining. There was the natty, paunchy, rich upstart; the slangy, kindly matron who wanted to marry everyone off; the professional matchmaker with his human goldbricks and his spiel. As these people clucked, strutted, bragged, fibbed, fenced they spilt over into caricature; but they boasted, for all that, a kind of solid tribal flesh.

While his older folk hold Behrman's looseleaf memory-book together, a younger generation is falling in love and inquiring of life. Chief of these, Willie, is an unstable college student, the friend and mentor of the Behrman-like teen-ager Tobey. Willie, forever losing himself in trying to find himself, unavailingly in love with one girl, unavailingly loved by another, seems—for all his lostness—an essentially comic type. Then suddenly, more out of *Winesburg, Ohio* than Worcester, Mass., he kills himself. Mr. Behrman nowhere anticipates such dark final chords; indeed Willie—and all the young people generally—seem rather flat-surfaced and hand-me-down. The play leaves a final impression that is friendly and touching; but all its Youth-Faces-Life side does more than blow a cold wind upon it; it throws cold water.

Make a Million concerned a Southern gal who is $100,000 ahead on a quiz show; she is also, it turns out, pregnant by an unknown soldier. To save the show's honor, the girl must be married at once. A piece of pure dedicated hackwork, one part farcical, one part topical, one part sexy, *Make a Million* stuck grimly to formula: in dashed the characters, out bounced the gags, up came the noise-maker, off fell the handle. There were some lively moments and funny gags, and there was Sam Levene who, when he could not help the show with his buoyant low comedy, could at least divert attention away from it.

The Third Best Sport—the first two being sex and baseball—is industrial conventions; and on the subject Eleanor and Leo Bayer wrote a satiric farce about a convention in Palm Beach. In it the rather sophisticated bride of a corporation executive suddenly learned all about cliché persiflage, canasta tournaments and we-must-all-hang-togetherness; she also showed a centipede's capacity for putting her foot in things, eventually insulting the star client's wife in the presence of an apoplectic Big Boss. However familiar by now,

Gertrude Berg and Cedric Hardwicke in "A Majority of One"

the organization man and the organization manner could make good stage fun; but even once around the floor with *The Third Best Sport* began to pall, and as it went round and round without ever changing the tune, it was a question who found things more boring, the heroine or the audience. The authors had still to learn how to impale conformity without inducing commonplaceness.

The Gazebo, by Alec Coppel, was a murder comedy that was at its best as a comedy murder, with Walter Slezak ticking off plans to kill a blackmailer with all the zestful efficiency of a hostess ticking off items for a dinner party. But for a good murder yarn, the play hadn't enough twists; nor, as something aimed at the funnybone rather than the spine, enough laughs. Everything about it except Slezak, who was extremely helpful, seemed too thin.

Tall Story was Howard Lindsay and Russel Crouse attempting a bit less and aiming a bit lower than men of their calibre might feel the need to do. Another college comedy, *Tall Story* centered its campus rumpus in a star basketball player who, because of his standing in two courses, can't play in the Big Game. Help is sought of the two crucial professors; but one of them, a stiffnecked absolutist, refuses to cooperate, and there is much tearing of hair before teacher has a change of heart. The play, beyond featuring love, bribery and academic satire, drops an ounce of moral seriousness into a gallon jug of farcical hullabaloo. If agreeably carpentered, *Tall Story* is yet plainly jerry-built; if its sermon against too rigid values is available to the brainier playgoer, it need never detain the cheerier type; if its jokes are often agreeable, they are oftener needlessly glib.

A Majority of One is the sort of popular comedy that preaches tolerance, and that is nicely enough done to invite it. Mrs. Jacobs, a kindhearted Brooklyn Jewish widow who lost a son in World War II, meets on shipboard Mr. Amato, a millionaire Buddhist Japanese widower who lost a daughter at Hiroshima. Gradually their hostility toward each other's country is dissolved in their feeling for each other. At the same time, the widow's diplomatic-corps son-in-law, by opposing the friendship, dangerously offends the powerful millionaire; and Mrs. Jacobs has to play Mrs. Fixit on the way to becoming Mrs. Amato.

By their delightful (and delightfully contrasted) acting, Gertrude Berg and Sir Cedric Hardwick made something appealing, something sprinkled with laughs and brushed with tears, of Leonard Spigelgass's moderately idiotic blending of Kind-hearts-are-more-than-coronets with Love-conquers-all. Mrs. Berg and Sir Cedric proved that two of the most mismated of characters were certainly made for each other on the stage. And if Mr. Spigelgass, while pretending to be a playwright, is really a spinner of fairy tales, and while having the look of a sociologist has only the aims of a marriage broker, there is something disarming about him. When "warmhearted" twaddle is as nicely done as this, it deserves its success.

In *Look After Lulu*, Noel Coward adapted Georges Feydeau's very famous and very farcical farce, *Occupe-toi-d'Amelie*—a bed-and-bedlam scamper that Cecil Beaton mounted with tropical extravagance and Cyril Ritchard staged with calisthenic abandon. At moments it seemed more laboriously frolicsome than funny, more wearing than gay, and the evening as a whole was never French and not often stylish. Nor did Mr. Coward himself right the balance with anything brilliantly British, or his own. Yet despite how far *Lulu* fell short in method no less than in madness, it seemed more fun, and better fun, than the season's run of wisecracking farces; at least it was a true romp, with something farcical always in the offing and something fizzy in the air.

Once again— it has virtually become standard—Broadway took almost no notice of the classics: it left the Greeks and the Elizabethans, Molière and Congreve, even Chekhov and Shaw, to visiting French or English troupes, to Off-Broadway or amateur ones. Perhaps it is just as well, since the absence in our professional theatre of an Old Vic or a Comédie Française—of all that a first-rate repertory theatre implies in purpose and achievement—can only mean revivals pivoting on star names and put together with what is available on short notice. For years Broadway has not boasted a single producing name that cared enough for the theatre's masterpieces to do anything about regularly producing them; nor, for all the power of its name directors, has a single one of them managed to devote even a single season to the classics. Accordingly, what Broadway itself got round to during 1958-59 was, rather than a revival, a first production of Sean O'Casey's first play, *The Shadow of a Gunman*—and not a very good production, at that; and, came spring, two one-acters of O'Casey's and a Chekhov monologue.

France, fortunately, was represented by the adventurous Jean Vilar's Théâtre National Populaire in a three-week visit that included such celebrated pieces as Molière's *Don Juan* and Corneille's *Le Cid* and that made a particular impression with Victor Hugo's *Marie Tudor* and Musset's *Lorenzaccio*. *Marie Tudor* won bravos for the performance of Maria Cesares; *Lorenzaccio*—which for all its strands of story and excess of scenes, has operatic stir and psychological bite—was a chance for the T.N.P. to provide a lesson in staging. Letting brilliant lighting and costumes compensate for an almost total absence of décor, this *Lorenzaccio*, with one scene flowing into another, achieved great cohesiveness and pace.

The Old Vic offered three of Shakespeare's plays—*Twelfth Night, Henry V* and *Hamlet*—and triumphed in the least promising one, *Twelfth Night*. The *Hamlet*, possessing an Edwardian air in the Court scenes, and elsewhere an expressionist one, had individualizing touches—a trim club-bore of a Polonius, an Ophelia obscenely mad; but in general it fell short, not least for John Neville's Gielgudish Hamlet that was not Gielgud enough. In *Henry V* Shakespeare wrote his greatest Success Story which is why, by severe standards, it is never high drama. More chronicle, indeed, than drama, the work more of a patriot than a poet, it made a splendid cinema pageant; but what were great battle scenes in Technicolor dwindled, on stage, into what looked like more flags than soldiers; while Laurence Harvey as Henry never seemed sufficiently vigorous at war or gay at wooing. As against such pleasantly unmemorable productions, *Twelfth Night*—which for all its verbal charm usually palls in the theatre—came off an entire delight. The plot, to be sure, did not suddenly sprint, nor did the jokes put on new leaves; but the poetry danced in and out of the prankishness, the air seemed filled with light, the Malvolio could be grandly absurd and really funny, the Viola girlishly charming whether in man's dress or woman's. The key to such success lay in ensemble playing: the Old Vic could thank its stars not to boast any. People who knew how to speak Shakespeare and be graceful or acrobatic, knew above all how to join hands. Add to this a delightful set, and there was for once in the theatre the sense of letting something deathless prove its mettle and not of beseeching something lifeless to move its limbs.

The Phoenix Theatre, in line with a plan for a season of plays by Nobel prizewinners, got off to a rewarding start with what should have been a revival—but was actually the first professional American production—of T. S. Eliot's *The Family Reunion*. However great its shortcomings, this verse play of Eliot's that is closest in intent to *The Cocktail Party* had not only a very special interest where it succeeded but even an academic interest where it failed. Thereafter the Phoenix shelved its plan of Nobel prizewinners and provided miscellaneous fare, whether adaptations of novels or musical shows, of varying worth.

Also, from time to time during the season, there were offerings that fell outside the standard categories. Betty Comden and Adolph Green provided a pleasant, and often pleasantly nostalgic, evening that drew heavily on their old Village Vanguard numbers. The two made an engaging team, not least for their flawless stage manners. Late in the season Jessica Tandy and Hume Cronyn offered, in *Triple Play*, the Chekhov monologue and O'Casey one-acters mentioned earlier, and a one-act play by Tennessee Williams. The evening, despite the names of the playwrights and the giftedness of the Cronyns, had something of the in-and-out quality common to such theatrical mixed bags. The Williams play, a water-color sketch of a Blanche DuBois, was all right enough but had more easy pathos than power. The famous Chekhov monologue on the Dangers of Tobacco, though good enough too and well delivered by Mr. Cronyn, seemed not quite worthy of its fame. O'Casey's post-office sketch was indifferent slapstick; it was only his *Bedtime Story*, a funny piece about a tart who fleeces the scared, Puritanical bachelor she has gone to bed with, that had something infectious about it—chiefly for Miss Tandy's delightful performance.

Norman Corwin's *The Rivalry* seemed to me in essence a special sort of event, for though Mr. Corwin contrived his own framework for presenting the Lincoln-Douglas debates, he set nothing creative, or that had to do with playwriting, or that ever smacked of being a play, inside the frame. And this had its own kind of merit, just as Richard Boone, who played Lincoln, had his own kind of quality for not looking like Lincoln. He and Martin Gabel, as Douglas, were well contrasted, in personality as in perspective, in their technique as political showmen as in their aims as men; and the slavery issue, in an age where segregation has become a focal one, gave to history the topical fillup that a mere stage piece seeks. By introducing Mrs. Douglas into the picture—or at any rate into the frame—and by clearly seeking to do justice to both men, Mr. Corwin contributed something further. I am not sure that, in the end, the added framework did much more than turn *The Rivalry* into a full-length evening, or that the debates themselves had quite the thrust and the fire one looked for; but *The Rivalry* was pleasantly different and eminently respectable.

Of the special occasions, by all odds the most memorable—conceivably, indeed, it was the season's most memorable event—was *Ages of Man,* in which a dinner-jacketed Sir John Gielgud came out on an unadorned stage and recited Shakespeare. In at least one respect it resembled an all-Bach or all-Beethoven recital, in that Gielgud, if only in excerpts, communicated the range, richness, greatness, above all uniqueness of his subject. That meant, of course, displaying his own richness and range; it meant, too—since Shakespeare was dramatist and poet both—being equally good at acting and speaking words. It was Shakespeare the poet, the magician with words, who bulked largest in the recital, and Gielgud had his own touch of magic—not from magnificence of voice or roll of theatrical thunder, but from a projection of feeling and rush of psychological light. But what perhaps stood out most of all was Gielgud's absorption in his subject, the sense toward Shakespeare of something loved and lifelong. It made any flashing virtuosity seem secondary; it made the essence of the evening not glitter but glow.

Musicals—America's ace-in-the-hole when her theatre is scrutinized or assailed, and indeed Broadway's particular contribution to the gaiety of nations—could not, during '58-'59, too easily bear scrutiny or survive assault. Very early in the season, to be sure, a non-Broadway, indeed a non-American product—as a matter of fact, a *revue* with a French title—did supply as gay an evening as could be asked for. But aside from *La Plume de Ma Tante* the musical field languished sadly till, late in April, *Destry* rode with at least a clatter of hoofs and some of the bang-bang of good popular entertainment. Earlier, there were fumbled musical attempts to put rings on Jane Austen's fingers and bells on Sean O'Casey's toes, along with less nobly descended shows that, whatever the routine competence of the better ones, never seemed festive or fresh.

Goldilocks, with a Walter and Jean Kerr book and music by Leroy Anderson, spoofed the pioneer cinema days when redskins swarmed all over Fort Lee. Concerned with a short-on-cash and long-on-ego moviemaker and a sizzle-tongued actress who throw verbal knives at each other without realizing that they are actually Cupid's darts, the show had an always professional air about it, and every so often Mrs. Kerr's *Please Don't Eat the Daisies* dewy, screwy touch. But the professionalism came at a price, set the packaging too much above the product, too often substituted mere method for point of view. Mrs. Kerr's daisies bloom better in suburban soil than Broadway asphalt; and early Westerns are not only satirically old hat, but somehow the nickelodeon, like the Model T, is fitter for nostalgia than satire. The show had Broadway know-how enough; what it lacked was 1958 freshness and 1913 charm.

As the work of Rodgers and Hammerstein, *Flower Drum Song* was perhaps the biggest disappointment in a season when disappointments loomed large. In a season that also made the Orient its dominant motif, *Flower Drum Song* was suitably if not very convincingly Oriental enough: it told a tale of San Francisco's Chinatown, it provided a conflict between Oriental parents and Americanized children, it had East meet West amid clashing customs and picturesque ceremonies. It had its pleasant performers and gorgeous costumes; the score offered proof of here a jolly Rodgers and there a dreamy one. The show was nowhere unprofessional, it sought everywhere to prove popular. You had only, however, to compare it to Rodgers and Hammerstein's previous Oriental effort—*The King and I*—to see how far it fell short. Doubtless, Rodgers and Hammerstein were determined that these two examples of East meets West should be as unlike as possible in effect; in any case, they were decidedly unlike in quality. Where, at least in musical-comedy terms, *The King and I* seemed truly exotic, and aromatically blended its fable, its score and its dancing, *Flower Drum Song* had nothing distinctive to blend, and was so little exotic as to make Chinatown almost indistinguishable from Broadway. What seemed worst about the show was not that it failed to be first-rate but that it gave no sense of ever trying to be. It seemed sadly routine; it called to mind how different from second-best Rodgers and Hammerstein was second-best Rodgers and Hart which, if it sagged, might also soar; if it starved the nightingale had something succulent for the mockingbird. The Hart wit would waltz to a Rodgers tune, and the Hart irreverence would puncture what, again and again, *Flower Drum Song* seemed all out to promote.

In a Broadway season gone a bit mad over the Far East, a shift to the Far West could have proved refreshing; but *Whoop-Up*, a musical about whites and Indians in Montana, was beyond geographical aid. That, compared to *Whoop-Up's* domesticated tribesmen, cigar-store Indians would have seemed frighteningly real, was perhaps the least of what was wrong. The whole show was a bust: no musical in years had been at once so frenzied and so immobile, so deafening and so dull. It had all the yelp of a great massacre without a trace of the excitement, and such bad gags as should have left the librettists redfaced themselves.

Not the Far East or the Far West, but France brought surcease: *La Plume de Ma Tante* spoke a sort of compound-fractured English but was in all other respects as French as it was funny. The question of speech hardly mattered anyhow, for *La Plume* was a revue that stressed the international comic language of leers and leaps, pratfalls and double-takes, cupboards and manholes. In contrast to the season's mechanical gag shows, that alone would call for thanks. But, with *La Plume*, the quality of *merci* was not strained; the show shone by more than contrast. Even where it fell flat, there were high spots to fall from, and actors who could plummet with gymnastic grace.

La Plume had three great merits: madness, precision and charm. The madness proved a sort of soufflé'd *Hellzapoppin'*, of things out of context or out of the blue—a man contentedly nibbling a dog biscuit, a wonderful high-kicking chorus line with one girl always kicking the wrong leg. And about all the proceedings there was a sort of dreamlike clockwork precision, part of it owing to a background use of gay, rhythmic, tinny music. But what most enhanced what was good in the show and most cushioned what was not could only be called charm. It lent a kind of glow to the delightful cast's zaniness, lure to the patter, appeal to the pranks. And it added something human and wistful to the calisthenic comedy of the unforgettable first-act finale, in which four monks pull, then intertwine and at length make jubilant Maypole madness with four bellropes. But of the whole evening, what seemed like elementary *la-plume-de-ma-tante* performing was in truth almost untranslatably idiomatic. The

Pat Suzuki and Miyoshi Um

"Flower Drum Song"

revue had two of Broadway's outstanding virtues without their accompanying defects: there was no aggression in its showmanship, or tension in its speed.

Sooner or later there was bound to be a musical made from *Pride and Prejudice*. *First Impressions* took its title, if not always its cue, from Jane Austen's original draft of the novel; and the sets and costumes were as consonant and captivating as Jane Austen herself could have asked for. Thereafter, things began to fall short of perfection. The score was sometimes pretty or prancing, but never very impressive. Abe Burrows' book was a display of piety tempered with ruthlessness—it retained a good deal, but what it excluded or revamped was often crucial. Thus Mr. Burrows reduced Mr. Bennet, the wittiest *character* in all Jane Austen, to a cipher who did a bit of gardening; and one Mr. B. was never a substitute for the other. Again, Mr. Collins was not only subtly altered as a person but was literally changed from a curate to a curator; and the added syllable represents the general nature of the Burrows adding machine. The most drastic change, however, was offering Hermione Gingold as Mrs. Bennet—which not merely made of the lady a quite different kind of vulgarian but turned her into the heroine of the evening—someone whose dedicated efforts to marry off her daughters met an approving response in all the quite un-Austenish middle-class matrons in the audience.

It matters not how much or how little of *Pride and Prejudice* was preserved in the letter: with Mr. Bennet ignored, with Mrs. Bennet made over, with Farley Grainger impossible as Darcy, the spirit was lost. But that *First Impressions* was not like enough to *Pride and Prejudice* matters much less than that it was not good enough as musical comedy; that it lacked an identity, a swing and a sparkle of its own. Once tone was to be tampered with, timidity was pointless. If Miss Gingold, who in her own way is splendid, was to play Mrs. Bennet, why should not Ethel Merman have played Lady Catherine, and Danny Kaye, Mr. Collins and Marlon Brando, Darcy: and by shifting things to the Deep South in 1870, Mr. Bennet could have died at Bull Run and been eliminated completely.

Juno, a musical version of *Juno and the Paycock* with a book and score by Marc Blitzstein, fell short on more honorable terms and in some sense for opposite reasons. Mr. Blitzstein's respect for O'Casey's play was great enough for him to respect every difficult part of it: there was no softening what was harsh in it, or glossing over what was painful. Indeed, it was the harsher side—which, being as often melodramatic as it is tragic, makes it the lesser side—

that was favored; and the comic side, which is what makes for one of the great works of the modern theatre, that seemed slighted. The Paycock and Joxer never rose to their full height, where the Charlie Benhams got more attention than they needed. No less crucially, *Juno* was hurt by the attempt—so frequent with musical drama—to create a balance between the book and the music, to establish a kind of William-and-Mary régime. As a result, the music seemed superimposed on the story, where it should have been integrated with it—or better still, and in line with opera, sovereign to it. *Juno,* in the end, was too much like *Juno and the Paycock* to need to be so much different: if it was to be changed at all, it should have been truly transformed.

Mr. Blitzstein's music, on its own terms, seemed pleasant and interesting; but here again there was a snag, since neither Shirley Booth as Juno, nor Melvyn Douglas as the Paycock could sing at all. Surely they would better have played O'Casey straight, and could hardly have done worse by Mr. Blitzstein. Some of Agnes De Mille's choreography—notably a fine second-act street scene—proved a help; but much more of a distinguished play was lost than a respectable musical could atone for.

Redhead starred Gwen Verdon—and so far, so good. But this tale, splashed with raffishness and romance, of the plain Victorian niece of two sisters who run a waxworks museum smacked a bit of a waxworks itself; there were pleasant period touches but there was little musical comedy excitement. Indeed, not till Miss Verdon shook off her plainness did she really begin to dance (and even then, with less than her usual magic). In any case, by the time she had found her feet the audience had all but lost interest in the show.

Destry Rides Again, reaching Broadway late in April, quite lacked distinction, but did at least give Broadway a straightforwardly lively, crudely picturesque old-style musical. That it ought, like the movie it was made from, to have had a distinctive rather than a merely conventional appeal, is true enough: here again, even when adapting *movies,* the adapter's curse is evident. As a result, *Destry* is at once rather too sentimental and too loud, as it also comes to seem too long. But if nowhere vintage, it is good *vin ordinaire.* It has the conventional color and the usual climaxes; Harold Rome's score has sometimes beat and sometimes lilt; Dolores Gray does well enough with her part as it is written; Andy Griffith fills his part with his own likeable charm; and Michael Kidd, at whatever cost in strenuousness and blare, has danced life into the show. For the tens of thousands who *don't* want the best, here was a nice popular blending of music, dancing and story.

Jack Klugman, Ethel Merman, Sandra Church, M

rnilova, Faith Dane and Chotzi Foley in "Gypsy"

The Nervous Set was a spoof of the Beat Generation, contrasted (for double satiric effect) with the squares. There were some direct hits in the dialogue and amusing potshots in the lyrics, but too often the mere name of something topical tried to pass as a joke about it, and too often vulgarity tried to masquerade as wit. The chief trouble, however, was the staging of the show; there were times, indeed, when *The Nervous Set* seemed most like a spoof of amateur productions.

Gypsy, which wound up the season amid reviewing huzzas, hardly seemed worthy of them. To be sure, it brought Ethel Merman back to Broadway, this time as a mother with ruthless stage ambitions for her two girls, the future June Havoc and Gypsy Rose Lee; and it told a "true" story that had much of the humor, color and hard facts of stage life about it. Furthermore, the virtually unfailing Jerome Robbins worked up some funny child-actress vaudeville routines, and made the show's low point in refinement its high point in réclame: the performance of three old-style bump-and-grind burlesque queens rates with the all-time musical-comedy numbers. Such things, together with Miss Merman's presence in the cast, must make *Gypsy* worth seeing.

All the same, Arthur Laurents' libretto is a touch commonplace and more than a touch repetitious; Jule Styne's score, though agreeable, is nowhere noteworthy, and Stephen Sondheim's lyrics, if sometimes spritely, are largely routine. All this is too run-of-the-mine to give *Gypsy* any sustained quality; and I fear that, gallantly playing an unsympathetic role that also means playing against herself, Ethel Merman cannot quite make the show's shortcomings seem negligible. In *Gypsy* she is the great showman she always is, and at moments the great performer; but the driving woman she impersonates proves much less rewarding than the superbly coarse, lowdown, good-humored gal that Ethel Merman is herself.

THE SEASON IN CHICAGO

By Claudia Cassidy

Drama Critic, Chicago *Tribune*

SOMETHING was stirring in the Chicago theatre season of 1958-59, something more provocative than the chronic rumble of discontent. There was an air of do it yourself on some playgoing fronts, tempering the temptation to call the season more edifice than edifying. But there is no doubt that it had a kind of building boom.

Two of our more charming theatres, the Civic and the Harris, now the Michael Todd, neglected souvenirs of the roaring twenties, were handsomely restored. A project was launched to build a new home for the Chicago Symphony Orchestra. Reclaiming the wonderful old Auditorium moved another snail's step toward the possible. And over on the lakefront at 23rd Street the huge new convention hall is building a stunning theatre in white, red and gold, opening on a lakeside plaza with adjoining restaurants—the work of Alfred Shaw, one of whose collaborators is Edward D. Stone.

On the other hand, several of the town's playhouses keep the lights low to hide the dirt and the peeling plaster, and a Loop building project dooms the Great Northern, a spacious old house dating from 1896, when it opened with Henry Miller in *Heartsease*. In recent years it has been falling apart, especially backstage, a place abhorred by many actors as the theatrical black hole of Calcutta. The Lunts demurred. When they played there in *The Great Sebastians* they called the house "an actor's dream," and loved it as fitting Jean Giraudoux's definition of a true theatre—"a large room." This season it was a ghost house, with three and one half weeks' booking.

But then it was a skimpy season all around, which makes you look twice at costly restoration of theatres which might capture no plays. Sentiment, with a reassuring streak of shrewdness, was back of both gestures. Reclaiming the Harris, for instance, was Michael Todd, Jr.'s way of completing a gesture toward Chicago begun by his showman father.

Side by side on Dearborn Street are "the twin temples of the seven arts of the stage," as the publicity man called them when they opened in the season of 1922-23. The Selwyn, generally in the

Georgian style, was the Archie and Edgar Selwyn project, launched with *The Circle,* starring John Drew and Mrs. Leslie Carter. Mike Todd took that one, called it the Cinestage, and installed *Around the World in 80 Days.* After his death his son took up the option on its neighbor, which Sam Harris had opened with Ernest Truex in *Six Cylinder Love.* Young Todd restored it to its Florentine luxury, renamed it the Michael Todd, and reopened it at Christmas with a first rate production of *Two for the Seesaw,* with Ruth Roman and Jeffrey Lynn. He now has the job of keeping it open.

The Civic, a rose, gold and green jewel box of a theatre, was part of the Samuel Insull dream to make Chicago Opera magnificently self-supporting. A small version of the big house, it opened in 1929 with a typical gesture of the times. Harley Clarke, then a big man in public utilities, liked Shakespeare. He handed Fritz Leiber $300,000 and said, play some. *Hamlet* was the first of a fairly deplorable lot. The original purpose of the little Civic, which was to give intimate opera the right setting, never came off either. At Christmas, 1944, the theatre had a splurge of glory when it saw the indelible first performance of *The Glass Menagerie.* For the last eleven years or so, it had been given over to television.

The rescuer in this case was Alan Carr, a twenty-one-year-old Chicagoan with a passion for theatre, a bank account, and what looks hopefully like a flair for being an impresario. With the house beautifully restored he ran into the usual shortage of bookings. *The Girls in 509* was not a strong opener, but it effectively displayed the New York production and cast. Second time out Mr. Carr struck gold with a superb production of *Garden District* co-starring Cathleen Nesbitt and a Diana Barrymore who proved that she comes of thoroughbred stock. The Civic wouldn't mind being the Tennessee Williams house—his plays find their resonance there—but Mr. Carr is ranging theatre fronts from ballet to puppetry and Off-Broadway fare to keep his theatre alive in the mind of the public.

For the shows from Broadway shrink. In 1922-23 when the twin theatres were built, Chicago had more than 100 theatre attractions playing nineteen theatres. In 1958-59 by the most generous count there were seventeen playing seven.

My Fair Lady ran its string to sixty-six weeks and departed. *The Music Man* marched in with Forrest Tucker to an advance sale of $400,000. *A Raisin in the Sun* came to kill time until it could get a Broadway theatre, and turned away a small fortune at the anguished box office. Peter Ustinov amused the town vastly in *Romanoff and Juliet,* and a remarkable company of *Look Back in*

Summertime at the straw-hat playhouses

Anger, headed by Donald Harron, Pippa Scott and Al Muscari, bulged the theatre for its brief engagement.

The Dark at the Top of the Stairs reached us with a competent cast and scrambled direction. *The Warm Peninsula* was such a dull play that Julie Harris turned shrill trying to put it over. The Old Vic crowded its *Twelfth Night, Henry V* and its bourgeois *Hamlet* into a two-week span. Constance Bennett was *Auntie Mame* without the free wheeling gusto. Eddie Bracken tackled *The Tunnel of Love*. *Li'l Abner* stumbled in by bus and truck and not even Al Capp could have loved it.

At the Studebaker, a producer allergic to critics opened his *Fun Time* without them, but discovered that not all critics have by-lines. One group of 300 or so refused to pay for their tickets, whereupon the producer shut up shop for that one night. Allegedly annoyed by Basil Rathbone, who was reciting Shakespeare, he instructed the orchestra to accompany the recitation with "Cow Cow Boogie." Allegedly annoyed by Jack Leonard, he fired him and announced his intention to replace him by making his own first appearance on any stage. This led to an AGVA meeting in which AGVA said its members did not appear with non-members. The producer became a member and the show went on.

On their own terms, John Gielgud's *Ages of Man* and the Judy Garland show restored the faith. Emlyn Williams came back in his Dylan Thomas show, and all Mary Martin admirers were relieved to discover that the fiasco of *An Evening with Mary Martin* was, after all, only a tryout for television.

Meanwhile, the record for 1958-59:

Shubert Theatre: 52 weeks—*My Fair Lady*, 36 weeks, 66 in all; *The Music Man*, 16 weeks, so far.

Erlanger Theatre: 28 weeks—*Auntie Mame*, 20 weeks; *The Warm Peninsula*, 4 weeks; *The Dark at the Top of the Stairs*, 4 weeks.

Blackstone Theatre: 18 weeks—*The Tunnel of Love*, 3 weeks; *Romanoff and Juliet*, 4 weeks; *Look Back in Anger*, 3 weeks; *A Raisin in the Sun*, 4 weeks; *Li'l Abner*, 2 weeks; *Les Ballets Africains*, 2 weeks.

Michael Todd Theatre: *Two for the Seesaw*, 15 weeks.

Civic Theatre: *The Girls in 509*, 6 weeks; *Garden District*, 2 weeks, so far.

Great Northern Theatre: 3½ weeks—*Mask and Gown*, 1½ weeks; Old Vic, 2 weeks.

Studebaker Theatre: *Fun Time*, 2 weeks.

THE SEASON IN LONDON

By Harold Hobson
Drama Critic, London *Sunday Times*
London Drama Critic, *The Christian Science Monitor*

AMERICAN musicals continue to prosper in London. *My Fair Lady* has survived the withdrawal of Rex Harrison, and the substitution in his place of Alec Clunes. And *West Side Story* has shown that the United States can do for Shakespeare almost as much as they did for Shaw. On the native side of talent, though T. S. Eliot's *Elder Statesman* disappointed, no season in recent years has been so successful as this. For years we have been scanning the horizon in vain for the appearance of new young dramatists. Except John Osborne, none arrived. But now no less than six have turned up; it is almost an army. At the least, it amounts to a formidable advance guard. But it must be recorded that these fresh juvenous abilities—Peter Shaffer, Brendan Behan, Shelagh Delaney, Willis Hall, John Arden and Donald Howarth—have come at a moment which has suddenly become perilous.

On the whole, these people—one of them a provincial girl of nineteen, another a man who has spent eight of his thirty-odd years in prison for his activities on behalf of the Irish Republican Army, and all of them young—represent a rebellious attitude towards life and society. With the exception of Shaffer, they write about working-class people; they assume that working-class people are shoddily treated, and that no other class in the community has any social value; they despise, implicitly or explicitly, royalty, the social hierarchy, religion, the Archbishop of Canterbury, all those forces which tend to preserve Britain more or less as it is. They are, in fact, offshoots—vigorous offshoots—of that movement which was started with brilliant success by John Osborne in *Look Back in Anger* and continued by him in *The Entertainer*.

Now John Osborne himself has put this entire movement—the most exciting and worth-while of any the London theatre has seen since the war—into danger. Osborne, a few years ago a poor man, is now rich. He has married a beautiful wife. He employs a chauffeur. He has been anxiously and maliciously watched to see if his revolutionary outlook shows any signs of amelioration under the softening glow of gold. There has been hope amongst his enemies—that is, amongst the unsuccessful—that this gold in the pockets would reveal clay in the boots. It was considered not impossible that his musical, *The World of Paul Slickey,* presented for the first time in London on Tuesday, May 5, 1959—a date that may become historical—would mark some betrayal of the causes Mr. Osborne had espoused in his days of poverty, bitterness and neglect.

Well, *The World of Paul Slickey* did nothing of the sort. The attacks on what is called The Establishment, the ordered constituents of British society, to be found in his previous plays are here carried further, on a wider front, and with less restraint. Far from being mollified by wealth, Osborne has become sharper, more acid, more merciless, ready to express himself, because of the fierceness of his scorn, his contempt, in terms downright scurrilous. He no longer thinks that the things he hates—the nobility, the press, the Church—are worth clean, hard hitting. In *The World of Paul Slickey* he adopts against them the weapons of the most savage satirists, the weapons of Swift and Juvenal—scabrousness and indecency.

Slickey is a gossip columnist; when urged to write stuff yet more debased than usual by his proprietor, he shuffles and prevaricates. His victims are a noble family that is less than half-witted, and concerned only to keep its head alive sufficiently long to reduce death duties. Its younger members are sexually promiscuous, and finally enter on medical experiments so that the men may become women and the women men. Nobody in Mr. Osborne's play has the courage to stand up his employers; nobody has the courage even to accept the responsibilities of his sex. Everything and everybody is rotten: the press, the notorious and the celebrated about whom the press writes, and, by implication, the people who are fools enough to read what is written by the press.

Mr. Osborne has, in fact, here drawn up an indictment of a whole nation. Burke, in the course of some remarks about America, said that this could not be done. The fate of *The World of Paul Slickey* suggests that Burke was right. At first the reception accorded to Osborne's latest work was friendly enough. Jokes about the stage, and about the Inland Revenue were well received. Satire against a pompous old Etonian Tory set all the dukes in the audience laughing, whilst even their duchesses smiled indulgently. The more jests against the aristocracy there were, the better the aristocrats in the audience seemed to be pleased.

This is what everyone expected. The staunchest supporters of anti-Establishment plays in England are the intelligent members of

In "Look After Lulu," Tammy Grimes is admired by Roddy Mc-Dowall, George Baker and Kurt Kasznar

the Establishment. The working classes know nothing about their defenders in the new theatrical movement. They are quite satisfied with their football pools and their Hollywood films. The whole anti-Establishment movement stems from the English Stage Company, on whose committee are a member of the royal family, a son of a former Governor-General of Canada, and the head of one of the most prosperous and largest capitalist enterprises in the world. The enormous strength of the English aristocracy is that it accepts and even supports attacks on itself if these attacks are made with ability; but when those attacks are without ability, its revenge is swift and sure.

A quarter of the way through *The World of Paul Slickey,* the audience suddenly and apparently capriciously decided that on this occasion ability was something that Mr. Osborne conspicuously lacked. The lyrics were wanting in the neatness that any one of half a dozen American writers could have given them. The story became confused. The jokes misfired. The music by Christopher Whelen was no more than sub-Bernstein. There came a scene in which a cigar-smoking clergyman danced a conga in mockery of the funeral rites of the Church of England. Normally the Church of England is fair game for any attack in the theatre, but at this moment personal rage against Mr. Osborne seemed to convulse every member of the gallery. Boos and screams broke out which were renewed at the end of the play. The two dukes in front of me in the stalls did not join in the hooting. They merely sat with aristocratically frozen faces and allowed the gallery to obliterate Mr. Osborne for them.

It is difficult to judge what the effect of all this will be. But the next night there was the first performance in England of Frederick Lonsdale's *Let Them Eat Cake*, which had been presented in America twenty years ago. The cast of characters is almost entirely composed of lords and ladies. In recent years the temper of the gallery has been such that aristocratic characters on the stage have had a very rough passage. Snobbery has been scented with preternatural acuteness. On this occasion the reaction from the night before was very evident. For the first time in years titles were received by the gallery with affection, almost with reverence. With the failure of *The World of Paul Slickey,* the proletariat-loving, Establishment-hating, revolutionary drama in Britain has received its first serious check.

The uproar about Mr. Osborne's latest play has obscured what might otherwise have been the outstanding theatrical development of the 1958-59 season. This was the decision of the Lord Chamberlain to soften the restrictions which he places upon the public presentation of drama in the British Isles. The world's first performance of Samuel Beckett's *Fin de Partie* was given, in French, by a French company, at the Royal Court Theatre in the early months of 1957. The Lord Chamberlain permitted the play, in the security of a foreign language, to be given uncut and unmodified. In particular he raised no objection to one of the characters describing God as *"un salaud."* But when it was proposed to present *Fin de Partie* in English, under the title of *End Game* at the same theatre, with *"salaud"* translated as "bastard," he interdicted it. Mr. Beckett's friends protested, and there was a long struggle. Finally the Lord Chamberlain had his way. *"Salaud"* was turned into "swine." This was a victory for the censorship, but apparently the Lord Chamberlain emerged from the battle a chastened man. Soon afterwards he formally declared that he would in future give a licence to plays dealing with homosexuality and lesbianism, provided these subjects were treated seriously.

The results have been less sensational than might have been expected. There has been no rush of excited dramatists anxious to exploit their new-found freedom to discuss sexual perversion. Just before Christmas, 1958, in a trivial farce by Denis Cannan, *Who's Your Father?*, the word "homosexuality" ("Was there much homosexuality at Eton?" "Oh, the usual amount.") was pronounced for the first time upon the public, as distinct from a club, stage in Britain. That is all the Lord Chamberlain's decision has resulted in, up to the present.

Two plays of the year, however, both produced originally before the Lord Chamberlain made his memorable advance into modern times, have had a strong undercurrent of homosexuality; they evaded the censorship by not mentioning the thing explicitly. They were Peter Shaffer's *Five Finger Exercise* and Shelagh Delaney's *A Taste of Honey*. Mr. Shaffer's play is about a family of middle-class people who are strangely disturbed by the arrival in their midst of a young German tutor. The play has the exquisite balance of a piece by Chekhov, and a remarkable delicacy of feeling. It has subsidiary themes of great beauty. The rich Philistine father's attempt and failure to understand why his son wishes to study so unutilitarian a thing as English literature at Cambridge, for example, is most touchingly and sympathetically observed.

Miss Delaney's milieu is a slum in Lancashire. She presents working-class life in all its rawness and squalor and vigor. Her most successful character is a young man of strong feminine qualities who displays extraordinary tenderness in encouraging a girl to look forward to the birth of her illegitimate child (of which, needless to say, he is not the father). Miss Delaney's strength here is that she treats this youth as if he were part of the normal order of nature, not as a freak or a warning or a pioneer. The result is extremely moving and generous-hearted.

The boy is played by Murray Melvin. Mr. Melvin also appeared as an English soldier in Brendan Behan's *The Hostage*. This is a wild, reckless piece about the tension between England and Ireland. It is a mixture of farce, comedy, satire, music hall and tragedy. It has things in it to offend both countries, and others to make them both proud. There is incompetence in it, and genius, too. Like *A Taste of Honey*, *The Hostage* is a product of the East End Theatre Workshop.

On the whole, it has been a Theatre Workshop and an English Stage Company (Royal Court) season. John Arden in *Live like*

Pigs wrote for the Court a play which boldly argues that if people wish to be filthy and degraded, then on the best principles of individual freedom they should be allowed to be so. The first thing his family of migrants do when they are put into a decent house is to put the water closet out of action. That is their gesture of liberty, and philosophically Mr. Arden approves it. In another Court play, *The Long and the Short and the Tall,* Willis Hall shows that the best soldiers are not necessarily the best men. He does it quite powerfully.

But perhaps the highest achievement of the year has not been British, but American. The last act of Eugene O'Neill's *Long Day's Journey into Night* was of incomparable pathos and beauty. It is comforting to think that part of its glory was due to quotations from an English poet, Swinburne ("Yea, though we sang as angels in her ear/She would not hear"); ironic, to reflect that Swinburne was a poet who had no success in the drama himself. Here the New World and the Old are in perfect accord.

OFF BROADWAY

By Henry Hewes

Drama Critic, *Saturday Review*

ENJOYING the 1958-59 Off-Broadway season required a greater sense of divination than ever before. There were more productions than ever, more reviews of each—even *The New Yorker* ran regular Off-Broadway reviews by a critic hired especially for that purpose—and almost any attraction could lift a blurb to deceive theatregoers. However, the top dozen events were first-rate theatre and showed a gratifying willingness to risk all on the playwright's intent rather than obscure that intent with success-obsessed production methods.

Circle-in-the-Square with its distinguished young director, José Quintero, continued to be New York's only producing organization to produce plays with a steadily distinctive high quality. Its opening play, *The Quare Fellow*, introduced Brendan Behan, the most exciting new playwright to come out of Ireland since O'Casey. The title is the nickname prisoners give to a man about to be hanged, and the play explored poetically and with humor the hard truth of life inside a jail where an incipient hanging brought out the best and the worst in the prisoners and the guards. Designer David Hays used a few wooden catwalks and a black wall on which had been painted in large letters "SILENCE," to capture the essence of the Irish prison. And in this set a large cast gave beautiful performances, the most memorable of which was Lester Rawlins' intense portrait of a religiously fanatic warder. And after a four-month run Mr. Quintero followed with an even more highly acclaimed revival of Thornton Wilder's *Our Town*, featuring John Beal, Jane McArthur and Clinton Kimbrough.

A new director was discovered in William Ball, who staged the first New York production of *Ivanov* at the Renata. This early Chekhov play proved to have more stage vitality than his later masterpieces. *Ivanov* is peppered with delightful little vaudevilles of rustic social life, and a fine cast played them for humor, trusting the tragic overtones to emerge by themselves, which they did.

The most pleasant surprise of the Off-Broadway season turned out to be a thirty-four-year-old TV actor named Hal Holbrook, who entertained audiences at the Forty-first Street Theatre with *Mark Twain Tonight*. In what seemed an amazingly good impersonation of the seventy-year-old author, Mr. Holbrook wandered about the stage toying with his cigar, or leafing through some tattered notes, and let his stories and jokes come out in reluctant sentences. The device of following what appeared to be the punch line of an anecdote with a long thoughtful pause and a second wry comment much funnier than the first was most effective.

While today's Off Broadway has failed to uncover another Eugene O'Neill or Paul Green, it occasionally exhibits a new playwright of quality. One such was Meade Roberts, whose *Maidens and Mistresses at Home at the Zoo* was a burning and hypnotic piece of theatre. In it Leueen MacGrath gave a superb performance as a lost and beautiful woman whose husband has become paralyzed through a life of debauchery. This play, along with Giraudoux's *Song of Songs*, was first performed as a special matinee at the New York Chapter of ANTA's Matinee Theatre Series. Its transference to a regular Off-Broadway theatre by producers repeated a pattern which led to the presentation of *Guests of the Nation* and *Aria da Capo* at the Theatre Marquee in July of 1958. The former was Neil McKenzie's excellent adaptation of Frank O'Connor's short story about two affable British prisoners shot reluctantly by the Irish in reprisal.

Although it did not go any further, Off Broadway's finest new play was Tennessee Williams' *I Rise in Flame Cried the Phoenix*, which was performed in the Matinee Theatre Series. This very pure work distilled the beauty and truth of D. H. Lawrence's life into a brief death scene. Alfred Ryder seemed to burn from the inside as he gave us the dying poet. And Viveca Lindfors and Nan Martin provided a study in contrasts as the visceral Frieda and the celibate Brett who hovered around him.

Of the new American plays by unestablished playwrights, perhaps the most interesting was poet William Carlos Williams' *Many Loves*, which constituted the opening bill at the Living Theatre's gaily decorated new headquarters at Fourteenth Street and Sixth Avenue. While the author's attitude was not always clear in an uneven production, it did face its subject matter with truthful insight and humor.

Also-rans in this category were Lonny Chapman's *The Buffalo Skinner*, an honestly written, well-produced autobiography of an Oklahoma boy who spends too long learning a little about life; Valgene Massey's *Chaparral*, the saga of a degenerate Texas family; Frank Merlin's *Foenix in Choir*, a play that takes place after the A-bomb has fallen; Wade Dent's *A Good Place to Raise a Boy*, an unsuccessful drama attacking the South for its attitude on segregation; Rock Anthony's *Jackknife*, a *Truck Stop* play with odd characters but one good scene spoofing insurance claim settlers; J. Fred Scollay's *Listen to the Quiet*, which dramatized the efforts of a totalitarian guard to break down the religious faith of a group of prisoners; Barry Stavis's *The Man Who Never Died*, a politically-minded tribute to labor leader Joe Hill; John Wulp's *The Saintliness of Margery Kempe*, a long-winded comedy set in the fourteenth century; Nathaniel Banks' *Season of Choice*, which condensed enough story for three plays into one family drama that made the South look more normal and less interesting than usual; and Thomas Barbour's *The Smokeweaver's Daughter*, a slight comedy. Also rating special mention were Bernard Evslin's *The Geranium Hat*, a children's play for not very demanding adults that dealt with a puppet master who could change people into tiny puppets and did; and James Dey's *The Redemptor*, inspired by Ionesco's *The Chairs* and taking much too long to treat a rather interesting situation—namely a kindly old professor who has worked all his life to invent a bomb that will destroy the world and gain him recognition.

If Off Broadway has not been very successful in the matter of developing new native playwrights, it has done a great deal to introduce foreign ones who are new to most of us. The aforementioned Brendan Behan topped this season's list, but also well-received was Hermann Gressieker, a German playwright whose *Royal Gambit* was a discursive but original play that postulated Henry VIII as the first modern man and presented its case through spotlighted conversations between Henry and each of his wives.

James Forsyth's *Heloise* somehow managed to get good notices despite a shabby production and a script that seemed only occasionally interesting. It had, however, the distinction of being the first of two plays this season to deal with the subject of castration. Also from England came Nigel Dennis's *The Making of Moo*, a Shavian satire on organized religion, and Bernard Kops' *The Hamlet of Stephey Green*, a strange transition of the *Hamlet* theme transferred to a Jewish family in a modern London suburb.

The more established foreign playwrights fared slightly better. Ionesco's *The Bald Soprano* and *Jack* ran several months despite a lukewarm reception. Jean Genet's *Deathwatch*, as directed and produced at Theatre East by Leo Garen, proved a remarkable poetic fantasy that looked unflinchingly into the subconscious desires of three incarcerated criminals. Thus it dealt with the very jungle Ionesco's characters avoid by frenziedly hanging on to society's clichés. Later in the season a newly formed Sunday night theatre club presented the world premiere of Yeats's *The Death of Cuchulain*. And Sean O'Casey's *Cock-a-Doodle Dandy* finally was seen in New York in a not very satisfactory production.

Except for *Ivanov*, the only other classic to receive a notable revival was the medieval *The Play of Daniel*, which, under the direction of Nikos Psacharopoulos, played ten times in Trinity Church. With a narration written by W. H. Auden and delivered impassionedly by Alvin Epstein, this perfectly costumed reconstruction proved a beautiful evening of theatre. Other revivals included Judith Evelyn in a sleepy *Electra*, Ellis Rabb in a doubleheader of Sophocles' *Philoctetes* followed by Gide's more humorous version of the same myth, and Ford's *'Tis Pity She's a Whore*, which ran into amusing problems because of its title. Shakespeare had a lean year with the Shakespearewrights' *King Lear*, featuring Sidney Walker in a noisy and monotonous production.

The efforts of Joseph Papp and his New York Shakespeare Festival in Central Park ran into problems. The free performances of *Othello* and *Twelfth Night* in the summer of 1958 continued to be an asset to Central Park, and a "reading" version of *Antony and Cleopatra* at the Heckscher Theatre introduced an effective method of presentation of this difficult play. Unfortunately, George Scott's Antony, modeled after General MacArthur, didn't work, and under the circumstances Colleen Dewhurst failed to flourish as Cleopatra. But worse trouble lay ahead. Unaccountably, Park Commissioner Robert Moses presented Mr. Papp with a demand that he charge admission to the 1959 performances in the park and give a percentage to the Park Department for the replacement of grass eroded by the audience's nightly visits.

Another important function of Off Broadway is the providing of recent Broadway plays with a second showing. At the Sheridan Square Playhouse a talented new director, Jack Ragotzy, directed two Arthur Laurents plays, *The Time of the Cuckoo* and *A Clearing in the Woods*, in ways which were more faithful to the author's original intentions than had been the Broadway productions. In the former Kathleen Maguire presented us with a less sympathetic but stronger Miss Samish than had Shirley Booth, and in the latter Nancy Wickwire gave a stylish and thoughtful performance in the role created by Kim Stanley. At the Gramercy Arts Theatre (formerly the Davenport), William Archibald's *The Innocents*, based on Henry James' novel *The Turn of the Screw*, seemed more effective than one remembers it in its Broadway outing. And a rather unsubtle but vigorous production of Arthur Miller's *An Enemy of the People* at the Actors Playhouse was nevertheless a solid hit.

Last season's in-the-round presentation of Mr. Miller's *The Crucible* at the Martinique had played 517 performances by the first of June and promised to run long enough to set a new record for Off-Broadway performances of a play. The record is now held by Circle-in-the-Square with 565 performances of *The Iceman Cometh*. In third place is the same organization's *Summer and Smoke* with 356.

Also seen Off Broadway in this category were *The Potting Shed, Look Back in Anger, A Trip to Bountiful, Waiting for Godot* (the San Francisco Actors Workshop production enroute to the Brussels World Fair), and *The Waltz of the Toreadors*. The Equity Library Theatre, in the fifteenth year of its existence, included in its schedule: *The Cave Dwellers, Separate Tables, The Rope Dancers, The Matchmaker, Night of the Auk, Orpheus Descending*, and *Billy Budd*.

If there was a discernible trend it was towards musicals. The pacemakers continued to be *The Threepenny Opera* and *The Boy Friend*, with the former chalking up 1550 performances through June 1 and moving into third place in the all-time list of musicals on or off Broadway. Of this season's musicals the most delightful was a revival of *Fashion*, with period songs collected by Deems Taylor that included the very catchy "Walking Down Broadway." The cast included Rosina Fernhoff, who, along with Anne Fielding of *Ivanov* and Jane McArthur of *Our Town*, seemed the most promising of the new actresses. Also achieving a considerable success were Barry Morse's production of the British musical, *Salad Days*, at the Barbizon-Plaza, which was better done here than in England, where it is still running after five years; and *She Shall Have Music*, Stuart Bishop's and Dede Meyer's musical version of *The Country Wife*, featuring Cherry Davis, the Off-Broadway Gwen Verdon. Ira Bilowit, Wilson Lehr and Alfred Brooks presented an extremely tasteful musical version of *Of Mice and Men*, with a fine cast featuring Leo Penn, Art Lund and Jo Sullivan. While the songs added little, they afforded a new excuse for seeing a well-acted performance of Steinbeck's moving play. An all-Negro musical based on *The Egg and I* and a Spanish comic-operetta called *Olé* rounded out the straight musicals. However, a promising new revue-writer was discovered in twenty-two-year-old Stephen Vinaver, who concocted *Diversions*, a revue acted by only five people. One of our theatre's first ladies, Ethel Waters, demonstrated how the intimacy of the small Renata Theatre could increase the effectiveness of a program she had performed on Broadway several seasons ago, but oddly enough it did poor business and had to close. Likewise the Broadway musical hit *On the Town* opened to fine notices at the Carnegie Hall Playhouse, but was somehow unsuccessful in getting attendance.

Dolly Haas in "Lute Song"

Fortunately the reverse was not true when musical-comedy writers Betty Comden and Adolph Green offered a special Monday night program of their material at the Cherry Lane, under the unpretentious title, *A Party*. They were able to move to Broadway and become a hit there as well.

But the most distinguished Off-Broadway musical event was the American premiere at the City Center of the Bertholt Brecht-Kurt Weill theatre piece, *The Seven Deadly Sins*. Lotte Lenya and the lovely dancer, Allegra Kent, performed brilliantly in this satire on middle-class hypocrisy, which shows the schizoid morality of a daughter who by means of sin helps pay for her self-righteous family's Louisiana home. City Center also gave impressive revivals to the Elmer Rice-Kurt Weill mixture of musical comedy and opera, *Street Scene*, and to Sidney Howard's and Raymond Scott's exquisite musical version of *Lute Song*, with Dolly Haas bringing a nice grace and sadness to the role of the faithful wife.

Finally, mention must be made of two important Off-Broadway events. The first was Oliver Saylor's and Marjorie Barkenstein's heroic effort to transfer the Nighttown sequence of James Joyce's *Ulysses* to the stage at the Rooftop Theatre. Director Burgess Meredith and choreographer Valerie Bettis did a fine job, and *Ulysses in Nighttown* became the talk of New York. While Zero Mostel may not have been Leopold Bloom, he surprised everyone with the deep sense of tragedy that he evoked despite his hilarious carryings-on. And Sven Swenson captured the essence of ribaldry with a short danced-sung refrain that outdistanced all of Joyce's dirty words.

And at the York, Maxwell Anderson paid tribute to Off Broadway by allowing it to have the New York debut of his final play, *The Golden Six*, which bit off a considerable gulp of Roman history. Unfortunately it was not well performed, and except for a much publicized bit of semi-nudity, offered a tame dramatization of some ironic and colorful history. This was a pity, for Mr. Anderson, like Mr. Sayler, devoted a lifetime to the theatre and earned a happier ending.

THE TEN BEST PLAYS

A TOUCH OF THE POET
A Play in Four Acts
BY EUGENE O'NEILL

[EUGENE O'NEILL *was born in New York in 1888, the son of a popular American actor, most famous for "The Count of Monte Cristo." O'Neill's early plays were staged by the Provincetown Players. They were mostly one-act dramas of the sea. He has been the winner of four Pulitzer Prizes—for "Beyond the Horizon" (1920), "Anna Christie" (1922), "Strange Interlude" (1928) and "Long Day's Journey into Night" (1957). Generally regarded as America's greatest playwright, he died in 1953.*]

[NOTE: *Because of the special circumstances surrounding the posthumous publication of "A Touch of the Poet," it was not possible for the publishers to secure the right to excerpt in the customary "Best Plays" fashion. Accordingly, the Editor has summarized the action without quotation.*]

For the cast listing, see page 293.

A Touch of the Poet takes place during the day and evening of July 27, 1828, at Melody's Tavern, a hundred-year-old inn fallen on evil days. Situated in a village a few miles from Boston, the tavern was once a prosperous stage-coach stop; since the stage-coach run was discontinued some years back, the tavern had been all but deserted. Its former handsome and spacious taproom is now divided by a flimsy, painted partition into a bar and dining room. When there are customers these days, they are for the most part local Irish freeloaders who hang out in the bar. The dining end, unadorned except for a large mirror on the wall, contains four tables of varying size, some straight chairs and a schoolmaster's desk, where the accounts are worked.

"A Touch of the Poet": By Eugene O'Neill. Unpublished dramatic composition copyrighted 1946 by Eugene O'Neill. First published in 1957 by Yale University Press and © reserved by Carlotta Monterey O'Neill. All rights reserved. All inquiries regarding this play should be addressed to the Richard J. Madden Play Co., Inc., 522 Fifth Avenue, New York, N. Y.

On this morning of July 27th, the young, sturdy barkeep, Mickey Maloy, takes it easy reading his newspaper in the dining room. Greeting an older and hung-over Irishman, James Cregan, Mickey takes pity on him and offers him a drink on the house from Con Melody's private stock cached in the dining room.

Warmed by the drink, Cregan rehashes last night's surprising meeting with Melody, whom he hadn't seen since the 1812 war in Spain. When he starts proudly displaying his face with its saber cut from the battle of Talavera, where he had been a corporal and Melody captain, Maloy indicates that he's heard all this before. Hoping uneasily that he hadn't talked too much the previous night, Cregan asks Maloy to repeat what he had said so he can recant if there were any lies.

Maloy tells of the dossier Cregan provided on Melody's background: Con Melody was not, as he pretends, of the landed gentry but the son of a thieving Irish innkeeper who got rich through trickery and usury. When he had amassed enough money, Con's father bought an estate, acquired a pack of hounds and a wife who died giving birth to Con. Though none of the gentry would deign to come near him, tough Melody senior was undeterred. He sent Con to a gentleman's school in Dublin, with large amounts of money to make him the equal of any.

Quickly finding out that the gentry would borrow his money and sneer behind his back, Con discovered no less quickly how to wipe the smile from their faces and at the same time bolster his pride by dueling. From then on Con was always seeking an excuse to challenge someone, and eventually his dueling ruined him. He killed a Spanish nobleman with whose wife he had been found. Disgraced right on the heels of his promotion to major, Con's fine record alone kept him from a court-martial.

Well aware that he has been indiscreet, Cregan brazens it out. He tells Maloy that if he had known Con in those days when, wearing his uniform and mounted on a thoroughbred, he was the handsomest man around, he would never doubt Con's drunken boasts of conquest. In Spain and Portugal, as opposed to Ireland, Con as an officer was welcome in the gentry's houses. At home, except for Nora, Con had only known whores. "It is the same thing here," says Maloy: Con has no chance among these stiff-necked Yankees to flaunt his prowess with women, and he's too proud to mingle with the few Irish whom he considers scum. Once in a while when a Yankee family does stop overnight Con overplays the gallant with the wife and daughter and boasts afterwards that he could have bedded them, given the chance. If Maloy had only known Con in the old days, maintains Cregan, he would never doubt any boast that Con ever made.

Maloy is sure that he has his own information about Nora. When he used to sleep in, Maloy would overhear Con's drunken accusations that Nora trapped him, with the help of the priests, into marriage. Cregan is outraged at this downright lie: Con Melody never did anything that he didn't want to do. When, shunned by the Irish gentry and lonely on his estate, Con discovered Nora, he fell very much in love with her, although he was at the same time ashamed that she came from ignorant peasant stock. He married her, then left her alone in the castle to have her child while he went off to war in Spain. Sent home in disgrace, he raised enough money to bring Nora and their daughter Sara to America, where no one would know him.

Finding it hard to believe that—in view of how he treats Nora today—Con ever loved her, Maloy just the same thanks Cregan for this new and apparently true picture, and for Nora's sake promises never to breathe a word of it.

At the first note of a girl's voice, Cregan, not caring to be blamed for the drinking bout of the night before, clears out; Maloy remains stubbornly behind.

An exceedingly pretty, youthful blend of aristocrat and peasant, Sara enters and peremptorily calls for Maloy's bar book. Maloy points out that Con has drunk up any possible profit. When Sara ignores him, he taunts her for the grand airs she's assumed ever since the young Yankee has been upstairs, sick in bed and too weak to defend himself. When sparks begin to fly, Maloy placates Sara with some news. Doing her accounts and seeming not to listen, she is at once all attention when Maloy says that a Yankee lady drove up early this morning in a grand coach with a Negro coachman, ostensibly to be shown the road to the lake but more likely to have a look at the waitress. Touchy at being called "the waitress," Sara hopes Maloy made clear that she was also the owner's daughter.

Disliking Yankees as much as Sara does, Maloy says that he not only made Sara's position clear but was very curt with the lady. Sara now starts worrying that Maloy might have been ill-mannered. Actually, she just wants to hear what the lady looked like. Though she was too delicate for Maloy's taste, he had yet found the lady surprisingly young, more like the young man's sweetheart than his mother. Youthfully confident that there is no sweetheart, Sara now worries that the lady had a needless hot drive and walk through the wood, when all the time her son was upstairs. Maloy had reasoned that since the lady never bothered to mention her son, he had no reason to tell her about him. Accepting this excuse and refusing to bother further, Sara goes back to her figures just as her mother appears at the door.

In contrast to the Yankee's young-looking mother, Nora, who must have been every bit as pretty as Sara when a girl, is old beyond her forty years. Dumpy and slovenly and too worn out by hard work to care about her appearance, Nora yet remains the gentle spirit she always was.

Fond of Nora and ever ready to take advantage of her kindness, Maloy asks if she will keep an eye on the bar while he runs to the store for some tobacco. Nora is agreeable; Maloy escapes, and Sara is furious.

Though her rheumatism pains her, Nora refuses to spend money on a doctor or a cure, but uses her last penny to buy eggs for a breakfast Con will not eat. As Sara bitterly points this out, Nora excuses last night's drinking as due to the chance encounter with James Cregan. Unimpressed, Sara finds it difficult to remember any night that Con was sober.

Her mind skipping to other unpleasant things, Nora mentions that if Neilan's grocery bill isn't settled by the end of the week, there'll be no more groceries. Fortunately she has been able to put aside the money to pay for his mare's overdue feed bill. Sara's Irish temper flares anew at the thought of her father putting his horse ahead of his family. Lapsing into a strong brogue, she asks God's pity on her mother; Nora's only response is that Sara is not speaking as she was taught in that school for gentlemen's daughters. Sara answers sharply that she was unable to remain there long since her father had neither the pride nor love enough to keep Nora from slaving her heart out. Since *she* had both, Sara left school to help out as best she could. Her father couldn't afford a waitress, but he can afford to preen and prance about on his mare. He can afford a barkeep, too, though he should be tending bar himself. However tenderly she feels toward Sara, Nora becomes indignant at her suggestion that Con Melody, a gentleman, should tend bar.

Refusing to acknowledge what they both know—that Con's pretense to fine lineage is fiction—Nora maintains stubbornly that, born rich in a castle and educated in college, Con is the gentleman he claims to be. No matter what Sara says, Nora will not condemn him or leave him. She declares that her pride is in her love for Con, and since Sara is possessed of the same devilish pride as her father, she will never know how to give all of herself—which is what love is. Sara, on the defensive, answers that she could give herself *if* she wanted to. But there are no "ifs" in Nora's world, and, impressed in spite of herself, Sara kisses her mother impulsively. A fraction of a second later, her defiance returning, Sara declaims that she will love to gain her freedom, not her slavery. Deeply hurt and quite defenseless, Nora begs her daughter to leave her the pride she has in her love; otherwise she is nothing.

Nora now sighs over Father Flynn's warning that Con had better stop sneering at the Irish. They are already incensed at his promise to vote, along with the Yankees, for Quincy Adams against Jackson and the Democrats. Sara, with undisguised contempt, recalls Con's crying out against mob rule like any of the Yankees who swindled him into buying this inn. What she most holds against him is his being such a great fool when he had every opportunity in America to become what he pretended to be. If she were a man, Sara asserts, there isn't a dream that she would not make come true. And, much like her own father, she adds that Father Flynn should mind his own business and remember that he's not dealing with shanty scum.

Finished with her accounts, Sara thinks that she'll now put on her Sunday best to blarney Neilan for further credit. Quite aware that Sara isn't bothering to change into her best for the grocer, Nora inquires after the young man upstairs. Suddenly coquettish, Sara says that her patient is well on the way to recovery and will soon be able to go back to his cabin by the lake.

Nora can't understand how a rich man's son can live like a tramp. Sara explains that Simon, after graduating from Harvard College, wanted to get away from his father's great shipping business: he didn't like being in trade. Since this is how a gentleman should feel, Nora is most sympathetic. But Sara, who can repeat with ease her young Yankee's plan to live at one with nature, far from man's greed, and to write a book filled with Utopian ideas, isn't so sure that his ideas aren't somewhat crazy. At any rate, she adds smugly, Simon of late has had no time to write the book; he has been writing love poems. Nora can see that Simon Hartford has a touch of the poet in him—just as Sara's father has. Sara scornfully asks God's help for her mother who can think Con Melody a poet because he shows off reciting Lord Byron.

Uneasily changing the subject, Nora notes that young Hartford is falling in love with Sara. Crying out triumphantly that he's already fallen head over heels, though he is too timid to tell her, Sara admits that she also is in love, but not too much. She's determined to marry him and rise in the world. Full of admiration, Nora yet warns her about his Yankee family, and that it may not be marriage that Simon has in mind. Angry at first, Sara answers smilingly that if it comes to seducing, she would have to be the seducer.

As her father enters and greets them with old-world courtesy, Sara answers curtly and goes upstairs.

Tall, broad-shouldered, full of tough peasant vitality, Cornelius Melody shows the ravages of dissipation only in his face. His polished manner is overdone; his bloodshot eyes anticipate insult; yet, in spite of all this, there is something singularly impressive about him. As Nora timidly offers him breakfast, Melody condescendingly and brusquely refuses it. Desiring only to help him, Nora next offers to put cold compresses on his forehead, but observing his shaky hands, she suggests the only possible thing: a hair of the dog. Con virtuously won't hear of it, but after the briefest encouragement drinks up eagerly.

Nora's meekness rubbing him the wrong way and her disheveled appearance repelling him, Con becomes thoroughly abusive. With drink in him, his confidence flowers and his manner becomes grand. Reading his newspaper, he remarks disdainfully that the idol of the riff-raff will be the next president, whatever the efforts of himself and men like him. Then noticing the date on the paper, he strikes the table with his fist and declares dramatically that he had all but forgotten the anniversary of Talavera, when, before the whole assembled army, the Duke of Wellington had commended him for bravery. Taking her cue and saying staunchly that such an anniversary must never be forgotten, Nora promises a special dinner tonight.

Eagerly welcoming this idea, Melody decides that he will ask to the dinner James Cregan, who by the barest good fortune has arrived here. Though of course Cregan is not a gentleman, he was a brave soldier, and may therefore have the honor of sitting at Con's right. Con also decides to include in the party those members of the rabble, O'Dowd, Riley and Roche, though he can't sink to sitting at the same table with them.

Nurturing her husband's dream of being a gentleman, Nora promises to get his uniform from the trunk, and promises further he will be so handsome that no woman could keep her eyes off him. Melody boastfully recounts his days of female conquest in Portugal and Spain, and then for a moment has the good grace to be ashamed of his talk. He vacillates constantly between vainglorious pride and a sense of apology toward Nora, just as he vacillates constantly between his hatred of the Yankees and the English and his blistering contempt for the illiterate Irish. He damns Nora's peasant brogue and the fact that her daughter seems to be acquiring it. Next he makes an elaborate apology for last night's behavior. He rewards a blissful Nora with a kiss, but suddenly shoves her away because her hair is so dirty. Thus dismissed, she goes meekly to prepare his eggs.

Feeling much better with his third drink in him, squaring his shoulders and surveying himself in the glass, Melody hammily recites from Byron's "Childe Harold." Observing such posturing with contempt, Sara refuses to acknowledge Melody's compliments on her pretty dress. She reminds him sharply of her blarneying visit to Neilan. Hearing nothing he does not want to, and retaining his gracious air, Melody asks for a quiet talk with her.

Sara's barbs get under Melody's skin, but with a brave show of tolerance, he expresses his approval of young Hartford. Furthermore, having investigated his family, he thinks it will pass muster. Though it is hard to forget Melody Castle and his stableful of hunters, Con, now that he is an American, refuses to be an old-world snob who looks down on trade. Bitter at such preposterous talk, Sara reminds her father of the bill for his thoroughbred. Provoked at last, Melody cries out defiantly that he will keep the mare even if it means starving himself. Then, getting control of himself, he resumes his ridiculous patronizing of the Hartford family. Assuming that he may shortly expect an interview from the young man, he mentions the financial arrangements that Simon's father and he will first have to settle. Hardly believing her ears, and trying to bring Con back to reality, Sara says stingingly that he should attend to his drinking and leave her alone. Exasperated and yet pleading, she cries out that even now, when he's nearly sober, he can no longer distinguish between lies and truth. Reached somehow, Melody becomes enraged.

Tumbling and pushing one another, Roche, O'Dowd and Riley enter the front door. Pulling himself together and calling them down for their filthy manners, Melody sends them into the bar. Disdainfully tolerant of their rabble ways, he offers them drinks on the house. Equally disdainful of her father and his drinking cronies, Sara leaves the inn.

Entering with his food, Nora begs Con to eat it before it gets cold. Paying no attention, he starts for the bar. Then, without even turning toward Nora, he says condescendingly that he's sorry that she has gone to this trouble but he isn't in the least hungry. Going into the bar, he closes the door behind him.

ACT II

Two drinks and a half-hour later, Melody, leaving the bar to brood over his memories, strikes a Byronic attitude. Sara, back from her humiliating errand for credit, does her best to avoid him. When he reminds her that it is the anniversary of Talavera, she replies that it's a great day then for spongers and a bad day for the inn. Breaking up what might prove another kind of pitched battle, Nora gives Sara a glass of milk for her patient. As Sara leaves, Melody fires the parting shot—that he pities Simon caught in this scheming peasant trap. If all else fails, he sneers, there's always that last way to hook Simon, by appealing to his honor.

Nora blarneys Melody back into good humor by telling him how irresistible he was and is. He answers gallantly that she was the prettiest girl in Ireland, but looking at her he winces. Nora ventures to be mildly scornful of Simon's shyness; agreeing, Melody is utterly contemptuous of the genus Yankee, so lacking as it is in romantic fire. Unwilling to face Sara's wrath, however, Melody goes back into the bar as she re-enters.

Sara blissfully reports to Nora that Simon kissed her at last, but in doing so he made her as bashful as himself. Determined to have her wits about her the next time, she is sure that she is as good as married. Too happy now to feel any bitterness for anyone, Sara offers to get Melody's uniform out of the attic trunk, and goes gaily upstairs with her mother.

Increasingly disdainful of his drinking companions with every drink he takes, Melody backs out of the bar. Drawn irresistibly to the mirror, he strikes a Byronic pose as before and quotes his favorite passage from Byron.

Deborah Hartford, coming quietly into the inn, observes this narcissistic performance with dry amusement. Dressed in white with calculated simplicity, she presents a tiny, unusual figure. Once he has got over his anger at being caught out and has regained his composure, Melody is on his mettle. At the sight of this delicate lady, he is all seductive charm. He holds a chair for her to be seated.

Puzzled by his manner, Deborah addresses him curtly as the innkeeper, Melody. Matching her in curtness, he informs her that he is Major Cornelius Melody, formerly of His Majesty's Seventh Dragoons. Once more the amused spectator, she apologizes. She is not permitted to remain the spectator for long: going into action, Melody pulls out his whole bag of seducer's wiles, and in spite of herself, Deborah becomes frightened and fascinated. Melody's tone, as he talks, assumes a caressing note and at length a downright passionate one. Drawing her hand into his and leaning over her, he is about to manage a kiss when the smell of whiskey on his breath does him in. Icily angry, Deborah makes plain that she finds him disgusting and his performance absurd. Melody, as if slapped, draws back and Deborah rises. At the door, Nora and Sara know at once what has happened.

Addressing her remarks to Sara in a cool, self-possessed fashion, astounding Melody by what she has to say, Mrs. Hartford inquires after her son. When Sara informs her of Simon's illness at the lake and of his recovery at the inn, Deborah graciously thanks both Sara and her mother for their care.

As Sara escorts Mrs. Hartford to her son's room, Melody, left with his wife, fumes and rages at the visitor's ridicule. To soothe him, Nora suggests he go to his room and put on the uniform that she and Sara have laid out for him. Suddenly seized with the idea that if Mrs. Hartford saw him in full regalia, she would not question his being a gentleman or think him a drunken liar, he agrees to putting it on. Then, planning a formal apology for their little misunderstanding and ordering Nora to hold Deborah Hartford until he returns, Melody struts upstairs.

Sara returns to her mother's side. Furious at her father for playing the fool, she is almost as upset by Mrs. Hartford's air of superiority. Then reversing herself, she crows at the snubbing her father received at the lady's hands. A second later, Sara is really disturbed that by timing her arrival as she did, Simon's mother may have prevented the marriage. Outside Simon's door, Sara had overheard his mother say that Simon's father, enraged by an anonymous letter about Sara and Simon, had forthwith left to see his lawyer. Forbidden to see him ever since he left home for his cabin at the lake, his mother had slipped out all the same to warn him, and now must hurry home before she is missed.

Finding Simon's mother strange, queer and very hard to figure out, Sara is still prepared to best her at whatever game she plays. When the two finally talk together, Sara finds her more difficult than ever to fathom. She talks in such a rapid, remote, detached way about her son—a dreamer, who comes from a family of strange dreamers, pursuers of liberty and incorruptible reformers. The point of her rambling disquisition is that Sara can have no idea what revengeful hate the Hartfords' pursuit of freedom has imposed on the women who shared their lives. Left with these dreamers, the women, makers and accumulators of money, who even made money in slaves, would have appreciated, says Mrs. Hartford, Sara's ambition and determination. She has come here not only to speak to Simon but to warn Sara that the Hartfords never part from their dreams even when they deny them. This book of Simon's may well never be written, but it is already written on his conscience.

Eric Portman, Betty Field, Helen Hay

...d Kim Stanley in "A Touch of the Poet"

Departing without Sara's really being able to talk to her after all, Deborah leaves frustration in her wake. Unable to count on help from any direction, Sara decides to play hard to get: she will stay away from Simon until he grows afraid of losing her. As for Melody, he had been prepared to bowl Deborah over in his red-coated uniform and now finds instead that she has left. Feeling humiliated and consequently enraged, he is on the verge of violence. Only Cregan's arrival saves him from himself. With liquor and Cregan's flattery to cheer him, Melody toasts the day and Corporal Cregan. Lifting his glass, enthusiastically toasting the day and Con, Cregan is rebuked for his familiarity. Angry at first, then actually admiring Melody's manner of putting him in his place, Cregan amends his toast "to the day and *Major* Melody." Melody then condescends to touch Cregan's glass.

ACT III

Looking handsome in his uniform, but drunker than any of the barflies he has invited to his dinner, Melody has celebrated long and well while his wife slaved in the kitchen and his daughter served her father and waited on the drunks. At the end of the meal, Melody is so nasty and condescending to Sara that he literally treats her like a scullery maid. Boiling with anger, she prays that someday when he is admiring himself in the mirror, something will make him see at last what he really is.

Shooing his guests back into the bar where they belong and wishing to have another of his "quiet" talks with Sara, Melody tells her how outrageously he has interfered in her affairs. He has taken it upon himself to ask Simon of his intentions, and on hearing that Simon wants to marry Sara, he has grandly announced that a settlement between the fathers must first be arranged, and that he fully agrees with Mrs. Hartford that a year's interval should elapse before the marriage. In the face of this preposterous meddling, Sara is helpless. But when she acidly inquires whether her father has considered that perhaps Mr. Hartford will not think it an honor for his son to marry Melody's daughter, Con is grander than ever and talks of Melody's castle as against this money-grubber's hovel. But Sara has, as usual, hit the mark. Her words rankle, and with increasing vindictiveness Melody offers another reason why he could not give young Hartford an immediate decision. Watching and examining his daughter's conduct, trying to be fair and make every possible allowance, he has concluded that she is a common, greedy, scheming peasant girl who has shamelessly thrown herself at this young man's head because of his family's money and position. He has accordingly decided that she must decline Simon Hartford's offer of marriage. Trying to control herself, recognizing the time-worn pattern of his drunken tirades, Sara tells him she doesn't give a damn what he has decided. As a gentleman, as someone who cannot but know what a tragic misalliance such a union would be, Melody feels honor bound to prevent it. On the other hand, the man regards as a perfect match for her his bartender, Mickey Maloy. Sara is wild, but Melody continues his brutal remarks. Sara finally hits home by saying that the dirty hovel he remembers is the one his father grew up in. Stung to fury, glaring at her, Con says of course if she tricked Hartford into getting her with child, he can't refuse his consent. Sara promises to remember.

Melody stalks to the bar door, then suddenly turns around contritely. But Sara is not there. Once again the mirror attracts him; he is proudly speaking his piece to it when there is a knock on the door.

Nicholas Gadsby, Mr. Henry Hartford's lawyer, goes through a difficult interview with Melody: he first runs into Melody's hate for the law, then into his insults to Gadsby's profession, and finally into utter confusion over the settlement Hartford has in mind. With his only child's happiness at stake, Melody says that he is prepared to make every possible effort. But it turns out that what Gadsby is talking about is that Mr. Hartford, unalterably opposed to any further relationship between his son and Melody's daughter, is prepared to buy the Melodys off. Sara is to sign an agreement relinquishing any claim on Simon whatsoever, and the whole family is to leave this part of the country. Sara, running in, prevents Melody from smashing Gadsby's face in by appealing to his pride. Agreeing that it would be beneath him to touch this lackey, Con gets his bar cronies to do the work for him. The whole mob tackle Gadsby enthusiastically, and he is last heard from while being kicked down the street.

Melody's rage and humiliation cloud his entire thinking. He is determined to win an apology from Hartford; otherwise there will be a duel in the morning. Sara tries to placate him: there is no longer any dueling in this part of America and, besides, Hartford would never accept the challenge. Threatening to put a whip to him, Melody shouts that Hartford will fight or be dragged out of his house and horsewhipped in the middle of the street. A frightened Sara pleads with her father that Hartford already, by way of Gadsby, knows his answer. What's more, it's plain that Melody could not even get by Hartford's servants, let alone see Hartford.

No longer even thinking of Sara in this matter—he wouldn't allow her to marry the son of a man who had insulted his honor—Melody begins to lose all control of himself. Calling Sara a slut and a whore, he would see her dead before allowing her to marry. He'd kill her himself. As Sara shrinks back, Cregan steps between them and suggests that they start off for Hartford's. Only stopping for another drink, Melody strides to the door. Sara's helpless cry—that by his actions he will force her to go to Simon—falls on deaf ears. He disappears into the noisy bar.

O'Dowd and company, laughing uproariously, claiming that the foe is in full retreat, return from the brawl. Finding no Major to report to, and Sara completely unresponsive, they all pile into the bar.

To Nora, joining her daughter, it seems like old times again. A certain kind of pride lights her face as she thinks of Con Melody off to another duel. As a raucous farewell takes place in the bar, Nora determines to be brave and not to worry. Sara says bitterly that her father can go his way and she'll go hers. She will show him that she too can play at the game of gentleman's honor, and, avoiding Nora's eyes, she says she's going to bed.

At first Nora is angry that her daughter could be so heartless as to sleep while Con is in danger. Then, remembering what a bad day Sara has had, Nora becomes tender and understanding. Always the believer in true love, she comforts Sara with the thought that no duel will be able to keep the lovers apart.

Kissing her mother impulsively, Sara goes upstairs. Waiting for Con, Nora finds the bar noise cheering and encouraging.

ACT IV

As, shivering with cold, worry and exhaustion, Nora keeps her lonely vigil in the dining room, Mickey Maloy comes out of the noisy bar. Hoping to cheer Nora and warm her with a drink, he reports that the bar is having a record night because of Con and Cregan's being on the warpath. All the Irishmen who hate Con, but who hate the Yankees more, are crowding into the bar in the hope that he will beat the living daylights out of Hartford. As Nora fiercely echoes this sentiment, Mickey Maloy grins. He'd certainly like to have a mother like Nora, or better yet—he tells her—a wife. Suddenly wonderfully coquettish, Nora tells him to save his blarney for the young. Having succeeded in cheering her ever so briefly, Maloy returns to the bar.

Sara appears silently in the door. Dressed in her nightgown and a faded wrapper, her hair streaming down her back and her face

A TOUCH OF THE POET

exultant, she seems unable to say a word. Sensing her presence, needing her comfort badly, Nora starts to sob. As Sara hugs and kisses her, Nora pours out all that worries her in a long monologue. It must be a duel, else Melody would be back by now. If it is to be a duel, he will have taken a room near the dueling ground and by dawn will have drunk too much to shoot his best. At this point Nora contradicts herself: Con's eye, no matter what his condition, always remains sharp. She then suddenly pushes Sara away, only to grab for her hand again. It now occurs to her that James Cregan hasn't come for Con's dueling pistols. Suddenly Nora's resentment overflows: why couldn't Con have sent James with a reassuring word for her? Nora now becomes openly critical of Melody's high-handed English-gentleman ways, of his "red livery av bloody England," and of his family pride, which is all a lie since he stems from a thief. Having for once in her life had her say, Nora becomes horrified at herself. Yet, reversing herself again, she becomes openly rebellious.

It is not the duel that causes Nora the greatest anxiety. What haunts her most is God's punishment for the mortal sin that she committed with Melody before they were married; and Melody's forcing her to leave the church so that she could not make her confession. It now occurs to her that it would serve Con right if she were to choose this moment to wake up the priest to hear her confession. With Sara smiling at her, Nora starts gamely for the door, but stops short. She knows it's no use pretending. Not seeming to hear, Nora continues that if she were now to confess, Melody would feel betrayed. In spite of his scorn for her, he knows full well that her love is all he has. And, she adds spiritedly, *her* honor is as proud as his any day. Sara adds softly that she too has learned about the honor of a woman's love.

As if realizing for the first time that Sara is at her side, Nora says acidly that she's glad that Sara has found her tongue. Noticing too how pretty and contented Sara looks, she finds it odd that she shouldn't be showing any concern for her father.

In an unconcerned, dreamy voice, Sara says that Simon has assured her that there will be no duel, that his father will never bring himself to participate in anything so unlawful as a duel—and for Sara, it really doesn't matter what happens now.

Her attention focused on her daughter, Nora stares at her. Resuming her far-off tone, Sara confesses that she is now held, body and soul, in a dream that will never end as long as she lives. She knows now that Simon is hers and that no one can take him from her. At first Nora is pleased and quite unsuspecting at the cause of this great joy. As Sara relates how she had gone to Simon's room with every dishonorable intention only to remain a blushing maiden, Nora is somewhat less pleased. Thinking of her daughter's appearance in a man's room in the middle of the night, she is thoroughly scandalized. It is now Sara's turn to deliver a monologue on her new-found joy, her new-found shyness, Simon's surprising boldness and his manhood.

Simon had put to rest all of Sara's fears concerning his mother's influence. No promise had been exacted from him to wait a full year. Simon had also assured Sara that his mother would undoubtedly be amused by his father's failure to buy off the Melodys, and his probable need for police protection. Aroused at mention of the police, Nora cries bloody vengeance on them, as Sara, unheeding, talks of kisses and love. As she speaks of her willingness to live in a hut and work herself to the bone for love of Simon, Nora, still preoccupied with thoughts of the police, gives her daughter a mechanical pat.

Simon had said that since he had a small cotton mill to run, it wouldn't be quite necessary to live in a hut, and since the mill would provide for a comfortable life, with time left over to write his book, he could maintain his ideas and not become a slave to greed but be happy with enough and no more. Sara cries to her mother that she had answered with a kiss and had sworn that all she wanted from life was his love and his happiness. Again Nora responds with an automatic pat.

Lost in a cloud of happiness, Sara continues her account of the exchange of kisses, of confidences, and of the light finally being put out. Lost in her own thoughts, Nora says she knows. Sara suddenly wonders guiltily just what her mother knows.

Abruptly made to realize what is up, Nora accuses Sara of being a wicked, sinful girl. With a toss of her head, Sara reminds her mother of her own pride in love, so that Nora can only say weakly that God will punish her. Sara is all for letting Him do His worst.

Hugging her mother to her, Sara recalls with a smile Simon's sense of guilt and repentance, and her own feelings that made her forget all thoughts of marriage. Teasing Nora lovingly, Sara says that her mother is not only the sweetest woman in the world but the wisest. She now proclaims that women are the slaves of love, not of men, and in spite of what Melody is, she can understand a little Nora's proud love for him.

This feeling passes quickly. In another second Sara's bitterness toward Melody returns. Sure that nothing has happened except his making a public disgrace of himself, Sara expects that he got his just deserts. She only hopes that the result may wake him from his lies, may make him face the truth about himself in the mirror; but she doesn't count on it.

Nora pays no attention to this last speech; she has heard a noise outside. Bloody and bruised, with a finger to his lips for silence, James Cregan sidles in. Making sure that no one in the bar sees Melody in his present condition, Cregan has Sara lock the bar door. Then half pulling and half pushing, Cregan manages to get Melody through the door. Not so much drunk as seemingly stupified from shock, Melody, his uniform torn and filthy, his face ghastly white and marred by bruises and clots of blood, stares unseeingly at the women and seats himself heavily at the center table.

Cregan denies categorically that Melody is drunk: he hasn't touched a drop since he left the inn, just as he refuses to drink even now. Cregan, after drinking what Melody won't touch, gives an account of Melody's grand entrance into the Hartford house, of the brawl with the servants that followed, and the fight, after that, with the police.

Sara with angry scorn reminds Cregan that this is just what she had prophesied. Ignoring her interruptions, Cregan describes the glorious fight with the police. Suddenly without any change of expression, Melody mumbles sarcastically that the hero of Talavera had acted like the drunken son of a thieving innkeeper, as all the while the pale bitch watched from her window and sneered with disgust.

Nora cries out that Melody has lost his mind, but Sara says toughly that he has come to his senses at last. As Cregan, undeterred, states that he and Con finally went down under the policemen's clubs for the glory of old Ireland, Melody mutters that they went down like drunken troopers outside a brothel on Saturday night. Then with a wild laugh, Melody gets to his feet and gropes his way to the door.

Cregan thinks that he's being sensible and going to bed, but both the women are thoroughly frightened, Nora so much so that she follows Con upstairs.

Alone with Sara, Cregan puts the whole blame squarely on her shoulders. Sara answers that she revenges her own wrongs. While her father was out playing the fool and getting sneered at by Mrs. Hartford, she beat the lady once and for all. The triumph leaving her voice, Sara asks God's forgiveness for such talk.

Cregan drunkenly wants to do all the talking anyway. Though he can remember the effect of a whip on his own head many years before, he is decidedly uneasy at Melody's strange behavior, and at his talk of the "pale, sneering bitch," and of his beautiful, dishonored mare.

Interrupting, Nora frantically begs Cregan to follow Con to the stable, where he has just gone with his dueling pistols. A moment after Cregan has gone, the women hear a pistol shot; and a few seconds afterwards, Cregan pushes Melody back into the room. Melody, he announces, has killed his mare. Then, wanting to get back to the gaiety of the barroom, and promising to speak only of the fight in the city, he slams the bar door behind him.

Sara's hysterical laughter seems somehow to pierce through Melody's dazed state. Speaking suddenly in the broadest brogue imaginable, saying that it takes more than a few clubs to dull his wits, Con insists emphatically that he is not taunting them or play-acting. That was the Major's game. Patting Nora's hand with genuine affection, he promises that the late lamented, lunatic and liar, Major Melody, will never torment her again. He will never show off before the Yankees or prance about on his beautiful mare, who is dead too. The shot that killed the mare killed the Major at the same time. There was no need, as he had intended, to use the other pistol on himself.

For a brief moment, Melody abandons his brogue as he grieves for the beautiful mare who understood him even at the very end. Starting to sob, wrenching himself out of this mood, he puts on the jeering broad brogue once more. Saying that he intends to bury the Major's accursed red livery, he proposes now to live at his ease in his proper station as old Nick Melody's son.

Now that what she had hoped for so long has arrived, Sara is upset and unhappy. Melody, handling her roughly, gives her some advice: it's to hell with honor if she wishes to rise in the world. Have the young Yankee bed her, then appeal tearfully to his honor, so that in marrying her, he will save hers. Goaded beyond endurance, Sara in a brogue matching Melody's own, answers that she took his advice while he was out fighting the police.

Melody's face freezes into the Major's cold glare. Groping for his other dueling pistol, his eye never leaving Sara, Melody lifts the pistol and aims it straight at Sara's heart. With a quick lunge Nora deflects it.

A dazed look comes over Melody's face as he says that he had wanted not to murder Sara but to congratulate her. Ever well-meaning, Nora tries to explain that Simon means to marry Sara as soon as possible, and has always intended to do so.

With a leering chuckle for Simon's fate at his daughter's hands, Melody proposes starting her on her upward path by giving her as a wedding present the land on which Simon built his cabin. Then seeing the pistol on the table, he says jeeringly that from now on he'll have no need for guns; his fists or a handy club will suffice. After all, didn't he and Jamie Cregan lick a whole regiment of police that night? Nora staunchly agrees. Grinning that never was there a loyaler wife, he kisses her and tells her he loves her and has always loved her. He promises furthermore to be a real husband and run the inn properly instead of being a sponge. He even suggests firing Mickey and tending bar himself; when Nora protests, Melody slyly begs her remember that at least he made the offer. He starts off for the bar.

Unable to bear this new coarseness of his any longer, Sara wishes that the Major were back, that the hero of Talavera, instead of joining the scum in the bar, would drink here with Jamie Cregan to keep him company. Answering to hell with Talavera, Melody catching a glimpse of himself in the glass says mockingly that it was in the glass that the old loon admired his mug, spouted his Byron and pretended to be a lord with a touch of the poet. Striking a pose, he burlesques his former performances.

Hearing a roar of laughter from the bar, he suddenly can't wait to tell the boys he's with them and all set to join the Democrats and Andy Jackson. Grabbing at him, Sara apologizes for all her taunts and sneers. She offers to do anything, even to telling Simon that she's too proud to marry him. Feeling his last hope of escape cut off, Melody crumples visibly; but with just a little encouragement from Nora, he recovers in a flash. Giving Sara a playful cuff, he knocks her off balance. This is to warn her once and for all not to raise the dead. And as for her not marrying Simon—has she no honor? Having seduced him, she is duty-bound to make an honest gentleman of him.

As Melody goes into the bar, Sara reflects that her father is beaten at last, and that the pride she inherited from the late Major is dead along with his. Hearing Melody toasting Andrew Jackson on the bar and acting as one of the crowd, Nora decides that if this brings him peace and companionship after his lonely life of pride, she'll play the game right along with him. She has no pride but that. Moved, wanting to be like her mother, Sara still can't help observing that, quite unknowingly, Patch Riley is playing a requiem on his pipes for the hero of Talavera. She suddenly bursts into tears.

THE PLEASURE OF HIS COMPANY

A Play in Two Acts

By Samuel Taylor, with Cornelia Otis Skinner

[Samuel Taylor *was born in Chicago in 1912. He grew up in San Francisco and attended the University of California, where he edited the campus humor magazine, "The Pelican." He then came to New York and got a job as a play reader. This gave him an opportunity to finish "What a Life," which George Abbott produced; its success led to Mr. Taylor's spending nine years in the field of radio writing further about the Henry Aldrich family. His "Sabrina Fair" proved a popular hit of the 1953-1954 season.*]

[Cornelia Otis Skinner, *the daughter of Otis Skinner, has long been a star in her own right. She was educated at the Baldwin School and at Bryn Mawr College. Aside from her starring roles on Broadway in "The Searching Wind," "Lady Windermere's Fan" and many other plays, she is the author of countless magazine articles as well as of a play, "Captain Fury," and of such books as "Dithers and Jitters," "Soap Behind the Ears" and (with Emily Kimbrough) "Our Hearts Were Young and Gay." She also wrote such volumes of autobiography as "Family Circle," "That's Me All Over" and "Happy Family." She was awarded honorary degrees by the University of Pennsylvania, the University of Rochester, St. Lawrence University, Temple University and Mills College. She was invested an Officer of the French Academy in 1954.*]

For the cast listing, see page 298.

THE *Pleasure of His Company* takes place in an old San Francisco house situated high on a hill overlooking the Golden Gate. Its living room, filled with objects from both San Francisco's interesting

---

"The Pleasure of His Company": By Samuel Taylor with Cornelia Otis Skinner. © Copyright 1958, as an unpublished work, by Samuel Taylor and Cornelia Otis Skinner and © Copyright 1959 by Samuel Taylor and Cornelia Otis Skinner. Reprinted by permission of Random House, Inc. See caution notice on copyright page. All inquiries should be addressed to the authors' agent: MCA Artists, Ltd., 598 Madison Avenue, New York 22, N. Y.

and moneyed past and her elegant present, provides a breathtaking view of the bay.

An entrance to a sun porch, now used as a bar, is at one end of the living room; at the other is the entrance hall that cannot be seen. There is a hall staircase with a landing that extends over the living room and provides a view of it for anyone ascending or descending the stairs.

Toy, an elderly Chinese houseman, is unwrapping wedding gifts spread around a Victorian ottoman. There appears to be a run on cocktail shakers of every size and shape—the last of which, in the form of a bell, Toy shakes optimistically. The telephone rings. The doorbell chimes. Picking up the phone and ordering whoever is on the other end to wait, Toy hurries to the hall door.

Biddeford Poole, "a man completely conscious of his charm and who uses it flagrantly," enters. Wearing a trenchcoat and carrying his hat in one hand and a tall, white-wrapped object in the other, he strides inquisitively into the living room. Pleased with the view from the bay window, the furniture and the various oil paintings, he particularly admires a portrait of a little girl by Augustus John.

He and Toy exchange pidgin English. "What name you got?" asks Poole. Learning it, Poole inquires if Toy was born here. "Me native son," states Toy. Poole tests him: "In 1906, was it an earthquake or a fire?" "Fire," says Toy unhesitatingly. Poole rests his case.

Without further small talk, Poole orders Toy to get him settled, run him a bath and, above all, fix him a whiskey and soda. Having had no such orders from his Missy, Toy balks. Removing a roll of bills from his pocket, Poole deftly slips a bill to Toy, who as deftly palms it. Then with a fine burst of Cantonese obscenity, Poole makes Toy his man forever. Delighted with the new visitor, Toy hurries to the sun porch for the whiskey and soda.

By this time there are very audible screeches from the telephone. Picking up the receiver and discovering a liquor merchant at the other end, Poole calmly orders fifteen cases of Dom Perignon '43 or '47. The splutterings at the other end don't faze Poole at all. Very grandly telling Mr. Rousseau that nothing is too good for his daughter's wedding, Poole asks Mr. Rousseau to gather himself together. Then with the further admonition that he is sure Mr. Rousseau can find what he wants "among his more reputable competitors," Poole hangs up abruptly.

Finding the father of the bride admiring the portrait of the little girl, Toy, who has overheard the telephone conversation, says realistically that Poole stayed away a long time. His daughter now is very pretty, very grown-up, and Poole won't recognize her. "I think I will," says Poole. "She'll be as her mother was, I think. No? Old Missy changed, Toy? Now just like one fat old woman?" "No," answers Toy. "Big girl, but no fat. Velly stlong 'oman, Missy Dougherty." Remembering grimly that she always was, Poole orders Toy to get the hell topside.

Having sown confusion at Mr. Rousseau's liquor shop, Poole now proceeds to do the same here. Refusing flatly to bed down in the guest room facing the street, he commandeers his host's own study because he fancies a view of the bay. Knowing he should put up a fight for his boss, Toy only needs to hear some more of Poole's Cantonese to capitulate. Shrieking with laughter while following in Poole's wake, Toy carries the suitcase upstairs.

Returning from a final shopping spree before the wedding, Kate Dougherty, handsome and self-possessed, drops the large box she is carrying onto a chair. Removing her hat and gloves, checking off a final item on her list, she thanks God that this day is over. While she examines a stack of mail on the secretary, her pretty daughter Jessica groans at the new batch of wedding presents. All brightness and gaiety, Jessica says she feels like a moocher. "You are cordially invited to my wedding," says she; "kindly remit gifts. Might as well pass the plate in church." "Hm," says Kate, looking up from a letter, "why hasn't anyone thought of that?"

Jim Dougherty, telegram in hand, follows the women into the room. A stocky, good-humored man, he is aware of Kate's tension as she opens the wire. When it proves to be from wedding guests wishing reservations at the Mark, Kate is obviously relieved, but Jessica is as obviously disappointed.

Hiding her feelings, wandering aimlessly about the room, Jessica discovers Poole's odd package; but acknowledging Toy's franchise ("Toy would never forgive me if I opened it first"), she doesn't touch it. On the other hand, loading the already opened presents into her arms and heading for the sun porch, she wonders why her parents' friends all seem to think she's an alcoholic.

Kate, making a last-minute check, asks Jim if he has taken care of the liquor for the reception. Jim says soothingly that everything is under control. Then having nothing concrete to worry over, Kate shifts to Jessica's cool behavior. But a telephone call from Mr. Rousseau gives her something else to think about.

Answering the phone, Jim cries: "You'll have to fly what in from New York? . . . What? . . . No!!" Turning to Kate, Jim asks: "Did you order fifteen cases of champagne at a hundred and fifty dollars a case?" Kate gives a startled "No." "No!" yells Jim into the phone. "Nobody ordered it!! . . . Well, *stop* looking around! . . . No! Yes! . . . All right! Thank you." Hanging up, Jim says: "That's the damndest thing." All Kate can think is: "Fifteen cases of champagne at a hundred and fifty dollars a case!"

Appearing in the doorway, Kate's father, Mackenzie Savage, murmurs: "Sounds like a good party." In his seventies, no longer surprised at anything, Savage has left his Monterey isolation just for his granddaughter's wedding, but he has chosen to stay at his club rather than with Kate. After greeting Jessica with very special affection, he wants his drink. As Jim goes to oblige, Kate none too subtly tries to get rid of Jessica. Instead, Jessica regales Savage with a description of the mink cape Jim has given her. When, however, she tells Savage of the change in her wedding trip plans, he is somewhat appalled that Roger will be taking her to Hawaii rather than Paris. "Well," says Jessica, "Roger got a notice of a big cattle auction in Hawaii, and there's a prize bull he thinks he might want to buy, so . . . we decided to kill two birds with one stone." "Practical, eh?" says Savage, glancing at Kate.

Having delivered the drink to Savage, Jim has been picking away at the strange, white-wrapped object. As he finally unveils an African primitive wood carving, Kate gives a yelp. "Really," she cries, "what a hell of a thing to send a bride!" And she isn't in the least surprised that Jim can find no card. Jessica, on the other hand, wins her grandfather's approval when she finds it oddly beautiful. Jim's contribution is to place an ash tray on its head to give it the functional touch it needs.

Kate wants her talk with her father. Firmly piling boxes and packages in Jessica's arms, she urges her to try on her new outfit so that they all can admire the effect. Lagging, Jessica overhears what is on Kate's mind. "Jim thinks you ought to be the one to give the bride away," Kate tells Savage, embarrassing both Jessica and Jim. "Oh? Why?" asks Savage, totally unembarrassed. As stepfather, Jim has felt that he hasn't this right, and besides Jessica worships Savage. "She worships you, too, Jim," says Savage. "She has an infinite capacity for worship."

As Jessica flees, Savage gathers that nothing has been heard from the rightful father, Biddeford Poole, Esquire. A letter written to him months ago, and a cable Jim sent last week, have gone unanswered. Kate, however, finds none of this strange. "In fifteen years," she says, "he's written to Jessica exactly three times. He's remembered her birthday exactly twice. And he never heard of

Christmas. Why should he let his daughter's wedding disturb his gay, roving life? The fabulous Pogo Poole! International playboy! Sportsman. Globetrotter. Heel." Savage detects a slight note of rancor. When Kate states that Savage *will* give Jessica away, Savage says he won't.

SAVAGE—I love and respect her too much to "give her away."
KATE—Why, so do we all, but . . .
SAVAGE—But convention demands it. What convention, daughter? That when a young woman reaches a certain age, she must be disposed of as quickly as possible? Why must marriage be thought of as a fixed law of nature, like gravity? She needn't be given away.
KATE (*studying him*)—Don't you approve of this marriage?
SAVAGE—No. I do not.
KATE—You've never said so.
SAVAGE—I've never been asked. I used to be a contentious man, but as I grew older, I lost my nerve. I wait to be asked, now.
JIM—Roger's a good boy, Mr. Savage.
SAVAGE—I'm sure. He's not my concern. But I have a granddaughter with wit and intelligence and a sweet love of life. She has an inquiring spirit and an eagerness to explore, and a capacity for living, that delight me. How will she use them now? Cut down in the prime of her life by marriage!

Savage knows very well that both Kate and Jim approve this marriage, that Kate had trained Jessica for exactly such a match, and though he may, as his daughter says, be a non-domestic male, this is not the case that he is pleading. To Savage the non-domestic male is a rapidly disappearing breed. "The young men," says he, "have become shy and frail and dispirited. They are the ones who need the security of marriage, the dull comfort of marriage, the sanctuary of marriage. Let them wait. All they can offer is an inclination to breed; why should we give them our daughters? No. Let the young women have the time of *their* lives, and breed at a time of *their* choosing." "Jessica wants to breed now!" Kate manages to get in. Dismissing this as a common confusion, Savage launches into morality. Knowing, from long practice, what's ahead, Kate asks for Jim's drink. Then cutting in on Savage, she asks slowly and quietly: "Will you walk down the aisle with Jessica?" "Yes," answers Savage firmly.

This being attended to, Jim and Savage seek more bourbon. As Savage reaches the sun room door, Kate asks: "You were never very happy with Mother, were you?" "Your mother," replies Savage, "was a saint, who made our home an outpost of heaven. It's why I spent so much time in saloons."

Alone, Kate makes a feeble effort to clean up the room; then giving up, she stands before the window staring across the bay. "Hello, Katherine," says Poole, poking his head over the staircase. Momentarily stunned, Kate makes a frantic but ineffectual effort to reach her compact before Poole comes into the living room. Like a questing bird dog, Poole circles around her. "How are you, Kate?" says he, leaning forward to kiss her. Kate holds her hand out quickly. "Well, Pogo," she says brightly.

Apologizing for arriving unannounced, Poole says he had been moving too fast, and besides had mislaid her address. The cable had only caught up with him the day before yesterday, and the letter had never reached him.

KATE—Did you bring your wife? I mentioned in my letter—oh, but then of course you didn't get it . . .
POOLE—I have no wife.
KATE—Again?
POOLE—I'm not very retentive, am I?
KATE—A bit slipshod. I take it she's divorced, not dead. (*He nods.*) And that makes—
POOLE—Only three. Counting you.
KATE—Yes, I suppose you have to count me.
POOLE—I insist on counting you. You're looking well, Kate.
KATE—Thank you. (*And now, aware that he still holds her hand, she disengages it.*) I suppose this is the moment for each of us to say: "You haven't changed."
POOLE—No point in saying it unless we have. Have you?
KATE—Of course!
POOLE (*dubiously*)—Oh? (*He steps back and examines her from head to toe, admiringly, then begins to circle her slowly as she stands stock-still. When he gets to her rear, he nods approvingly.*) Very good.
KATE—Would you like to look at my teeth? (*She bares them.*)
POOLE—I'm quite impressed.
KATE—What did you expect in fifteen years? Fatty degeneration?
POOLE—You've borne the burden of the years very nicely.
KATE—You've had the same amount of burden, you know.
POOLE (*with tender affection. He has moved in to stand close to her, a little too close*)—Ah, but you're one of those lucky ones that improve with age. You've . . . ripened.

KATE (*tenderly, matching his tone*)—I shall go on a diet tomorrow.

That concluded, Kate ever so politely asks where Poole is staying, and not so politely receives the information that the father of the bride has chosen to stay right here. Poole reminds her reproachfully to think of their daughter. With a grim look, Kate inquires: "Did Toy get you settled?" "Beautifully settled," answers Poole. "Delightful room; delicious view." "Of Green Street?" says Kate. "I'm surprised you didn't pre-empt one of the rooms looking out on the bay." It is Poole's turn to smile, sweetly.

Prowling about the room, Poole says how crazy he is about the house, and in all seriousness Kate answers how much she loves this house and its past. "I've become," she confesses, "a part of something that is sure and settled and . . . permanent; that's been lived in." "By Doughertys," says Poole. "I'm a Dougherty," Kate assures him, but she admits that there is much of Pogo in Jessica. According to Kate, Jessica has all of Pogo's charm and his gift for music. Though, Kate adds, "She'll always be a gifted . . . amateur." "Like me," says Poole. As far as Kate can discover, she and Jessica resemble each other only in the way they bump into furniture.

Poole would now like to hear about Dougherty, though Kate would prefer that Poole form his own opinion. "He is your age," Kate says. "Exactly. He's an attorney. It's an old family firm, highly respected. He is a native son in the best meaning of the term, head of the Harbor Commission, a strong power in California politics, extremely popular—"

POOLE—I'm not asking for his business, political and social credentials. What's he like with you?

KATE—Oh, Pogo, you sound like a social worker! "Does your husband treat you good?"

POOLE—Well? Does he?

KATE (*childishly defiant*)—Damn good! He's a wonderful guy, and I'm extremely happy with him!

POOLE—So there!

KATE—I wish you'd stop trying to make me feel as though I had a run in my stocking.

POOLE (*lightly*)—You have.

So off-balance is Kate, that as Jim enters with a drink, she introduces Pogo as her husband. Letting her off lightly, Jim says: "It's all right, Kate. I can prove I'm your husband." "And I," adds Pogo, "can prove that I'm not. It sounds as though we should congratulate each other, but somehow it would seem rude, wouldn't it?" He then proceeds to charm Jim, who responds charmingly, until Kate, not being able to listen to any more of this, exclaims: "Oh, will you two stop being so . . . chummy!"

Once again, Poole admires Jim's house. "Yes, it's a good one," replies Jim. "My grandfather built it. You'll find him there in that picture alongside James J. Hill. It's the driving of the Golden Spike when they completed the first transcontinental railroad." "Charming," murmurs Poole.

Returning for his newspaper, Savage shows no surprise whatever on seeing Poole and greets him as if he had just left him an hour ago: "How are you, Biddeford?" Assuming that Poole has come from a great distance to give the bride away, Savage comments that he is well-traveled. Poole starts one of his social travelogues. "I do seem to get about a bit, don't I?" he says. "Actually, the cable caught up with me high up on the Tanganyika border. It was really a miracle that the runner found me . . ." One question from Jim and Poole is off, and back, from Nairobi to Cairo, Cairo to Rome, Rome to Paris, Paris to New York, and New York to San Francisco —where Jessica, calling from the balcony, discovers him.

Her meeting with her father is sudden and tentative. Poole takes Jessica in his arms, as she, with loving pride, says: "Hello, Father." "Hello, daughter," says Poole. "And did you come from the ends of the earth?" asks Jessica, nodding happily as he replies: "The green hills of Africa." Now she knows where the wood carving came from.

Launching into a presentation speech, Poole says the carving is for Kate: "The moment I set eyes on it, it reminded me of . . . no, that could be misconstrued. But I remembered how you fell madly in love with primitive art, our first year in Paris, and I thought you might like it." He tells Jessica: "Your mother discovered that sort of thing long before it became a vogue. She had a wonderful eye. Painters liked her because she could see what they saw. Most people can't." Under Savage's eye, Kate shrugs this off uncomfortably.

With another flourish, Poole goes into high gear. Taking a velvet jewel case from his pocket, he says to Jessica with gentle romanticism: "It belonged to my grandmother. She left it to me with a simple instruction: that I must keep it, and give it, one day, to someone that she might have loved. I've kept it for you." Kate snorts, but watches intently as Poole places an emerald and diamond necklace around the neck of his overwhelmed daughter. "Mother!"

Jessica cries. "Look! I'm speechless." "So am I," Kate answers grimly.

Observing all this, Savage is highly amused, while Jim wonders about the stones. "It's an old Italian piece," says Poole. "Forty-eight diamonds and . . . I don't remember how many emeralds." "Thirty-two," Kate says distinctly.

As Jessica, looking at Poole with deep affection, would settle for his love without these jewels, Jim feels somewhat left out of things. He excuses himself; then starting to leave the room, he remembers to inquire where Poole is staying. With a great, sweet smile, Kate says: "He's staying here." Recovering, Jim says heartily that of course Poole must stay here. They have all the room in the world. "I'll try not to be a nuisance," says Poole. "Anything I can do to get you settled?" Jim says. "Thank you," Poole replies, "I've been very well taken care of." "Good!" says Jim, after a quick look at Kate.

Completely at home now, Poole admires his womenfolk, thinking mother and daughter make a lovely picture together. Feeling self-conscious, Kate offers him a drink, just as a very angry Jim pokes his head over the balcony and asks to see her. Kate goes up.

Alone, father and daughter admire one another and, against a background of slamming doors and upstairs rumblings, make up for lost time. But in describing her Roger to Poole, Jessica finds herself on the defensive in much the same way that Kate had been before her. Will she, asks Poole, like ranch life enough to stay put forever? Jessica thinks that they'll be able to get about after Roger has the ranch running as he wishes. Anyway, she remarks, Kate and Jim once took her to Europe for six weeks, when Poole was either in India or Pakistan.

It comes out that Jessica always knew where Poole was from news photographs in the English and Continental illustrated magazines. In fact, she kept scrapbooks of his travels that reminded her of the adventure books she used to read as a child: " 'Pogo Poole in the Scottish Highland,' 'Pogo Poole at Ascot,' 'Pogo Poole in the Isles of Greece,' 'Pogo Poole and His Racing Car' . . . I always looked forward to finding something new," Jessica says. And adds with a gentle smile: "It let me feel that I . . . had you."

POOLE (*touched and troubled*)—In the only way you could. (*Pause.*) I'm not very good about letters.

JESSICA—It didn't matter.

POOLE—And things like birthdays slip by. I've many things to be sorry for.

La Plume de Ma Tante

Photo by Philippe Halsman for LIFE, © TIME, Inc.

OUTSTANDING BROADWAY

SIDNEY POITIER
as Walter Lee Younger,
  CLAUDIA McNEIL
  as Lena Younger
in "A Raisin in the Sun"

GERALDINE PAGE
as The Princess
in "Sweet Bird of Youth"

EILEEN HERLIE   **ROBERT STEPHENS**
as Ruth Gray,   as George Dillon
in "Epitaph for George Dillon"

CYRIL RITCHARD
as Biddeford Poole
in "The Pleasure of His Company"

JASON ROBARDS, JR.
as Manley Halliday
in "The Disenchanted"

CHRISTOPHER PLUMMER
as Nickles
in "J. B."

PERFORMANCES 1958-1959

JOHN GIELGUD
in Shakespeare's
"Ages of Man"

ERIC PORTMAN
as Cornelius Melody,

KIM STANLEY
as Sara Melody
in "A Touch of the Poet"

GERTRUDE BERG
as Mrs. Jacoby,

CEDRIC HARDWICKE
as Koichi Asano
in "A Majority of One"

PIERRE OLAF
Performing
in "La Plume de Ma
Tante"

ROBERT DHÉRY
Performing
in "La Plume de Ma
Tante"

ANDY GRIFFITH
as Destry
in "Destry Rides Again"

Ralph Morse—LIFE, © TIME, Inc.

Juanita Hall, Conrad Yama and Miyoshi Umeki in "Flower Drum Song"

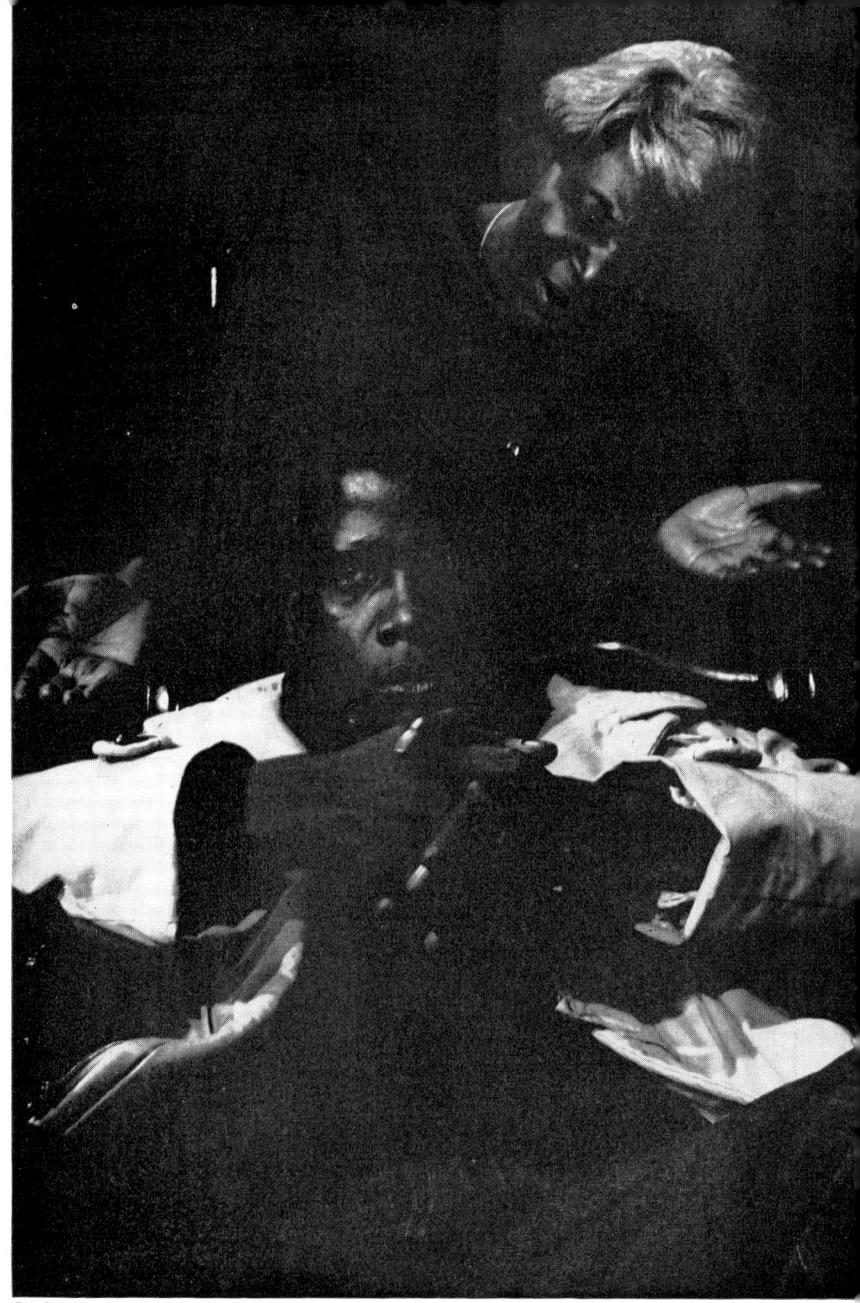

Gordon Parks—LIFE, © *TIME, Inc.*

Sidney Poitier and Claudia McNeil in "A Raisin in the Sun"

Roddy McDowall, Tammy Grimes and Jack Gilford in "Look After Lulu"

Photo by Vandamm

Dolores Hart, Cyril Ritchard and ... in "The Pleasure...

Robert Stephens, Alison Leggatt and Avril Elgar in "Epitaph for George Dillon"

Sig Arno and Maureen Stapleton in "The Cold Wind and the Warm"

Photo by Fred Fehl

Backdrop for "Juno" designed by Oliver Smith

Ben Edwards' set design for
"A Touch of the Poet"

Costume sketches for "Redhead" by Rouben Ter-Arutunian

Design by Rouben Ter-Arutunian for a drop in "Redhead"

Costume designs: "A Touch of the Poet" by Ben Edwards, and "Juno" by Irene Sharaff

Boris Aronson's set design for "J. B."

Costume designs by Alvin Colt for "Destry Rides Again" and "First Impressions"

Set design by Oliver Smith for "Destry Rides Again"

Costume designs by Irene Sharaff for "Flower Drum Song"

Backdrop design by Oliver Smith for "Flower Drum Song"

Scene from "A Majority of One," with Gertrude Berg and Cedric Hardwicke

Photo by Friedman-Abeles

Rosemary Harris and Jason Robards, Jr., in "The Disenchanted"

Yale Joel—LIFE, © *TIME, Inc.*

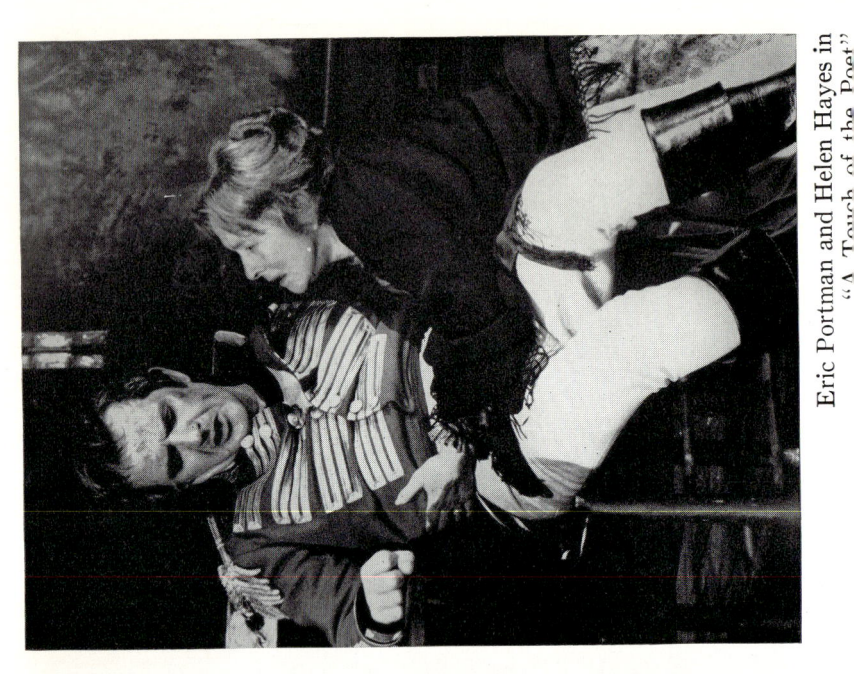

Eric Portman and Helen Hayes in
"A Touch of the Poet"

Gwen Verdon in "Redhead"

JESSICA—No, you haven't.
POOLE—"Pogo Poole and His Mechanical Heart." And now I've returned, to give away something I never had.

Jessica disproves this by pouring out her love for her father, and Poole, responding, reveals himself to be a man who had always demanded last things first and who, above all, went about his business of pleasure.

JESSICA—What?
POOLE—Pleasure.
JESSICA (*troubled*)—I don't believe it was as simple as that.
POOLE—It wasn't simple at all. A life of pleasure demands a concentration and self-discipline far beyond the capabilities of most. One may be trivial about many things, but never about pleasure. Don't ever try it; it's frightfully exhausting. (JESSICA *laughs*.) There's so much to see, and so much to do. And so little time. So little time . . .
JESSICA—I know.
POOLE (*amused*)—You?
JESSICA—Oh, I worry terribly about people dying before they can do all the things they want to do. Sometime, when I'm playing Mozart, I find myself crying because he died so young. And when I read Keats, or Shelley . . . ! I'm a terrible weeper.
POOLE—Do not weep for Adonais—he is dead.
JESSICA—But—
POOLE—Weep for the quick, not the dead. The ones who have to keep running. "But at my back I always hear/ Time's wingèd chariot hurrying near." Do you know that one? . . . Andrew Marvell. Actually, he was making love to a young lady and was getting a bit impatient, but still . . .
JESSICA (*laughing*)—What's it called?
POOLE—"To His Coy Mistress."
JESSICA—Oh, Father!

Having conquered Jessica, Poole is ready to take on Kate, who has changed into a new dress in his honor. When Roger's loud arrival draws Jessica out into the hall, Kate is left alone with Poole.

POOLE (*genially*)—She really is pleased with the necklace, isn't she?
KATE—She should be. I was, too.
POOLE—What do you mean?

KATE—When you gave it to me.

POOLE—I never gave it to you.

KATE (*suddenly angry*)—You gave it to me the night before we were married! And then you took it away when you left! That's . . . stealing!

POOLE—Nonsense. Why would I give it to you, when I always knew I would keep it for my daughter? You're confusing yourself with somebody else. It was Mona I took it away from.

KATE—Who?

POOLE—The second Mrs. Poole.

KATE—I've never had the pleasure of meeting the second Mrs. Poole!

POOLE—The pleasure was negligible. Or it may have been Natalie, the next one. Yes, you're confusing yourself with both.

KATE—I'm confusing myself with no one! You put it around my neck in the very same way, I was touched and moved because you used the very same words! Do you think a woman forgets a thing like that? (*Bitterly, mocking.*) Your grandmother's simple instruction! "I must keep it, and give it, one day, to someone that she might have loved. I've kept it for you." (*She growls.*) Your grandmother must be whirling in her grave!

POOLE—My grandmother was a sweet, sedentary old lady, and still is, I hope. And since you've brought up the unpleasant subject of stealing, let me point out that that is mine— (*He starts a quick tour of the room, pointing out the best French paintings.*) —and *that* . . . and *that* . . . (*He comes to the painting of the driving of the Golden Spike.*) You may keep *that* . . . and the Augustus John portrait of Jessica—

KATE—If you lay a hand on that portrait, I'll— (*And then she realizes it is gone.*) Where is it?

POOLE—I took it up to my room!

KATE—You will bring it back down!

POOLE—Never!

KATE—And you will get the hell out of Jim's study!

POOLE—I consider that extremely petty.

All excited, Jessica drags Roger into the room to meet her father. Usually a sure-footed and graceful outdoors man, Roger becomes a clumsy target for Poole's "charm." "So," says Poole, "you're the young man who's taking my little girl away from me." Kate stares at this new line. Replying sturdily and nicely to Poole's "father-of-the-bride" remarks, Roger shakes Poole's hand. Feeling he has done his job brilliantly, Poole turns about and smiles in self-approval at Kate.

Doing his unmusical best, Roger has bought the best piano to be found in San Francisco for Jessica. In announcing this bit of news, Roger can't help making several boners. As Kate tries to cover up, Poole stares at her with polite attention. "I'm afraid," Roger tells Poole ruefully, "Jessica's going to have a tough time with me, sir. But she's going to teach me about music and poetry if it kills her. It'll probably kill me." "I'm sure you'll catch on," Poole says.

On Jim's icy entrance, Poole assumes a sunny air. Apologizing to Jim for taking over his quarters, he forces Jim to answer in kind. Then, having been put on this spot, Jim realizes that Kate is all dressed up.

Trying to explain her clothes away, Kate has her embarrassment compounded by her father's entrance. Observant as ever, Savage—having overheard Jim and Kate—remarks: "That's a pretty dress, daughter." Kate is exasperated.

A phone call from Roger's ranch confuses things even more. Roger's prize bull is so sick that Roger feels he must be at its side. Though disappointed that the health of his bull takes precedence with Roger over party-going with his fiancée, Jessica offers at once to go with him to the ranch. "Don't be silly," Roger says. "This party's for you; you have to show up."

Kate's insistence that Jessica must attend the party in her honor enables Poole to offer a solution to the problem: himself. "To go to the ranch?" Kate asks coldly. "No," says Poole, "I'm not much of a veterinarian. But I can dance." Roger is relieved; Jessica is overjoyed. An irritated Kate does her best: "Ah, no! It's sweet of your father to offer, dear, but I'm afraid he wouldn't have a very good time . . . with all the young. . . ." Jim, backing her up, says: "And he must be terribly tired, after flying all the way from . . . Africa." Poole says cooly that he isn't in the least tired. Savage takes his part. Kate glares at her father. Poole reassures Roger: "I'll never leave her side." Jessica can't wait to have the girls see Poole. She knows she will be trampled in the rush. Poole is inclined to agree.

Goodbyes are said to Roger, who in turn promises to be back by Wednesday to dine with Poole. Left with Jessica under his wing, Poole asks to hear her play, and she leads him towards the music room. From the door, Poole beams at Kate and Jim: he's so glad they asked him.

Kate and Jim, side by side on the ottoman, stare stolidly ahead.

After a long silence, Savage wanders back into the room. Kate looks at him coldly.

KATE—You were a great help, Old Philosopher.
SAVAGE—I've changed my mind, daughter. I think I *will* move in. (*Another silence; then the piano is heard in a brilliant, romantic attack on the waltz from Schumann's* Carnaval.)
JIM (*finally*)—I'm damned if I'll call him Pogo! (*They listen to the music.*)
KATE (*finally, quietly*)—Everybody . . . calls him Pogo.
SAVAGE (*finally, cheerfully*)—Not I. I call him Biddeford. (*The music goes on.*)

ACT II

Two evenings later, in a living room now drenched with mimosa, Poole is still dancing with his bewitched daughter. Jessica is still raving over the impression Poole made on the women of San Francisco, while Roger watches from the side lines in disgust.

After putting Jessica through some tricky steps that a Duchess once taught him, Poole lights a cigarette as his daughter hurries out to stop the record.

POOLE—Wonderful exercise, dancing. Keeps everything loose. You're getting an enchanting girl, Roger. I hope you know that.
ROGER (*staring straight ahead*)—Yes, sir, I do.
POOLE (*looking after her with a proud laugh*)—Ah, if I were your age, and not her father, I'd make you fight me for her, boy.
ROGER (*grimly*)—I wish I could.

On her return, Jessica perches on the arm of Roger's chair, while Poole, gazing out into the San Francisco fog, assumes a Byronic stance. Poole proceeds to quote in romantic tones "The sea has many voices" . . . causing Roger to rise abruptly from his chair and almost knock Jessica onto the floor. "Sorry, Jess," he says, "I've been up two nights with that bull, and I'm flaked out."

Poole even manages to beat Roger to a farewell scene and bids Jessica a fond good night. Old hand that he is, Poole brings her down to earth with a gentle kiss, says good night to Roger and leaves the room—but not for long. On his way upstairs, he can't resist an appearance on the balcony—in the rule of Juliet. At last he retires.

Giving Roger her belated attention, Jessica fails to understand what is wrong. What with all the French that was spoken tonight, and the mention of Duchesses, and the quoting of poetry, Roger is mighty depressed: "I'm not the Continental type, that's all! Look, you go ahead and have a ball with your father, and I'll see you at the church Saturday! Good night." Jessica pleads that Poole went to all kinds of trouble planning tonight's dinner so he could get acquainted with Roger.

ROGER—Well, it didn't take; my French isn't good enough.
JESSICA—We didn't speak French all evening.
ROGER—I wonder what it was?
JESSICA—And it just so happens that we were in a French restaurant. And the proprietor was a Frenchman. And when you speak to a Frenchman, you speak French.
ROGER—Not if he's been in America for thirty years! and speaks English better than I do!
JESSICA—You seem to be weak in all languages.
ROGER—My French is just as good as yours. *Épatant! Merveilleux! La salade était magnifique!* It was salad! Plain, ordinary salad!
JESSICA—It *wasn't* plain, ordinary salad! It had upland cress in it, and wild dandelion leaves!
ROGER—That's what my cattle eat! And you don't see them dancing around yelling, "*Épatant! Merveilleux!*"
JESSICA—Oh, you and your cattle!
ROGER—And let me tell you something as a cattleman!
JESSICA (*overlapping*)—That's all I ever hear!
ROGER—That beef we had! It's a crime to take good prime beef and pour brown gunk all over it!
JESSICA—Brown gunk! Do you mean to call that heavenly sauce brown gunk?
ROGER—Brown gunk! And what makes you think your father discovered that "little French restaurant"? My Aunt Sarah goes there for dinner twice a week!

Rushing in, in negligee and pajamas, Kate and Jim hear simultaneous complaints from Jessica and Roger. "Well, I suppose I could have warned you," Kate says. "I was way out in left field, all evening!" cries Roger. Feeling that he acted like a sullen, unappreciative oaf, Jessica is close to tears: "Oh, Mother, it was a wonderful dinner!" she wails. "Father went down to the restaurant yesterday, twenty-four hours ahead, and planned the whole thing with the chef, so it would be perfect." Bursting into tears, Jessica states the final and lasting injury: "And then when they served the beef, *he* scraped the sauce off!" Amused, Jim thinks Roger acted courageously; Kate merely says: "The evening's over, your father's gone to bed, and when you're married you can serve the sauce on the side."

Soothing her daughter, Kate asks: "Did you have trouble getting home in the fog?" Wiping her nose, Jessica says they walked. Kate says brightly that that must have been fun. And when they came home, Jessica says further, they danced. "Well, that was fun!" contributes Jim. "You and Roger danced while your father watched." "No," says Roger flatly. "Oh," says Jim. Jim does manage, however, to have the young couple kiss and make up before Roger leaves. Then, with a look from Kate, he too retires.

Alone with her daughter, Kate knows just what the evening program entailed, what wines were ordered, and how much Jessica drank. She also knows that Jessica is suffering from a common but not fatal complaint: a violent attack of Pogo Poole. In Kate's day she'd seen it run through a party of females like wildfire. She herself had one of the most serious attacks on record, but had happily got over it. "And still," Kate smiles, "it's one of the more grateful diseases. Once you've had an attack, you're immune, but not sorry you had it. It's like vaccination."

"All my life," says Jessica, "I've romanticized my father. I'd built up a picture in my mind of the gayest, most charming, most exciting man in the world. And then he came back. And I wasn't disappointed, or disillusioned, or let down." Touched, saying it should be that way, especially now, Kate adds: "I suspect he's between people for the moment. And that's always hard for him. He has to have someone—not crowds of people, though he dearly loves an audience—but some *one* to love him, to look to him for joy and amusement, to give him substance. He's much more dependent on others than he would ever admit." Nodding, Jessica remembers Poole's saying that "Time had become the enemy."

Jessica thinks Poole should have someone like Kate; but laughing this off, Kate says Poole has found someone else: "His newly discovered daughter. It's as though he'd just given birth to you, full-grown, and he's entranced with what he produced. You're his new toy." Jessica wishes ruefully that he had come back five years ago. Kate does, too, for both of their sakes. "But he missed the boat. You're taken. You see that, don't you?" And though Jessica says Yes, Kate finds no satisfaction in any part of this situation.

Jessica surmises that having Poole in Jim's house must be strange for Kate.

KATE—I do feel a bit illegal.
JESSICA—And when he swept in with all that mimosa, just as he did in the old days . . .
KATE—Well?
JESSICA—Didn't you feel a slight quiver?
KATE (*moving to mimosa tree*)—Not even a quiver. I only wondered if it would keep until Saturday. I'm afraid it won't. (POOLE *appears in doorway; she sees him.*) That's the trouble with mimosa. It dries up.

Offering his indigestion as an excuse for a brandy and soda, Poole happily barges in on mother and daughter. As Jessica goes out to get him his drink, Poole starts cutting Roger down to size. He found him strong, silent and glum. "Oh," says Kate, "he can talk—if given a chance." Poole tries another tactic. Kate answers frankly: "You underestimate the enemy, Pogo. He's a tough, strongminded young man who knows where he's going and knows what he wants. And he's got her. It's as simple as that." Smiling charmingly, Poole says: "It's never that simple."

A telephone call from Roger brightens life considerably for Jessica, and crying that "All's well," she heads for the kitchen for milk and cake.

Not one to waste time, Poole starts in rewooing Kate. He runs into a blank wall. She remains untouched by mimosa, old songs and him. She asserts that she is a contented, happy woman now enjoying blessed tranquility. Poole doesn't let her stay tranquil for long. As he expresses exaggerated pity for the more conventional pleasures of her life with Jim, Kate begins to boil. "Poor Kate," says Poole softly.

KATE—Don't you "poor Kate" me!
POOLE—You're wasted, Kate. And it's my fault, isn't it?
KATE—Oh, please don't blame yourself!
POOLE (*attacking*)—You once had a rage to live—
KATE—Still have!
POOLE—and the things you learned with me—
KATE—What things? To stand on my head in the Place Pigalle and whistle "Dixie"? In six years of being an international gypsy with you, I learned four languages and how to cook! I still speak

the languages, and my dinner parties are the best in San Francisco. What else?

POOLE—Everything else, poor Kate! And the mimosa does bring it back, doesn't it? You're lovely against the mimosa, Kate. And I can remember— (*She moves quickly away from the flowers—he grins.*) It isn't that easy. You're still there. High on a hill now, against a dark sky, wind-blown and eager, fresh and young—

KATE—We're high on a hill in San Francisco, and it's a thousand and eighty years later, and I'm wind-blown every day of my life! Don't you turn it on for me, Pogo Poole! I'm an elderly, overweight clubwoman, and I like it, I like it, I like it! (*Stricken,* POOLE *turns away.*)

POOLE—It wasn't "Dixie." It was "Swanee River."

KATE—I despise seedy reminiscence!

And what's more, she orders Poole to leave Jessica alone. "There's no need," she says, "for this elaborate seduction! She's yours; the birth certificate says so!" "I had no idea," Poole answers indignantly, "that the normal attention of a loving father came under the heading of seduction!" Starting for the stairs, Kate needs only one more remark from Poole to set her off. She slaps his face, then droops with embarrassment. And he, in full control, making the most of the situation and accepting her apologies charmingly, exploits his advantage. As of old, the slap leads to a kiss. It is a nice kiss, not a passionate one, but, unfortunately, at that precise moment, Jim pokes his head over the balcony. Tripping in his anger, hurtling downstairs, Jim crash-lands amidst "Ows!" and "God damn its."

Kate offers Jim unwanted sympathy. Poole, thoroughly happy, offers Jim some of his drink. "I don't want your liquor," Jim shouts. "It's yours," says Poole. "How civilized!" Jim says. "How terribly, terribly urbane! A man makes love to his former wife, in her present husband's home, and when he's discovered, says: 'Can I get you a drink?' Shall we dance?"

Cutting this short because of Jessica's return, Jim tells Poole he'll see him in the morning, and stumbles upstairs. Rushing after her husband, Kate cries: "Jessica, I want you to come right to bed."

Jessica, sharing cake with her father, says: "This isn't our night." "On the contrary," says Poole, "it isn't theirs." Pleased with himself, Poole admits that the pass he had made at Kate was a form of testing. Though finding this all immoral, Jessica can't help giggling.

Poole and Jessica sit side by side, happy in each other's company. Savoring each mouthful of cake, Poole suddenly wonders if Toy might be interested in traveling. Jessica at once calls Poole to account for trying to steal Toy, but she is curious whether he would have gone on making love to her mother if Kate had been receptive. When Poole answers, "Yes," Jessica says she isn't shocked, but she is intrigued. "That's my girl," he says, "we're two of a kind."

In a much used gambit that sounds familiar even to himself, Poole offers to show Jessica the Grecian Islands. He says: "We'd sail into the Gulf of Corinth, the water so blue it's unreal, with the whitewashed houses of Delphi in the distance, and Parnassus looking just as it did when Agamemnon consulted the oracle. A friend of mine has a boat, a sleek white yawl; I can have it whenever I want it. Tomorrow. All I have to do is send him a cable . . ." This sounds heavenly to Jessica. Poole comes to the point: "Shall I send it now?" "What?" says Jessica. "The cable," says Poole, "to say that I must have the boat, now that I have found the most enchanting girl of my life, and want to show her the world?"

Jessica is so overwhelmed that she thinks of asking Roger to go there instead of Hawaii. Poole is cold to this idea. He is not suggesting that he be the guide on their honeymoon. What he has in mind is for them to send Roger a postcard from Greece. "But we're getting married Saturday!" cries Jessica.

POOLE—You can always get married!
JESSICA—But what would I say to him?
POOLE—Just "goodbye."
JESSICA—Father! Oh . . . you! You really are wicked. I know. You're testing again, aren't you?
POOLE—Yes. Just testing.
JESSICA—Really! You mustn't make love to me, Father. It's taboo.
POOLE—It's the only way I know to talk to a woman—even my daughter. I'm sorry.

Jessica is disturbed that she will never do all these things she had dreamt of doing with her father. Someday she and Roger might do them, but that was not part of her dream.

As outside the foghorns groan and wail, Poole says, by way of changing the subject: "Variations on a theme—San Francisco on a foggy night." Assigning a horn to Jessica, he asks her to imitate it. Then picking out the notes, Poole and Jessica sing a foghorn duet, having a wonderful time all the while.

Scene II

Waiting for Saturday has become almost too much for Kate. She tells Jim that, having spent six years with that "aging adolescent," she knows he's up to something, and having eavesdropped on his sending a cable to France this morning, she's practically convinced.

When an answer to the cable is brought in for Poole, Kate grabs it. While Jim, trying to soothe her, assures her that everything is going to be all right, that his idea for today was quite brilliant, Kate bets money that it doesn't work. "Bound to," says Jim. "When I talked to Roger this morning, he thought it was a great idea. Get Pogo out to the ranch for the day, let Jessica see him against the background of Roger's good simple life—it's bound to turn the trick. Jessica's no fool." "No," says Kate, engrossed in prying open the cable, "but you and Roger are."

Jim was outraged at Kate's eavesdropping; now he is horrified that she should read someone else's mail. Savage's entrance doesn't deter her.

JIM—Your daughter has criminal instincts.
SAVAGE—She got them from me.
JIM—That's absolutely unforgivable. Give me that!
KATE—You keep away. I'm fighting for my daughter's happiness!
JIM—Happiness my eye! You're just curious! You can't read someone else's mail!
KATE—It's not mail, it's a cable.
JIM—That's worse.
SAVAGE—A cable for Biddeford?
KATE—Besides, he reads our mail. I caught him down here yesterday going through everything on this desk, including your doctor's report!
JIM—I don't believe it.
KATE—The things he knows about *you!* And do you think for a minute he hasn't been through the desk in your study? Who do you think taught me this? There! (*She shows the open envelope.*) Now, who would know?

In spite of Jim's real indignation, Kate reads: "My boat is berthed at Monte Carlo. All yours for six weeks. Who's the girl?" "Well, who's the girl?" Jim asks. "Who do you think?" says Kate. "Oh, come on, Kate," Jim says. "After the wedding he's going back to Europe. He's got a date with a girl, and he's borrowed a boat to go cruising. What could be more simple?" "You, for one thing," Kate answers.

Savage and Kate can well imagine who the girl is. "Kate, Jessica is being married on Saturday," argues Jim. "No man would do a thing like that to his own daughter!" Waving the cable, Kate howls: "He'd do a thing like that to his own mother!" "That would take a bit of doing," says Savage. Kate knows that what Pogo wants he takes, and he now wants to show his daughter off to the world. Kate cries: "Oh, my poor baby! Why couldn't he have been lost in darkest Africa? And been trampled by elephants?"

Hearing someone at the front door, Kate makes a frantic leap to the desk, starts shoving things about and cries: "Where's the glue? Where the hell's the glue?" When at last she finds a little bottle, she wildly smears the flap of the cable, pounds it, leaves the envelope on the desk and assumes a composure she obviously doesn't feel, just as a small procession enters the room.

With a rakish plaster over one eye and his left arm in a sling, Poole manages his entrance with the aid of a cane. Jessica can't be sufficiently helpful to her father, or sufficiently furious at Roger, who in turn is extremely impatient with Poole's performance. Playing the gallant, injured hero, Poole listens with a patient air as Jessica accuses Roger of deliberately throwing Poole to the wild horses and steers. Roger protests that he wouldn't dare a man to ride a wild steer. "I'm not out of my mind! He might have been killed." "Oh! Yes!" Kate thinks rather enthusiastically. "Nonsense!" says Poole; "I just didn't get settled right on him, that's all. I'd like to try that again, sometime." "Tomorrow?" Kate hopes.

Jim remembers the cable. With pleased innocence, Poole can't imagine it's for him, but the minute his fingers touch the glue, he gives Kate an amused glance, reads the message, pockets it, consents to a drink—and asks where he can wash his hands. He goes out to the bar, with Jessica at his side.

Roger yowls impotently: "I don't *like* taking this kind of beating! She hates me! Honest to God, she hates me!" He looks to Savage for solace but gets none. All that remains, as far as Roger can see, is to call off the wedding and elope this very night. "I don't think that I can last until Saturday!" he cries.

From the doorway, where Jessica and Poole have overheard this outburst, Jessica coldly inquires why Roger can't last till Saturday. "Because of him," Roger answers. "Perhaps," says Jessica, "you won't have to last until Saturday."

It's now all out in the open, and the only one who enjoys it is Poole, who says jocularly: "You're not suggesting that Jessica choose between us, are you, Roger? You're on dangerous ground, my boy." Roger is all for taking his chances. Jim suggests that Roger and Jessica walk in the garden. "He'd come along," Roger says. "We may as well stay." "I wouldn't want to intrude," Poole smiles. "You do," says Roger.

POOLE—Careful. (*He smiles, but his eyes narrow.*) I *am* her father.

ROGER—No—you're not. I know about that; I raise bulls. I send out the seed, and the calves are born, but the bulls don't feel responsible. They don't care.

Poole, according to Roger, has done things to Jessica that scare him. He has made her think that life with Roger would be dull, and that the idle, wandering life he leads is romantic. Jessica jumps in angrily, protecting her father. "But you don't have to sneer at *his* life!" she cries. "I don't sneer at . . . yes, I do!" says Roger. "You're damned right I do!" Kate tries to interfere, but Roger is not to be stopped. "I don't like idle people!" he cries. "I don't think there's anything romantic about a man who doesn't work! My father! My father, who started from scratch, and fought his way through a depression, and built up a ranch and a life for his family—he's the most romantic guy in the world compared to *him!*" "You were right," Poole says to Kate. "He *can* talk."

Heroically, Poole asks Jim to get him a plane ticket that night for Paris. Poole couldn't possibly give his daughter away now, and doesn't wish to start trading punches with Roger at the altar. Realizing that Poole is certainly giving them a good start, Roger asks Jessica to go for a walk. When she shakes her head, he says: "All right. But look. You don't have to get married. Nobody's going to force you; nobody's tying you down. But you've got to know what you want, and you've got to make up your mind. Because if you marry me, it's for keeps." After a long, hard look at Jessica, Roger takes his leave.

Left victorious and pulling out all the stops, Poole plays straight to Jessica. Undeterred by muttered barbs from Kate, he lays it on so thick that he is literally quoting Sydney Carton on the scaffold before the curtain mercifully falls.

Scene III

Playing solitaire with a bottle of bourbon nearby, Savage sings all the verses of "Mighty Lak a Rose." His "sweetest little feller, everybody knows . . ." brings Poole on the scene in a larcenous mood.

Dressed for travel, his bags at his side, Poole—while handing Toy a bill—looks speculatively upstairs. He then broaches the subject of seeing the world to Toy. "Go way from San Francisco?" answers Toy impassively. "I need someone to take care of me, Toy," says Poole. "And you're an awfully good man with a shirt. I'd take you to Paris and Rome and London, and places you never heard of. You're a native-born Californian, Toy. Wouldn't you like to see the Orient? Would you like to see Hong Kong? We can't get into Canton, but—" Toy is as impassive as ever. "Ah, the hell with it," shrugs Poole. "Take the bags out, Toy." "He wouldn't even like," says Savage, "to see Los Angeles."

Picking up his drink where he had left it, Poole joins Savage, who admits to being puzzled by Jessica. "She has a good mind," says Savage. "I'm proud of her mind, and yet she didn't recognize the sham behind the heroics. Why?" "Too much emotion," says Poole. "Mmm. And yet she will, in time," Savage says; "you realize that." "But then," Poole answers lightly, "perhaps later in time she'll realize—that behind the sham there was a kind of . . . truth?" Savage won't accept that. Playing his cards carefully, he adds: "Ah, but then again in time she may realize—that in back of the truth was a sly, Machiavellian duplicity. What then?" With a grin, Poole says: "I would hope that she'd laugh."

Having been a newspaperman, Savage confesses to an early-acquired fondness for scoundrels that has never left him. Savage thought Poole had won out for a while, and wonders what licked him. Poole says it was something basic: the sexual appeal of a young bull in his prime, with which no father could compete. "Not," says Savage, "unless he wants to be thrown in jail."

Philosophers both, they are rocked by Jessica's sudden arrival. Wearing traveling clothes and toting traveling bags, she is ready to depart with Poole. "Sex," cries Poole, "isn't everything!" "It's what I keep telling myself," remarks Savage.

Determined on a quick getaway, Poole is blocked by Kate. Ordering Jessica—to no avail—back to her room, Kate asks her to think of Roger. "If I am old enough to marry him, I am old enough to jilt him," cries Jessica. Obviously receiving no help from Poole, Kate appeals to her father. Savage has gone over to the enemy.

All for taking Jessica away from her trivial existence, Poole is shocked by her confession of liking it here, and by her intention of returning to Roger in a year's time. Jessica wants to marry Roger, wants to have his children and share his life, but is willing to take this awful chance of losing him. She has something she must do for her father first.

Jessica can't bear to leave Poole alone: she wishes to give him love, comfort and unquestioning worship. Poole is shattered. "You have your revenge, Kate," he says softly. And then he asks of Savage: "Old man—is this how one falls into old age? Pushed from behind?"

Reading what she has done in her mother's eyes, Jessica, smiling almost wickedly, says: "But then—there is another thing, too. I *am* my father's daughter. And it *would* be such glorious *fun!*" With a triumphant whoop, Poole cries: "Blood will tell!" And Jessica, now riding high, exclaims: "Mother! I want to live in every direction!" Kate realizes that this *is* her father's daughter. As both plead with her to let them go, Kate just yearns for a gun. Savage joins the chorus of pleaders. He and Jessica call in Thoreau to help them.

Kate can resist Thoreau, but Poole's plea starts to wear her down: "Kate, give me a chance to make up for lost years! My years with you were such glorious years! Give me the chance to relive them with her!" "You can't go back!" cries Kate. But as Poole plays back his record of memories relentlessly, Kate weakens, softens and finally gives in. "Go quick," Kate calls blindly.

Savage is so caught up by the prevailing atmosphere that for a moment he thinks he too will go off with Poole. As Poole and Jessica urge him to come, Savage remembers suddenly that he is the man in the ivory tower. "That was a close one," he says ruefully. "I almost lost my pose, didn't I?"

Carrying one of Jessica's bags, Poole bids Kate a truly grateful goodbye. As Jessica and Poole go out, Kate comes suddenly to efficient life. She yells after Jessica to be sure about her passport and re-entry card. Then, as the laughter fades and the front door slams, Kate stops at the mimosa tree and stares out the window. Back at his solitaire and bourbon, Savage sings:

> "Sweetest little feller . . .
> Everybody knows . . .
> Don't know what to call him . . .
> (*He turns over a card*)
> But he's mighty lak a rose . . ."

EPITAPH FOR GEORGE DILLON
A Play in Three Acts

BY JOHN OSBORNE AND ANTHONY CREIGHTON

[JOHN OSBORNE *was born and brought up in London's Chelsea. He was educated at Oxford, where he was president of the Oxford University Dramatic Society. He began writing for trade magazines, then switched to acting. He was an actor-manager in provincial repertory before joining the English Stage Company, acting in "Don Juan," "The Death of Satan," "The Making of Moo" and "Cards of Destiny." His "Look Back in Anger" and "The Entertainer" have been successfully produced in theatres throughout Europe as well as on Broadway. He has directed television for the B.B.C.*]

[ANTHONY CREIGHTON *is a young English actor who was with Mr. Osborne in repertory and came to London with him. It was while acting together that they wrote "Epitaph for George Dillon," which had considerable success in England. At the moment Mr. Creighton is working on a play of his own.*]

For the cast listing, see pages 301 and 317.

JUST outside London, among many equally modest dwellings, stands the Elliot house. The sitting room and hall have an immediate and depressing effect on the viewer. The Elliot family possessions—an ornate "cocktail cabinet," a "radiogram," painted ducks on a wall, a tinted wedding picture—all contribute to the impression.

A hatch, when raised, reveals the kitchen beyond the sitting room. The front hall with its hat-and-coat stand, tumbled with clothing and magazines, even sports a vase of artificial flowers in this spring

"Epitaph for George Dillon": By John Osborne and Anthony Creighton. Reprinted by permission of the publisher, Criterion Books, Inc., 257 Fourth Avenue, New York 10, N. Y. Copyright © 1958 by John Osborne and Anthony Creighton. See CAUTION notice on copyright page. All inquiries should be addressed to Harold Freedman, Brandt and Brandt Dramatic Department, 101 Park Avenue, New York, N. Y.

of the year. A suggested wall, in which the door alone is actual, divides the hall from the sitting room, and under the arch formed by the hall stairs, is the door leading into the "lounge" that houses the television set.

Twenty-year-old Josie Elliot, sloppy in stained slacks, pretty in a hard, frilly way, and with curlers in hair, sprawls in a chair. Reading a magazine and doing her best to ignore the Mozart on the radio, she is passing the time while waiting for a collect package in "vicious idleness." When the doorbell finally rings, she pays off the messenger and comes back excitedly with her prize. Undoing the package, then taking a cigarette from her handbag, then simultaneously kicking off her slippers and unzipping her slacks, she next goes to the radiogram. Having got out of her slacks and left them, with one leg inside out, on the floor, she chooses a record. Waiting for a New Orleans trumpet blast, she hurriedly puts on her new black "jazz trousers." Delightedly patting herself on the seat, Josie examines herself in a mirror. Lighting her cigarette, she strikes an elegant pose. Then smoke clouding from her cigarette, she dances sexily about the room, and at last lies with her back on the floor and her knees in the air.

When the front door opens, Josie—as she calls out "Mum"—hastily pulls off her new slacks. Entering the room, Ruth catches her amidships. Picking up the old slacks, Ruth, while tossing them to Josie, asks if she's looking for them.

Ruth, who is fortyish, slim and attractive, puts down her weekend case and inquires none too hopefully whether Josie has made any tea. Knowing the answer, Ruth goes herself to put the kettle on. Begging a cigarette of Josie, all she gets is inquisitive questions. Josie, eyeing the suitcase, wants to know where Ruth has been. Getting no satisfaction, Josie says that a small package came for Ruth, but she wouldn't know what's in it.

RUTH (*off*)—Didn't you open it?

JOSIE—What do you mean? Course I didn't open it.

RUTH (*coming back*)—If you must fry food when you're feeling ill, you might have the decency to clear up afterwards. The gas stove is covered in grease and muck—it's filthy. (*Examining package.*) Is this it? . . . You've even left the breakfast things in the sink. (*Holding her package of cigarettes,* JOSIE *watches her curiously.*)

JOSIE—Typewritten.

RUTH—You've had damn-all to do all day. It's like a slum when your mother comes in.

Josie—Aren't you going to open it?
Ruth—I said you're a slut.
Josie—Oh, did you? I didn't hear. (Josie *slips her cigarettes back in her bag.*)

Unwrapping the package under Josie's ever-watchful eyes, Ruth takes out a man's wrist watch and a letter. After a moment, Ruth asks again, in tired tones, for that cigarette. Josie just gives her a cup of tea.

As Josie's mother, Mrs. Elliot, comes in the house, Ruth warns Josie to clean up the kitchen so that her mother can cook the supper without having to clean up Josie's mess first. Josie hurriedly asks Ruth: "You're not in any trouble are you, Auntie?" "In trouble?" answers Ruth. "Do you mean in the general or the popular sense?"

Carrying a large paper bag of groceries, Mrs. Elliot, the minute she enters, is off in all directions at once. Mildly upbraiding Josie for the messy kitchen, wondering if George likes parsley sauce, hoping that Josie's trouble this morning wasn't food poisoning, Mrs. Elliot has something that she wants to ask Ruth, but the messy kitchen puts it out of her mind for the moment. "Now try to help me a little, Josie, I'm rather cross with you over that kitchen, my girl," says her mother. Ruth pitches in to help, and to lay the table next to the kitchen hatch. Seeing everyone else working, Josie collapses feet up over a chair, and wonders why all the panic. "Young George is coming, that's all," says Mrs. Elliot. Pinned down, she says it is George Dillon who works at her place. Ruth remembers about this young, rather superior young man, and wonders that he's still holding down the job that wasn't good enough for him.

Mrs. Elliot—I've always felt a bit sorry for him, that's all. He seemed so much on his own all the time. And, one day, I started telling him about our Raymond, and he was most interested. He was in the services as well, you see.
Ruth—Quite a coincidence.
Mrs. Elliot—Yes. He went right through the war.
Ruth—I had an idea we all did. (*Pause.*)
Mrs. Elliot—No, Ruth, some boys didn't get to see the end of it.
Ruth—I'm sorry, Kate. I've had a bit of a day, I'm afraid. I'm not in the right frame of mind to talk to young men, refined or not. If I can't do anything for you down here, I'll go and run myself a bath, if you don't mind.

Not wanting to go into any rigmarole, Mrs. Elliot breaks the news that she has asked George to live with them for the time being, and if Ruth wouldn't mind, would she give up Raymond's old room and move in with Norah. Ruth would mind. Not having time to discuss it, Mrs. Elliot appoints Josie to move in with Norah. As Ruth apologizes, Mrs. Elliot says: "I just thought it would be nicer, that's all. It doesn't matter, dear. And there's no fuss, Madame Josie, thank you. God pays debts without money, I always say."

Preoccupied and headachy, Ruth starts upstairs, only to be reminded to put out a towel for George. Back at the dinner table, Mrs. Elliot wonders: "Now, where are we?" Going next to the cocktail cabinet, she brings forth from its neon-lit depths a bottle of sherry. Josie exclaims: "My, we're posh, aren't we? Sherry! Anybody'd think it was Christmas." Mrs. Elliot merely requests that Josie go up and make herself presentable for George. She returns to the kitchen.

Gliding about the room, Josie chants: "Georgie Porgie . . ." Then, with further urging from Mrs. Elliot to get dressed and to draw the sitting room curtains, she goes into her song:

> "Why don't you give me . . .
> Give me. Give me.
> All that you—
> All that you
> Have to share . . ."

Her eyes lighting on Ruth's package, Josie sidles up to it, removes its letter and reads: "My dear—You have just left, and I have found that you have left two pounds for me on the desk. How thoughtful of you, and, after that catechism of smug deficiencies you had just recited to me, how very practical and how like you. I suppose you must have slipped it there while I was swallowed up in the damned misery of our situation. Make no mistake—for the money, I'm grateful. But your setting up as a kind of emotional soup kitchen makes me spit.

"If you had any understanding at all, you would know what a bitter taste this kind of watery gruel must have. This is the Brown Windsor of love all right, and the only fit place for it is the sink. If this is the kind of thing you and your pals would dole out for the proletariat and its poor, grubby artists, you had better think again. I'm just going out for some beer. Ps. Was just going to post this, when I thought I would return this watch to you. It seems to be the one thing I have left that you ever gave me. I'd like to think that my returning it would hurt you, but I know it won't." Pocketing the letter, Josie goes upstairs.

When naively simple Norah arrives home from work, Mrs. Elliot rushes her to the table. Over Norah's protests that she really doesn't want any supper, Mrs. Elliot says: "Too many sweets, my girl, that's your trouble. You know what a state your teeth are in already." Having placed a plate of food in front of Norah, Mrs. Elliot hurries to the foot of the stairs to urge Ruth to come down and to remind her once more about George's towel.

Percy Elliot is the next to arrive home; taking a paper from his brief case, he comes into the living room. A mean, small man, obviously disliked by Norah and ignored by his wife, he refuses supper and demands tea. Hearing about George, Percy snarls that his wife is cradle-snatching, among her other sins. Controlling herself, Mrs. Elliot tells Percy off: this is *her* house, bought with *her* money, and as far as she is concerned, Percy merely lodges here. As Mrs. Elliot elaborates on this theme, Norah mildly remonstrates. "I'm sorry, Norah," says Mrs. Elliot, "but there it is. There are times when your father goes too far with his insults. And I'll have you know this, too: George is a fine, clean, upright young man. And he's clever too. He's in the theatrical line, he is, and one day he's going to be as famous as that Laurence Olivier, you see, and then perhaps you'll laugh on the other side of your face." When Percy snaps that he probably doesn't have any money, Mrs. Elliot agrees that at the moment George doesn't have much. She admits, too, that as of today George no longer has a job. All approving of his having walked out, Mrs. Elliot says it was no place anyway for him to waste his time and talent on. An irate Percy would like to know what the neighbors will think. "No more than they do now, believe me," retorts Mrs. Elliot. "They know very well what you're like. I haven't forgotten yesterday either—shouting and swearing at the top of your voice. At the front door too. The humiliation of it! I don't mind your swearing at the back door, but the front door—well—"

Respectably dressed, Josie would pass up supper for television, but her mother tells her to forget the "telly" and sit down. Then, as long as everyone is eating, Mrs. Elliot feels she might as well bring in a plate for herself. As they all set to, Josie says: "Silence in the pig-market, let the old sow speak first." "Pudding, Percy?" says Mrs. Elliot. Over Percy's protests, and with her mother's consent, Josie puts on a record to liven things up.

There is a knocking that no one in the sitting room can hear. Ruth, on her way downstairs, answers the door. Carrying his bags, George—"not good looking but with an anti-romantic kind of charm" —comes into the hall. George can register all emotions and attitudes, can be all things, sometimes all at the same time. Feeling his way at the moment, George is being shy. As Ruth introduces herself to the young man, he says: "I seem to think we've met somewhere before." Ruth, too, is struck by this.

Hearing talk in the hall, Mrs. Elliot comes out. Almost without drawing a breath, Mrs. Elliot greets George, approves his mode of transportation, offers him supper, wants to show him his room, and leads him upstairs, with Ruth and Josie looking up after them. Deciding out of curiosity to hang around home tonight, Josie goes into the lounge for the "telly." Referring to the guest as "Henry Irving," Percy shortly follows.

On Mrs. Elliot's return, Ruth turns down supper in favor of some hot milk. Picking up the little box containing the watch, she discovers that her letter is missing. Noticing her sister's disturbed air, Mrs. Elliot says: "Now Ruth, dear, don't go upsetting yourself over a little thing like that. I expect you'll come across it later on. You go upstairs and I'll bring you some hot milk later on."

Halfway upstairs, Ruth turns around and calls Josie out of the lounge. Insolent and sullen, Josie doesn't know what Ruth is talking about. Told she damn well knows, Josie reluctantly withdraws the letter from her jumper.

RUTH—Thank you very much. Kindly learn to keep your nose clean in the future, will you?

JOSIE—So that's where you've been all these week-ends, with Jock. Does he wear a kilt?

RUTH—Mind your own damn business. (*Gives her a resounding smack.* JOSIE *yells.*)

MRS. ELLIOT—Why, whatever's going on?

JOSIE—Going on! It's Auntie Ruth what's been going on. *Carrying* on more like—with a man—and paying him for it what's more.

RUTH—Just you dare read my letters again, and I'll do more than slap your face.

JOSIE—Don't you talk to me like that—you're not my mum.

MRS. ELLIOT—If what Ruth says is true, Josie, then I'm very ashamed. I thought I'd brought you up to behave like a lady. Never, never do that again, do you hear? Now kindly leave the room—but first say you're sorry to Auntie Ruth.

JOSIE (*after some hesitation*)—I'm sorry, Auntie Ruth. (*Goes off to the lounge, singing* "If Jock could love me, love me . . .")

RUTH—Slut! Slut! Slut!

MRS. ELLIOT—Ruth—that's no way to talk, and you know it. So things didn't work out then?

RUTH—No—I've just walked out on him, for better or for worse.

MRS. ELLIOT—But I don't understand. Josie said something about paying him—

RUTH—I don't have to buy my love—or do I? Yes, I gave him the odd pound or two, to keep him alive.

MRS. ELLIOT—But surely he could do a job of work?

RUTH—Job of work? He's a writer—the original starving artist in the attic—and I believed he had promise.

MRS. ELLIOT—Then why did you leave him?

RUTH—He's been a promising young man for too long. Youthful promise doesn't look too well with receding hair. I've misjudged him—he's the complete flop, and I've spent nearly six years giving all I could to him, giving my love to him—such as it is.

MRS. ELLIOT—It's beyond me, dear. It's funny—you're the only one in the family who doesn't have patience or understanding. While you were enjoying yourself at college, we all had to go out to work. I can only say that college gave you a lot of funny ideas.

RUTH—That's right. Funny enough to make me do an inexcusable thing. When he told me he hadn't a penny, not even the price of a packet of cigarettes, I went to his jacket pocket, and inside I found a cheque for eight guineas for some book review or other he'd written. He hadn't even told me about it. Not only did he lie about the money, but he even kept his piffling little success from me. A brainless, cheap little lie. And that did it—the whole works collapsed, the whole flimsy works. (*She walks to the door.*) I suppose that's really why I left him. (*Exits upstairs.*)

George, passing Ruth on the stairs, comes into the sitting room. Almost unable to hear herself talk, Mrs. Elliot calls to her family to turn down the "telly." Settling George in Percy's place at the table, Mrs. Elliot begs him to make this his home. George says he doesn't know what to say; but putting out his hand, he says: "I can only say that I won't impose myself on you for one minute longer than I can help. You're so very kind." Pointing to a photograph, Mrs. Elliot confesses that she feels that by taking in George she is, in some small way, helping her son Raymond, who was killed in the war. Mothering George, appreciating him, Mrs. Elliot begs him never to go short of money. Raymond's savings will be put to good use if they help him. Coughing slightly, George blesses her and once more protests his unworthiness: "I only hope I'll prove worthy of your kindness. I promise I won't let you down in any way. I promise you that."

As Mrs. Elliot goes into the kitchen for George's special vegetarian dinner, he stares at the birds on the wall. Mrs. Elliot pops her head through the kitchen hatch to say: "Yes, Ray painted those. I told you he was artistic, didn't I?" The hatch slams down. Ambling about the room, looking at everything, George stops in front of Raymond's picture, picks it up, remarks out loud: "You stupid looking bastard."

ACT II

It is now summer, with the family sitting around the dinner table in their accustomed places. Things are just as before except for a new gadget in their lives: as a convenience to George, Mrs. Elliot has had a telephone installed. With its very first ring, Percy snarls: "What a racket—wireless, TV, and now the blinking telephone." The phone's maiden call is from George himself, who—though on his way home—couldn't wait to report there was news about a job and his play.

JOSIE (*from the kitchen*)—Must be something good for him to ring up like that.

MRS. ELLIOT—Yes—silly boy. He was only at the station. He'll be home in a minute. I'm so glad. That awful day he left that office, he swore he'd stick it out until he got something really worthwhile. (NORAH *comes in with teapot.*)

MRS. ELLIOT—And it's turned up at last. He always said he wouldn't take anything tatty.

NORAH—What's "tatty"?

MRS. ELLIOT—I don't really know, dear—George is always saying it.

JOSIE—Well, now I can really tell the whole of Targon Broadway that we've got a real actor staying with us. That's if he doesn't get too stuck up, and want to go and live in Berkeley Square or something.

MRS. ELLIOT—Of course he won't. George has settled down here very well. This is his home now. There's no reason at all why he should have to go.

JOSIE—Well, he'll have to get married sometime, won't he?

MRS. ELLIOT—Well, yes, there is that, of course.

Teasing Josie about being quite gone on George, Mrs. Elliot asks about her erstwhile beau, Len Cook. George, Josie answers, will fill in nicely while Len is doing his National Service in Germany, though she wouldn't mind going to Germany with Len. To do that, Norah chirps, Josie would have to marry Len first.

JOSIE—Oh, I don't know. I don't mind what I do or where I go, so long as my man's got money.

PERCY—The trouble with young girls today is that they spend too much time thinking about love and S-E-X.
JOSIE—S-E-X? Oh, sex. Sex doesn't mean a thing to me. To my way of thinking, love is the most important and beautiful thing in this world and that's got nothing to do with sex.
PERCY—Well, I may be a crank and all that, but if I can persuade the council to close the park gates after dark, I shall die a happy man.
NORAH—What on earth's that got to do with sex?
MRS. ELLIOT—Well, I don't think we need go on with this conversation—but Josie is quite right. You keep those beautiful thoughts, dear, and you can be sure you won't come to any harm—

Waving a bottle of wine as he barges in through the French windows, George urges everyone to celebrate. He himself would appear to have started celebrating somewhat earlier.

Answering the barrage of questions gaily, George reels off a description of a day that started badly with interviews but ended triumphantly with a job. Pouring wine and receiving congratulations, he tells the Elliots that there's every chance of his play going on at the Trident Theatre in Bayswater—not exactly the West End but at least where agents and managers can see it. Next, George reports that he has a part in a film coming up soon. And lastly he announces that he will have a job on TV in three weeks' time.

Suddenly reminded that Mr. Colwyn-Stuart is coming to take her to the meeting, Mrs. Elliot hurries into the kitchen to get things out of the way. Reminded that it's jazz night, Josie hurries off to change into suitable clothes, while George and Percy are united for once over the idiocy of Mrs. Elliot's churchy companion, Colwyn-Stuart. Percy even thanks George for the wine. Soothed by this sudden good nature, George is quickly brought up sharp by Percy's next remark: "I certainly hope that now you are earning money, you will be able to pay for yourself instead of sponging off other people." Before George can answer, the doorbell rings.

Elegant and pale, Geoffrey Colwyn-Stuart follows Ruth into the sitting room. As Ruth sits down at the table for tea, Geoffrey gushingly greets Mrs. Elliot. When she goes upstairs to get ready to go out, Geoffrey turns his cheeriness on the unresponsive men in the room. He commiserates with Percy on his sleepless nights. "It's just that I have a lot of things on my mind," snaps Percy.

GEOFFREY—In your own words, Mr. Elliot. Exactly. The old ravelled sleeve of care, am I right, George?
GEORGE (*absently*)—Eh?

RUTH—Shakespeare, George. Aren't you supposed to stand to attention, or something?
GEOFFREY—The number of people one sees every day, with tired, haggard eyes, dark circles of care underneath them.
GEORGE—I always thought that had another significance.
GEOFFREY (*smiling*)—You're a pretty free sort of chap, aren't you? I hope you don't shock everyone in this respectable household with your Bohemian ways.
GEORGE—By "Bohemian" I suppose you mean crummy. It's rather like calling bad breath "halitosis," don't you think?
RUTH—He's straight out of *Trilby*—didn't you know?
GEORGE—Frankly, I always touch mine up with a brown liner.
GEOFFREY—What?
GEORGE—The rings under my eyes—helps me when I play clergymen's parts. I'm rather good at them.
GEOFFREY (*refusing to be stung*)—You know, you surprise me a little, George. You seem such an intelligent, vital young man, so much in the swim. After all, it's not even considered fashionable to be skeptical nowadays. The really *smart* thing is the spiritual thing.
RUTH—That's true enough.
GEOFFREY—And you too, Ruth. Of course, your interests are political, I know. But shall I tell you something? If I were to invite the Foreign Secretary, say, down here to speak, he wouldn't be able to half fill the Jubilee Hall.
RUTH—Are we supposed to be surprised?
GEOFFREY—On the other hand, if I were to invite someone like Billy Graham—well, take my word for it, you wouldn't be able to get within a mile of the place.
RUTH—With his message of love and all that? Love isn't everything, you know, Mr. Stuart.
GEOFFREY—That's where we disagree, Ruth. I believe that it is.
RUTH—Take justice away from love, and it doesn't mean a thing.
GEOFFREY—Love can change the face of the world.
RUTH—Tell that to the poor black devils in South Africa. Why don't you do something for them?
GEOFFREY—Dear, oh dear—we're going to get involved already if we're not careful. I can see that. Oh, there's nothing I enjoy more than a good old intellectual rough and tumble, and I only wish I could stay and slog it out with the two of you, but there isn't time, unfortunately. The fact is, we've probably got a great deal in common. You know: I've discovered a new way of judging people.

Geoffrey Colwyn-Stuart's system is to ask himself whether people's "lamps are shining." Getting into the act, Ruth and George focus

Geoffrey's attention on Percy's lamp, which doesn't seem to be shining very brightly. To Percy's irritation and the fascinated boredom of the others, Geoffrey goes on sermonizing. When Mrs. Elliot returns, Geoffrey—complimenting her spirit—sums up the whole thing: "It's all a question of what we call synchronizing yourself with Providence. Of getting in step with the almighty." As Mrs. Elliot starts to go, George, who hasn't been paying much attention to all Stuart's talk, suddenly comes to.

GEORGE—Yes. If only it were as simple as that, Mr. Stuart. But life isn't simple, and, if you've any brains in your head at all, it's frankly a pain in the arse.
MRS. ELLIOT—George! Really!
GEORGE—I'm sorry. I apologize. But I've said it now. You see, to me there is something contemptible about a man who can't face it all without drugging himself up to the rings round his eyes with a lot of comforting myths—like all these bird-brains who batten off the National Health. I don't care who it is—you or anyone—you must have a secret doubt somewhere. You know that the only reason you do believe these things is because they *are* comforting.

Not at all put out, Geoffrey leads George step by step to say what he does believe in. "I believe in evidence," says George, "and faith is believing in something for which there *is* no evidence. You don't say I have faith that two and two are four, do you? Or that the earth is round? And why? Because they're both easily verified.

GEOFFREY—So it all has to be verified for you, does it, George? I think I understand you better than you know.
GEORGE—Oh?
GEOFFREY—You see I come into contact with a great many artistic people. What *do* you believe in? Yourself?
GEORGE—Right. (*Adding in vocal parenthesis—*) He said, striking attitude of genius.
GEOFFREY—You have faith. You have faith in yourself—in your talent. Am I right?
GEORGE—Well?
GEOFFREY—Your talent, George. You believe in that with all your heart. And your evidence? Where is that, George? Can you show it to me? (*Pause. They all look at him.*)
RUTH—*Touché.*

Leaving them with their lamps burning, Colwyn-Stuart escorts Mrs. Elliot off to the meeting. Percy goes into the lounge to look at television. Noticing that George is a bit shaken from the treatment he's just received, Ruth says: "You aren't very impressed with Geoffrey, I take it." "Right," answers George. "What the Americans call 'strictly for the birds.' If there should be any heavenly purpose at all behind Mr. Colwyn-phony-Stuart, it's that he's God's own gift to the birds. Hope I didn't upset Mrs. Elliot, though. She's obviously pretty taken up with the whole racket." "It might help," says Ruth, "if you weren't quite so vicious about it. You sound like a man with a secret doubt yourself." "Why is it you distrust me so much?" asks George. "I had a feeling we were the same kind." "Did you? I suppose it's given poor Kate something to think about since Raymond was killed," Ruth says. Suddenly feeling a member of the family, she doesn't want George to pitch into Kate, his only friend. Nor is she in the mood tonight for his shoddy little gags. "I looked up the Party secretary tonight," Ruth explains.

GEORGE—So you've packed it in at last.

RUTH—No doubt you think it's pretty funny.

GEORGE—No. I don't think it's funny.

RUTH—Seventeen years. It's rather like walking out on a lover. All over, finished, kaput. He hardly listened to my explanation—just sat there with a sneer all over his face. He didn't even have the manners to get up and show me out. I think that's what I've hated most of all, all these years—the sheer, damned bad manners of the lot of them.

GEORGE—Farther left you go, the worse the manners seem to get.

RUTH—Well! The house is still fairly ringing with the bloody shovel of *your* opinions.

GEORGE—I have a sense of humor. "Bloody shovel of your opinions"! Is that a quotation?

RUTH—Just someone I used to know. Someone rather like you, in fact.

GEORGE—I thought you'd tied me up with someone the moment I met you.

RUTH—Where are you going tonight?

GEORGE—Dancing, I believe. Somewhere Josie knows.

RUTH—Don't sound so apologetic about it. It doesn't suit you. Pass my handbag, will you? Looks as though you've a long wait ahead of you, my lad. (*She offers him a cigarette.*)

GEORGE—Have one of mine. (*Fumbles in his pockets.*)

RUTH—You needn't go through the pantomime for me, George. Take one.

GEORGE—No, thank you.
RUTH—Oh, don't look like that, for God's sake! You make me feel as though I'm setting up as a soup kitchen or something. Please.

Leaning over Ruth for a light from her lighter, George says how young she looks sometimes. A few moments later, in the course of their conversation, George asks Ruth what she is doing this evening. The atmosphere grows increasingly intimate. Learning that George has pawned his watch, Ruth gives him the wrist watch that was returned to her.

GEORGE—I shan't pawn it, I promise you. I think it must be the nicest present I've had. How do you fix it?
RUTH—Here. (*She adjusts it for him as he watches her.*)
GEORGE—Your . . . friend?
RUTH—Oh, he doesn't want it any more. He told me.
GEORGE—Can you get the Third Programme on it?
RUTH—There!
GEORGE—Perhaps it'll change my luck.
RUTH—Superstitious, too?
GEORGE—Thank you. Very much. (*She still has his hand in hers.*)
RUTH—How beautiful your hands are—they're like marble, so white and clear.
GEORGE—Nonsense.
RUTH—But they are. I've never seen such beautiful hands.
GEORGE—You make it sound as if I were half dead already.

As Ruth, disturbed, looks up, George quite suddenly kisses her. Recovering, she moves away, and continues to make conversation. George apologizes for kissing her. Admitting that she was flattered for a moment, Ruth murmurs it's the first time she had tasted the Brown Windsor of love.
One moment unbelievably exhausted, the next moment George turns the elaborate cocktail cabinet into an organ, and puts on a full-blown act of a movie palace organist. George is pleased by Ruth's laughter: "That's the first time you've ever laughed." "Oh, yes, you can be funny, George," says Ruth. "These flashes of frenzy, the torrent of ideas they can be quite funny, even exciting at times. If I don't laugh, it's because I know I shall see fatigue and fear in your eyes sooner or later." Ruth would like to know why he is burning himself out. For what? Does he have any real integrity?

she wonders. She asks about the television job and finds that it is a walk-on; that the film assignment was just the "old keep-in-touch" line; as for the Trident Theatre, it's a "so-called club theatre, meaning a preciously over decorated flea-pit, principally famous," according to George, "for its rather tarty bar, and frequented almost exclusively by intense students, incompetent longhairs, and rather flashy deadbeats." Ruth offers to read some of his work, and George says in an unpleasant tone that he'll think about it. "Perhaps," says Ruth, "your sense of humor has deserted you after all. My politics and your art—they seem to be like Kate's religion, better not discussed. Rationally, at any rate."

Urging George to leave this house where he is being unfair to himself and everyone in it, Ruth is thrown off balance by his counter-attack. Ferociously dissecting each Elliot, George wants to know why Ruth lives here. He does such a nasty job on Josie and her "night starvation" and on poor Norah, "a hole in the air," that Ruth breaks in: "You've a lot to learn yet, George. If there weren't people like the Elliots, people like you couldn't exist. Don't forget that. Don't think it's the other way around, because it's not. They can do without you, take my word for it. But without them, you're lost—nothing." Landing into her for her life of mysterious week-ends, George retorts that Ruth can't afford to sneer at him. She admits that he's made his point. She can't move elsewhere because she spends too much on clothes and cigarettes. Holding up the wrist watch, George adds: "Incidentals?" Perhaps she also lacks the courage to leave her hideously boring job and try for something new. "At least," Ruth confesses, "I'm safe. And so I go on, from spring, through summer, to the autumn and another winter, meaningless; just another caricature."

Bursting into a long tirade as to why he hates the Elliots, George cites their lack of apprehension, curiosity and humility. Ruth laughs out loud at the word "humility." "Good old George," she says, and adds in amusement: "Perhaps you have got talent, George. I don't know. Who can tell? Even the experts can't always recognize it when they see it. You may even be great. But don't make a disease out of it. You're sick with it." George reminds Ruth that others would like to have this disease, which moreover is incurable. "Gal-loping," says Ruth, "like consumption." "What did that mean?" asks George sharply. "Nothing," says Ruth.

Listening to George reminisce dramatically, Ruth says: "You can't tell what's real and what isn't any more, can you, George? I can't sit here driveling all night." She turns to go.

GEORGE (*taking her arm*)—And what if I do? What does it matter? My motives aren't as simple as you like to think—
RUTH—You're being phony, George, aren't you? We're a pair of—
GEORGE—What if I am? Or you, for that matter? It's just as—
RUTH (*sings*)—"It's a Barnum and Bailey world,
    Just as phony as it can be!"
You've got us both acting it now—
GEORGE—just as serious and as complex as any other attitude, Ruth! Believe me, it isn't any less—
RUTH—haven't you, George? Cutting in on each other's lives—
GEORGE—real or sincere. You just never stop standing outside—
RUTH—fluffing your emotions—
GEORGE—it's a penance—
RUTH—that's the word, isn't it? You're fluffing it—
GEORGE—the actor's second sense—
RUTH—all studied, premeditated—
GEORGE—watching, observing, watching me now, commenting, analyzing, giggling—
RUTH—timed for effect, deliberate, suspect—
GEORGE—just at this moment, don't you want me more than anything else—
RUTH—I've had my lot, George.
GEORGE—More than anything?
RUTH—We've both had our lots!
GEORGE—You're as arrogant as I am!
RUTH—You know what, George?
GEORGE—That's one of the reasons you're drawn to me! If only you knew—how much—at this moment—
RUTH—No, not me. Somebody else—not me!
GEORGE—I mean it, damn you!
RUTH—Strictly for the birds, George! Strictly for the birds!
GEORGE—Ruth!
RUTH—Let me go!
GEORGE (*he does so*)—I've botched it. (*Pause.*) Haven't I?
RUTH—I'm not sure what has happened. Nothing, I suppose. We're just two rather lost people—nothing extraordinary. Anyway, I'm past the stage for casual affairs. (*Turns away.*) You can't go on being Bohemian at forty.

Running downstairs in her "jazz" pants, Josie calls to ask George if he is ready. As Ruth moves quickly through the French windows,

George pulls himself together. Offering Josie a drink before they go, he replies to her giggled "Cheers": "It'll be tonight, Josephine."

While they finish their drinks, Josie suggests a bit of dancing. But after the record has been chosen and they start to dance, Josie finds it a bit boring.

GEORGE—The preliminaries always are, Josie, my girl. But they make anticipation all the more exciting. Are you ever excited by anticipation?

JOSIE—No, not really. Only when I see fellows like Len Cook, he's lovely.

GEORGE—That's not anticipation, Josie, that's lust, plain lust. Although it never is really plain. Do you know what lust is, Josie?

JOSIE—Of course I do, silly.

GEORGE—Lust, the harshest detergent of them all, the expense of spirit in a waste of shame. Or as Jean-Paul Sartre put it—sex.

JOSIE—We were only talking about sex a little while ago. Boring, I think.

GEORGE—Do you? Shall we go?

In the hall, stopping Josie, George asks if she has ever been kissed. "Hundreds of times," says Josie. "Like this?" says George, kissing her fiercely. The lounge door opens and they do not see Percy standing there. At the same time, Ruth comes through the French windows and switches out the main light. Over Josie's startled protests, George starts dragging her upstairs. He smothers her cry with another kiss. "Silly girl," says George. "But George," cries Josie, "what will Mum say?"

As the two are lost in the darkness, Percy looks up the stairs, then goes into the sitting room and looks for a moment at Ruth. "Why, Percy, how long have you been there?" she asks. "Long enough, I think," says Percy. "Quite long enough."

ACT III

It is autumn now. Feeling "a bit whacked," George is getting all the extra attention imaginable from Mrs. Elliot. She urges him to stay in bed; she brings him his food on a tray. Concerned that he can't eat and seems so feeble, she is delighted when a man arrives to see him.

Left alone with George, the man introduces himself as from the National Assistance Board. He has come in answer to George's letter. Claiming that he was an out-of-work actor, paying thirty shillings rent a week, George had applied for relief. Learning that when he has no "rent book" to show he gets no check, a very much put-out George pleads: "This money means rather a lot at the moment. I need—something—to show, you see." At the same time George is anxious that no one in the Elliot house learn about this. The man is understanding, but unfortunately Percy enters and sits down.

MAN—Well, Mr. Dillon, I can only hand in my report as I see things, and see what happens. The board is very hesitant about— paying out money to strong, healthy men.
GEORGE—Of course. Is there anything else? (*Looking at* PERCY.)
MAN—There's just the little matter of your last job. When was that?
GEORGE—Oh, about three months ago—television.
PERCY—Accch! You don't call that a job, do you? You could hardly see it was him. *We* knew it was him all right—but you had to be sharp to catch him.
MAN—Well, that'll be all, I think, Mr. Dillon. (*Rising.*) You won't forget your rent book, will you?
PERCY—Rent book. Rent book! He hasn't got one! Shouldn't think he's ever paid any!

Josie, on her way in her dressing gown to the kitchen for some hot milk, inquires for Ruth. Coming back from getting rid of the Assistance man, George says that Ruth has gone after his medical report for him.
"Not content with taking the money we bring home, you're even trying to get hold of the money we pay in income tax," cries Percy. "You're getting it all ways, aren't you, George?" Percy knows all about him. Through the credit firm he works for, he has checked up and knows that George owes bills all over the place. Percy wouldn't be the least bit surprised to have the Police coming after him for debt. "Imagine that!" cries Percy. "Police coming to my house—to me that's never owed a farthing to anybody in all his life." Whereupon the doorbell rings, and there's a loud knocking. Oddly enough, knowing a "copper's knock" when he hears it, Percy disappears quickly into the kitchen.
On his way to Brighton for the week-end, Barney Evans barges in on George. Expensively dressed, though rumpled in appearance, this "poor man's Binkie" sprays self-assurance about him. Having got hold of George's script, Evans says that if George is interested

in big money and willing to let art slide, he's Barney's man. "Dialogue's not bad," he announces, "but these great long speeches—that's a mistake. People want action, excitement. I know—*you* think you're Bernard Shaw. But where's he today? Eh? People won't listen to him. Anyway, politics are out—you ought to know that. Now, take *My Skin Is My Enemy!* I've got that on the road at the moment. That and *Slasher Girl!*" A great admirer of Hitler's ruthlessness, Barney feels that George's play has possibilities: "Act One and Two won't be so bad provided you cut out all the highbrow stuff, give it pace—you know: dirty it up a bit, you see." Although the Third Act is weak, Barney feels that George's getting the girl in a family way is something that never fails.

Reminding George to be absolutely ruthless, Barney tells him to redraft the whole play. George will hear from him. As his impatient date left in the car outside honks at the horn, Barney comes up with what he thinks a smashing title for George's play: "Telephone Tart." Leaving, Barney says: "You string along with me, George. I'll see you're all right."

On top of this, Ruth comes in with George's medical report. Drawing him into the lounge, she speaks to him privately. Irritated over being excluded, Josie turns the phonograph on full blast.

When Mrs. Elliot returns to her wildly noisy house, Percy greets her with the news that George has T.B. Confirming this, Ruth reports that the doctor will be coming soon to announce the arrangements for George's going away. Full of pity, Mrs. Elliot hurries up to George, while Percy enumerates, at the top of his lungs, all the things that will have to be burnt. In the midst of the excitement, Josie asks piteously: "Oh, my God. Auntie Ruth! What's going to happen? What about me?"

Scene II

It is now winter. Back from the hospital, George is upstairs with Josie. Mrs. Elliot, confronted with more bad news about George from Percy, is as protective as ever. She maintains that George will show them all. "God always pays debts without money," says Mrs. Elliot. "I've got down on my knees at night, and prayed for that boy. I've prayed that he'll be well, and get on, and be happy—here with us."

Percy has told Mrs. Elliot not only that George already has a wife, but that, in his opinion, George carried on with Ruth, too. Although Ruth's sudden departure from the house had struck her as odd, Mrs. Elliot considers this accusation ridiculous: "Why, she's old enough to be his mother."

Returning to the house for her things, Ruth lets herself in for another farewell. She meets George as she comes through the front door. He pleads with her, and asks: "What's going to happen to me?" She orders him to try and help a little. "Isn't it hell—loving people?" says George.

Ruth asks if George has seen Josie. "God! What a farce!" he cries. "What pure, screaming farce!" Starting to laugh, George has just remembered "how to make sure of your Third Act." Pulling himself together, he begs Ruth once more not to leave him on his own, then abruptly asks why Ruth hasn't mentioned his success. Ruth hadn't known whether he wanted to be congratulated or not. "Second week of tour," recites George. "I've got the returns here. Look: Empire Theatre, Llandrindod Wells—week's gross takings £647 18s. 4d. Long hair drama gets a haircut from Mr. Barney Evans!" Not wanting to watch him hurt himself any more, Ruth turns away. George rattles on, but Ruth starts to go. "No, wait," says George. "Shall I recite my epitaph to you? Yes, do recite your epitaph to me. Here lies the body of George Dillon, aged thirty-four—or thereabouts—who thought, who hoped, he was that mysterious, ridiculous being called an artist. He never allowed himself one day of peace. He worshipped the physical things of this world, and was betrayed by his own body. He loved also things of the mind, but his own brain was a cripple from the waist down. He achieved nothing he set out to do. He made no one happy, no one looked up with excitement when he entered the room. He was always troubled with wind round his heart, but he loved no one successfully. He was a bit of a bore, and frankly, rather useless. But the germs loved him." George doesn't see Ruth leave, and continues: "Even his sentimental epitaph is probably a pastiche of someone or other, but he doesn't quite know who. And, in the end, it doesn't really matter."

Ruth may have left, but Norah and Mrs. Elliot swarm affectionately about George. As Norah goes upstairs for their homecoming present for George, Percy confronts him with his firm's evidence of a 1943 marriage. Blandly admitting that it's true, George insists that it changes nothing. "But what about Josie?" asks Mrs. Elliot. Assuring her that nothing is changed, George explains that it was simply that his busy actress wife had never bothered with a divorce, and that he never had the money for one. "But it's all easily settled," says George. "There's nothing to worry about. I promise you." He's come home, George tells Mrs. Elliot. One more thing, however, bothers her: "Now that—well—now that you're a success, how do you know that your wife won't want you back?" "Somehow," answers George, "I don't think that will influence her!"

Annoyed that no one has told him George's news, and agog over the play's financial success, Percy quickly turns sycophant. Then Norah returns with the homecoming present—a typewriter. George —as son-in-law, brother-in-law and husband—is trapped among the Elliots.

THE DISENCHANTED

A Play in Three Acts

By Budd Schulberg and Harvey Breit

[Budd Schulberg. *Following his graduation from Los Angeles High School, he matriculated at Dartmouth in preparation for a career in archaeology. During his academic years, however, he wrote for school publications and eventually found a commercial market for his work. His first novel "What Makes Sammy Run?" became a best-seller and established his reputation. His novel "The Disenchanted" was also a best-seller, and he adapted his subsequent book "On the Waterfront" into an Oscar-winning film. He also wrote an original screen play, "A Face in the Crowd." "The Disenchanted" —made from his novel—is his first play.*]

[Harvey Breit *was born in New York and began his literary career in New Mexico in the 1930s. This resulted in his book of poems, "There Falls Tom Fool." In the middle 1940s he went to work for "The New York Times," first in the magazine section and later in the book section. He has written introductions to William Faulkner's "Absalom, Absalom!" and to J. F. Byrne's "Silent Years" (an autobiography containing memoirs of James Joyce). In 1952 he took a six months' leave from the "Times" to go to India for the Ford Foundation, where he edited a collection of contemporary Indian writing, "Perspective of India." "The Disenchanted" is his first play.*]

For the cast listing, see page 308.

IT is a winter's evening in 1939. Shep Stearns, a young screen writer, and Victor Milgrim, a producer, have come by appointment to Manley Halliday's beach shack, but he is not around. "Are all

"The Disenchanted": By Budd Schulberg and Harvey Breit. © Copyright 1959 by Budd Schulberg and Harvey Breit. Based on the novel of the same name, Copyright 1950 by Budd Schulberg. Reprinted by permission of Random House, Inc. See CAUTION notice on copyright page. All inquiries should be addressed to the authors' agent: Ad Schulberg, 277 Park Avenue, New York 17, N. Y.

writers unable to be punctual even when they insist on having appointments in their own—" Milgrim looks around at the shack's meagre furnishings—"quarters? Stearns, the last time I saw Manley Halliday, he was living in a thirty-room mansion overlooking Beverly Hills." "Maybe he read my script," cracks Stearns, "and walked out into the ocean, like Freddy March at the end of *A Star Is Born*." Looking at an autographed snapshot of Hemingway, Stearns finds it hard to believe that a Pulitzer Prize winner like Halliday should turn up on the "available list" like any hack, and be prepared to work with him on *Love on Ice*. "I know what you saw in the idea," says Stearns, "and I tried my best to give it to you, but what can a novelist like Manley Halliday see in it?"

MILGRIM—At the moment, Stearns, he doesn't see anything in it. He left word at my office that he and your script are incompatible. That's why I'm here. There are two things a good executive producer must have: the ability to decide on the objective—and then use the personnel best equipped to attain it. My objective with *Love on Ice* is a freshly written college musical that will please the public without offending the college authorities. My choice of personnel—an energetic, disciplined junior writer, teamed with a man who was once the darling of the Ivy League. According to the critics, the only writer ever able to capture the true spirit of American college life. Ten years ago I offered Manley Halliday a small fortune to write for me, and he turned me down with a quip. Ten years—especially his ten years—is a long time. I'm here to change his mind . . .

Manley Halliday, entering the shack at this point, apologizes for keeping them waiting. In his early forties, his face perennially youthful, however ravaged, his clothes a little worn and old-fashioned, Halliday shakes hands with Milgrim, accepts the introduction to Stearns, and turns down *Love on Ice*.

MILGRIM (*ignoring the rejection*)—I don't expect to win an Oscar with this one—as I did last year. But I know with your help we can make a pleasing valentine out of it. I think you'll find it an interesting challenge.

HALLIDAY—Victor, I don't mind challenges. It may seem erratic; I ask you for a job . . . then I turn you down, but, surely, there must be something you need that I'd be better suited for.

MILGRIM—My approach to pictures is this: do a bread-and-butter film like *Love on Ice*—commercially sound, but of course with what I like to think of as the Milgrim quality. And then something offbeat, serious, tragic, Dostoievsky, Faulkner—maybe Halliday. But my next picture is *Love on Ice*. (*He pauses to allow his softening-up operation to work; then rapidly presses on.*) And I'm prepared to guarantee you ten weeks' work at fifteen hundred dollars a week.

HALLIDAY—I'd forgotten there were weeks like that.

MILGRIM—This could be the start of a very happy relationship. If we score with *Love on Ice,* as I know we can with the Halliday touch, then we'll talk about a forty-week contract at fifteen hundred a week with an escalator clause.

HALLIDAY—Victor, I don't want to get on your escalator. I'm afraid I might not be able to get off.

MILGRIM—If it's money you're after . . .

HALLIDAY—I'm not after money, period; I'm after money, comma.

Then, since all he has in mind is a polishing job, Milgrim urges him to take the ten weeks. According to Halliday, this script needs a new script. That, too, is all right with Milgrim. Saying that Halliday can throw out the whole story line if he wants to, just so he keeps the external values of Webster College, the winter Mardi Gras and so forth, Milgrim says he'd be "free to supply the internal values —real people, believable dialogue, wit instead of gags—" Feeling like Faust, Halliday capitulates.

Delighted, Milgrim stipulates that Stearns, too, will be kept on— "Most writers here," he explains, "find it useful to have someone they can bounce ideas against." Though he hasn't collaborated with anyone since his Hasty Pudding days, Halliday agrees to this too.

Suddenly all business, Milgrim says that his second-unit crew will be covering the Webster Mardi Gras this week-end and will need a "step sheet" by Friday night. Stearns explains for Halliday: "A 'step sheet' is just an outline of the action step-by-step. It usually isn't more than ten or twelve pages." Such a deadline doesn't bother Halliday, who once wrote a pretty fair novel in a hundred and seven days. *"Shadow Ball,"* exclaims Stearns. "I've been wanting to read that again. Why don't they reprint it? I love that book." "The critics didn't love it," says Halliday bitterly. " 'Typical of the irresponsibility of the twenties.' Quote. 'In a new decade, Mr. Halliday seems to be entering a strange house to which he was not invited.' " Breaking in on Shep's enthusiasm, Milgrim says that all refinements on the script can await their return from New York and Webster.

Deeply disturbed at the thought of being uprooted, Halliday begs to do his work here. Maintaining that he's not stubborn, just stationary, Halliday seems curiously intense about a trip to New York.

MILGRIM (*suspiciously, but suavely*)—There's nothing wrong with you? A screen writer needs a strong back as well as a good mind. You have been taking care of yourself?

HALLIDAY (*indignation, mounting to anger*)—Victor, I'm too old for euphemisms. Am I positively off the booze? That's what you mean, isn't it? For two hundred and seventy-nine days I have been drinking nothing stronger than Sunkist orange juice. (*He pulls a whiskey bottle from a closet.*) Take a good look at this bottle—a decent, well-behaved bottle—it's lived with me for nine months and still a virgin. . . . I've learned to eat and sleep and live and work on this workbench. I function here. I don't have to go out into the world. I've had the world. I can bring it here.

Pouring on the persuasion, assuring Halliday that exactly one week from today he will be back *here,* Milgrim seems to be getting nowhere. "There must be something about this you're not telling me," he says. "Isn't there always?" answers Halliday. "Victor, I'm not telling you. I'm asking you to let me do this piece of work here, where we are now, right here." Instead, Milgrim sits down and writes a check for two thousand dollars, his top salary for writers. And if, he adds urbanely, Halliday decides next morning not to keep it, he should simply return it to his office. With a jovial farewell, Milgrim starts for the door, where, with studied casualness, he remarks: "By the way, you have a tuxedo. The dinner for us on Saturday night is black tie." After he leaves, there is a silence, broken by Halliday's saying: "What a lovely world this must have been before Victor Milgrim invented money." Crumpling the check, he tosses it into the wastebasket.

Picking up his script, Stearns starts quietly to leave. At the door he turns in mute appeal, but Halliday's back is to him. Without looking up, Halliday says: "So you read *Shadow Ball?*" Spinning around, Stearns begs: "Mr. Halliday, please come to New York with me! *Shadow Ball. Friends and Foes. The Lamps Along the Park. Friends and Foes* was my bible. Mr. Halliday, it's my first writing job. I waited three years for this chance. I took a hundred odd jobs and wrote movie scripts at night in order to break through, and now I've finally done it."

Although he finds Shep's scenario dreadful, Halliday concedes that ever so often Shep's real voice comes through. But the question remains: "Where was *Love on Ice* born? Not inside you—not inside

Victor Milgrim. It is a celluloid baby, born of artificial insemination on a box-office counter." "But you can't condemn the whole medium because of this one," protests Stearns. "Serious movies combine all the arts—and they carry a hell of a message all over the world. It's practically the first international language. Look at Chaplin, *The Informer, Ten Days That Shook the World*—I have no illusions about this one, but if what you feel about me is true, I can say a little more the next time out, and then a little more after that and then—one of these days I can do a picture I really believe in—about the dust bowl, Mexican wetbacks . . ." "Ever higher and higher!" says Halliday. "Don't you see you're kidding yourself? If you write three bad scripts, the fourth will be worse, not better. The mask becomes the face, whether in politics or art . . . remember that."

Right now, Stearns is only concerned with this one. If Halliday takes it on, it will be a different story. Promising to protect him from New York—they'll lock themselves in—Stearns says: "I'll pull up the drawbridge. I'll stand guard at the door. I'll type like a tiger." Appreciative, Halliday is surprised that anyone of Shep's generation even remembers *Friends and Foes*. Wound up, Shep tells of his excitement at the chance to work with Halliday—as if he were to work with Thomas Hardy or Joseph Conrad. "In fact," Stearns gaffes, "I didn't think you were still—" "Still alive?" says Halliday. "Reports on my death have been exaggerated—or should I say only slightly exaggerated?" Stearns suggests that it was because the pace of those times was so fast and that he caught it so well, that when the jazz age died— Why, Halliday protests, does he only remember the party scenes? There were other things, too.

STEARNS—I used to quote that whole chapter on the argument between General Pershing and the Unknown Soldier. Funny, when I was working my way through Webster, we were all for proletarian literature. We used to tear you apart as middle-class, decadent, defeatist. But late at night, alone in my room, I found myself thinking through your ideas, living out your experiences, knowing your characters better than I knew my roommates. And your heroines— I fell in love with them all. What a parade of marvelous girls! That Leonore Woodbury. The way you first brought her in, wearing that polar-bear coat and nothing but that polar-bear coat. She was so real my dates used to get jealous, I talked so much about her. I suppose you've been asked this a thousand times, but was Leonore a real person? Did you really know a golden-eyed jazz-baby like that?

HALLIDAY (*troubled*)—No . . . she wasn't a real person. (JERE *laughs offstage.* HALLIDAY *appears haunted and dazed. Since* JERE *exists only in his mind, her laughter is not heard by* STEARNS.)

STEARNS—I thought I read somewhere she was based on your wife.

HALLIDAY—She was fiction. She bears no relation to any person living or dead. (JERE'S *laugh is heard again.*) She was fiction. I created her from the champagne threads and vapors of the times.

As the past encroaches on the present, a Parisian army canteen establishes itself right on the beach shack. To the tune of "Smiles," played by a trumpet and piano, and the laughing and singing of uniformed couples and their shouts of *"Fini la guerre"* and *"Vive l'armistice,"* a beautiful girl with red-gold hair dances into the room. Dressed in a ball gown of the period, she cries: "I feel champagne-yellow tonight!" Halliday, now the attractive young captain of 1918, finds her the most beautiful woman he's ever seen. With a broad French accent, Jere says: "That is not important." Clearly fascinated by one another, as the other couples whirl and dance around them, Halliday persists: "Perhaps mademoiselle will be good enough to say what is important?" "Dancing. Pleasure," answers Jere. "To be gay—these are the only truths." "But are you not too attractive," says Halliday, "to bother about definitions of truth?" "Ho-hum," says Jere. "I bore you?" says Halliday. "Being told I'm beautiful? Why shouldn't it bore me? Generals and privates tell me. Even handsome captains—" Halliday salutes smartly. "I have eyes. I can see that I am beautiful. I look into the glass after the bath and I say to myself, 'How much more beautiful you are than those stupid pink nudes of Renoir.'" "Perhaps," says Halliday, "some day soon I shall be fortunate enough to be permitted to agree with you." "Ish kabibble," answers Jere.

Telling her to come clean, she's not French, Halliday asks Jere why she isn't in uniform. In her roundabout way, she finally says: "Armistice night—let them court-martial me! If I have to face a firing squad I'll die as a woman—not as a corporal—" As the music stops and Jere moves toward the crowd, Halliday tells her to sit down, he has to talk to her. It's now Jere's turn to find out about him.

HALLIDAY—Some days I'm Christopher Wren building my own cathedral. Some nights I'm Toulouse-Lautrec on the prowl with paints and brushes. I might even try to be a writer.

JERE—That's it. You are a writer.

HALLIDAY—How do you know?

JERE—It's the one you find hardest to say.
HALLIDAY (*thoughtfully quiet*)—One day I met a German soldier in Belleau Wood leaning against a shattered tree, writing a sonnet. And we talked about Schiller.
JERE—In the very eye of the holocaust two enemies meet and talk quietly together about Schiller. And your commander would have hated you both.
HALLIDAY—If I could be a novelist, that's what I'd write about.
JERE—*Friends and Foes.* That's your novel!
HALLIDAY—*Friends and Foes,* by Manley Halliday! I like it.
JERE (*standing up*)—Then, Manley Halliday, write it! I'll make you write it. If you don't, I'll haunt you.
HALLIDAY (*standing up facing her*)—Who are you?
JERE—I am me and me is I—
  Lawless, flawless Lorelei—
  If I should die before I try—
  Will you put a penny on my eye?
HALLIDAY—You'll never die. You're my eternal jazz-baby Lorelei.

Hearing "Till We Meet Again" played, Jere is right on the job: she has to leave and say good night to everybody. She loves her job. "I wish," she confides, "that wars would go on and on and on, only without any shooting, so that these patriotic orgies would go on and on too. It makes me feel so conscientiously promiscuous." "Just be promiscuous with me," says Halliday. And ushering the crowd out good-naturedly, promising that they'll catch up with them in an hour at the Ritz, Halliday has Jere to himself.
Asking if he should take her seriously, Jere says: "Never completely, but always a little." "I'll always remember that," Halliday assures her. *"O terrible frisson des amours novices sur le sol sanglant!* Oh, the agony of new love on bleeding earth. Rimbaud and bright lights never seem right together," says Jere; "he wrote by the light of hellfire!" Halliday turns off the overhead lamp. "One of these days I'm going to astonish the world with my translations. But now when I try to put Rimbaud into English it goes so dingy—and blah!"
Taking Jere in his arms, Halliday feels he has never wanted anyone or anything so much. As he kisses her and begins to unbutton her dress, Jere says: "Mannie, I hate that feeling . . . fingers under my clothes." Pleading with her, Halliday insists that she must. "There isn't anything in this world that I must!" cries Jere. "Except die. And I'll never forgive God for that!" "You'll never die," says Halliday. "You're ageless and timeless. Promise me you'll

look exactly as you do this moment a hundred years from now."

As Jere backs sexily away, the Paris scene fades. . . . Striking the table, Halliday shouts that she never existed. Stearns murmurs what the critics had said.

HALLIDAY—I don't care what the critics say. Oh, why in God's name don't the critics write about the sins in our books instead of titillating the public with our personal lives? I'm through with personal lives. Until today, no more than two people crossed the threshold in the last nine months.

STEARNS—How did you ever wind up in a—hideout like this?

HALLIDAY—One day I was twenty-eight—and the next day I was forty. And when you're forty, you think about all the books you should have written. How little time there is left to do them in. On my fortieth birthday, I hadn't worked on a book for eight years. I found myself walking along the beach until I came here. It looked like me. Ramshackle—on shaky stilts, a few leaks in the roof. This is where I make my stand, I told myself. I went into training; tough daily workouts on that Corona; eat, work, walk, sleep—eat, work, work— (*He falters and, with* STEARNS' *help, lowers himself into a chair.*)

A worried Stearns asks if he should call a doctor. Passing it off casually as merely having forgotten to take his insulin, Halliday says that he gets shaky when he neglects it. Stearns is now sure this is why Halliday is avoiding New York. "New York is a terrible chance," says Halliday, "and it's too late for chances. The stakes are too high." "Sure they're high," answers Stearns, "but together we're a cinch to satisfy Milgrim." "Do you think I'd subject myself to the ignominy of Victor Milgrim's available list if I didn't have an end beyond the end of merely satisfying Milgrim? No, Stearns, no. These are the stakes I'm talking about!" He strikes his piled up manuscript, but warns Stearns away from it. Stearns just gets a glimpse of the title, *Folly and Farewell*, before he steps back from the table. Halliday will allow no one to look at it until it is finished, but how to finish it, what with all his debts, is something else. Stearns can't understand why his publishers won't get him off the hook, after his fantastic success.

HALLIDAY—Fantastic success! But commit the unforgivable sin of failure and the temple doors are slammed in your face—the gods of Manhattan are more ruthless than Jehovah. Stearns, on my last visit to New York I stayed in a third-class hotel and ate Fig Newtons.

I couldn't call my best friend in the world—my editor, Burt Seixas—because I owed him two thousand I knew he could use. I was afraid to go down to the lobby for fear that some enterprising sob sister would trap me for one of those riches-to-rags human-interest yarns. Nothing fails like success. God, I hate that city.

STEARNS—But this time it has to be different! The Waldorf, a Milgrim picture, a fat expense account—that's the way to go to New York. What a place it is . . . the life of that city.

HALLIDAY—The dead of that city . . . and the crazy thing is I know I'm on to the one big book of my life. I'll show them: the doubters, the scoffers and, goddamn them, the forgetters! The trick is to endure.

What to do appears very simple to Stearns: if the movie job provides the solution to Halliday's money worries, then do it as fast as you can, get it over with, and get back to the book. For Halliday it's not that easy. He is convinced that "every time a man betrays his total gift—his unique ability, the universe fails." At worst, says Stearns, it falters—Halliday can come back with a clean bank account, a free mind and a clear conscience.

Deducting his debts—what he owes for Jere's hospital and alimony, Douglas's tuition and allowance and personal obligations, Halliday finds he will clear about seventy-three hundred dollars if he takes the job. Persuaded against his better judgment, feeling as if he were "making a pilgrimage to his own grave," he says goodbye to his manuscript—he may have to leave it for a while.

Stearns cries exuberantly: "This calls for a drink." Getting the bottle, Halliday says most amiably that Stearns can drink for both of them. "It's a dream going back to the old Alma Mater with Manley Halliday," cries Stearns. "Boy, will the old school eat that up! His enthusiasm is infectious. Halliday does his best to enter into the spirit of the occasion: "The Rover boys at the Waldorf." He still needs reassurance, though. "Oh, it's going to be a lot better than all right," says Stearns expansively. "According to the Milgrim Law of Cinematics, with your brain and my back we ought to make one hell of a screen writer." Halliday suddenly feels that things are working out for him, too. He's all ready to wind up that obstinate Chapter Six tonight so that on his return, he'll be set for Part Two of *Folly and Farewell*. He feels like a writer again.

When Stearns has gone, Halliday settles down at once to work. As he writes "the color of their moods . . . the living and the loving . . ." Jere enters their Paris studio. "Darling," she says, "I feel all aquamarine today." Lovingly, Halliday tries to shoo her away.

Sprawled on his stomach, trying to write, he doesn't want to think about her now. Jere, however, has to model her surprise for him: a Reboux hat that took every sou of their week's food allowance. "Our last four hundred francs," exclaims Halliday. "Jere, you moonstruck desperado, what am I going to do with you?" "Thank me, darling," she replies. "My extravagance will bring us luck. The time to celebrate a triumph is before it happens, because—that will make it happen. Tomorrow the world will go out of its mind over *Friends and Foes*." Loving her every moment, Halliday still tries to have her leave him alone. He needs an hour. "Go fix Rimbaud. Knock him dead," he orders. Jere, however, has decided to give up that horrible Rimbaud. Her idea is, if people want to read him, let them learn French. Urging her to go away, not far away, just far enough, Halliday pleads for an hour. One big hour. One tenweek hour. As the past slowly yields to the present, Jere continues her tempting prattle against the counterpoint of Halliday's plea for a second chance. His determination is weakened. He ends up crying, "I can do it!," but he is less certain.

ACT II

It is four days later in a suite at the Waldorf. Stearns tries to type in the living room strewn with discarded balled-up paper, while Halliday, feeling the need of fresh air, has gone out.

A knock at the door sends Stearns rushing hopefully to answer it. Instead of Halliday it is his editor Burt Seixas who, having read, not without qualms, of their arrival, has come to pay a call.

Stearns, exasperated by how little has been accomplished on the script and by the constant flow of wires from Milgrim (the last of which showed considerable irritation), answers Burt's inquiries about Halliday none too sympathetically. He has never run into anyone who roots around so much in his memory. Knowing well these ghosts of Halliday's, Seixas asks if there have been any phone calls at crazy hours. "Yeah," says Stearns, "we did have a couple. But we decided it was that insomniac Milgrim, so we let it ring." Seixas asks if Halliday wasn't anxious to hear from anyone else—to see his wife, Jere.

STEARNS—From everything he's told me, she's the last person he'd want to see.

SEIXAS—She was always the last person he wanted to see and she was always the first person he did see.

STEARNS (*agitated*)—Do you think that's where he's gone?

SEIXAS—I hope to God not. The last time he came to New York I begged him not to see her, but—of course he did. It was a nightmare. Manley disappeared. I hunted for him in three states. I hate to tell you what condition I found him in.

STEARNS—Oh, my God! Now and then it hits me how sure I am about what I don't know. . . . Between Milgrim's telegrams and Manley's ghosts I'll be an old man at twenty-six. Here, Mr. Seixas, you can publish them— "The Collected Telegrams of Victor Milgrim." (*Shouting crazily.*) Manley . . . where the hell are you? . . . I'm sorry, Mr. Manley . . . Mr. Seixas. You see, I think I'm going out of my mind. On Monday I was a normal, healthy, well-adjusted junior writer. You want to play a game of chess?

SEIXAS—Stearns, has Manley been drinking?

STEARNS—No, not a drop. He's solidly on the wagon!

SEIXAS—Thank God! I always worry about that when he's near Jere.

STEARNS (*indignant*)—What happens? Every time he climbs up she drags him down?

SEIXAS—It was never as simple as something one did to the other. It was always the two of them doing it to each one of them. They danced in a champagne haze on the rooftop of the world. Jere could have made a first-rate poet if she had any discipline or any confidence. They always had too much money and always needed more. She could do so many things so brilliantly and all the time she was a failure, and though it seemed incredible at the time, he was failing, too. He caught the writer's most dreaded disease—silence—years and years of silence. I could never get him started again.

Stearns breaks the news that Halliday *is* writing again: he carries the manuscript of *Folly and Farewell* around as if it were a live bird in his pocket. "After all these years," says Seixas. "That manuscript has been accident-prone. One draft was lost on a train. Another version he tossed into the sea. 'Flaubert wouldn't have liked it,' he said. A third time . . . there was a third time." Thinking only about Halliday's coming back to work, Stearns can feel "Milgrim's propeller slicing off the top of my head." At this point, Seixas thinks he'd better call Jere. It's unnecessary. Looking fresh and revived by his walk, Halliday quietly enters the room.

Since plainly there is going to be no work while Seixas is here, Stearns decides to grab a shower. First, however—bringing Halliday up to date on the latest wire received from Milgrim—Stearns warns him that any minute they'll be hearing from Milgrim in person. Asking for a mere five minutes, throwing in that he had a few notions for

Love on Ice on his walk, Halliday temporarily soothes Stearns.

"Manley, Manley, after all these years!" cries Seixas. "After the fire, I heard a thousand conflicting stories from a thousand different friends." "I never had a thousand friends," says Halliday, "I had nine hundred and ninety-nine hangers-on and you." "Well, the past is the past. You've survived fire and ice," Seixas says. "And now, you secretive, conspiratorial so-and-so, you're writing again, you're rewriting *Folly and Farewell*. I'll take the first chapters with me and go over them tonight." "No," answers Halliday.

Overriding Burt's protests, Halliday presents his side: "It's as simple as this: I don't want you fighting for my unfinished symphonies ever again, suffering through those announcements of a new Halliday novel for the fall list, the spring list, the never-never list. . . ." But he assures Burt triumphantly that he has a book. Recognizing this tone from long ago, Seixas is pleased. He warns Halliday, however, against the treacherous pitfalls of New York expeditions and warns him particularly against Jere. "Now that you've decided to survive," Seixas says, "you've got to think of her as dead." This is just what Halliday has been trying to do for these past ten years. Seixas further urges him to dedicate himself to himself. Taking his hat and coat, a highly encouraged Seixas tries once more to see the book—for old time's sake. "For new time's sake, let me do it my way," answers Halliday. So with a final warning not to answer the phone, Seixas departs.

Halliday, after a moment, calls for Shep so that they can get on the ball. Disappointing Stearns again because the ideas he had on his walk now don't seem worth repeating, Halliday tries to review some of their old ideas. As Halliday picks up a ball of crumpled paper, the phone rings. Once again Stearns puts off Jere, but the work mood is broken. Halliday reads his crumpled page with difficulty. Stearns suggests they go back to his "waitress." "This time," he says, "she's not a gum-chewer. She's sort of a social-register Hepburn type who's had a hassle with her old man. He threw her out and . . ."

HALLIDAY—Have you ever heard of a waitress who turned out Main Line?

STEARNS—Hell, if you applied that test to every script, you'd have no movies.

HALLIDAY—What I want to know is what makes a girl like that do a thing like that. I knew a girl on Long Island who was brought up in the most proper blue-stocking way. Even when she was eighteen her parents had to approve her beaux and she had to be home by eleven. It was the insecurity that comes with money.

"Who will love me for myself alone?" When she busted out, it was a Vesuvius. Last I heard of her . . .

STEARNS (*jumping up with excitement*)—Say! That's an idea. We get a girl who's in the middle of an adolescent rebellion, really wild! I knew a girl like that. A sixteen-year-old kid, daughter of a minister across the river from Webster, and hot as a pistol. Polly Ann Dean! The boys called her Dizzy. One night a quarterback brought her into the dorm and sold chances on her. She stayed nine days and that boy made his tuition.

HALLIDAY (*laughing*)—Dizzy Dean! That's a good one!

STEARNS—The campus cops moved in and took Dizzy home. The quarterback was expelled.

HALLIDAY—Oh, that's too bad.

STEARNS (*quietly*)—He was only third string.

HALLIDAY (*after a pause, thoughtfully*)—For the movies we might have to clean it up a little. We could get Jeannette MacDonald and give her a few songs to sing.

STEARNS (*laughing*)—MacDonald would be terrific! We could get George Raft for the boy. Poor third-string quarterback working his way through college. (*He flips an imaginary coin in the familiar Raft manner.*)

When the cast comes to include May West and Peter Lorre, and when Krafft-Ebing and Advanced Rape I become part of the Webster curriculum, Stearns, roaring with laughter, realizes that he's laughing at his own funeral. Halliday apologizes; Stearns goes to the typewriter; but in another moment, Halliday is recalling something funny that happened to him and Jere in St. Moritz. Cutting in on him, Stearns tries to bring him back to the dull world of Victor Milgrim. "Okay, laddie, okay, okay, okay," says Halliday, "let's box it. I feel a little of Victor Milgrim's breath on my neck too. And it makes me sick." Guessing that he's had no insulin, Stearns now has to worry whether Halliday can work without it. It suddenly isn't a question of work: Halliday now plans to rely on "the blue sky-rack," that something that you pull out of the blue. "Everything hangs from it. Reach for that blue sky-rack," he says. "Suddenly everything fits, everything is solved." By now fed up as well as indignant, Stearns cries: "Bunk!" "How would you know?" answers Halliday. "It wasn't only me—it happened to all of us. We were the generation of the blue sky-rack." Fed to the teeth with Halliday's generation, Stearns shouts that it was bankrupt from the start. This, instead of stopping Halliday, merely goads him into delivering a paean of praise to the writers, the wits, the actresses, the magazines, the songs and even the movie stars of his Golden Age. He strikes his high note with the name of Lindy: "God how we loved Lindy! Coming out of nowhere and going into everywhere—a living symbol of the blue sky-rack." Lindbergh's name breaks the spell for Stearns: "Billie Dove, 'Ain't Misbehavin',' all those writers in one year—you make it sound like all the joys, the pure untroubled joys we Depression kids were cheated out of. But Lindbergh! You can have your Lindbergh. We give him back to you!" With Lindbergh's name the scrap starts. Halliday is passionate about his non-political romantic age. Stearns is furious that after their party was over his generation was left to clean up their mess—"Breadlines and small civil wars between strikers and state police, and young writers so busy starving and picketing for writers' projects that they had not time to write." Answering that those boys, those junior Lenins, weren't writers—otherwise they would have found time to write, even in jail—Halliday starts a verbal row over art vs. social justice. Stearns ends up shouting that at this stage in the game he's not interested in debating man's true interest, there's a gun pointed at his head and he wants to do something about it. He is even beginning to doubt that Halliday's novel consists of more than some words written down without his knowing what's the score.

Halliday is horrified. He knows what Stearns is thinking: "Lindy outlived his time and so did Manley Halliday." "You're right," shouts Stearns. "You're exactly right, Mr. Halliday." What's more, as Halliday desperately refers to his novel, Stearns cries: "You write a novel? You can't even write a lousy movie script! You're all talk now." Accepting this as a challenge, Halliday painfully and reluctantly puts his manuscript in Stearns' hands. "Now you go ahead and read that. If it doesn't say something to your new, Depression-proud, cocksure generation—if it doesn't say anything—I mean it, if it doesn't—I'll tear it up. You be the judge—you yourself." As Stearns hesitantly takes it, but turns with concern toward the typewriter, Halliday stops him. "You read. I'll write . . . And don't worry—the blue sky-rack." As Stearns goes into the other room, Halliday, at the typewriter, begins to muse aloud, a preliminary to work: "Ski captain . . . waitress . . . Put them through what I know . . . throw them into my whole sad, funny world . . ."

. . . The Hallidays are throwing a huge party this December of 1929. Their Hollywood mansion swarms with guests they don't even know. Halliday is cornered by Milgrim, "the youngest genius" in Hollywood.

MILGRIM—There you are, Manley. Beautiful party, Halliday. I suppose it's no use trying to lure you into doing a picture for me?

Halliday—Pictures—what are they?
Milgrim (*chuckling*)—Just our blood . . . Not even if I signed the check and let you fill in the amount?
Halliday—I'd write it for ten million, I'd buy the studio and close it down.
Milgrim—Forget I mentioned it.

Having looked for Jere all evening, when he finally has her to himself, Halliday tries to make her face the grim reality of their finances. Not wanting her party spoiled by statistics, Jere asks what happened to the money they had last week. Reaching for her elaborate necklace, jerking it off, Halliday snaps: "You're wearing it tonight!" Sobbing, Jere cries that now her party is spoilt.

Halliday—One of these days there won't be any party. You never used to cry. Are you crying because you're drinking or drinking because you're crying?
Jere (*violently*)—Stop analyzing me! Will people never stop analyzing me? First that horrible doctor in Vienna you made me go to.
Halliday—He was doing you some good. You should've stayed.
Jere—He was an old goat with lascivious fingers. I hated him!
Halliday—It was the truth you hated. You're lying to yourself. For months I've been trying to get you to help me draw up our balance sheet. Not just our finances, but of our lives, where we're going, what we're doing to each other. Oh, Jere, Jere, let's not get stuck in this tunnel of lovelessness.

Instead, Jere, like a bit of quicksilver, slips away with an amorous movie star. As the party becomes more and more drunk and disorderly, Halliday, through a drunken haze, discovers Burt Seixas. Here to break the news that Halliday's fed-up publishers will give no more advances, Seixas is unable to find further excuses for him: he's run out of ammunition, and now with the crash it's impossible. "Just look at this crazy house," cries Seixas; "how the devil could even a hack writer work here?" He urges Halliday to break away: "You've got your talent. That bank hasn't gone under yet, and never will. Just change this terrible, terrible life—" Then, not being able to stand the party another moment, Seixas leaves abruptly.

A liquored-up Halliday, nabbing Jere, tries to communicate what Seixas had been telling him. "It's not fun any more," says Jere. Trying to make her face the grown-up truth, Halliday says they are broke. Jere simply can't bear grubbing around and becomes indignant when Halliday tells her that Seixas has turned him down. "Christ, you know how he could," answers Halliday. "You know the worst of my session with Burt? He didn't ask to see it . . . the novel . . . even if it wasn't finished. He never asked to see it. And you never asked to see it! Used to hang on my shoulder. Used to love to watch me work. Not any more! You never looked at this one. Why?" He takes hold of her arm fiercely. "Too damn busy! Too damn many buddies!" "They're not my buddies," cries Jere; "your buddies. Tell them to leave me alone—" "Just the last page!" says Halliday drunkenly. "About us. The whole truth about us. The intimate, intricate, inanimate truth about us. Read it. Pat it on the head like a dog. Wait right here. Don't move! Be right back."

Although she gives way to tears of confusion, Jere quickly dabs them away when Wister La Salle tracks her down. Incapable of making any decision of her own, she agrees to go to his hideaway with him as soon as she tells Halliday. Back with his manuscript, observing their amorous goings-on, Halliday shouts: "Go, bitch! Go on. Have your night!" As in the distance the orchestra plays "Ain't We Got Fun," Jere asks Halliday to say she *can't* go. "I'm breaking into a thousand pieces and only you can put me together again," she cries. "I've tried putting you together," shouts Halliday, "now let Wister La Salle try . . . let all the king's horses and all the king's men!" As Jere runs off, the party seems to reach a frenzied pitch. In a maniacal rage, Halliday starts heaving his guests out bodily. Then alone, despairing, he cries: "Jere . . . you couldn't. Not with La Salle. With nobody. With nobody!" Halliday now finds that he has torn the manuscript in two. Stunned, then with drunken deliberation, he tears the paper to shreds, makes a heap of paper on the floor, lights a match to it, and starts to burn down the house. "Oh, Jere! Jere!," he cries. "How do we get out of this amusement park?"

The present finds Milgrim at the door, Stearns trying to bluff, and Halliday admitting that they have no story. Listening to their ineffectual answers, noticing Shep's bottle, Milgrim asks angrily if they've been drinking. "Victor," says Halliday, "we've had one hell of a time getting acquainted. A collaboration is like a marriage."

MILGRIM—Dammit, don't give me any of your highbrow analogies!
STEARNS—Mr. Milgrim, we keep looking for something better.
MILGRIM—Look, gentlemen, I'm a perfectionist myself, up to a point. Then I become a realist. Now what are the realities? I'm paying you, Manley, two thousand dollars a week. I'm paying you,

Stearns, the maximum junior writer's salary. And what have I got to show for it? (*He snatches up the wastebasket and dumps its contents on the floor.*) Crumpled paper, perfection! I don't want a wastebasket full of perfection. What I want—and what I intend to get—is a coherent, detailed shooting outline that I can put in the hands of my director in the morning. And that you can present to the dean and his staff at five o'clock tomorrow afternoon. Stay up all night if you have to. Take Benzedrine if you need it. Only don't fail me. I'm warning you, Manley—both of you—you better not fail me. We're all committed now, we're locked together. (*He goes to the door.*) It's been snowing in Webster all day. The weather is perfect for winter sports and photography. All the elements are ready too. Ah . . . (*He tries to remember if he has omitted anything.*) Good night, gentlemen. (*He exits.*)

After this whipping, Stearns is even ready for Halliday's blue skyrack. Then there is another knock and Halliday opens the door upon a macabre, middle-aged version of the young, enthralling Jere.

Striving for her old gaiety, she gets nowhere. Saying they need every moment to meet their deadline, Stearns tries nervously to have her leave. "One minute," says Jere, "and I'll disappear like a pumpkin coach." "It's all right, Shep, we won't be long," Halliday reassures him. Unable to cope with this new interruption, Stearns, taking Halliday's manuscript with him, goes into the bedroom.

While Halliday tries to keep his distance Jere, talking of many things in a strained fashion, does her best to introduce a personal note. She can't imagine his writing for the movies. . . . It looks like New Directions is going to publish her Rimbaud. . . . Seeing the whiskey bottle, Jere launches into a lecture on the benefits of A.A. "Look, Jere," says Halliday, "I don't need A.A. I haven't had a drink in almost a year now." "But, Mannie, darling, once you take the step it's such a satisfaction," she persists. "I don't want to spend the rest of my life nursing drunks. I've got to *work*," cries Halliday. "I've lost so much time." Jere switches the conversation to Halliday's appearance: he looks ghastly, she says, and tries to straighten his tie—but he moves away. The tension is coming more to the surface. Trying to gossip about their old crowd, whom Manley doesn't see, Jere gets nowhere. She comes to the point: "Mannie, I hate to bring up the horrid subject of money the first time I see you in years. But there's all that back alimony—"

HALLIDAY—I sent you some money three days ago.
JERE—Yes, but it wasn't that much. It didn't last me a day.
HALLIDAY—It was half my check—a thousand dollars!

JERE—But I was two months behind in my rent—that was six hundred right there—

HALLIDAY—I wrote you years ago that you couldn't afford your apartment any more. I'm not made of gold. I can't keep you in the style of a—

JERE—I've got all our lovely things there. I'd just die if I had to leave it. Besides, it isn't only me. It's a place for Douglas to come home to from School. And, Mannie, that's the main reason I came. Do you know what you've done?

Jere now accuses Halliday of hurting his son by being so late in sending the boy's tuition that he ran away from school. "He came home sobbing," continues Jere, "because he didn't have enough money to invite a girl to the junior prom." Pointing out that his only reason for doing this damn movie is to provide for *them*, Halliday pleads for help from Jere. But, blind and deaf to what he asks, Jere replies with tears. Instinct demands that he comfort her but he stops short. Clutching at him, begging his pity and his love, Jere wants to start all over. "Jere," says Halliday, "I simply haven't the time or strength to go through all this with you again."

JERE—I know it isn't going to be easy for either of us. We'll never solve our problems by running away from them. Mannie, you have to learn to face yourself.

HALLIDAY (*wearily*)—Jere, don't start lecturing me again. I'm in no mood for lectures these days.

JERE—I believe I know what's best for both of us, I've learned to make sacrifices—they're good for the soul.

Her irrational talk drives Halliday wild. As he shows his anger, Jere's neurotic statements grow loud and more pronounced: "I know why you're against it, because I'm for it. You always were against everything I tried to do. You told me I'd never finish my translation. But in spite of your jealousy, I am finishing it!" She becomes so violent she slaps Halliday hard across the face. Worse still, she becomes loving. Halliday in despair tries to get her to go—to leave him alone. He'll send her money, but she is to stay away from him. As she starts for the door, she says in a voice filled with patience: "One of these days you'll want me back. And I'll come back." As Stearns enters, Jere fires her parting shot: "I know us so well now." She leaves.

Halliday's and Stearns' eyes meet. They stare at each other for a long moment. "Stearns, I wonder if a man can ever really love a woman without hating her too," says Halliday. "Like the shipwrecked mariner, the rock on which I flounder is the rock to which I cling." Fighting to control his anguish, Halliday disappears into the bedroom.

Waiting only a moment, Stearns makes an urgent call to Seixas: "I've been reading *Folly and Farewell*. I know all his books—but this one—this one is so much more—you've got to read it right away because he may turn against it and tear it up. Mrs. Halliday was just here. He's coming. I'll leave it at the desk."

Halliday, coming back into the room, apparently determined that this night belongs to Victor Milgrim, watches Stearns pour himself a drink.

HALLIDAY (*raising an imaginary glass*)—To our heroine, who is either a buxom red-headed waitress in a hash joint, or a bony *Harper's Bazaar* model—or a fantastic combination of both.

STEARNS (*laughing, his spirits soaring*)—Tonight the blue sky-rack. Tomorrow Webster! We're off to the frozen North. Mush!

HALLIDAY (*quietly, painfully*)—That's what we've got to write—mush! (*He stares at his empty hand for a long moment, then stares at the bottle on the table for a moment. Suddenly, almost involuntarily, he pours himself a drink, hesitates for a split second, then convulsively gulps the drink down as* STEARNS, *shocked and fearful, slowly rises.*)

ACT III

That Saturday afternoon, in their attic room at the Webster Inn, with their five o'clock deadline just an hour away, Halliday sprawls on a chaise. Unshaven and somewhat drunk, Halliday is nothing but a nuisance to Stearns, who is still trying to get something down on paper.

Barging in unannounced and surveying the bottle-scarred scene, Milgrim reads the two the riot act. Calling to their attention that his unemployed second-unit crew is whiling away the time throwing snowballs, Milgrim is ready to cite Halliday and Stearns for "contractual irresponsibility." "Stearns, you find the director," orders Milgrim. "He's pacing the lobby. If you have anything—or can think of something up on the way—give it to him. And then come back on the double." Seeing that Halliday is in sudden pain, Stearns hesitates; but, brought up sharp by Milgrim's shouts, he does as he is told.

Milgrim is desperate enough to plead with Halliday: he *must* find a story for them and it *must* reflect credit on Webster. Drunk as he is, Halliday flushes out Milgrim's hope for an honorary degree. On the defensive, saying that whether or not he and Halliday like it, they are tied together, Milgrim starts to leave with Halliday's bottle. Halliday's outstretched hand stops Milgrim. His frustration complete, Milgrim tosses the bottle back to Halliday, saying weakly: "Be ready at five."

Stearns, returning to this room that reeks of booze and tobacco, says: "Funny, ever since they sprung me out of here five years ago, I've had dreams how I'd come back in style. Showing up with someone like you or Hemingway. And now it's just something to go through, to get over with as painlessly as possible." Observing that Halliday is cockeyed drunk, Stearns thinks that the best thing Halliday can do when five o'clock rolls round is just smile and look famous. Towards this end, Stearns hands him a fresh shirt and tells him to put his shoes on. Balking at having to go to Milgrim's rooms, Halliday says: "If I'm going to be a monkey act in Milgrim's circus, let it be in my own cage."

STEARNS—Manley, you know what this means to me. It should mean a hell of a lot more to *you*. That novel of yours! You've always known how—

HALLIDAY (*poignantly*)—Haven't you finished it yet? Give it back to me. I need it. I feel unarmed without it.

STEARNS (*pushing* HALLIDAY *into a chair*)—Listen to me, you're not! That book's like a Colt forty-five. It knocks you down . . . I can't give it back to you yet. I gave it to Mr. Seixas.

HALLIDAY (*playfully tapping* STEARNS' *jaw with a woefully weak fist*)—You betrayed me.

STEARNS—You've always known what! You've even known how, but now you know why! You showed me why. I'm not even sure you know what a book that is. Mr. Seixas thinks it's the best five and one-half chapters you ever wrote, and so do I.

HALLIDAY—Ah, pour it in, pour it in, it's better than insulin, better than blood and glucose.

"That book's got to be finished," says Stearns. Halliday, knowing that he can't walk, asks Stearns to bring everyone up here. Giving in once more, Stearns warns Manley: "If you need an insulin shot, take it; whatever you need except whiskey, take it." "Okay, laddie," answers Halliday. "Okay, okay, okay." "I descend to the first circle of Hell," groans Stearns.

Picking up pencil and paper, all poised to write, Halliday finds himself in the past, in a sun-drenched beach house at La Jolla, with

Jere. Recuperating from the effects of the Hollywood party fire, Halliday feels like a new man. Grateful for the fire that wiped out their merry-go-round, refusing henceforth to be whirled about, he is determined to be a "miser of time." Jere insists that she too misses nothing that was lost except *Folly and Farewell.* Unwilling to be sad even about that, Halliday feels sure that when he is ready he will write it again, only better. In complete agreement on such things as no parties, no friends and no bottles, Halliday and Jere seemingly have recaptured their old feelings for each other.

Yet their weakness is such that the first visitors who track them down lead them astray. Jere can't say "no" to the champagne her friends offer and gaily leads Halliday right back to destruction. Accepting an invitation to a wild yachting party, Jere calls back: "Mannie, you coming?" . . . In his attic room a staggering Halliday cries: "Yes, I'm coming. I'm just having trouble finding my way."

STEARNS (*entering rapidly*)—Manley, Milgrim just gave me hell but they're coming up here, so start thinking. We're about to get the heaveroo.

HALLIDAY—Heaveroo? Never heard the word. You make it up? Or is it generic?

STEARNS—Who the hell cares what it is? I did my share. Now, come on, you do yours.

HALLIDAY—Stick with me, laddie. Okay, Shep, okay, laddie. Help me.

STEARNS—Help yourself. Save your own goddamn life. From here on in, I don't care what the hell happens to you.

HALLIDAY—Stearns, tell you a secret . . . Want Jere. Need Jere. Shep, do me a favor—call her. You got to call her.

STEARNS (*sarcastically*)—Anything you want!

HALLIDAY—Want Jere. Want a new heart, a fresh start, a drink. (*He shakily reaches into his valise for his tuxedo jacket and struggles into it while still sitting.*)

As the Webster faculty group converges on Halliday's room, Milgrim takes one disapproving look at Halliday and does his best to cover up for his appearance. After introductions are made all around, the chairman of the Webster English department, Professor Connelly, is unwise enough to ask Halliday if he remembers that they spoke on the same platform some twenty years ago. Not only does Halliday remember precisely the man's full name and the lengthy, scholarly title of his topic, he also remembers the unpardonable length of its delivery.

The uncomfortable atmosphere created first by Halliday's appearance, and then by what he says, is not helped by the college wives' banal remarks. Hoping they can begin, Milgrim instructs Halliday to tell the story. Halliday reacts blankly. Jumping into the breach, Stearns dredges up the "ski-captain" hero. Milgrim cuts him short: "Thank you, Stearns, but we've gathered here to listen to Manley Halliday. Manley, curtain's up and you're on." But Halliday fails to react.

STEARNS (*urgently*)—Blue sky-rack!

HALLIDAY (*he hears* STEARNS, *takes his hand, rises shakily, then after a long tense pause he begins to talk in an almost trance-like fashion*)—We see a white fairyland in the Green Mountains. A tiny dark figure appears and starts sweeping down toward our camera. Faster and faster he flies over the freshly fallen snow, a perfect carpet for the Lone Skier. Youth charging down into the virgin field of trackless snow . . . (*He pauses. His audience is attentively silent.*) At the bottom of this white world we see a winding road. Rounding into view comes an elegant touring car, carrying a single passenger, a girl whose face is aglow with the cold of the air and the warmth of being alive. She is the Princess Rimbaud. As her innocent, vivid young eyes lift to take in everything, she sees our skier, a breathtaking masculine blur of green against the snow-white slope . . ."

Milgrim is relieved and excited; the faculty is impressed; and Stearns cries: "Manley, you've got hold of the rack!" As Halliday concludes his vignette of "the Boy and Girl forever losing, finding, and not keeping, even in Fairyland," Stearns urges him on. Halliday falters. Milgrim prompts: "The boy, the girl, they meet . . . and—" After a trembling pause, Halliday says: "And . . . and they never see each other again." Milgrim gets up and insists that that's just an introduction. It's good but there has to be more. Halliday heads for the door: he is going to Jere. Stearns begs Halliday to come back and finish. Milgrim insists that he finish. Coming back to reality, Halliday gives them more in a mounting demoniacal frenzy: "From the slick surface of the ski jump we dissolve to the slick surface of the faculty mind. From the beautiful snow-white surface of a ski trail we dissolve to the hand of Victor Milgrim as it moves up the beautiful snowy-white surface of a thigh—of Mrs. Connelly's thigh. And as Victor Milgrim's hand moves up and up and up . . ." There is general chaos in the room.

MILGRIM—I don't know when the next train leaves, but you two bastards better be on it!

Halliday (*shouting*)—I told you there wasn't any more. It was all over, finished, a lifetime in a minute. Pure poetry and pure crap. Exactly right for a movie script. Now this party is over . . . done . . . fini . . . kaput! Out!

As the Dean leaves with his group, he has serious doubts that Webster can have anything further to do with this project. After more recriminations Milgrim leaves Halliday alone with Stearns, whose turn it now is: "Once, when I heard you were alive, and going to work on *Love on Ice,* I couldn't believe it. I thought you were dead. You are dead, aren't you? Tell me . . . are you dead?" As Stearns moves in furiously to strike him, he catches and embraces him instead. Halliday begins to sink down. He is gasping for breath and groans in pain. Begging him to hold on, Stearns rushes out for a doctor.

Appearing to the faint tinkle of long-remembered music, a phantom Jere interferes with Halliday's last, spasmodic effort to write. Halliday cries: "Take her away! Take her away! This woman is smothering me!" The pencil dropping from his hand, he falls back dead: simultaneously Jere disappears.

Rushing back with the word that the doctor is on his way, Stearns becomes frenzied when he discovers Halliday's death. Then noticing a slip of paper clutched in Halliday's hand, Stearns gently removes it. He reads slowly: "A second chance—that was our delusion. A first chance—that's all we have. Remember that, laddie." Crumpling the paper in deep anguish Stearns, with increasing resolution, replies: "Okay, laddie, okay, okay, okay—"

THE COLD WIND AND THE WARM
A Play in Three Acts

By S. N. Behrman

[Samuel Nathaniel Behrman *was born in Worcester, Mass., in 1893. He attended Clark College and later Harvard, where he studied under George Pierce Baker. He earned his M.A. degree at Columbia University. He wrote his first play, "Bedside Manners," with Kenyon Nicholson in 1923. He has been a play reader and a theatrical press agent, has contributed many stories and articles to magazines and written many films for Hollywood. He was one of the founders of the Playwrights' Company. Among his many plays are "The Second Man," "Brief Moment," "Biography," "End of Summer," "No Time for Comedy," "Jacobowsky and the Colonel," "I Know My Love" and "Jane."*]

For the cast listing, see page 309.

WITH a lovely, plaintive melody—the oboe passage from Handel's *Water Music*—as accompaniment, Tobey's voice can be heard: Tobey, as he grows older, thinks back more and more to his friendship with Willie when they were young and happy in Worcester, Massachusetts. Tobey's voice recalls that "Willie was always preoccupied with mystery—the mystery of life—the mystery of death. He used to illuminate all my childish problems for me. But he left me an inheritance of the greatest mystery of all: why he killed himself, why he felt he had to do it. . . ." The one thing Tobey knows

"The Cold Wind and the Warm": By S. N. Behrman. Suggested by his *New Yorker* series and book, "The Worcester Account." © Copyright 1958, as an unpublished work, by S. N. Behrman. © Copyright 1959 by S. N. Behrman. Reprinted by permission of Random House, Inc. "The Cold Wind and the Warm" is the sole property of the author and is fully protected by copyright. It may not be acted by professionals or amateurs without formal permission and the payment of a royalty. See caution notice on copyright page. All inquiries should be addressed to the author's agent: Harold Freedman, Brandt and Brandt Dramatic Department, Inc., 101 Park Avenue, New York, N. Y.

now is that Willie was the "most life-giving person" he had ever known.

On an early summer evening in 1908, twenty-year-old Willie Lavin and his twelve-year-old, bespectacled friend Tobey stand deep in conversation. Tobey is asking Willie a lot of questions that his father says he's better off not thinking about.

TOBEY—We're standing here, aren't we—at the corner of Exchange and Green?
WILLIE—Precisely.
TOBEY—Above us is the sky. Right?
WILLIE—Right.
TOBEY—Now above that sky—let's say a million miles away—there's another sky.
WILLIE—I'll grant that.
TOBEY—Let's say there are a million skies beyond that sky. A trillion. All right?
WILLIE—I'm with you, Tobey—at the trillionth sky.
TOBEY (*his voice rising in triumph*)—Well, what's beyond the *last* sky? There *must* be an end to it some place. At night I build a big wall to end it. But what's beyond the wall?
WILLIE—Infinity.
TOBEY—That's what Father says I mustn't think about!
WILLIE—I disagree with your father. It's a problem—like other problems. It can be analyzed. Resolved into its component parts.

Hearing Dr. Jim Nightingale's oboe, they decide to look in on him at his office. Willie wants to know what else Tobey's father asks him not to think about. "It seems," says Tobey, "that the Lord has many names but no one knows the *True* Name." His father says that those who come close to it are destroyed. "Perhaps if you solved infinity," muses Willie, "you'd find out the True Name of the Lord also. Perhaps there's only one mystery—the key to everything—and you'd get it in one blinding flash."
Annoyed for the moment at being interrupted during his oboe playing, Dr. Jim is delighted that it's not patients, but Willie and Tobey. Settling Tobey on the sagging horsehair sofa and offering him a magazine, Jim winks at Willie: "Manual of Obstetrics. The kids come in here and devour the illustrations." Blushing furiously, Tobey refuses to look at it. As Jim urges it on him, Tobey becomes

hideously embarrassed. Willie interferes and Tobey is allowed to look at *Puck* instead.

Catching up on Willie's chemistry studies, Jim wishes to hell that *he* had stuck to science. "Medicine may be science but practising isn't," he says. "Good God, the women who come in here with their imaginary pains—they're bored with their husbands—" Reminded of Tobey's presence, Jim asks Tobey when his mother is coming home. Unable to say, Tobey returns to *Puck*. "They haven't got the money to rent a piano for the kid," says Jim to Willie, "but to send his mother to New York." "Well," says Willie by way of excuse, "when it's a question of health." Saying bluntly that she's got chronic asthma, that he's done all he can for her and still they send her to Professor Jacobi in New York, Jim bemoans his type of practice. Then, looking with love at his oboe, he curses a ringing telephone and lets it ring. Tobey is shocked. "But maybe somebody is dying!" he cries. Amused by Tobey's concern, Jim goes to take the call.

For all his cynicism, Willie assures Tobey, Jim is very goodhearted. Tobey knows this, as he knows no one pays Jim and that he never presses anyone for payment. Longing for a piano of his own, Tobey admires the way Jim goes to Boston twice a week for music lessons.

Coming back, Dr. Jim announces cheerfully that Tobey was right, somebody *is* dying. Reassuring Tobey that it won't happen that night, he says it's diabetes. "Who?" asks Willie casually. No less casually, Jim, violating professional confidence, tells Willie it is his friend Dan Eisner. "It's not possible!" cries Willie. "Dan is getting married." "Marriage," answers Jim, "is no cure for diabetes." Thinking of Myra, Willie asks whether she knows. "If he's told her, she knows. If he hasn't, she doesn't. None of my business," says Jim. "But if it's true—then Myra . . ." cries Willie. "In three or four years she'll be a beautiful widow," says Jim; "that's a good kind of widow to be!" Suddenly aware of how affected Willie is, Jim adds: "Oh, I forgot. You're in love with Myra yourself. Well, bide your time, Willie. . . ."

Visibly upset, Willie tells Tobey that they have to go. Refusing a restaurant dinner invitation from Jim, and wanting to get off the subject of Dan and Myra, Willie asks whether Jim can't afford to replace his sagging sofa. "Symbol of conquest," crows Jim. "I've been treating bored wives on that sofa for twenty years!" "Please," shushes Willie, "not in front of the boy!"

Passing Dan on the way home, Tobey can't get over how, if this carbon-copy of John Drew is dying, he can take so much trouble over his appearance. But Willie's mind, occupied with Tobey's piano problem, has just found the solution: Willie will buy the piano and pay for the lessons himself. "All your friends wonder," says Tobey, "why you spend so much time with me." "Can't discuss abstract questions with my friends," Willie answers. "Nice fellows but they're a bit excessively down to earth. I have great faith in your future." Glowing, Tobey feels very lucky.

By the time they reach the stoop in front of Tobey's house, Dan is once more in their thoughts. Willie is thinking of Myra, but Tobey is thinking of what Dan should do about the Dark Angel— the Angel of Death. "Dan should do what I do," he says, "he should hold on tight—to the bedposts. Like this." He illustrates what he means by clinging to the railing.

WILLIE (*humors him*)—You don't think the Dark Angel might be stronger?

TOBEY—No. You can outfight him if you hold on fast enough. He comes at night. He's always at our house you know, Willie—to take my mother. Every night Father says his night prayer, about those four good angels . . . and I have confidence in them so I fall asleep. But then I wake up—and he's standing there, the Dark One, grabbing at me, to take me away . . .

WILLIE (*fascinated*)—What's he look like?

TOBEY—He hasn't got any face—yet he looks at you—with *something*. He's not angry or anything—he just wants to take you.

WILLIE—And you don't let him?

TOBEY—No. I hold on to the bedposts. The more he tugs, the more I hold on. That's what Mother should do and that's what Dan should do!

WILLIE—Have you told your mother?

TOBEY—When she has one of her attacks—I can't—her hands look so weak . . . her hands, Willie . . .

WILLIE (*quietly*)—Yes, Tobey?

TOBEY—Her hands look as if they already belonged to the Dark One.

WILLIE (*after a moment*)—I think maybe, Tobey . . . I think maybe you read too much.

Coming out on her apartment porch (Worcester calls it "piazza"), obviously looking for someone, Tobey's Aunt Ida calls down: "What you two have to talk about all the time I don't know, but any minute I'm expecting Leah from Fitchburg." The entire hill, according to Willie, is expecting Leah from Fitchburg, whom Ida is marrying off to a "very rich millionaire," a "high-toned" furrier from Atlanta. Fitchburg being no place to meet a bride, Ida is having him meet Leah here tomorrow. "When your uncle—may he rest in peace—married me," Ida tells Tobey, "he took me for a honeymoon to Fitchburg on the streetcar. It spoiled the whole honeymoon. So be sure, Willie, and bring her up the moment she gets here."

Going back into her apartment, Ida surveys it approvingly. Her daughter, Ren, sprawled on the couch reading "The Ancient Mariner," tries to sidestep her mother's suggestion to go pick flowers. "I'm trying to do my homework!" cries Ren. "So," says Ida, "you'll be a schoolteacher two weeks later!"

REN (*with scorn*)—I have a feeling that this furrier is nowhere near as high-tone as you think he is!

IDA—What are you talking, Ren? So rich is the furrier that his apartment is furnished by an interior man. I showed you his picture, Ren?

REN—Looks more like a trapper than a furrier.

IDA (*studying photograph with detachment*)—Handsome he is but he has no neck.

Torn from her book, Ren wonders why her father was so concerned about Leah. Ida says that before she died, Leah's mother had begged him: "Please, Harry, ask your wife she should find for Leah!" "Well," says Ren, "that's your specialty. Finding! Why didn't you?" Admitting that she didn't trust herself, Ida felt that she needed a professional on the job, like Rappaport from Boston. "So," says Ida, "he found Atlanta. Leah's picture he sent to Atlanta. Atlanta's picture he sent to Leah."

Worcester may be better than Fitchburg, but to Ren it's boring: she wants to move to New York. One step ahead of her, Ida says that she has already written to her father, the Ramov, about moving there, and the Ramov advises that when Ren is through high school, she should go to City College in New York. Accusing her mother of staying in Worcester for another reason, Ren confronts Ida with loving their landlord, Mr. Mandel. "I am not in love," cries Ida indignantly, "until I find out if I am loved back!"

While Willie and Tobey, listening for the streetcar, sit out on the stoop, Myra and Dan's younger brother Aaron come down the hill. Bubbly and flirtatious, Myra runs right up to Willie. "That's the awful thing about being engaged," cries Myra, "everybody drops you!" She just adores having boys around who adore her and whom she can adore back. "That's all the fun—flirting," she says. "With me flirting is almost everything. If I flirt with anybody that means I'm a little bit in love with them . . ." Sulking on the sidelines, Aaron urges Myra to keep her promise and listen to his poem. Announcing that Aaron dedicates *all* his poems to her, Myra avoids giving Willie a direct answer about the date of the wedding. She says coyly that they may even elope.

As Aaron takes her indoors, Tobey wonders whether everybody is in love with Myra, and whether Aunt Ida arranged this marriage. "No," says Willie, "Aunt Ida had nothing to do with that. That was spontaneous combustion."

Having escorted Tobey upstairs, Willie returns to the street. Bumping into Rappaport from Boston, he directs him to Ida's apartment.

Ida, seeing Rappaport with a little nosegay clutched in his hand, assumes that everything is settled. Instead, Rappaport denounces the furrier as a coarse fellow, and then resorts to coughing. Not caring for such evasiveness, Ida asks him to explain himself. As a preliminary, Rappaport says: "With you, Mrs. Feinberg, matchmaking is a hobby. You don't make from it. But hobbies, *I* can't afford. From matchmaking I have to make a living, Mrs. Feinberg." It turns out that Rappaport not only sent Leah's picture to Atlanta, but took the precaution of sending a second picture, that of Goldie from Revere Beach. Ida says scornfully: "Goldie from Revere Beach: then I'm not worried. To Goldie I brought myself three men. They all ran away. Goldie from Revere Beach speaks with a palate. With Goldie you can't tell whether she is saying yes or no." "To the furrier," answers Rappaport, "she said yes."

Ida, in a real fury, says that she "could tear him from each limb." Rappaport, wanting to stay in her good graces, pleads with her to no avail. She tells him off majestically: "Rappaport! That you are a nudnick I always knew. Only now I find out that besides being a nudnick you are also—do you hear me, Rappaport?—a no-good-Benedict-the-traitor!" As for that furrier, Ida, picking up his photograph, demonstrates to Rappaport what she'd like to do: "A neck he hasn't got or I'd break it!" Tearing the photograph to bits, she hurls the pieces at Rappaport's face.

Rappaport slinks away, leaving Ida to wonder what she can possibly tell poor Leah. Kissing her, Ren assures her: "You'll think of something. You always do."

Tobey's father, Mr. Sacher, coming home tired and late from his grocery store, finds that Tobey has stayed up to tell him that Willie, who is in a dilemma, will be in to see him. Wishing Tobey sweet dreams, Mr. Sacher sees him off to bed. Then pacing about the room, he says his night prayers: "And may the angel Michael be at my right hand, Gabriel at my left, before me Uriel, behind me Raphael, and over my head the divine presence of God."

Willie and his ethical dilemma interrupt Mr. Sacher's prayers. Awkwardly Willie explains that this afternoon he found out by accident that Dan Eisner has diabetes. Jim Nightingale told him it was only a question of time. Willie wants to know should he or should he not tell Myra. Mr. Sacher questions Willie as to his motives and makes him squirm. "Is Jim Nightingale God?" asks Sacher. "He's a damn good doctor," answers Willie. "Can he read the future?" pursues Sacher. "How does he know that some cure will not be discovered? Or that Dan may not be the exception who recovers? My dear wife has been given up several times. Yet God has seen fit to spare her." Tobey's father advises Willie to look into his soul: "I know how you feel about Myra. If anyone tells Myra—it shouldn't be you."

WILLIE (*suddenly*)—Why don't *you* tell her?

FATHER—I'm a poor stumbling creature. I am not God. In any case, Willie—

WILLIE—Well?

FATHER—You know—according to the ancient law—if Dan should die . . .

WILLIE (*truculent*)—Well?

FATHER—Myra would be bound, unless released by Dan's family, to marry Dan's younger brother, Aaron, who professes to be in love with her too.

Taking books from the shelves, Mr. Sacher shows Willie many things written on the Levirate Law. As Willie reads in these books, Myra and Aaron emerge, hand in hand, to sit on the stoop.

Myra adores to see the love in Aaron's eyes. "Oh, Aaron!" she cries, "you'll always love me, won't you? Even after I'm married to Dan? Won't you? When you become a famous poet you'll dedicate your poems to me, and I'll tell you everything and you'll tell me everything. We'll have no secrets from each other—" As a starter, Aaron blurts out that his poems are no good. According to his teacher, they're *banal*. Taking but a moment's time to comfort him, Myra rattles on about going on her honeymoon with Dan to the Hotel Astor in New York.

MYRA—It's on Broadway and Forty-second Street—right in the middle of *everything!* I'll be Right There! Can you imagine? I've never been farther than Framingham. I'll miss *you*, darling; I wish you were coming. Do you think Dan would think it's funny if I asked him to bring you? (*In ecstasy at every prospect.*) Oh, Aaron—Aaron!

AARON (*in misery*)—Oh, Myra—Myra—

MYRA—I love everything. All the world. I love myself—and everybody else. I love you, Aaron—in the most special way—I *love* you, Aaron!

AARON—If you loved me you wouldn't—

MYRA (*pedantically*)—Marriage is an experience every girl should have. You're too young to marry. Why, you're still in college.

Shutting the books, Willie dismisses the Levirate Law as medieval nonsense. Sternly disagreeing with him, Mr. Sacher says: "This will only bring us back to our old argument . . . faith versus reason. You are a good boy, Willie—" Mr. Sacher smiles at him—"though a scientist! You came to ask my advice. People who ask your advice usually want it to justify a course they have already decided on. You have probably decided, already, to tell Myra . . ." Willie protests. "Then," says Mr. Sacher, "all I can say is . . . look into your heart—ask yourself why you're doing it. Is it to save Myra? Or to save her for yourself? . . . Go home, my son, and think." Knowing that Mr. Sacher has hit on the truth, Willie thanks him and leaves.

Willie, coming out on the stoop, is waylaid by Myra. As she pulls him to her side, Aaron, tearing up his poems, runs wildly down the hill. "Guess you're not satisfied with Dan," says Willie. "You want his brother too."

Just then Dan struts into view. Effusive but condescending toward Willie, teasing him about being up to his old tricks with Myra, Dan takes over. Waving a three-carat engagement ring in front of Myra, he quickly gets her attention. While she tries on the ring, Dan boasts of having, during the afternoon, swum across the lake. It took an hour and twenty minutes, and he had no boat to follow him. "That's dangerous," says Willie, "you might get a cramp." Flexing his muscles, Dan says he never gets cramps.

Sneaking out of his apartment in his nightgown, Tobey, with a sense of mission, comes down to give Dan advice about the Angel. "What angel?" asks Dan. "The Angel of Death," answers Tobey. "I know he's after you." Horrified, Willie tries to shush Tobey, but the boy proceeds: "I heard Father say—you mustn't do it—so I have to do it . . ."

As Tobey persists with his instructions on how to treat the Angel,

Dan turns ashen. Enraged, he is ready to hit the boy, but Willie shields him.

WILLIE—You know with his mother sick all the time he has these fantasies at night. . . . He's afraid he's going to lose his mother . . .

MYRA—But why to Dan?

DAN (*trembling with anger and fear*)—I won't forget this—I'll tell you—

MYRA—Dan! Is there anything wrong with you?

DAN (*shouting*)—I'm in great shape, I tell you! Never felt better in my life!

MYRA—Then why are you so . . . so . . . ?

DAN (*in better control*)—It's that jealous . . . (*Points to* WILLIE.) He put the kid up to it. Won't do you a bit of good, my friend. (*To* MYRA, *masterfully*.) You come upstairs with me. Away from these . . . How do you like the ring? Let me see it *on* you.

Completely hypnotized by the ring, Myra follows Dan. "They're bound to notice it," she says; "don't you think so, Willie, in the lobby of the Hotel Astor?"

Alone with Tobey, Willie assures him that he isn't angry at him. He shocks and scares Tobey, however, when he announces his decision to wait for Myra. As a matter of fact, Willie confesses to being scared himself. Well-tutored in the Law, Tobey reminds Willie of Aaron's rights should anything happen to Dan.

WILLIE—I'd like to see them try it! I'm beginning to think you're much too preoccupied with angels. (*Sits beside him.*) Might be a good idea if you cultivated an outdoor hobby.

TOBEY (*that would settle it*)—Have *you* got one?

WILLIE—I am beginning to think seriously about fishing.

TOBEY—Why don't you?

WILLIE—First I have to master the theory of fishing. There's a considerable literature, you know, on fishing—different methods, different techniques.

TOBEY—Allie Seidenberg just fishes.

WILLIE—Well, he's just an empiricist.

TOBEY—What's an empiricist?

WILLIE—I'll explain that to you on one of our walks. (*Smiles.*) The peripatetic method.

Hearing the streetcar stop up the hill, they peer into the dark to see who it is. Hoping that it's his mother, Tobey expresses disappointment that it's only a girl. Carrying a cheap suitcase, Leah comes down the hill. The first to greet her, with the gallant remark that her "reputation has preceded her," Willie not only helps Leah with her suitcase, but in no time is helping her get out of a marriage to a man she has never met.

Shy, upset and faint from the strain, Leah is putty in Willie's helpful hands.

WILLIE—Have you got cold feet, Leah?
LEAH—Oh, Mr. Lavin . . .
WILLIE—Willie.
LEAH—Oh, Willie, I feel *so ungrateful!*
WILLIE (*cracks his knuckles*)—I can very well imagine a situation where at the very altar . . . where at the very altar, the bride will relinquish the groom. I will go so far as to say . . . that unless the impulse toward this person is *overwhelming,* it is your *duty* to break off this engagement.
LEAH—But Ida has been so kind and for a stranger, you might say. She hardly knows me. She's taken *so* much trouble.
WILLIE—Ida, out of the goodness of her heart, has found husbands for the halt, the lame and the blind—she will have no problem whatever with you, Leah.

Willie's taking such a load off her mind has made Leah feel much better. She tries to express her gratitude to Willie. "It is the highest function of human beings to help each other," he answers, "especially in moments of crisis. I venture to say that the opportunity may some day come for *you* to help *me.*" As Leah hopes for that time, dudish, forty-ish Norbert Mandel swaggers home up the hill. Ginger-colored in dress and mustachios, Norbert is a man who is never seen without a cane. Seeing Willie, he condescends to nod; then, noticing Leah, whom Willie introduces, he says good evening.

MANDEL—I am Norbert Mandel. I am the proprietor of this property. My own residence is just on the top of the hill, very noticeable by its stain-glass window.
LEAH—How nice.
MANDEL—I am a close personal friend of Mrs. Feinberg and had I known she had so charming a client, Norbert Mandel would have expressed a personal interest.
LEAH (*in agony*)—Thank you.
MANDEL—I have just completed the purchase of a Winton Six. Consider it will be at your service any time should you care to see

our fair countryside. Good night. (*He continues his stately progress up the hill.*)

Once more upset that everyone knows about the Atlanta gentleman, Leah wonders what Mrs. Feinberg will say. Willie offers to straighten things out with her: holding open the door for Leah, he ushers her into the house, while shooing Tobey to bed.

Warmly greeted by Ida, Leah, looking around the apartment, exclaims: "What a beautiful tenement!" "That's your room," says Ida, pointing to the porch; "there from the piazza you can see the whole world." Leah goes out and looks down the street. She tells Ida that she has already met her nephew Tobey. Deducing that if Leah has met Tobey, she has met Willie, Ida is struck with a brilliant idea: "To meet Willie Lavin, that's a good start. I want you should have a good time in Worcester."

Wanting to get the unpleasantness over with, Leah starts to take the plunge, but Ida gets there first: "About that furrier from Atlanta I found out such things that I apologize I ever got you mixed up with such a no-good." Leah is greatly relieved.

IDA (*squaring off*)—It's a miracle I found out in time. It's like a special delivery from God.

LEAH—What did you find out?

IDA—In the first place I met somebody who knows him close and his face is with pimples. In the photograph you can't see because the photographer took them all out with an eraser. This is right away dishonest. In his leg he has a vein. And, over and above, he's not even a furrier. What he sells is from cats. So now the mayor of Atlanta is after him with a subpoena.

LEAH (*happy to be absolved, playing along*)—Then how can I face him when he comes tomorrow?

IDA—You think I would let a no-good low-life that steals cats set foot in this house? Today I sent him a telegram he should save himself the trouble.

LEAH—To tell you the truth I'm relieved.

IDA—Relieved is nothing. You are salvaged!

LEAH—I do want to get married. But somehow—I want . . .

IDA—You'll get!

This happily out of the way for both women, Ida insists that Leah stay with her: "Stay you will for company. Here are people coming and going. In the afternoon we go to Easton's Drug Store—five o'clock it's full of prospects with milk shakes. Already you met

Willie Lavin. I bet he right away melted." Poking his head in the door to see how Leah is managing, Willie gets trapped. Ida disappears into the kitchen, and Leah and Willie, embarrassed at her maneuver, carry on a stilted conversation.

Willie does his awkward best to be sociable, and even suggests that he will take Leah to the White City Amusement Park some evening. But he can't have a date tonight because of an important exam in the morning. As Willie gets up to go, Myra comes out on her piazza above.

Waving good night to Dan, Myra decides she needs more company. All she has to do is whistle, to call Willie's name, for Willie to drop everything and dash upstairs to her apartment.

Leah calls to Ida, and tells her that at the siren's call Willie went right up.

IDA—Myra?
LEAH—Yes. That's her name. Myra. I couldn't see in the dark. Is she attractive?
IDA (*with contempt*)—She's thin and she giggles.
LEAH—Well, I guess she's attractive enough to make Willie forget his important examination tomorrow morning.
IDA—Leah darling, about that hitzel-dritzel you don't have to worry, Leah, because in two weeks she's getting married!

ACT II

Two years have passed. Since Tobey's mother's death, Ida has been mothering the boy, and feeding him and Mr. Sacher. Dan, too, has died, and Willie, now, is fighting the windmill of the Levirate Law.

Calling for Tobey to take him for a walk, Willie has another argument with Mr. Sacher. Mr. Sacher finally cries: "Willie—Willie—you've thrown over chemistry—now you're studying law—you change your profession overnight. But about Myra you're steadfast. I wish it were the other way round . . ."

Willie accuses Ida, too, of siding with the families and invoking the Law against him. "From laws I know nothing," says Ida. "I go by what is good for you, Willie, and to get Myra safely settled with Aaron would be a load off. Aaron I hope is healthy enough to stay a while."

With Tobey and Willie out for a walk, and Mr. Sacher back at his grocery store, Ida is in a tizzy when Mandel pays her a visit. Hoping to land him for herself, Ida swoons with admiration over his incredible riding outfit.

IDA—Tell me, Mandel, in this suit are you coming or going?
MANDEL—Going.
IDA—It is a pleasure to look on you, Mandel. You smell from solid leather!
MANDEL (*formally*)—Thank you for the compliment, Mrs. Feinberg.
IDA—So tell me, with this suit where are you going?
MANDEL—Sundays is usual with me horseback. Sundays I canter. I am a habitué.
IDA (*stares at him, rapt*)—A peace on you, Mandel!
Mandel—Thank you for the thought, but peace I don't want. Peace I'll have in my grave. Norbert Mandel wants action!

Inquiring for Leah, finding that she is not at home, Mandel says that's too bad because now he has an appointment with his groom. Wanting to hold him, to feed him, to entertain him, to keep him at her side and have him finally come to terms, Ida asks Mandel to listen to her. He immediately turns cagey. "I have decided I would like for a change to be a private woman!" cries Ida. Affecting incredulity, Mandel answers: "Give up matchmaking! You wouldn't. It's in your blood." Her professionalism getting the better of her, Ida says: "You should get married, Mandel—even if it's not to me!" Mandel promptly announces that he is attracted by Ida's boarder, Miss Long. This is too much for Ida. She protests that Leah is a young girl: "Even for the prime Leah is too young. Leah is in the beginning. Besides—for Leah I am already arranging—"

MANDEL (*tensely*)—The fact is that in Norbert Mandel your lodger arouses the flame.
IDA—At our age let me tell you from the shoulder, Mandel, marriage is no flame.
MANDEL—For less Norbert Mandel will not settle!
IDA (*fighting a losing action*)—At our age a good marriage is to have steam heat in winter and an icebox in the summer.

Leah, coming home, is surprised to see Mandel. She tells Ida happily: "I just bumped into Willie Lavin and Tobey—Willie asked me to White City tonight." Giving Mandel a meaningful look, Ida says: "You see, Mandel! A fine canter to you, Mandel." But

THE COLD WIND AND THE WARM 157

through force of habit, Ida leaves the two of them alone.

Wishing to excuse herself, Leah is prevented from leaving. Mandel, holding her back, asks how such a lovely person is not married. It is simply, she says, that no one has ever asked her. As again she turns to go, Mandel again holds her back. He blurts out: *"I ask you, Miss Long!"* However upset, Leah manages to tell him that she is in love. "Willie Lavin? Now that Myra is a widow you will get no place with Willie Lavin!" shouts Mandel. Equally angry, Leah answers: "In any case I could never marry you." "And why not?" asks Mandel; "do you intend, perhaps, to remain an old maid?" "Rather than marry you—yes!" cries Leah, and she runs from the room.

Outraged, Mandel shouts for Ida, and crying in imperious tones that he is on fire, he orders her to arrange for him with Leah Long. "Norbert Mandel," he adds, "will never forget you!" "It's a funny way, Mandel, to preserve me in your mind!" answers Ida.

MANDEL—For your benefit, Mrs. Feinberg, I can tell you in confidence—recently I took out a big policy with the Prudential Insurance Company.

IDA—You're sick, Mandel?

MANDEL—Norbert Mandel was never in better health in his life. But get me yes from Miss Long and overnight she becomes the beneficiary. On my policies with the Prudential Insurance Company is featured a big rock. Norbert Mandel is like that rock. Stable. Gilt-edged. Pass that to Miss Long; she should know on which side is the butter.

IDA—I'll pass.

MANDEL—Good day, Mrs. Feinberg!

LEAH—Has he gone?

IDA—Gone he has. And, Leah, you should know if the worst, God forbid, comes to the worst, you have in reserve a *big rock!*

On the stoop, the story of unrequited love continues. Tobey asks Willie: "Don't you think then, that the *first* thing you should do is to find out how Myra feels? Oughtn't that be the first step?" Joking, Willie says that he's taking the second step first. But he adds: "Seriously, Myra or no Myra—I've got to upset the *concept*—the concept of the dead hand." With that comes thunder and lightning. "Applause from Heaven," says Willie.

Tobey has his own candidate: he finds Leah like his music. In fact he even thinks of her at night. "Do you?" says Willie. "It used to be the Dark Angel and holding onto the bedposts." "I've forgotten about them. It's Leah now," says Tobey. One reason for loving Leah is that she thinks Willie is wonderful; when he talks to Myra about Willie, they always end up talking about Myra.

Getting away from her nagging mother, Myra, wearing widow's weeds, joins Willie. "Go on up and practice your piece," Willie tells Tobey.

A thunderstorm that keeps Willie and Myra from leaving the porch throws Myra into a panic and then into Willie's arms. When the storm subsides, Myra confesses that since Dan's death everything frightens her more than ever. There's the problem of Aaron—Myra admits that she'd rather marry Willie than Aaron, but sometimes she thinks she'll just run away to New York. She knows that she'll be welcome at the Astor: when Dan took ill on their honeymoon, the manager of the Astor told Myra that any time she wanted a job just to let him know. "But Myra," Willie cries, "I've waited for you." "I know," she says, "I used to think—during that dreadful time—Willie loves me—Willie's waiting for me." This consoled her while she too waited. "For me?" asks Willie. "Were you waiting for me?" "I'm waiting for a promise," answers Myra, "that no one made me but which I've always felt. It's a kind of feeling that there is—there must be—love—which will make life . . ."

Close to her, overcome with his love for her, Willie for once finds it difficult to talk. Myra asks if he's going to marry Leah. "How can I," cries Willie, "when it's you I love?" Myra says: "I love you. But shall I tell you something? Don't wait for me. Love me. Don't forget me ever. But don't wait for me."

Then finding her mourning dress hateful, feeling rebellious, needing only the smallest encouragement from Willie, Myra dashes upstairs to change into something gay for him.

Aaron, clutching his umbrella, does his sullen best to brush by Willie. Willie stops him. Aaron dislikes Willie intensely and shows it. Undeterred, Willie proposes that they change their tactics with Myra. Angry at Willie's use of the plural, Aaron says heatedly: "I'm marrying Myra. You're not." "She'll marry neither of us," says Willie, "if we don't change our tactics. You are basing your whole claim on this old law. I am basing mine on demolishing the law. We are both misguided, Aaron, and do you know why? Because Myra is lawless . . ."

Myra, feeling ever so much more cheerful in her bright yellow dress, is quite ready to stand up to Aaron. Horrified that she has cast aside her mourning, Aaron accuses her of playing the harlot to tempt Willie. All worked up, he orders Willie to leave Myra alone. "I am Dan's brother," he shouts. "I have the right. She's mine by law. Get out!"

Aaron's tactics *are* wrong. Myra promptly says that she has never loved him and that now she doesn't even like him any more. She doesn't care about that law. Aaron's menacing tone and threats fall on deaf ears; he is even cheated of his effect by a clap of thunder, which again throws Myra into Willie's arms. As Aaron goes indoors to report Myra's sinful behavior to her mother, Myra begs Willie, the only one who loves her, never to leave her. Holding her in his arms and kissing her hair, Willie happily assures her that he never will.

Scene II

Late the next afternoon, while Mr. Sacher and his fellow-scholars of the Talmud have their annual celebration, Tobey sits outside with Willie on the stoop. Hearing that Willie has a date with Myra that evening, Tobey reports that everybody says Myra has given up Aaron for him. "So far," corrects Willie, "she's only given up Aaron." Then just as Mr. Sacher joins them, Ida calls down from her piazza that Willie's hitzel-dritzel Myra "flew away the coop." "She ran away," Ida cries. "A note she left that she'll write a note. So why didn't she write it now? For you too she left a note." Willie needn't run to read it, because Ida is able to tell him it's the same kind of note as the other.

WILLIE—I knew this would happen!
IDA (*matter-of-factly*)—So if you knew, why didn't you stop?
WILLIE (*dejected*)—You've driven her out, all of you. The loveliest thing in this God-obsessed community—you've driven her out!
MR. SACHER—No one forced Myra to go . . .
WILLIE (*in despair*)—All the bickering. All the wrangling. That fanatical father of Aaron's—Aaron himself.
MR. SACHER—You are not fanatical, Willie. Could you keep her?
WILLIE—I'll go to New York. She asked me never to leave her.
MR. SACHER—So then she promptly left you.

As Willie starts up the hill, Tobey wants to follow, but his father says that Willie needs solitude. Ida finds Myra's behavior all to the good: she can now arrange things for Willie and Leah.
Tobey asks: "Father, do you think Willie will get over this?"

MR. SACHER—That's a question I can't answer, Tobey. When I see the troubles of the young, it's a positive relief to be old.
TOBEY—Father—is it possible, Father, to be in love without being unhappy?
FATHER—It's possible, but highly unlikely.

Scene III

A month has passed, in which time Ren too is beginnning to find boys troublesome. As Ida explains to Willie: "Day and night they whistle for Ren."

As Tobey, upstairs, plays Schubert, Ida tries to talk to Willie about Leah. Pointing to a dress form that holds one of Leah's creations, Ida says that Filene's in Boston want Leah for a buyer, that Marshall Field's in Chicago want her, and that Norbert Mandel is hot on her trail.

Ida says she's worried about Willie: the whole hill is asking questions about him. She asks Willie to tell her in plain language what is the matter with him. "The fact is, dear Ida," says Willie, "I am afflicted by a syndrome of perplexities—a syndrome, dear Ida—" "Syndrome—pindrome, you've got to live!" she cries. "That, darling, is the heart of my problem," answers Willie.

When Leah comes in, Willie teases Ida about growing cool to Norbert Mandel, but when she goes out he confesses: "To be anchored to the bread and wine of life like Ida—to the near horizons—how enviable! Have you noticed? With Ida everything is factual—serious—a Heaven and Earth bounded by marriage." "Well," says Leah lightly, "what *are* Heaven and Earth bounded by?" Then Leah self-consciously switches the subject to Myra. Willie never tires of talking about her and Leah encourages him. At last she asks the question that most disturbs her: "Did you have an affair with Myra?" Myra, it turns out, hadn't consented to this, either.

No longer wanting to go to White City, Leah listens to Tobey's music. "It was very sweet of you, Willie, to give Tobey that piano," says Leah. Willie is proud of Tobey. After a pause, Willie adds: "It's only fair to tell you, Leah, I'm going to New York for good." He plans to be there when Myra needs him. Saying bluntly that Willie will just be waiting for the parade to pass, Leah lashes out: "Myra does what she likes. She takes what she likes. What's vulnerable about Myra?"

Revealing all the things that have hurt her for a long time, Leah confesses that she was happy when Myra ran away: now she knows that she will never be rid of her. Willie moves close to her. "Leah, dearest Leah," he says. Crying for him not to come near her, Leah wishes Myra were dead. But as Willie whispers endearments, Leah cries passionately: "She doesn't love you—but I do. That's why she won't sleep with you—because she doesn't love you—but I love you, Willie." He kisses her. The kiss becomes long and passionate.

SCENE IV

A few days later Willie arrives at the Sachers' with his suitcase: he has come to say farewell. But soon the old argument flares up between Mr. Sacher and him. Willie accuses Mr. Sacher of living in a closed world; Mr. Sacher counters that Willie lives in a limitless one. "That," he says, "is your danger. Too much room. Because there must be limits—that's what sanity is—a sense of limitation." "What are limits for you are chains for me!" cries Willie.

Mr. Sacher advises him to declare a loss on Myra, who doesn't love him, and to turn to someone else. Willie says that he couldn't do without his feelings for Myra, that by now they have nothing to do with her really. "Evidently you prefer mystery to light," says Mr. Sacher, "the riddle to the answer. All your gifts will go for nothing."

Angrily grabbing his suitcase and saying he'll write to Tobey, Willie rushes out. A woebegone Tobey follows. Knowing that Tobey's father is right, Willie says he still feels compelled to meet whatever is waiting for him. But promising to keep in touch with Tobey, Willie asks him to work hard. As Willie starts up the hill, Tobey cries: "Don't go, Willie, don't go."

ACT III

In New York, five years later, Tobey, a hard-working, aspiring composer of twenty, shares a garret room with Willie. Ida has brought Ren to New York, too; they have an apartment and Ren goes to college. Ida is still "finding."

As Tobey plays a few notes on his old upright and is writing them down, Ida telephones to inquire for Willie. Told he has a date with Myra, Ida cries: "So why is he chasing with that Myra when she is crazy in love with another man?" "That's a tough question to answer," says Tobey. "I find it hard to pin Willie down these days—a bit like trying to put mist in a bottle." The reason for Ida's call is that Leah and her adopted baby have returned from Chicago, and Ida wants Tobey and Willie for dinner. *"With* Myra?" asks Tobey. "Better without," concedes Ida, "but if I have to I have to." Smiling as he hangs up the phone, Tobey tosses aside his manuscript, picks up his jacket and starts for Ida's.

Hanging up at her end, Ida picks up the phone again as it rings.

IDA (*on phone*)—So why are you? . . . Oh, Mrs. Grodberg from Fourteen F . . . Tell me, Mrs. Grodberg, do I know you? . . . At my stepmother's funeral was the whole city of New York so I'm sorry I don't remember you, Mrs. Grodberg. . . . To my father you want an introduction? . . . Tell me, Mrs. Grodberg, are you healthy? . . . Are you pious? . . . I had in mind a Boston woman with whom my father could live out his life. . . . Well, promises I can't make, Mrs. Grodberg, but I will keep you in mind. . . . Yes, yes, I will mention to Poppa . . . (*Kindly.*) On pins and needles you shouldn't be sitting because a long time you may be sitting . . . so goodbye, Mrs. Grodberg. (*She hangs up and looks at* REN.) Till I find for Poppa I won't have a moment's peace!

Wanting to know whether Myra is coming for dinner, Ren practically swoons over how glamorous she is and how beautiful she was in the show. Hating to admit it, Ida says: "Beautiful she was, but so undressed I thought any minute they would turn the shower bath on her. What do you think, Ren? From Mandel I had a ring." Mandel, it turns out, is on his way up here. This is just one too many for Ren. She's having a terrible time with a French major at Columbia who won't pay any attention to her, but her mother is so busy marrying off other people that she doesn't even notice her. Ida says soothingly: "Don't worry, darling, when the time comes for you I'll find." "The time is *now*, Ma!" cries Ren. "Now is the time," says Ida, "I wish you would go in the kitchen and peel some onions."

The sight of Mandel on her doorstep, tanned from the Florida sun, twirling his cane and shiny in a sharkskin suit, proves too much for Ida. She had been cool to him, but now the very sight of him makes her palpitate. Mandel, as always, wants Leah from Fitchburg. Told to forget her, he cries: "Norbert Mandel is faithful! Norbert Mandel is steadfast! He don't switch!" When crossed, however, Mandel can still become nasty. When Leah comes in and, paying little or no attention to him excuses herself to go to her baby, Mandel remarks: "Norbert Mandel likes children, Miss Long. Maybe it is better for the baby you should the sooner the better be *Mrs.* Long." Furious at this insinuation, Ida cries: "Listen to me, Mandel. Cool I was to you already. Now I am frozen!" Ignoring her, Mandel says: "At your feet, Miss Long, Norbert Mandel lays his heart—baby or no baby. Should you care to communicate with me I am in Rooms Two Thirty-four, Two Thirty-five in the Waldorf-Astoria Hotel on Thirty-fourth Street and Fifth Avenue." Fascinated in spite of herself, Ida asks about the *two* rooms. "Norbert Mandel always takes two rooms," he says. "One is for sitting."

"Mandel," says Ida, "you should not come here again. Go to your rooms and sit in both of them." Appealing to Ida with fervor, Mandel begs her to tell Leah that what he feels for her occurs once in a lifetime: "I want her to do me the honor to be my bride. Where is she now? A buyer with an adapted baby that is not adapted. Let her marry me and overnight she becomes Mrs. Norbert Mandel. It's like with the glass slipper. That is the last word of Norbert Mandel."

After he's left Ida, still furious, says she'll never again arrange for him. "It's true, though," Leah says quietly. "To such slanders," says Ida, "you shouldn't even listen!" "But *I* am telling you, Ida," replies Leah. Overcome with shock, Ida manages: "Oh, I forgot. You I have to believe."

Taking the blame entirely upon herself, Leah says that Willie Lavin is the child's father. Leah went to Chicago five years ago so that Willie wouldn't know. To Ida's insistence that Willie must marry her at once, Leah answers that Willie doesn't know, that she doesn't want him to know, and that she trusts Ida not to tell him. Having Willie's child is what she wants: she has no wish to marry. Ida, her universe turned upside down, is in a state of emotional turmoil. When Leah, going to look after the child, reminds Ida that she is to tell nobody, Ida sits on in a daze.

On Tobey's arrival, he senses at once that something is wrong. Ida says repeatedly: "Don't ask me." Suddenly, turning to him, she pours out her secret in strictest confidence. Tobey mustn't tell a living soul. He promises.

IDA—You heard that in Chicago Leah adapted a baby?
TOBEY—Yes. I did.
IDA—*She didn't adapt.* She *had.*
TOBEY (*surprised*)—Are you sure?
IDA—More sure I couldn't be! But I have your promise, Tobey—not to tell anybody in the whole world.
TOBEY (*sincerely*)—Of course you have!
IDA (*abruptly*)—Except Willie Lavin! Him you can tell!

SCENE II

Trying to tell Willie is difficult. To begin with, during the past twenty-four hours Tobey hasn't even had a glimpse of him. When he finally finds him in their room, Willie doesn't let him get a word in edgewise.

Pacing restlessly up and down, Willie says that having passed his bar examinations, he wants Tobey to do him a favor: he wants Tobey to go back to Worcester with him for a visit.

WILLIE—Impulse to revisit the scenes of our youth. Think things over. Get back to first principles. I've come to a kind of conclusion, Tobey—it'll probably seem strange to you. I passed the bar exam with flying colors, but the thought of practicing law revolts me. Now for the first time I feel I know what I want to do.

TOBEY—Now listen to me, Willie.

WILLIE (*sitting on the bed*)—Here's the thing. I'm sick of the endless revolutions of my thoughts. I'm sick of pondering the mysteries that are insoluble. Everything is a question, everything is a dilemma. I long for the simple, the finite, the concrete.

Happy to hear him say this, Tobey would like to speak his piece before Willie is off on another tangent. But Willie is now full of the factory job he plans to take so that there'll be no need for him to think, so that at the end of the day, he'll be dead tired and fall into a dreamless sleep.

Deeply disturbed, Tobey tries to catch Willie's attention; instead Willie says offhandedly that Myra is going to dine with them tonight, that the director on whom she was counting for her career, and with whom she was very much in love, has jilted her. "All her hopes have vanished . . . to such a degree," says Willie, "that she wants to marry me." And the truth is that Willie doesn't want to marry her. "I don't believe that," says Tobey. "Myra doesn't either," Willie answers. "You know, Tobey, I've lived so long with this obsession for Myra that without it—I'd feel—unemployed."

TOBEY—Willie, now for God's sake listen to me. If you really want the finite, the concrete, you don't have to go to a factory in Worcester. Because they're all right here for you.

WILLIE—How?

TOBEY—You have a responsibility here—to Leah.

WILLIE—How can you trace responsibility to its ultimate source?

TOBEY (*rises*)—God damn it! Why do you talk about ultimate responsibility when you have an immediate one? Leah's adopted child is your child.

This had occurred to Willie, but he had let himself accept Leah's fiction. And he is now off on another tangent. Asking Tobey to remember that he thought once there might be only one mystery, the key to everything—well, it now occurs to Willie that even if he did hit on it, it might turn out to be something quite simple really—even a bore. Tobey, not in the least amused, jumps up, cuts off Willie's stream of words, and lays it on the line: "Listen, Willie. I owe you more than I can ever possibly repay. You made me see life as a wonder and as an adventure. I owe you everything—even the truth. And the truth is that you have wasted yourself—scattered your gifts, as my father warned you. I remember your arguments with my father. He was right—all the way. You feel this need for the concrete, so you turn to manual labor, which will probably bore you to death after one week. Another horizon, another mirage, another postponement. Chemistry. Law. What you know, what you have, you turn your back on. It is the unknowable that lures you. Even my talent is an unknown quantity and you made a concept out of that. Willie, the near things, the achievable things, the warm winds of affection, of friendship, of love, don't seem to touch you any more."

Almost childlike in his acceptance of all that Tobey says and tells him to do, Willie agrees to ask Leah to marry him. Tobey then promises to take Myra out to dinner to leave the path clear for Willie and Leah. With everything seemingly arranged, Willie keeps insisting that Tobey telephone him at Ida's.

Scene III

Mystified by Willie's visit and even more mystified by his proposal, Leah suddenly guesses that he has been told about the child. Insisting that Myra is now out of his life, Willie demands an answer. Although she will never love anyone else, Leah, because of this perpetual threat of Myra, refuses Willie. He becomes quite manic. His voice rises. He just wants her to say yes and to stop cross-examining him: *"Can't you just accept the fact?* I love you. I admire you. Isn't that enough for you? Have a heart, Leah! Give me a chance, can't you? You don't risk anything." "I risk this hold Myra has over you," cries Leah. "It's broken, I tell you," Willie yells back. "How many times do I have to tell you? There's no hope in Myra— not only for me—for anybody. Nor for herself. Shall I tell you why? She's in pursuit of a romantic ideal. She'll pursue it endlessly. It will elude her endlessly."

On her return, Ida finds a presumably happy engaged couple. When Leah goes off contentedly to wake the baby, Ida says: "Willie, darling, so long I waited to see this day I thought it would never come."

WILLIE (*after a pause*)—Perhaps it's come too late, darling.
IDA—What too late?
WILLIE—Too late for the near horizons—I abdicate!
IDA—What are you talking?
WILLIE (*his exuberance gone*)—Ida. Ida. Ida. (*As he sinks into the sofa.*)

Distraught, Ida is crying "Willie! Willie!" when Tobey's call comes through. Answering the call, Willie seems delighted with Tobey's news that his piece of music has been accepted for a concert. Telling Tobey that he'll meet him at the apartment, Willie hangs up. "Tobey's having his first performance," says Willie. "Isn't that wonderful? I feel as happy about this as you do, Ida, when you pull off a match. It's a funny thing, Ida, that the only responsibility I have ever recognized is my responsibility to Tobey. He's grown up—surpassed me as I knew he would. But my faith in Tobey and what he might do . . . that was tangible—that was real—and not as Tobey thinks—a concept. . . . Goodbye . . . I love you . . ." Telling Ida to give Tobey a message for him, in case he should miss him, Willie rushes out. Ida is frantic. First she starts to get Leah, then she calls Tobey. Saying how worried she is, how settled Willie was with Leah, and how he suddenly ran out to see Tobey, Ida cries: "He said goodbye to me as if he was saying goodbye. . . . Go down stairs to the sidewalk—wait for him, Tobey—grab him, Tobey!" Tobey promises, but when Ida gives him Willie's message, the receiver falls from his limp hand. "Something else he told me to tell you," says Ida, "crazy it sounded—he said I should tell you that no longer he's holding onto the bedposts . . ."

SCENE IV

Back to Worcester to recapture the happy times before Willie's death and his own despair, Tobey seeks out Dr. Jim, whose office and oboe-playing are unchanged.

Jim assures Tobey that there was no way he could have helped Willie: for him to come back to Worcester would have done no good. "Willie was without an anchor," explains Jim, "the anchor of reality. He couldn't face the everyday responsibilities of a permanent attachment . . . not only to a woman but to a job." "And yet," Tobey answers with bitter self-reproach, "the last time I saw him—I pushed him into reality." "It had nothing to do with you," argues Jim. "Life was doing it. Suicide, you know, is self-criticism in its acute form." Still Tobey is full of guilt for thinking about his music rather than about Willie. So involved was he with his performance that he had no time for Willie when Willie needed him, and even now he is more concerned with that concert—which was a colossal failure— than with anything else. "Look, Jim," says Tobey, "it is a world without Willie, and still the ego twitches." "Thank God," says Jim. "Once the ego stops twitching not even a great doctor like myself can do anything! What are you doing for dinner?" Agreeing to pick Jim up at eight for dinner at Putnam and Thurston's, Tobey starts out, then stops and says: "Jim, now that I'm back here, the whole past is like a heavy sack around me. All the dead—my father and mother—Dan and Willie—the anonymous dead . . . What does it all mean, anyway?" "Why does life have to have meaning?" asks Jim. "It's good in itself. That oboe is good. What Willie gave you was good. Dinner tonight will be good—I hope! You speak of the anonymous dead. They're not anonymous. They're figures in the tapestry in which we ourselves are figures. They've given us what we are. When you're young, you try to get away from them. But when you're mature, you return to them. You'll embrace them. And they'll support you, I promise you. Every breath you draw—every thought you have—every note you set down—you're living off them. . . . Now, clear out!"

Going to the door, looking out into the twilight, Tobey says: "The seven hills of Worcester." "Lift your eyes to them," says Jim brusquely. "See you at eight!"

J. B.

A Play in Two Acts

By Archibald MacLeish

[ARCHIBALD MACLEISH *was born in Glencoe, Ill., in 1892. He attended the Hotchkiss School in Lakeville, Conn., Yale University and the Harvard Law School. He won a Pulitzer Prize in 1932 with his narrative poem "Conquistador." He has been an editor, a lecturer, Librarian of Congress, Director of the Office of Facts and Figures in World War II and Assistant Secretary of State. His second Pulitzer Prize came in 1953 for his "Collected Poems, 1917-52."*]

For the cast listing, see page 312.

THE scene is that of a "traveling circus which has been on the roads of the world for a long time."

A couple of roustabouts amble on stage, adjusting ropes. Following them, women in coveralls set a table with a few glasses and a basket of fruit, throw a dustcover over the table, and depart. Pulling on the ropes of the ancient, battered tent, one roustabout says: "We sweat it up, they swat it down, night after night after . . ." Then inspecting their work, he adds: "That does it." Everything is set.

Entering the empty tent, Nickles, a sardonic young popcorn vendor, surveys the ring. Following him comes the balloon man, Mr. Zuss, an old actor fallen on evil days. Looking at the ring, the high perch and platform where "they play the play," Mr. Zuss is depressed and contemptuous. Nickles, climbing up on the stage, gestures: "Heaven and earth . . . that platform's Heaven." Earth, where the table is, will be where Job will sit. Gesturing to platform and perch, Nickles continues: "God and Satan lean above."

His contempt turning to apprehension, Mr. Zuss wonders whether

---

"J. B.": By Archibald MacLeish. Copyright © 1956, 1957, 1958 by Archibald MacLeish. Selections reprinted by permission of and arrangement with Houghton Mifflin Company, the authorized publishers. See CAUTION notice on copyright page. All inquiries should be addressed to Houghton Mifflin Company, 2 Park Street, Boston 7, Mass.

they should go on with this acting assignment. "At least," he comforts himself, "we're actors. They're not actors. Never acted anything." Under his breath, Nickles says: "That's right. They only own the show."

Ready to strut his stuff, unstrapping his popcorn tray and kicking it out of his way, Nickles says: "Poor Job! That perfect creature. . . ." Throwing down his jacket, he continues: "Crumpled on the dung of the earth. . . ." "Challenging *God!*" cries Zuss. "Crying to God!" corrects Nickles.

MR. ZUSS— Demanding *justice*. Of God!
NICKLES— Imagine
That! Asking God for justice!
(*He strikes an attitude.*)
I heard upon his dry dung heap
That man cry out who cannot sleep:
"If God is God He is not good.
If God is good He is not . . ."
Shall we
Start? You'll play the part of . . .
MR. ZUSS (*removing his vendor's jacket*)—
Naturally.

"Naturally," mocks Nickles.

Balking when told he must wear a mask, taunted into wearing one, finally impressed by the fact that he will be playing the maker of the world, Zuss asks: What kind of mask? "You'll find it somewhere," answers Nickles with an upward gesture. "Heaven's the great lost-and-found. Try Heaven!" As Zuss starts laboriously up the ladder to the platform above, Nickles sings out mockingly:

"If God should laugh
The mare would calf,
The cow would foal . . .
Diddle my soul."

Looking down sharply, Zuss retorts: "God never laughs! In the whole Bible!" "How *could* he laugh?" says Nickles. "He made it—the toy Top—the world—the dirty whirler!"

Squatting on the floor, thinking he is to play Job, Nickles starts miming the role. Zuss disabuses him of this idea: Job isn't the part he is to play. Brought up short, Nickles asks: "You wouldn't think of me for Job? What would you think of?" "Oh, there's always someone playing Job," replies Zuss. "There must be thousands!" cries Nickles.

> "What's that got to do with it?
> Millions and millions of mankind
> Burned, crushed, broken, mutilated,
> Slaughtered, and for what? For thinking!
> For walking round the world in the wrong
> Skin, the wrong-shaped noses, eyelids:
> Living at the wrong address—
> London, Berlin, Hiroshima,
> Wrong night, wrong city.
> There never could have been so many
> Suffered more for less. But where do
> I come in?
> . . . Play the dung heap?"

Assuring Nickles that all they have to do is start, and that Job will join them, Mr. Zuss is uncomfortable about Nickles' role. He had assumed that Nickles knew. "I think of you and me as 'opposites,'" says Zuss. "Nice of you," says Nickles.

When Zuss comes forth on the platform with the masks he has found, he hesitates in giving Nickles his, since "Evil is never very pretty." Reaching up for the mask, Nickles takes it.

> "Evil you call it!
> Look at those lips. They've tasted something
> Bitter as the broth of blood
> And spat the sup out. Was that evil?
> Was it?
> Spitefulness you say—
> You call that grin of anguish spite?
> Eyes that suffer: lips that spit—
> I'd rather wear this ache of loathing
> Night after night than wear that other
> Once—that . . . white indifference!"

Telling Zuss to put his on, Nickles calls for his lines. There is an ominous silence; then a sound of wind and out of the wind an urgent, distant voice.

DISTANT VOICE—
Whence comest thou?

Elia Kazan, the director of "J. B."

(MR. ZUSS *and* NICKLES *stand perfectly still, then, slowly taking off their masks, look at each other.*)
   NICKLES— Who said that?
(*There is only silence.*)
   DISTANT VOICE (*imperatively*)—
         Whence comest thou?
   MR. ZUSS (*a whisper*)—
         That was my line.

Nickles doesn't know what he's to say. "It's in the Bible," says Zuss. "I'm supposed to speak the *Bible!*" cries Nickles. "Maybe the mask can speak it," says Zuss scornfully; "ought to know the lines by now."

The Godmask gives the cue, and the Satanmask takes over: "*From going to and fro in the earth* " there is a snicker of suppressed laughter—"*and from walking up and down in it.*" There is a great guffaw: Nickles tears his mask off and throws it onto the stage, where it goes on laughing until it chokes into silence. Pulling his mask off angrily, Zuss calls for "Lights!"

Berated for laughing, Nickles, his face wry with pain, says that if Zuss had seen what he had seen, he'd never laugh again or weep either. Calmly explaining his part to him, Zuss says that it is a simple scene. "Let's get on," he says. The two maids come in to remove the dustcloth from the table. "Let's play the play." "You really think we're . . . playing?" asks Nickles.

As the masks repeat their lines, the maids, having finished their work, stand aside. Big, handsome, sanguine J. B. enters the ring.
   GODMASK— *Hast thou considered my servant Job*
         That there is none like him on the earth . . .
(SARAH, *a fine, pretty-faced woman, younger than J. B., follows him.*)
         A perfect and an upright man . . .
(*The five children, all blond, all beautiful, laughing and crowding one another, follow their parents.*)
         That feareth God and escheweth evil. . . .

"Heaven" is in half-light, as J. B., standing at the table's head, says grace: "Our Father which art in Heaven. Give us this day our daily bread." "That was short and sweet, my darling," says Sarah. J. B. answers cheerfully that it had all the essentials.

When the mammoth turkey and all the trimmings are carried in by the maids, J. B. asks the children what day it is. Screaming with laughter, they dub it everything from Turkey Day to a day when they all can eat too much. Calling them to order, Sarah tells them to answer their father. Jonathan says: "Thanksgiving Day" and David says: "The day we give thanks to God." "And did you, David?" asks Sarah. "Did you, Mary? Has any one of you thanked God? Really thanked him?" Mr. Zuss, who is high on his perch, leans down. "Thanked Him for everything?" pursues Sarah. If they do their part, she says, God does His, but should the children forget Him, He will forget. Trying to smooth things over, J. B. says reassuringly that children know the grace of God better than most people. Sarah remains concerned. "Forgive me, Sal," says J. B., "I'm sorry. But they do. They understand a little."

Putting down his knife and fork, J. B. asks for everyone's attention. No one is able to answer J. B.'s question why they eat this food. Little Rebecca pipes up: "Because it's good?" "Baby! Ah, my poor baby!" Sarah says.

J. B.— Why your poor baby?
She's right, isn't she? It is. It's good.
SARAH— Good . . . and *God* has sent it to us.
J. B.— She knows that.
SARAH— Does she?
Job! . . .
Do *you?*
NICKLES (*whispering up at* MR. ZUSS)—
What do *you* think? Think he knows?
Think he knows what God can send him?
SARAH— Oh, I think you do . . .
only . . .
I get so frightened, Job. We have so
Much.
J. B. (*dead serious*)—
You ought to think I know.
Even if no one else should, you should.
Never since I learned to tell
My shadow from my shirt, not once.
Not for a watch-tick, have I doubted
God was on my side—was helping me.
NICKLES (*to the audience*)—
That's our pigeon!

J. B. has always known that God was with him, and he has tried to show it in more than words. Touched, Sarah says that if anyone deserved it, J. B. did. "Nobody deserves it, Sarah," J. B. corrects her. "Not the world that God has given us." Laughing, J. B. says that he, at any rate, believes in it, and trusts his luck, his life, their life—God's goodness to him. A frightened Sarah doesn't find it that simple and doesn't wish the children to think it is. "God punishes," says Sarah; "God rewards and God can punish." Why has He kept each one from harm? Because of J. B.'s faithfulness. "No," says J. B.; "because He's just." Turning to David, he points out that a man can count on Him. Then raising a glass to Sarah, J. B. asks her to "Trust our luck!"

This is too much for Nickles, who promptly doubles up with laughter. Mr. Zuss, on the other hand, thinks the family feast a true Thanksgiving. Only—Mr. Zuss wonders whether J. B. knows that he's in the play. "Piety is hard enough to take among the poor who *have* to practice it," complains Nickles. "This man *has* it—and he's grateful," says Zuss.

GODMASK—
*Hast thou considered my servant Job
That there is none like him on the earth,
A perfect and an upright man, one
That feareth God and escheweth evil?*
SATANMASK (*insinuatingly*)—
*Doth Job fear God for naught?
Hast thou not made an hedge about him
And about his house
And about all that he hath on every side?
Thou hast blessed the work of his hands
And his substance is increased.*
(SATANMASK *voice drops.*)
*But put forth thine hand now and touch
All that he hath . . .
                and he will
Curse thee to thy face!*
GODMASK (*in great, furious voice*)—
*Behold!
All that he hath is in thy power!*
(NICKLES *bows mockingly, removes mask.*)
DISTANT VOICE—
*Only
Upon himself
Put not forth thy hand!*

To the accompaniment of band music, the two roustabouts, dressed now as soldiers, move through a crowd of soldiers and girls and heave drunkenly into view. Sarah notices that they are staring at

J. B.

her house; J. B. decides that they are "plastered." When the soldiers ring the doorbell, Sarah is convinced that they are messengers.

Acting as butler and announcing the soldiers as friends of Mr. David, Nickles ushers them in. Fumbling in their replies to Sarah while trying to cadge drinks, the soldiers tell garbled stories about David. J. B. is skeptical. Through the hazy remarks about knowing David, there suddenly emerges something else.

SECOND SOLDIER—
>How, by night, by chance, darkling . . .
>By dark of chance . . .

(*Loses train of thought.*)
FIRST SOLDIER—
>He's drunk.

SECOND SOLDIER—
>The war done . . .
>
>>the guns silent . . .

(*He raises his head.*)
>No one knows who gave the order.

FIRST SOLDIER (*raising his voice*)—
>Like I say, because he said to.
>Any friend of his he said to.
>Just to tell you we knew David.

But oddly enough, the question of doing their best with the wrong length of lumber comes into the conversation. At J. B.'s horrified reaction, the First Soldier discovers that the Army had never told J. B. Crying "Jesus!" the First Soldier, having had enough of this hospitality, dashes out of the house.

High on his perch, lifting a large, padded drumstick, Mr. Zuss asks Nickles if he's ready. "Got to be, don't they?" Nickles answers snottily. "I meant *you*," says Zuss. "They've got no choice. Disasters—deaths—mankind are always ready," answers Nickles.

With a downswing of the drumstick, J. B. gasps: "It isn't true . . . It isn't possible. . . . We had a letter from him . . . after the end of it. . . ."

SECOND SOLDIER—
>What shall I say to you?
>What I saw?
>What I believe I saw?
>>Or what
>I must have seen . . .
>>and have forgotten.

SARAH—	David is our son, our son, *our* son!
NICKLES—	Can't be happening to us. It can't be.
J. B.—	David's all right. He is. He has to be.
NICKLES—	God won't let it happen. Not to Job, the perfect and the upright man.
J. B.—	I know he is. The war is over.
NICKLES—	Job *deserves* his luck. He's earned it.
J. B.—	It never could have happened. Never. Never in this world.
NICKLES—	This world! This world! Suppose it did, though—suppose it did! What would this world be made of then?
SARAH (*to the* SECOND SOLDIER, *touching his face*)—	David's all right. I know he is.
SECOND SOLDIER—	*I only am escaped alone to tell thee.*

Nickles says nastily to Zuss: "Even a perfect and upright man, teach him long enough, might learn!"

Once started, Nickles keeps the ball rolling. Creating reporters out of the roustabouts, grabbing a pretty tart from the shadows, Nickles sets up a tabloid sob story as the next blow to J. B.

On their way home one evening, J. B. and Sarah are accosted by the girl, who maneuvers their attention while the reporters close in. In the glare of flashbulbs, Sarah and J. B. find out that two of their children were killed in an automobile crash. The Second Reporter says almost in a whisper: "I who have understood nothing . . . have known nothing . . . have been answered nothing . . . I only am escaped alone. . . ."

J. B.'s immediate reaction is directed violently against the vanishing reporters. Sarah asks: "Why did you follow *them?* It wasn't *they* that did it. . . . It wasn't *they.*" After a long silence, she says: "What had they done to Him—those children?"

Nickles grins up at Zuss, who, almost in a whisper, says: "*Shall we take the good and not the evil?*"

Thus prompted, J. B. reminds Sarah: "We have to take the evil. Evil with good. It doesn't mean there *is* no good." Not wishing to listen, Sarah runs off.

"Starting, isn't it?" says Nickles. And having no intention of leaving J. B. alone for a minute, Nickles gives the roustabouts black, shiny policeman coats. Zuss pleads with him. "Who? Me?" answers Nickles. "Am I God? Why should we leave him alone? He's suffering—it's an old role . . . played like a mouth organ. Any fool on earth can learn despair in six, short, easy lessons!" He whistles, a police siren echoes, and J. B. meets the two police officers. Nickles goes on: "Give him another little, needling nudge between the withers and the works: He'll learn . . . he's desperate now. . . . You'll teach him."

The police have arrived at J. B.'s call. Little Rebecca is missing. Having looked for her everywhere, they have reported it to the police. Sarah, beside herself, cries: "We believe in our luck in this house! We've earned the right to! We believe in it . . . All but the bad!"

NICKLES—   That's telling him!
            That's telling him!
            If God is Will
            And Will is well
            Then what is ill?
            God still?
            Dew tell!

Checking what the child wore when last seen, the First Policeman asks if Rebecca had a little red umbrella.

Zuss brings the drumstick down heavily. Bringing forth reluctantly a parcel, the Second Policeman cuts the strings that hold Rebecca's parasol. The First Policeman is left to tell of a hophead's murder of the child.

In a wheedling voice, Nickles says: "Now's the time to say it, Mister." "Now is the time," says Zuss.

J. B.—   *The Lord giveth . . .*
(*His voice breaks.*)
              The Lord taketh away.
MR. ZUSS (*urgently*)—
              Finish it! *Blessed be the . . .*
NICKLES—   What should he finish when he's said it all?
MR. ZUSS—   Go on!
NICKLES—   To what? To where? He's got there, hasn't he?
              Now that he's said it, now he knows.
              He knows Who gives. He knows Who *takes* . . .
MR. ZUSS—   Knows and accepts it all. All of it.
NICKLES (*a cough of bitter, disgusted, mirthless mirth*)—
              Accepts it all! Accepts! a son
              Destroyed by some fool officer's stupidity!

                             Two children smeared across a road
                             At midnight by a drunken child!
                             A daughter raped and murdered by an idiot!
                             And all with God's consent! Foreknowledge! . . .
                             He *accepts* it!
Mr. Zuss—   He accepts it
                             All. And more. And blesses God.
Nickles—   No! He'll curse Him to His face!

With the knife used to cut open the parcel, Nickles slashes at the ropes that hold the canvas; it falls. Against a black sky there is the scream of sirens and the crash of falling walls. Then there is silence. Slowly out of the dark, figures stumble forward. Several derelict old women and a child have survived the holocaust. Huddling together for body warmth, one cries: "Know what there was in the crib of the arc when the world went down? Four old women."

The roustabouts, now Civil Defense officers, appear carrying the body of a woman. Covered with dust, his clothing torn, J. B. arrives in the ring. He takes Sarah from the arms of the men. She had been found under a wall, where the Second Officer had heard her. "I heard two words," he says; "I don't know what they mean—Ruth! Ruth! . . ."

   First Civil Defense Officer—
                             Nobody answered.
                             Nobody could have.
                                                  You been down there?
                             Whole block's gone. Bank block. All of it.
                             J. B.'s bank, you know. Just gone.
                             Nothing left to show it ever.
                             Just the hole
                                           J. B.'s millions!
                             That's a laugh now—J. B.'s millions!
                             All he's got is just the hole.
                             Plant went too—all of it—everything.

Tonelessly, like a voice counting, Sarah can be heard saying: "David . . . Jonathan . . . Mary . . . Ruth. I cannot say the last." His hand in hers, J. B. says: "Rebecca." To the Second Officer, he asks: "There wasn't . . . anyone beside?" Gently the officer replies: *"I only am escaped alone to tell thee."*

Nickles rails against the indecency of J. B. taking it all. "You don't lose gracefully, do you?" asks Zuss. "I don't lose," snarls Nickles. "You have," says Zuss.

Christopher Plummer, Pat Hingle and Raymond Massey in "J. B."

The rushing sound of wind is heard. "Put on your mask," commands Zuss.

The Distant Voice—
>*Hast Thou considered my servant Job*
>*That there is none like him on the earth . . .*
>*And still he holdeth fast his integrity*
>*Although thou movedst me against him*
>*To destroy him . . .*
>   *without cause.*

(Nickles *lifts the* Satanmask *to his face.*)
Satanmask— *Skin for skin, yea, all that a man*
>*Hath will he give for his life.*
>*But put forth thine hand now and touch*
>*His bone and his flesh*
>*And he will curse thee to thy face!*

Godmask— *Behold . . .*
(*The drumstick rises, hesitates, comes soundlessly down. The play is out of* Mr. Zuss's *control and he knows it.*)
>*He is in thine hand . . .*
>   *but . . .*
>*Save his life!*

Sealing in his scorched, encrusted sack of skin, a shuddering J. B. begs God to let him die. Above, Zuss says placidly that J. B. will support this proof of pain. "No," says Nickles. "Job will make his own cold peace. A man can always cease— It's something: A judgment any way—reject the whole creation with a stale, pink pill."

The old women, not wanting to look at J. B. but unable to tear their eyes from him, find his skin looking as if it had been flayed. One old woman croons: "Poor soul, poor soul." Sarah says God won't let J. B. die: "God is our enemy." "Don't say that, Sarah," J. B. manages; "God has something hidden from our hearts to show."

Turning his head painfully towards his wife, J. B. urges her to sleep: "Out of sleep something of our own comes back to us. . . ." Sobbing, Sarah dozes off. "All that's left him now," says one old woman, "is her."

Suddenly shrieking, Sarah wakes up. God has even shut the night against her: horror blazes everywhere. "I know . . . I know those waking eyes," says J. B. "His will is everywhere against me even in my sleep . . . my dreams."

Above, Nickles is ready to spring. This is the moment he has been waiting for. Lifting his head, J. B. calls out passionately: "If I knew! If I knew why! What I can't bear is . . . the blindness . . . mean-

J. B. 181

ingless . . . the numb blow fallen in the stumbling night." "Even this," says Sarah bitterly; "has it no meaning?" J. B. thinks that God will not punish without cause. God is unthinkable if they are innocent. He repeats: "God is just!" Sarah won't accept this. Through her desperate defiance, J. B. tries to reach her. Catching her hand, he begs her to repeat after him: *"The Lord giveth . . . The Lord taketh away . . ."*

SARAH (*flinging his hand from her*)—
    Takes!
(*Her voice rises to a shriek.*)
    Kills! Kills! Kills! Kills!
J. B.—   *Blessed be the name of the Lord.*
SARAH—   They are
    Dead! And they were innocent! I will not
    Let you sacrifice their deaths
    To make injustice justice and God good!
    Must we buy quiet with their innocence—
    Theirs or yours?
                      I cannot stay here—
    I cannot stay here if you cringe,
    Connive in death's injustice, kneel to it—
    Not if you betray my children.
J. B. (*a cry*)—
    I have no choice but to be guilty.
SARAH (*at the end of her strength*)—
    We have the choice to live or die,
    All of us.
(*She stands over him.*)
    Curse God and die!
    Curse God . . . and die!
J. B.—   *Blessed be the name of the Lord.*

Sarah runs away. Blindly, J. B. calls out to her, and is answered by silence. "Now he knows," a woman says. Another adds: "And he's alone now."

The Old Women ask J. B. to join their circle for shelter and warmth. Giving them no answer, he cries to the heavens: *"Show me my guilt, O God!"*

"Well," says Nickles to Mr. Zuss: "You going to show him?" "Wait!" orders Zuss. Again J. B. repeats his cry. Raising his arms, he begs: *"Show me my guilt, O God!"* The Old Women huddle around him.

ACT II

Mr. Zuss inquires whether Nickles can hear J. B. cursing God: "God has done everything you asked for; God has destroyed him without cause." Acknowledging that indeed God has destroyed J. B.'s wealth, children and flesh, Nickles points out that J. B. *himself* God has not touched. "Teach his soul," he demands. "Show him that there are no reasons!" "Touch him in the soul," permits Zuss; "you've lost."

Still crying out to be shown his guilt, J. B. is answered only by silence. "The still silence of the stars," leers Nickles. In a drowning man's voice, J. B. begs repeatedly for an answer. He receives none. Then, suddenly out of the darkness come three men.

The first man, Eliphaz, wears the office uniform of a psychiatrist; the second, Bildad, wears an ancient windbreaker; the third, Zophar, is dressed as a cleric—without collar. Startled, Nickles shouts: "Zuss! Who *are* they?" Knowing the Book, Zuss says calmly: "Comforters. . . . Every time they play this play, Job's comforters come by. To comfort him." "You mean," snarls Nickles, "to justify the ways of God to God by making Job responsible? Making him worthy of his wretchedness? Giving him that dear gift of guilt, that putrid poultice of the soul that pulls the poison in, not out? That dirty thumb our generation sucks at?"

Looking at the comforters, the old women decide: "They hate each other! Each one knows the truth—alone." The doctor's appearance gives them the creeps: "That leather-backed old bucket," cries one old woman, indicating Bildad, "calls you Comrade in the park—blows your brains out in the cellar!" Another woman is sure that Zophar will damn your soul to Hell for saying prayers that he doesn't say. But J. B. thanks God for sending these comforters to him. With no self-pity, he puts his case before them: he is bereft of his children and of love. Astonished, Bildad spits out: "Love! What's love to Him! One man's misery!" J. B. asks timidly: "If I am innocent?"

BILDAD— Innocent? Innocent?
Nations have perished in their innocence.
Classes have perished in their innocence.
Young men in slaughtered cities
Offering their silly throats
Against the tanks in innocence have perished.
What's your innocence to theirs?

> God is History. If you offend Him
> Will not History dispense with you?
> History has no time for innocence.

J. B. maintains that God is just. Refusing to recognize the individual, Bildad shouts: "Screw your justice!" Making known that eventually there will be justice for all, Bildad is equally dogmatic that until then it doesn't matter. "He calls that comfort?" says Zuss. "Millions do," answers Nickles.

Persisting that guilt matters, J. B. holds that unless it matters, the whole world is meaningless and God is nothing. Dismissing J. B.'s argument, Bildad says:

> "Guilt is a sociological accident.
> Wrong class: wrong century.
> You pay for your luck with your licks,
>   that's all."

Eliphaz, breaking in like a seminar professor, dismisses guilt as a psychophenomenal situation—a mere illusion. And Zophar in turn pontificates that all mankind are guilty *always*. Thoroughly puzzled, Zuss says: "They don't sound much like comforters to me." "Every generation has its own," answers Nickles.

Having heard out Bildad and Eliphaz, J. B. answers passionately:

> "I'd rather suffer
> Every unspeakable suffering God sends,
> Knowing it was I that suffered,
> I that earned the need to suffer,
> I that acted, I that chose,
> Than wash my hands with yours in that
> Defiling innocence. Can we be men
> And make irresponsible ignorance
> Responsible for everything?
> I will not listen to you."

Praising J. B. for his sense of guilt, Zophar says: "Happy is the man whom God correcteth." J. B. begs Zophar to show him his transgression. "No, no, my son," says Zophar, "you show me." He suggests some ways in which J. B. might have easily erred. Rejecting such things, J. B. maintains that his is no childish fault, no mere nastiness or prurient act; his sin is more flagrant: "Worth of death, many deaths, of shame, loss, hurt—indignities such as *these!*" He raises his scorched arms for Zophar to see, but Zophar merely tells

J. B. that he is a venal man, like any other. A statistic—like any other, adds Bildad. A case-history, contributes Eliphaz. Zophar's explanation seems to J. B. the cruelest comfort of them all: "Making the creator of the Universe the miscreator of mankind. A party to the crime He punishes . . . Making my sin a horror—a deformity." "If it were otherwise," mumbles Zophar, "we could not bear it."

J. B.— I can bear anything a man can bear
If I can *be* one—if my life
Somehow can justify my living—
If my own self can answer. You
Refuse me even that. You tell me
One man's guilt is meaningless:
History has no time for guilt—
Science has no sign for guilt—
God created all men guilty.
Comforters you call yourselves!
I tell you those old women by the wall
Who sleep there shivering have given comfort
Greater than all of yours together.
They gave their misery to keep me warm.

(*He huddles in his rags, his head down.*)

Bitterly triumphant, Nickles now supposes that J. B. will curse God; but as the proselytizing comforters depart, J. B. once again cries: *"My God—answer me."*

J. B.— *I cry out of wrong but I am not heard . . .*
I cry aloud but there is no judgment . . .
(*Silence.*) *Though He slay me, yet will I trust in Him—*
(*Silence.*) *But I will maintain my own ways before Him.*
(J. B. *can find God nowhere. The wind brings forth the* DISTANT VOICE.)
DISTANT VOICE—
Who is this that darkeneth counsel
By words without knowledge? . . .
Where wast
Thou when I laid the foundations of the earth . . .
When the morning stars sang together
And all the sons of God shouted for joy?

J. B.

> *Hast thou commanded the morning?*
> *Have the gates of death been opened unto thee?* ...

Reproved by God, J. B. prostrates himself. Listening to the majestic words, he cowers lower and lower. Finally, in the voice of prayer, J. B. answers that Distant Voice:

> *"I know that Thou canst do everything . . .*
> *And that no thought can be withholden from Thee.*
> *Wherefore have I uttered that I understand not,*
> *Things too wonderful for me . . . which I understood*
> *Not. Hear, I beseech thee, and I will speak.*
> *I have heard of Thee by the hearing of the ear.*
> *But now mine eye seeth thee, wherefore*
> *I abhore myself and repent."*

For both Nickles and Zuss, that concludes matters. Telling a beaming Zuss that he has won, Nickles shows his disgust very plainly. But Zuss, exalted by God's words, cries out that not only has J. B. heard God, but he has also seen Him:

> "Marvel beyond the maze of mind,
> The whole creation: searchless power
> Burning upon the hearth of stars . . ."

"Where did I put that popcorn?" says Nickles.

To Nickles, J. B.'s repentance is like swallowing the swill of the world . . . and that alone is God's triumph. "Is God to be forgiven?" thunders Zuss. "Isn't He?" answers Nickles as he starts to leave. There is yet another scene, announces Zuss: "The scene that ends it. God restores him at the end."

NICKLES— God restores us all. That's normal.
That's God's mercy to mankind.
We never asked Him to be born.
We never chose the lives we die of.
They beat our rumps to make us breathe.
But, God, if we have suffered patiently,
Borne it in silence, stood the stench,
Rewards us! . . .
                     Gives our dirty souls back.
MR. ZUSS— God restores him *here*. On *earth*.

                    Gives him all he ever had and
                    More!
NICKLES (*starting out*)—
                    Sure! His wife. His children.
MR. ZUSS— He gets his wife back, and the children
                    Follow in nature's course.
NICKLES— You're lying.
MR. ZUSS— I'm not lying.
NICKLES (*passionately*)—
                    I say you're lying.
MR. ZUSS— Why should I lie? It's in the Book.
NICKLES (*racing back down the aisle, vaulting onto the stage*)—
                    Wife back! Wife! He wouldn't touch her.
                    He wouldn't take her with a glove!
                    After all that filth and blood and
                    Fury to begin again!
                    After life like his to take
                    The seed up of the sad creation
                    Planting the hopeful world again . . .
                    He can't. He won't. He wouldn't touch her.
MR. ZUSS— He does, though.
NICKLES— Live his life again?
                    Not even the most ignorant, obstinate,
                    Stupid or degraded man
                    This filthy planet ever farrowed
                    Offered the opportunity to live
                    His bodily life twice over, would accept it . . .
                    Least of all Job; poor, trampled bastard!
                    It can't be borne twice over. Can't be!
MR. ZUSS— It is, though. Time and again it is . . .
                    Every blessed generation. . . .

J. B. has meanwhile risen to his feet, and is questioning, in his old strong voice, the fact of his mortality. Is he wicked solely because, as a mortal, he is weak? Must his breath, his breathing, be forgiven him? Mr. Zuss is dumbfounded; Nickles grins. "Time and again, eh?" says Nickles. "Time and again? Not this generation, Mister."

Sidling up to J. B., Nickles asks him how he's going to play the end. J. B. knows of only one: he's begged for death, he's prayed for it. "Then," says Nickles, "the worst thing can't be death. He gives it back to you."

Incredulously, J. B. sees now that his arms are healed. In wheedling tones, Nickles tries to tell him how to play the end: "Any man was screwed as Job was . . ." As Nickle's voice rises urgently, Sarah—like Eurydice, appears at the edge of the circle of light. Nickles begs J. B. to listen to him:

> "Think of all the mucked-up millions
> Since this buggered world began
> Said No!—said Thank you! took a rope's end—
> Took a window for a door—
> Swallowed something—gagged on something . . ."

Seeing Sarah, Nickles shows desperation: "Not one of them had known what you know. Not one was taught *Job's* truth!" Shouting that Job won't take it, that Job will fling it in God's face, Nickles rushes to the stairs of the perch. Attempting to scale them, he collapses.

Grim and bitter, J. B. keeps his head turned away from Sarah. He wants to be let alone: he *is* alone. Prompted by Zuss, J. B. turns violently upon him. He refuses to bow again to the thunder, even though God kill him. As a man, J. B. must know. Nickles, himself defeated, grins sardonically. Mr. Zuss is deeply offended. With nothing left for them to do, Nickles and Zuss are yet reluctant to leave the scene.

Unable to take her own life, Sarah has come back because she loves J. B. To J. B. nothing is certain but the loss of love, love's inevitable heartbreak. Knowing all this, Sarah, with a cup, an old lantern, and an apple or two, has begun to busy herself in domestic fashion. Struggling with the lantern, she calls out that she has nothing to light the lantern with.

J. B. (*mocking himself and her*)—
>> You have our *love* to light it with!
>> Blow on the coal of the heart, poor Sarah!

SARAH (*taking the words for her own*)—
>> Blow on the coal of the heart . . . ?

J. B.— The candles in churches are out,
>> The lights have gone out in the sky!

SARAH— The candles in churches are out,
>> The lights have gone out in the sky,
>> Blow on the coal of the heart
>> And we'll see by and by . . .
>>>>> we'll see where we are.
>> We'll know. We'll know.

J. B. (*his head falls forward*)—
>>>> We can never *know*.

He answered me like the . . .
>stillness of a star

That silences us asking . . .
>No, Sarah, no!

We *are*—and that is all our answer.
We are, and what we are can suffer . . .
(*He looks at* SARAH *and at last* sees *her.*)
>But . . .

(*Silence.*)
>what suffers, loves. . . .

REQUIEM FOR A NUN

A Play in Three Acts

By RUTH FORD and WILLIAM FAULKNER

(Based on the novel by Mr. Faulkner)

[WILLIAM FAULKNER, *who was born in New Albany, Miss., in 1897, studied at the Oxford, Miss., high school and the University of Mississippi for two years. He served with the British Royal Air Force during World War I. He is the author of some 20 books, best known among which are "Sanctuary," "Light in August," "As I Lay Dying," "The Sound and the Fury" and "Intruder in the Dust." The last two have been made into motion pictures. He was awarded the Nobel Prize for Literature in 1950 and the same year was presented the William Dean Howells Medal for Fiction by the American Institute of Arts and Letters. "The Fable" won him a Pulitzer Prize in 1955.*]

For the cast listing, see page 319.

IN the town of Jefferson, Yoknapatawpha County, Mississippi, Negress Nancy Mannigoe is on trial for murder. At 5:30 P.M., this November 13th, a bell begins to toll and Nancy Mannigoe stands to hear the judge's verdict. Seemingly unaware of the crowded courtroom, this thirty-year-old woman has a calm, impenetrable look. From a distance the disembodied Judicial Voice speaks: "Have you anything to say before the sentence of the court is pronounced upon you? . . . That you, Nancy Mannigoe, did on the thirteenth day of June, wilfully and with malice aforethought kill and murder the infant child of Mr. and Mrs. Gowan Stevens in the town of Jefferson and the County of Yoknapatawpha. . . . It is the sentence of this court that you be taken from hence back to the county jail of Yok-

"Requiem for a Nun": By William Faulkner and Ruth Ford. From the novel by William Faulkner, adapted to the stage by Ruth Ford. Copyright 1950, 1951, by William Faulkner and © Copyright 1959 by William Faulkner and Ruth Ford. Reprinted by permission of Random House, Inc. See CAUTION notice on copyright page. All inquiries should be addressed to the authors' agent: Harold Ober Associates, Inc., 40 East 49th Street, New York 17, N. Y.

napatawpha County and there on the thirteenth day of March be hanged by the neck until you are dead. And may God have mercy on your soul." Quite loud in the silence, and to no one, Nancy says: "Yes, Lord. Thank you, Lord." The bell resumes its tolling.

Scene II

A half-hour later, accompanied by her husband Gowan and his uncle Gavin Stevens, the lawyer for the defense of Nancy Mannigoe, Temple Stevens enters her house. Coming into the living room, dressed all in black with no relieving touches, Temple seems brittle and tense. "Yes, God. Guilty, God. Thank you, God," mimics Temple harshly. "If that's your attitude toward being hung, what else can you expect from a judge and jury except to accommodate you?" Her hysteria nearing the surface, she orders Gowan to get drinks right away so that they can as quickly as possible be rid of his uncle. Wishing to avoid any kind of scene, Gowan hurries obediently to the kitchen.

The war of nerves begins as soon as Temple is alone with Stevens. First he offers her a handkerchief to wipe her dry eyes. "What's that for?" Temple asks calmly. "It's all right," says Stevens, "it's dry too." And still extending the unaccepted handkerchief, he adds: "For tomorrow, then." Appearing not to have understood, Temple announces that tomorrow they will be in California, and in the spring they might even go on to Hawaii or Canada. "So," she says, "why the handkerchief? Not a threat, because you don't have anything to threaten me with. I must not have anything you want, so it can't be a bribe either, can it?" Hearing the clink of glasses as Gowan approaches, Temple finishes by saying that whatever Stevens wants, he's not going to get it from her, and instead she has a question of her own: "How much do you—?" Changing smoothly in mid-sentence as Gowan enters she continues: "As her lawyer, she must have talked to you; even a dope fiend that murders a little baby must have what she calls some excuse for it, even a—" "I said stop it, Boots," interrupts Gowan. Passing the drinks, he thinks that for a change he'll have one himself: "After all these years. Why not?" "Why not?" echoes Temple. It is now Gowan's turn to find out why his uncle is here. Stevens answers evenly that he has just come to say goodbye. "Then say it," says Gowan. "One more for the road, and where's your hat, huh?"

TEMPLE (*she sets her untasted drink back on the tray*)—And put ice in it this time, and maybe even a little water. But first, take Uncle Gavin's coat.

Ruth Ford, Zachary Scott and Bertice Reading in "Requiem for a Nun"

GOWAN (*making a highball for* STEVENS)—That won't be necessary. If he could raise his arm in a white courtroom to defend a murdering nigger, he can certainly bend it in nothing but a wool overcoat—at least to take a drink with the victim's mother.

TEMPLE (*watching* STEVENS, *who watches her gravely*)—Don't forget the father too, dear.

GOWAN (*mixing the drink*)—Why should I, dear? How could I, dear? except that the child's father is unfortunately just a man. In the eyes of the law, men are not supposed to suffer. The law is tender only of women and children—particularly of women, particularly particular of nigger dope-fiend whores who murder white children. (*Hands highball to* STEVENS.) So why should we expect Defense Attorney Stevens to be tender of a man or a woman who just happened to be the parents of the child that got murdered?

Temple harshly puts a stop to this. Noticing that she hasn't touched her drink, Gowan inquires if she'd like some milk. "Please," says Temple. "Right," answers Gowan. "I thought of that, too. I put a pan on to heat while I was getting the drinks." Asking Stevens not to leave before he comes back, Gowan goes off to the kitchen.

Temple demands now how much Stevens knows. "Don't lie to me," she says; "don't you see there's not time?" Nancy, Stevens answers, still has four months—until the 13th of March. It comes out that what Temple means is no time for herself. "Oh, God, oh, God," she cries, "I talk about no time . . . and it's playing me button, button. She hasn't told you anything. It's me; I'm the one that's—don't you see? It's that I cannot believe—will not believe—impossible—" "Impossible to believe that all human beings really don't—stink?" suggests Stevens. "No," he adds, "she has told me nothing more." "Even if there was anything more?" prompts Temple. "Even if there was," Stevens answers.

Stevens thinks, however, that there was a man here that night. Saying in one breath that she'd been right about Stevens and in the next wanting to know if Stevens frightened this bit of information out of Nancy or just bought it off her, Temple next denies it categorically. Then she adds that when she goes to say good night to Bucky, she'll leave Gowan with Stevens . . . "And who knows what you might tell each other?"

Taking the milk and napkin that Gowan brings her on a tray, Temple offers her thanks. "Right, dear," says Gowan, receiving his kiss, then turns to Stevens: "You see? Not just a napkin; the *right* napkin. That's how I'm trained."

At the door, Temple turns to Stevens. "If," she says, "someone wants to go to heaven, who am I to stop them? Good night. Goodbye."

Urging his uncle to drink up, without touching his own glass, Gowan says: "Maybe you had better go on and leave us to our revenge." "I wish it could comfort you," answers Stevens.

GOWAN—I wish to God it could. I wish to God that what I wanted was only revenge. An eye for an eye—were ever words emptier? Only, you have got to have lost the eye to know it.
STEVENS—Yet she still has to die.
GOWAN—Why not? Even if she would be any loss—a nigger whore, a drunkard, a dope fiend—
STEVENS—A vagabond, a tramp, hopeless until one day Mr. and Mrs. Gowan Stevens out of simple pity and humanity picked her up out of the gutter to give her one more chance. (GOWAN *stands motionless, his hand tightening slowly about the glass.*) And then in return for it—

Upset, telling his uncle to get the hell out, saying he hadn't instigated the suit, that his only connection was that he was the father of the dead child, Gowan starts laughing hysterically. Pouring liquor into a glass, he keeps pouring and slopping until Stevens stops him. Holding his untasted drink, Gowan says: "All those years on the wagon—and this is what I got for it: my child murdered. You see? All these years without the drink, and so I got whatever it was I was buying by not drinking, and now I've got whatever it was I was paying for and it's paid for and so I can drink again. And now I don't want the drink. So I have a laugh coming. That's triumph. Because I got a bargain even in what I didn't want. Half price: a child, and a dope-fiend nigger whore on a public gallows: that's all I had to pay for immunity."

STEVENS—There's no such thing.
GOWAN—From the past. From my folly. My drunkenness. My cowardice—if you like—
STEVENS—There's no such thing as past either.
GOWAN—That is a laugh, that one. Only, not so loud, huh? to disturb the ladies—disturb Miss Drake—Miss Temple Drake. Now, Mrs. Gowan Stevens— Sure, why not cowardice? Only call it overtraining. You know? Gowan Stevens, trained at Virginia to drink like a gentleman, gets drunk as ten gentlemen, takes a college girl— who knows? maybe even a virgin—cross-country by car to another

college ball game, gets drunker than twenty gentlemen, gets lost, gets still drunker than forty gentlemen, wrecks the car, passes eighty gentlemen now, passes completely out while the virgin is being kidnapped into a Memphis whorehouse—(*he mumbles*)—and loved it.

Catching up Gowan about "the prisoner in the whorehouse," Stevens remarks: "You said 'and loved it.' Is that what you can never forgive her for?—for having created that moment in your life which you can never forget nor condone nor even stop thinking about, because she herself didn't even suffer but, on the contrary, even liked it. That you had to lose not only your bachelor freedom, but your man's self-respect, to pay for something your wife didn't even regret? Is that why this poor lost doomed crazy Negro woman must die?"

Told to get out, Stevens asks what else happened during that month that only Temple and Gowan know about, and possibly not even Gowan. Staring hard at Stevens, slowly and deliberately swinging the bottle over his head heedless of the liquor pouring down his arm, Gowan—ready to strike—cries: "So help me, Christ . . . So help me, Christ." With no sign of haste Stevens picks up his coat and hat and leaves.

Scene III

It is ten o'clock on the night of March 11th. Driven back to Jefferson by a telegram from Stevens reading "You have a week until the 13th— But where will you go then?" and by her son Bucky's asking the same question at the same time, Temple is now alone with Gavin Stevens in her living room. Gowan presumably is asleep under a barbiturate that Temple has given him.

"So Nancy must be saved," says Temple. "Apparently I know something I haven't told yet, or maybe you know?" Stevens says nothing. "All right," she persists, "why do you think there is something I haven't told yet?" Stevens offers several reasons: Temple has come all the way back from California; Temple, the bereaved mother, sat coolly through the entire trial—when she should have been far too grieved to think of revenge or even to bear to look at the child's murderer. Extremely casual, Temple, picking up a cigarette, says: "Now let Grandmama teach you how to suck an egg. It doesn't matter what I know, what you think I know, what might have happened. Because we won't even need it. All we need is an affidavit that she is crazy. Has been for years."

Stevens tells her patiently that it's too late for an affidavit—that in the eyes of the law Nancy Mannigoe is already dead. Equally patient, Temple says that *she* is the affidavit—otherwise what are they doing here at ten o'clock at night, barely a day from Nancy's execution? The thought of the prosecution's chief witness perjuring herself, and being in contempt of court, appals Stevens. "Then Temple Drake will have to save her," he remarks. "Mrs. Gowan Stevens will," she persists. Because a new sworn affidavit has to be based on new evidence, Stevens inquires what will it contain that they hadn't seen fit to bring up before. Temple dumps this right back in Stevens' lap: "What do such affidavits need, to—to make them work?" "Temple Drake," Stevens answers. And overriding Temple, he announces that he will settle for nothing less than Temple Drake and the "Truth" . . . the truth that can cope with injustice—as love or pity or courage or honesty can, or, Stevens concludes, a simple desire for the right to sleep at night. Having years ago learned how to ignore her sleeplessness, Temple is not impressed. "When you go before the Supreme Court what you will need will be facts—sworn documents," she says drily. "We're not going to the Supreme Court. We're going to the Governor. Tonight," says Stevens.

Even if the Governor fails to save Nancy, Stevens wants Temple to go for the sake of the truth. Temple is still not ready to give in completely. Stevens points out that she did come back. "Mrs. Gowan Stevens did," she says once more. "Temple Drake did," says he once more. "Mrs. Gowan Stevens is not even fighting in this class. This is Temple Drake's." "Temple Drake," she insists, "is dead." "The past," says Stevens, "is never dead. It's not even past."

Even though she realizes that she won't believe him, Temple wants Stevens to swear that he knows nothing. He complies. Then Temple asks how much he *thinks* he knows.

STEVENS—There was a man here that night.
TEMPLE (*quickly*)—Gowan.
STEVENS—Let's agree that this is for your life too. So nobody but a fool would believe you foolish enough to mistake a straw for a cudgel. Gowan wasn't here then. He and Bucky left at six o'clock that morning for New Orleans to go fishing. It was Gowan himself who gave you away—something he said to me without knowing he was doing it, which showed who planned that trip, to get not only Gowan but Bucky out of this house. I'm surprised you didn't send Nancy away too— (*He stops, obviously reacts to something he sees in* TEMPLE'S *face.*) Why, you did! You did try, and she refused. Yes. There was a man here that night.
TEMPLE—Prove it.
STEVENS—I can't. Don't I keep on saying that Nancy has refused to tell me anything about that night?

TEMPLE—Now listen to me. Listen carefully, because I don't intend to say this again. Temple Drake is dead. Temple Drake will have been dead years longer than Nancy Mannigoe will ever be. If there is anything that Mrs. Gowan Stevens can sign or swear to or lie to, to save Nancy Mannigoe, I will do it. But if all Nancy Mannigoe has left to save her is Temple Drake, then God help Nancy Mannigoe. Now get out of here. (STEVENS *leaves*.)

Having overheard much of this conversation, Gowan forcibly prevents Temple from suddenly wanting to telephone Gavin Stevens' house, while at the same time he flips a capsule onto the telephone table.

GOWAN—There's *your* pill too. Why don't you tell me about that man that Gavin says was here that night? Come on. You won't even have to think hard. Just tell me he was an uncle of Bucky's that you just forgot to tell me about.

TEMPLE—Would you believe me if I said there wasn't one?

GOWAN—Sure I would. Anything you say. I always have. That's what has sunk us. I even believed right up until tonight that it was me that planned that fishing trip. Everybody but me knew better, but that was all right, nobody needed to be fooled but me and I was already on my back when I came in. Thanks, though. But I can still see, even if I don't know until years afterward what I was looking at. But try the truth maybe; there surely must be something you can tell me that I won't believe. Maybe Gavin was right and his business wasn't with my wife but with Temple Drake. Maybe it was Bucky's papa, huh, just dropped in on the way through town—

TEMPLE—Gowan, hush. Why can't you hush? (*She indicates where the child is sleeping.*)

GOWAN—Don't worry, you were the one who seems to worry about waking him. I'm not going to make that much noise. I'm not going to hit you. I never hit a woman in my life, not even a whore, not even a Memphis whore, an ex-Memphis whore— Jesus, they say there are two women every man is entitled to hit once: his wife, and his whore. And just look at me; I can hit both of mine at one time, with one swing, one lick—

The thing that Gowan can't figure out is how "a man's wife just treating herself to a little extracurricular poontang should cause the murder of their child—" "That's right," says Temple, "go ahead. Then maybe we can stop." "Because you really do believe it, don't you," continues Gowan, "that there really is some price, some point where you can stop paying, some last nickel you've got in the world that they won't ask of you, that you won't have to pay for just one mistake—mistake—mistake? Jesus, let's laugh. Come on, laugh, just don't stand there—"

Speaking of his sin like a record played many times before, Gowan remembers that he got drunk that day to get up the courage to handle a little Mississippi country girl who'd never been away before. Answering that he didn't have to "twist her arm," Temple says that all he had to do was "suggest." "Will you shut up?" cries Gowan. "Will you? Let me have a good whine while I'm at it. Tell me what you probably think I've been telling myself all these years: how, if it hadn't been for you, I might have married a good girl—a decent girl that never heard of hot pants until her husband taught her." Dragging his hand over his face, Gowan says: "God, we must have loved each other once. We must have. Can't you remember?" "Yes," answers Temple. "Yes, what?" asks Gowan. "Loved one another once. We must have," she answers unconvincingly. "Can't you remember?" he says; "can't you?" Temple is silent. "Come here," Gowan orders. "No," says Temple flatly.

Gowan now orders Temple to stay away from the phone. He is certain that there was a man here that night, and since his Uncle Gavin knows it he supposes everybody else in Jefferson knows it. Even so, he still can't figure out the connection between that and the murder of his baby. "Maybe," he guesses, "Nancy caught you laying him, and killed Dee Dee in spite or excitement or something. Or maybe the excitement wasn't Nancy's; that in your hurry you forgot to move Dee Dee out of the bed, and in the general thrashing around— You see? You see what I am capable of? I don't even have to half try." But with another bit of illogic, Gowan says that since Temple hasn't told Gavin what happened here that night, he doesn't want to know. And now nobody is to know ever. She is not to call Gavin or tell the Governor or anybody else. "You said it yourself: if all that Nancy Mannigoe's got to save her is Temple Drake, then God help Nancy Mannigoe. Okay?" "No," says Temple. He begs her, then threatens her that if she calls Gavin, he quits. But asking Gowan to take his hand off the telephone, Temple picks up the receiver.

ACT II

It is two o'clock in the morning of March 12th: the Governor of the state, in his dressing gown, waits in his office. Seeing Gowan hurry in, the Governor shoos him silently back in the direction he came just as Stevens, escorting Temple, enters.

Offering Temple a cigarette, the Governor wants to know what Mrs. Gowan Stevens has to tell him. Corrected, he asks what Temple Drake can tell about Nancy.

TEMPLE—She was a dope-fiend whore that my husband and I took out of the gutter to nurse our children. She murdered one of them and is to be hung tomorrow morning. We—her lawyer and I—have come to ask you to save her.

GOVERNOR—Yes. I know all that. Why?

TEMPLE—Because I have forgiven her. Because she was crazy. All right. You don't mean why I am asking you to save her, but why I hired a whore and a tramp and a dope fiend to nurse our children. To give her another chance—a human being too.

STEVENS—No, Temple, not for that reason.

TEMPLE—Why can't I stop lying?

GOVERNOR—Yes. Go on.

TEMPLE—Whore, dope fiend; hopeless, already damned before she was ever born, whose only reason for living was to get the chance to die on the gallows. Who made her debut into public life lying in the gutter with a white man trying to kick her teeth down her throat. You remember, Gavin: what was his name? the pillar of the church. Well, this Monday morning and still drunk, Nancy comes up while he is unlocking the front door of the bank and fifty people standing at his back to get in, and Nancy comes into the crowd and right up to him and says, "Where's my two dollars, white man?" and he turned and struck her, knocked her across the pavement into the gutter, stomping and kicking at her face or anyway her voice which was still saying "Where's my two dollars, white man? It was two dollars more than two weeks ago and you done been back twice since—" So now I've got to tell all of it. Because that was just Nancy Mannigoe. Temple Drake was in more than just a two-dollar Saturday-night house.

She never thought anything on earth would make her tell about Temple Drake, least of all the murder of her child. The Governor says he remembers who Temple Drake was: the young woman who disappeared from a special train of students and reappeared six weeks later as a witness in a murder trial in Jefferson. Stevens fills in for him that it was his nephew Gowan Stevens who had met the train when drunk, and had driven Temple to the moonshiners' house where the murder happened, and from where the murderer kidnapped

Temple to Memphis to hold her for his alibi. "It was Gowan," says Stevens, "who knew the moonshiner and insisted on going there." "And married me for it," answers Temple harshly. "Does he have to pay for it twice? It wasn't really worth paying for once, was it?"

The Governor soon becomes aware that Temple is going to tell him something that Gowan doesn't know. Under further prodding, she says that even if Gowan was here, she now would speak out.

When kidnapped by Popeye, the murderer, Temple had ample opportunity as she was driven through small towns on her way to Memphis, to scream for help. She could have been returned to school or home; instead she chose the murderer and was carried to a Memphis brothel. For six weeks she was locked in a room guarded by a Negro maid stationed at the door; she was showered by Popeye with perfume, underwear, negligees, a fur coat. Her reason for waking the Governor at 2 A.M. now unfolds: as she could have been saved from the kidnapper had she wanted to be, so she could have escaped from the brothel, out the window and down the rainspout. But she didn't want to.

". . . hanging bone dry and safe in the middle of sin and pleasure like being suspended twenty fathoms deep in an ocean diving bell. Because he wanted her to be contented, you see. But Temple didn't want to be just contented. So she had to do what us sporting girls call fall in love."

STEVENS (*to the* GOVERNOR)—Popeye brought the man there himself. He—the young man—

TEMPLE—Gavin! No, I tell you!

STEVENS (*to the* GOVERNOR)—He was known in his own circles as Red, Alabama Red. He was the bouncer at the nightclub on the outskirts of town, which Popeye owned.

GOVERNOR—I see. This—Popeye—

STEVENS—He was a hybrid, impotent. He should have been crushed somehow under a vast and mindless boot, like a spider. He didn't sell her. He was a purist: he did not even murder for base profit. It was not even for simple lust. He was a gourmet, a sybarite.

The Governor is having difficulty understanding. Telling him not to try, Temple reveals the one thing that he should understand. She fell in love and wrote some letters. "So you fell in love," says the Governor. "Thank you for that. I mean the love," says Temple. "Except that I didn't even fall, I was already there. So I wrote the letters. I would write one each time . . . afterward, after they—he left." Pulled up sharp, the Governor asks: "Am I being told that this . . . Popeye would be there in the room, too?" "Yes," interrupts Stevens, "he was sexually incapable. That was why he brought Red. You see now what I meant by connoisseur and gourmet."

Explaining that the letters were explicit, that they were the kind of letters no husband should see no matter what he thought of a wife's past, Temple says this is all. She tries to stop. Stevens again insists that she continue. The letters, as blackmail, reappeared later on. "And being Temple Drake, the first way to buy them back that Temple Drake thought of was to produce the material for another set of them. Then," says Temple, "I found out that I not only hadn't forgot about the letters, I hadn't even reformed." "The young man Red died—" says the Governor.

TEMPLE—Yes—died, shot from a car while he was slipping up the alley behind the house, climbing up the drainpipe to see me—the one time, the only time when we thought we had dodged, fooled Popeye, could be alone together, just the two of us, after all the—other ones. If love can mean anything, except the newness, the learning, the peace, the privacy: no shame: not even conscious that you are naked because you are just using nakedness because that's a part of it; then he was killed, shot down right in the middle of thinking about me, when in just one more minute he would have been in the room with me, when all of him except just his body was already in the room with me; and then it was all over as though it had never happened.

Temple was the witness Popeye wanted at his trial; she lied for him and he was acquitted. And when she was shipped off to Europe for a year, she no longer cared about anything. That winter, when Gowan went to Paris and married her, Temple hoped that the two of them could confess their sins and be forgiven: "And then maybe there would be love this time—the peace, the quiet, the no shame that I . . . missed the other time . . ." Temple was wrong in expecting that forgiveness would hold them together, or maybe it was the gratitude that had to be constantly given and received that was even worse. Stevens suggests that it was Gowan's *vanity* that made things wrong. Because after about a year, he began to doubt the paternity of their child. The Governor, at this point, wishes Temple to speak for herself.

TEMPLE—I'm trying to. Let's see, we'd got back to Jefferson, back home. You know; face it: the disgrace: the shame, face it down, good and down forever. The Gowan Stevenses, young, popular: a new house on the right street, a country club, a pew in the right church.

STEVENS—Then the son and heir came; and now we are back to Nancy; guide, catalyst, glue, whatever you want to call it, holding the whole lot of them together: the only animal in Jefferson that spoke Temple Drake's language.

TEMPLE—Oh, yes, I'm going to tell that too. A confidante. Two sisters in sin swapping trade or anyway avocational secrets over Coca-Colas in the quiet kitchen. Somebody to talk to, as we all seem to need. Which is all that people really want, really need. I mean, to behave themselves, keep out of one another's hair.

STEVENS—Now she couldn't escape; she had waited too long. But it was worse than that. It was as though she realized for the first time that you—everyone—must, or anyway may have to, pay for your past. But she found a hope: which was the child's own tender and defenseless innocence: that God—if there was one—would protect the child—not her: that when He said "Suffer little children to come unto Me" He meant exactly that: He meant *suffer;* that the adults, the fathers, the old and capable of sin, must be ready and willing—nay eager—to suffer at any time, that the little children shall come unto Him unanguished, unterrified, undefiled. Do you accept that?

GOVERNOR—Go on.

STEVENS—So at least she had ease. Not hope: ease. It was precarious of course, but she could walk a tightrope too. It was as though she had struck an armistice with God. She had not tried to cheat.

GOVERNOR—Go on.

STEVENS—So you can take your choice about the second child. Perhaps she was too busy between the three of them to be careful enough: between the three of them: the doom, the fate, the past; the bargain with God; the forgiveness and the gratitude. She just didn't have time to be careful enough. Anyway, she was pregnant again, and she probably knew fifteen months before the murder of her child that this was the end. (*The lights begin to dim.*) She had merely been wondering for fifteen months what form the doom would take. Now tell it.

SCENE II

On the night of the previous June 13th, Temple, packed and ready to travel, is at the telephone. In supposedly trying to locate Nancy, she is putting on a show for the benefit of Pete, an "untamed" handsome young man who paces up and down the living room. When

Temple reports that no one knows where Nancy is, Pete is not the least surprised. "It's two thousand dollars. Besides the jewelry. What do you suggest then? Call the cops?" Temple has an out for him: he can quit now. Leave. Then all he has to do is, wait till her husband gets back and start over. He doesn't seem to understand. "You've still got the letters, haven't you?" asks Temple. As if he hadn't been thinking of them at all, he reaches inside his coat and hands them to Temple. "I told you two days ago I didn't want them," she says. "Sure," says Pete, "that was two days ago. Go ahead. Burn them. The other time I gave them to you, you turned them down so you could always change your mind and back out. Burn them." As Temple simply stands with the packet in one hand and a burning match in the other, not really making a move to burn them, Pete orders her to put the junk down and come to him. She obeys. Neither of them sees Nancy's shadow at the door. Putting his arms around Temple, Pete says: "I offered you an out too." Drawing her closer, he murmurs: "Baby." "Don't call me that," says Temple. Tightening his arms in a savage caress Pete says: "Red did. I'm as good a man as my brother was. Ain't I?" As they kiss, Nancy moves into the living room and watches them. Sensing her presence, they stop.

Angry that Nancy has come back to spy, Temple orders Pete to take the bags and go out to the car: "Go on, I tell you! Let's for God's sake get away from here." Loth to leave without roughing up Nancy a little to find out what she did with the money, Pete goes to the mantel, takes up the packet of letters, then drops them back on the mantel. "Maybe," he says, "you better not forget those, huh?" And he goes out.

NANCY—Maybe I was wrong to think that just hiding that money and diamonds was going to stop you. Maybe I ought to have give it to him yesterday as soon as I found where you had hid it. Then wouldn't nobody between here and Chicago or Texas seen anything of him but his dust.

TEMPLE—So you did steal it. And you saw what good that did, didn't you?

NANCY—If you can call it stealing, then so can I. Because wasn't but part of it yours to begin with. Just the diamonds was yours. Besides he ain't even worried about whether or not you'll have any money at all when you get out to the car. He knows that all he's got to do is, just wait and keep his hand on you and maybe just mash hard enough with it, and you'll get another passel of money and diamonds too out of your husband or your pa. Only, this time he'll have his hand on you and you'll have a little trouble telling him it's— (TEMPLE *slaps* NANCY *across the face. Stepping back,* NANCY *throws the packet of money and diamonds on the floor.*)

Nancy realizes that it isn't even the letters any more: "Maybe it never was. It was already there in whoever could write the kind of letters that years afterward could still make grief and ruin. The letters never did matter. You could have got them back at any time; he even tried to give them to you twice." And she is not thinking of Temple or her husband now, only of the two little children. "So am I," asserts Temple. "Why else do you think I sent Bucky on to his grandmother, except to get him out of a house where the man he has been taught to call his father, may at any moment decide to tell him he has none? As clever a spy as you must surely have heard my husband—" "I've heard him," Nancy answers, "and I heard you too. You fought back—that time. Not for yourself, but for that little child. But now you have quit." With Bucky now out of the way at his grandmother's, Nancy brings up the problem that Temple still has to solve: that of her six-months-old baby. "You can't no more leave a six-months-old baby with nobody while you run away from your husband with another man, than you can take a six-months baby with you on that trip . . ." Of course, Nancy says, it can always be left alone in the locked-up empty house until Gowan returns in a week—or it can be taken along until the first time Gowan or her pa refuse to send money, and Pete throws Temple and the baby out. Then, Nancy improvises: "You can just drop it into a garbage can and no more trouble to you or anybody, because then you will be rid of both of them."

Furious, Temple tells Nancy to hush. "I've hushed," says Nancy. Then not to Temple, but to someone else, she says: "I've tried. I've tried everything I know. You can see that." "Oh, yes, nobody will dispute that you tried," says Temple. "You threatened me with my children, and even with my husband. You even stole my elopement money. Though at least you brought it back—" Apologizing a moment later for hitting out at her when she has always been so good to her children, Temple says that Nancy has been good to her husband and her too, and "trying to hold us together in a household, a family, that anybody should have known all the time couldn't possibly hold together, even in decency, let alone happiness." Nancy isn't thinking of households or happiness. "I'm talking about two little children," she says. "Do you want them to know shame like us?" Crying for her to hush, saying that she's going ahead anyway, money or no money, children or no children, Temple orders Nancy out of the house. On her way, Nancy stops to get the baby's bottle which she says she's going to warm in the bathroom. "I tried everything I knowed," repeats Nancy. "You can see that," says Temple.

As Temple hastily puts money in her bag, and the baby's things in the baby's bag, Nancy comes back from the nursery. Temple asks her not to think too badly of her. "If it ever comes up," promises Temple, "I'll tell everybody you did your best. You tried. But you were right. It wasn't even the letters. It was me— Goodbye, Nancy, you've got your key."

Nancy stands there. Crossing to the nursery with the baby's blanket, Temple disappears. Then, backing slowly into the living room, frantic, clutching at Nancy, she screams. As Nancy walks slowly away, the bell begins to toll.

Scene III

As Temple comes back to the present, Gowan sits in the Governor's chair. The Governor is no longer in his office. Knowing instinctively that the Governor isn't going to save Nancy, that all this was in reality for the good of her own soul, Temple asks for one word of the Governor. Gowan, rising out of the Governor's chair, says: "Bitch." Temple notices him for the first time.

Realizing that Stevens had arranged this whole "plant," Temple says: "I'm sorry. I was the one that started us hiding things on each other, wasn't I?" Thinking that they hadn't started hiding things soon enough, Gowan asks for the letters: "I guess the guy will try to sell them to me direct this time. Which he may do, since I won't swap him for a lay." Stevens says that he now has the letters, which Nancy took that night and gave to him. Laughing bitterly, Gowan cries: "Not even a lay."

Turning to leave, Gowan announces his plan to get drunk—unless he has forgotten how in all these years. "What about Bucky?" asks Stevens. "He's at your house with Maggie. Isn't that safe?" asks Gowan. "They don't murder babies there too, do they?" He starts to leave, then, turning back, he remembers he's probably still supposed to use the spy's entrance. "Oh, God. Again," says Temple. Tomorrow and tomorrow—" "He will wreck the car again against the wrong tree, in the wrong place, and you will have to forgive him again, until," says Stevens, "he can wreck the car again in the wrong place, against the wrong tree— Come on. It's late."

Holding back, Temple wants to know why the Governor said "No." He couldn't do anything else, says Stevens. "The Governor wasn't even talking about justice. He was talking about a child, a little boy—the same little boy to hold whose normal and natural home together Nancy didn't hesitate to cast the last gambit she knew and had: her own debased and worthless life."

Finding out that the Governor said all of this a good week ago, Temple cries wildly that this confession of hers amounted to nothing, just pointless suffering.

STEVENS—You came here to affirm the very thing for which Nancy is going to die tomorrow morning: that little children, as long as they are little children, shall be intact, unanguished, untorn, unterrified.
TEMPLE—All right. I have done that. Can we go home now?
STEVENS—Yes.
TEMPLE (*to no one, still with that sleepwalking air*)—To save my soul—if I have a soul. If there is a God to save it—a God who wants it—

ACT III

At ten-thirty on the morning of March 12th Stevens and Temple arrive at the jail. Tubbs, a typical small-town turnkey, whose unending flow of talk ranges from straight brutishness to sheer sentimentality, opens up for these respected visitors. Temple and Stevens listen patiently as Tubbs talks on and on. Having missed Lawyer Stevens the night before, having expected him for his usual Sunday-night session, Tubbs explains to Temple: "Lawyer here"—indicating Stevens—"and Nancy have been singing hymns in her cell. The first time, he just stood out there on the sidewalk while she stood in that window yonder. Which was all right, not doing no harm, just singing church hymns. Because all of us home folks here in Jefferson and Yoknapatawpha County both know Lawyer Stevens even if some of us might have thought he got out of line—defending a nigger murderer, let alone when it was his own niece was mur— maybe suppose some stranger say, some durn Yankee tourist, happened to be passing through in a car, when we get enough durn criticism from Yankees like it is—besides, a white man standing out there in the cold, while a durned nigger murderer is up here all warm and comfortable; so it happened that me and Mrs. Tubbs hadn't went to prayer meeting that night, so we invited him to come in; and to tell the truth, we come to enjoy it too. Because as soon as they found out there wasn't going to be no objection to it, the other prisoners joined in too, and by the second or third Sunday night, folks was stopping along the street to listen to them instead of going to regular church. Of course, the other niggers would just be in and out over Saturday and Sunday night for fighting or gambling or drunk, so just about the time they would begin to get in tune, the whole choir would be a complete turnover. In fact, I had a idea at one time to have the Marshal comb the nigger dives and joints not for drunks and gamblers, but basses and baritones. . . ."

Tubbs even offers Temple refreshments, but refusing politely, Temple asks to see Nancy. As Tubbs goes off, Temple says: "People. They're really innately, inherently gentle and kind. That's what wrenches . . . something. Your entrails, maybe. The member of the mob who holds up the whole ceremony while he dislodges a family of bugs or lizards from the log he is about to put on the fire—"

Delivering Nancy, Tubbs asks how much time Stevens wants. "Ten minutes should be enough," says Stevens. Locking the door behind him, Tubbs leaves the three alone.

Calm, unchanged, Nancy asks Stevens if he followed her instructions. Told that the letters were delivered to Gowan, Nancy reckons that by now they're burned. Reacting wildly, Temple accuses Stevens of lying to her: "Don't you see? It's all a waste? You lied to me when you didn't have to, you gave him the letters when he didn't even need them—it's all a waste, of lying and letters, too." Nancy has no doubts about Gowan's burning them. "He can't quit now," she says levelly; "if he read them, maybe he could. But he burned them up, quick, so he wouldn't even have to not read them any more. Any quitting now, you'll have to do it."

Temple says that she came back. Nancy had heard that she'd come back all the way from California and had gone last night with Stevens to see the Governor. And furthermore, no one need tell her what the Governor said: maybe she could have told them last night and saved them the trip. Only she didn't.

TEMPLE—Why didn't you, Nancy?
NANCY—Because I went on hoping. The hardest thing of all to get rid of, let go of, the last thing of all poor sinning man will turn aloose. Maybe it's because that's all he's got. Leastways, he holds on to it, even with salvation already in his hand and all he needs is just to shut his fingers, old sin is still too strong for him, and sometimes before he even knows it, he has throwed salvation away just grabbing back at hoping. But it's all right.
STEVENS—You mean, when you have salvation, you don't have hope?
NANCY—You don't even need it. All you need, all you have to do, is just believe.
STEVENS—Believe what?
NANCY—Just believe. I know what the Big Man told you. And

it's all right. I finished all that a long time back, that same day in the judge's court. No: before that even: in the nursery that night, before I even lifted my hand—
TEMPLE (*convulsively*)—Hush. Hush.
NANCY—All right. I've hushed. Because it's all right. I can get low for Jesus too. I can get low for Him too.

First telling Nancy not to blaspheme, Temple next says that she too would get low for Him if that's all He wants. She'll do anything He wants if He'll just tell her what to do. "Trust in Him," says Nancy. Maybe, she figures, that's their pay for the suffering.

STEVENS—Then you believe that salvation of the world is in a man's suffering. Is that it?
NANCY—Yes, sir.
STEVENS—How?
NANCY—I don't know. Maybe when folks are suffering, they will be too busy to get into devilment, won't have time to worry and meddle one another.
TEMPLE—But why must it be suffering? Why couldn't He have invented something else? Or, if it's got to be suffering, why can't it be just your own? Why can't you buy back your own sins with your own agony? Why do you and my little baby both have to suffer just because I decided to go to a baseball game? Do you have to suffer everybody else's anguish just to believe in God? What kind of God is it that has to blackmail His customers with the whole world's grief and ruin?

Nancy thinks He might just be too busy, have too many people to look after. She compares the Lord to a man with too many mules. It's a ticklish business watching over them, and He knows that they can't help but sin: "You ain't *got* to. You can't help it. And He knows that. But you can suffer. And He knows that too. He don't tell you not to sin, He just asks you not to. And he don't tell you to suffer. But He gives you the chance. He gives you the best He can think of, that you are capable of doing. And He will save you."
Trustingly, Nancy believes that she, a murderess, can be used in Heaven as a general houseworker and to look after the children and keep them from harm. "Maybe even that baby?" says Stevens. "That one too," answers Nancy. "A heaven where the little child will remember nothing of my hands but gentleness because now this earth will have been nothing but a dream that didn't matter. Because

I loved that baby, even at the moment I raised my hand against it."
Nancy believes, she does not know what, but she believes. As Tubbs comes to take her away, Temple asks quickly: "Nancy, you're going to be all right, but—what about me? Even if there is a heaven and somebody waiting in it to forgive me, there's still tomorrow and tomorrow. And suppose tomorrow and tomorrow, and then nobody there, nobody waiting to forgive me—" Following Tubbs unhesitatingly, Nancy tells her to just believe.

Momentarily overcome, Temple wavers, then pulls herself together. "Anyone to save it," she says, "anyone who wants it. If there is none, I'm sunk. We all are. Doomed . . . Damned . . . Finished." "Of course we are," says Stevens. "Hasn't He been telling us that for going on two thousand years?"

Beyond the door Tubbs can be heard greeting Gowan. "Temple!" Gowan calls. "Coming," she answers.

SWEET BIRD OF YOUTH
A Play in Three Acts
By Tennessee Williams

[TENNESSEE WILLIAMS *was born Thomas Lanier Williams 45 years ago in Columbus, Miss. He disliked the name and took "Tennessee" instead. He graduated from the State University of Iowa and has been a clerk in a shoe company, an elevator operator, a bellhop, a movie usher, a waiter and a teletyper. "Battle of Angels," the original of "Orpheus Descending," was his first long play to gain production but did not get to Broadway. "The Glass Menagerie," however, did—and won the Drama Critics Circle Award. In the season of 1947-48 his "Streetcar Named Desire" won both this award and the Pulitzer Prize. Williams has also written "You Touched Me" (with Donald Windham), "Summer and Smoke," "The Rose Tattoo," "Camino Real" and "Cat on a Hot Tin Roof," which also won both the Critics Circle Award and the Pulitzer Prize.*]

For the cast listing, see page 328.

IN THE BEDROOM of an old-fashioned but still fashionable Gulf Coast hotel, among numerous pieces of luggage, piles of thrown-down clothing, and the remains of last night's supper and drinks, stands a huge double bed, on which lies a sleeping woman. As "Princess Kosmonopolis" breathes hard and tosses about, Chance Wayne, a young man, still in his pajamas, lights the first cigarette of the day.

Opening the door to a room-service waiter's knock, Chance orders him to put down his tray, mix him a bromo and open the shutters a little. "Hey, I said a little, not that much, not that much. ♪ . . I didn't know it was Sunday." Kneeling to pick up the tray of drinks, the waiter says that it's Easter Sunday. The singing is from the Episcopal Church, and the bells that can be heard are from the

---

"Sweet Bird of Youth": By Tennessee Williams. Copyright © 1959 by Two Rivers Enterprises, Inc. All rights reserved. Reprinted by permission of New Directions. See CAUTION notice on copyright page. All inquiries should be addressed to the author's agent: Audrey Wood, MCA Artists, Ltd., 598 Madison Avenue, New York 22, N. Y.

Catholic Church. Chance just tells him to put his tip on the bill. Thanking him by name, the waiter remembers: "I waited tables in the Grand Ballroom when you used to come to the dances on Saturday nights, with that real pretty girl you used to dance so good with, Mr. Boss Finley's daughter." Increasing the tip to five dollars, in return for which the waiter is not to remember to recognize him, Chance tells him to leave quietly. As the waiter opens the door, Chance has an unexpected and unwelcome visitor.

SCUDDER—The assistant manager that checked you in here last night phoned me this morning that you'd come back to Saint Cloud.
CHANCE—So you came right over to welcome me home?
SCUDDER—Your lady friend sounds like she's coming out of ether.
CHANCE—The Princess had a rough night.
SCUDDER—You're latched onto a Princess? Gee.
CHANCE—She's traveling incognito.
SCUDDER—Golly, I should think she would, if she's checking in hotels with you.

Having only a few minutes to talk before he has to report to the hospital—where he's chief-of-staff—Scudder asks why Chance has come back, and won't accept Chance's story that he has come back to see his sick mother. "Your mother," says Scudder, "died a couple of weeks ago." "Why wasn't I notified?" Chance wants to know.

SCUDDER—You were. A wire was sent you three days before she died at the last address she had for you which was general delivery, Los Angeles. We got no answer from that, and another wire was sent you after she died, the same day of her death, and we got no response from that either. Here's the church record. The church took up a collection for her hospital and funeral expenses. She was buried nicely in your family plot and the church has also given her a very nice headstone. . . . I'm giving you these details in spite of the fact that I know and everyone here in town knows that you had no interest in her, less than people who knew her only slightly, such as myself.

CHANCE—How did she go?
SCUDDER—She had a long illness, Chance. You know that.
CHANCE—Yes. She was sick when I left here the last time.
SCUDDER—She was sick at heart as well as sick in her body at that time, Chance. But people were very good to her, especially

people who knew her in the church, and the Reverend Walker was with her at the end.

CHANCE—She never had any luck.

Scudder hopes that Chance hasn't forgotten the letter he wrote to Chance after his last visit to St. Cloud. Having been moving around, Chance says he never received it and asks what was in it. Wanting to speak quietly about this, Scudder draws Chance further away from the bed. "In this letter," says Scudder, "I just told you that a certain girl we know had to go through an awful experience, a tragic ordeal, because of past contact with you. I told you that I was only giving you this information so that you would know better than to come back to Saint Cloud, but you didn't know better." Saying he got no letter, Chance wants to know what ordeal and what girl. "Heavenly? Heavenly, George?" Seeing it's not going to be easy to have a quiet talk, Scudder starts to leave. When Chance blocks his way, Scudder warns him that he is not to see this girl and that he is to leave before her father and brother hear that he is in town. He wants to impress on Chance the gravity of his position. Wanting no names mentioned—for they are not alone in the room—Scudder says he's going to tell Hatcher, the assistant manager, that Chance wants to check out—"So you'd better get Sleeping Beauty and yourself ready to travel, and I suggest that you keep on traveling till you've crossed the state line. . . ."

CHANCE—You're not going to leave this room till you've explained to me what you've been hinting at about my girl in St. Cloud.

SCUDDER—There's a lot more to this which we feel ought not to be talked about to anyone, least of all to you, since you have turned into a criminal degenerate, the only right term for you, but Chance, I think I ought to remind you that once long ago the father of this girl wrote out a prescription for you, a sort of medical prescription, which is castration. You'd better think about that—that would deprive you of all you've got to get by on.

CHANCE—I'm used to that threat. I'm not going to leave St. Cloud without my girl.

SCUDDER—You don't have a girl in St. Cloud. Heavenly and I are going to be married next month.

The minute Scudder has left, Chance rushes to the phone and calls "Aunt Nonnie," but apparently she won't talk to him. The Princess, moaning, sits up abruptly. Flinging down her black eye mask, she cries: "Who are you? Help!" Asking her to hush, offering her the consoling thought that *he's* with her, Chance merely compounds her confusion. Reaching over the edge of the bed, groping about, she cries: "Oxygen! Mask!" "Why, do you feel short-winded?" asks Chance. "Yes!" she gasps. "I have . . . air . . . shortage!" Chance, having unlocked the suitcase they are in, removes the oxygen tank and mask. With the Princess' scream of "Hurry!" as accompaniment, Chance gives her the mask and twists the tank's valve.

PRINCESS (*after breathing in some oxygen*)—Why in hell did you lock it up in that case?
CHANCE—You said to put all your valuables in that case.
PRINCESS—I meant my jewelry, and you know it, you, bast—tard!
CHANCE—Princess, I didn't think you'd have these attacks any more. I thought that having me with you to protect you would stop these attacks of panic, I . . .
PRINCESS—Give me a pill.
CHANCE—Which pill?
PRINCESS—A pink one, a pinkie and . . . vodka. . . .

Putting down the tank, giving the Princess a pill, Chance reaches for a bottle just as the telephone rings. The house manager requests that they vacate the room at once.

Despite the Princess' loud protests that he must not use her name, Chance repeatedly lets it be known that Alexandre Del Lago cannot be moved in her present state of exhaustion, that he will not take the responsibility for Miss Del Lago's leaving today. The Princess shouts at him to hang up. Obligingly he puts up the receiver and crosses to her side with the bottle of vodka. Drinking and telling Chance to shut up, the Princess says that she's forgetting, that she's commanding herself to forget. Once more she throws herself on the bed.

Putting down the bottle, Chance goes into action. Picking up a tape recorder, he dashes back, puts it on the floor next to the bed and connects it. The Princess by now has had enough oxygen and orders Chance to take the mask away and to check the cylinder before putting it back in its case. Noticing her hard breathing, Chance asks if he should get a doctor. Shrieking that she doesn't need doctors, the Princess says that what happened is nothing at all. "Something disturbs me . . . adrenalin's pumped in my blood and I get short-winded, that's all, that's all there is to it. . . . I woke up, I didn't know where I was or who I was with, I got panicky. . . . Adrenalin was released and I got short-winded." Kneeling on her bed, helping her with the pillows, Chance says: "You're full of com-

Paul Newman and Geraldine Page in "Sweet Bird of Youth"

plexes, plump lady." He tells her she put on a good deal of weight after that disappointment last month. Hitting him with a small pillow, she says she doesn't remember any disappointment. "Can you control your memory like that?" asks Chance. "Yes. I've had to learn to," says the Princess. "What is this place, a hospital? And you, what are you, a male nurse?" "I take care of you but I'm not your nurse," he says. "But you're employed by me, aren't you?" she asks. "For some purpose or other?" He's on no salary, says Chance; she's just footing the bills.

Rubbing her eyes, the Princess also seems to be having a hard time seeing. "My vision's so cloudy. Don't I wear glasses, don't I have any glasses?" Last night she had an accident with them: she fell flat on her face, says Chance. "Well, please give me the remnants," orders the Princess. "I don't mind waking up in a . . . intimate situation with someone, but I like to see who it's with, so I can make whatever adjustments seem called for. . . ." She has no idea or memory of what Chance looks like. As he searches for the glasses, Princess wants to know just what happened last night.

CHANCE—You knocked yourself out.
PRINCESS—Did we sleep here together?
CHANCE—Yes, but I didn't molest you.
PRINCESS—Should I thank you for that, or accuse you of cheating?
CHANCE—I like you, you're a nice monster.
PRINCESS—Your voice sounds young. Are you young?
CHANCE—My age is twenty-nine years.
PRINCESS—That's young for anyone but an Arab. Are you very good looking?

Chance claims to have been the best-looking boy in this town. He reaches over the headboard and hands her her cracked, broken glasses. Putting them on, she looks him over. Then motioning him to come nearer, she puts her hand on his naked chest and feels him. "Well," she says, "I may have done better, but God knows I've done worse."

CHANCE—What are you doing now, Princess?
PRINCESS—The tactile approach.
CHANCE—You do that like you were feeling a piece of goods to see if it was genuine silk or phony. . . .
PRINCESS—It feels like silk, genuine! This much I do remember, that I like bodies to be hairless silky smooth gold.
CHANCE—Do I meet those requirements?
PRINCESS—You seem to meet those requirements. But I still have a feeling that something is not satisfied in the relation between us.
CHANCE—You've had your experiences, I've had mine. You can't expect everything to be settled at once. . . . Two different experiences of two different people. Naturally there's some things that have to be settled between them before there's any absolute agreement.

Tossing aside the splintered lenses, Princess asks the time. Taking her watch from his pocket, Chance inquires if it's platinum. The Princess says she never travels with anything expensive. "Why?" asks Chance. "Do you get robbed much? Huh? Do you get rolled often?" Ignoring him, she now demands the phone. Princess wishes to inquire where she is and *who* is with her. Preventing her from phoning, getting on the bed beside her, pulling her back to lean against him, Chance asks if she doesn't now feel secure with him.

Trapped by her memory block, she says: "I feel as if someone I loved had died lately, and I don't want to remember who it could be—" Reminding her that in Palm Beach he discovered her real name and that she admitted to it, Chance brings her back to reality too quickly.

The Princess demands that she be left to get back her memory in her own way. . . . The last place that she remembers was Tallahassee, where, according to Chance, they laid in a supply of vodka to carry them through this dry Sunday. Except for the one bottle that the Princess consumed by herself in the back seat of the car, their supplies are still holding up.

The Princess now has a yen to get up and look out of the window to see where they are. "I can describe the view to you," says Chance. "I'm not sure I'd trust your description. *WELL!*" says the Princess. With an "oopsa-daisy," Chance propels her across the room. Landing in a chair, the Princess yowls: "My God! I said help me, not toss me onto the carpet!" Seeing the Palm Gardens, the highway and beach and bathers and the endless stretch of water, suddenly remembering the one thing she didn't want to think of, the Princess heads back to bed with Chance's help. Turning down his offer of oxygen, she now demands "the stuff." Chance has hidden it under the mattress which, says the fuming Princess, is a downright stupid place for it. Not recognizing her brand, Chance asks what it is. "This isn't pot," says he. "What is it?"

PRINCESS—Wouldn't that be pretty? A year in jail in one of those model prisons for distinguished addicts. What is it? Do you know what it is, you beautiful, stupid young man? It's hashish, Moroccan, the finest.

CHANCE—Oh, hash! How did you get it through customs when you came back for your comeback?

PRINCESS—I didn't get it through customs. The ship's doctor gave me injections while this stuff was winging over the ocean to a shifty young gentleman that thought he could blackmail me for it.

CHANCE—Couldn't he?

PRINCESS—Of course not. I called his bluff.

Observing that Chance talks too much and asks far too many questions, the Princess asks him to hurry up and fix it. She needs some quick.

CHANCE—I'm a new hand at this.

PRINCESS—I'm sure, or you wouldn't discuss it in a hotel room.

... For years they all told me that it was ridiculous of me to feel that I couldn't go back to the screen or the stage as a middle-aged woman. They told me I was an artist, not just a star whose career depended on youth. But I knew in my heart that the legend of Alexandra Del Lago couldn't be separated from an appearance of youth. ... There's no more valuable knowledge than knowing the right time to go. I knew it. I went at the right time to go. Retired! Where to? To what? to that dead planet, the moon ... there's nowhere else to retire to when you retire from an art because, believe it or not, I really was once an artist. So I retired to the moon, but the atmosphere of the moon doesn't have any oxygen in it. I began to feel breathless, in the withered, withering country, of time coming after time not meant to come after, and so I discovered ... Haven't you fixed it yet? (CHANCE *rises and crosses to her with stick; he returns to bed.*) Discovered this! And other practices like it, to put to sleep the tiger that raged in my nerves. ... Why the unsatisfied tiger? In the nerves jungle? Why is anything, anywhere, unsatisfied and raging? ... Ask somebody's good doctor. But don't believe his answer because it isn't ... the answer. ... If I had just been old! But you see, I wasn't old ... I just wasn't young, not young, young ... I just wasn't young any more. ...

Smoking her hashish, the Princess enumerates the practices she's indulged in, including the taking on of young lovers, the last of whom is Chance: but he came after "the comeback." She lives through the horror of seeing herself on the screen, seeing a close-up of herself that made people gasp, her headlong flight, her tripping over her train and falling down the marble stairs and "rolled, rolled, like a sailor's drunk whore to the bottom ... hands, merciful hands without faces, assisted me to get up. After that? Flight, just flight, not interrupted until I woke up this morning. ... Oh God, it's gone out. ..." Every once in a while, offering her another stick, Chance pointedly breaks in. It occurs to the Princess that she is being most indiscreet. Ordinarily she takes the most fantastic precautions against detection. It occurs to her, too, that Chance seems to be trying to prove something.

CHANCE—You brought it into the country, you smuggled it through customs into the U.S.A. and you had a fair supply of it at that hotel in Palm Beach and were asked to check out before you were ready to do so, because its aroma drifted into the corridor one breezy night.

PRINCESS—What are you trying to prove?

CHANCE—You don't deny that you introduced me to it?
PRINCESS—Boy, I doubt very much that I have any vice that I'd need to introduce to you. . . .

On his high horse, Chance maintains that all his vices were caught from other people, but the Princess's memory is now working as it should. She remembers vividly that it was this joint practice that brought them together. She remembers that he was using the name "Carl." Saying he always carries an extra name in his pocket, he asks her now to call him Chance. "You're not a criminal, are you?" asks the Princess. "No, ma'am, not me," says Chance. "You're the one that's committed a federal offense." And he tells her that in Palm Beach she, too, was using a phony name. "Yes, to avoid any reports or condolences on the disaster I ran from," says the Princess. She can see that they have not yet reached an agreement. Chance is holding out for a guarantee that she will go through with the contract she gave him.

CHANCE—You said that you had a large block of stock, more than half ownership in a sort of second-rate Hollywood studio, and could put me under contract. I doubted your word about that. You're not like any phony I've met before, but phonies come in all types and sizes. So I held out, even after we locked your cabana door for the papaya cream rubs. . . . You wired for some contract papers we signed. It was notarized and witnessed by three strangers found in a bar.
PRINCESS—Then why did you hold out, still?
CHANCE—I didn't have much faith in it. You know, you can buy those things for six bits in novelty stores. I've been conned and tricked too often to put much faith in anything that could possibly still be phony.
PRINCESS—You're wise. However, I have the impression that there's been a certain amount of intimacy between us. (*She stands over him—between his legs.*)
CHANCE—A certain amount. No more. I wanted to hold your interest.

He hazards a guess that there were plenty of loopholes in the contract. Agreeing, the Princess wants to know if he has any talent. "For what?" asks Chance. "Acting, baby, ACTING!" she answers. He, who had so many chances, and almost but not quite made the grade every time, is blocked by terror. . . . "Otherwise would I be your goddamn caretaker, hauling you across the country?

Picking you up when you fall? Well, would I, except for that block, be anything less than a star?" "CARL!" cries the Princess. "Chance," he says, "Chance Wayne. You're stoned."

Pulling him to the bed, leaning over him and kissing him, the Princess asks that they comfort each other a little. Instead, Chance chooses this moment to show that he has her over a barrel: he plays back the tapes. Familiar enough with blackmail to recognize it immediately, the Princess shouts for an immediate inventory of all her possessions: mink stole, jewels insured by Lloyd's of London. She's not worried about money: she only carries traveler's checks. Having already found this out, Chance offers her his fountain pen.

She wonders whether he is really serious in this attempt to blackmail her. "You'd better believe it. Your trades turned to dirt on you, Princess," says Chance. "You understand that language?" "The language of the gutter," answers the Princess, "is understood anywhere that anyone ever fell in it."

Chance now threatens her with *Confidential* and other scandal rags, with the F.B.I., and with the making of additional copies of the tapes. She merely observes that he's sweating, that he's obviously not an old hand at this. "Here! Here! Start signing . . . or . . ." "Or WHAT?" says the Princess. "Go take a shower under cold water. I don't like hot sweaty bodies in a tropical climate."

Ignoring his efforts, the Princess makes clear her conditions for payment, which she can easily afford, but which she will make only after delivery. Chance is forbidden to mention who she was, or the ruin of that legend; he is not to mention her heart disease nor death. Her last rule for him is: "When I say *now,* the answer must not be *later.* I have only one way to forget these things I don't want to remember and that's through the act of lovemaking. That's the only dependable distraction so when I say *now,* because I need that distraction, it has to be now, not later. . . . Chance, I need that distraction." Taking the pen, she throws it away. "It's time for me to find out if you're able to give it to me. You mustn't hang onto your silly little idea that you can increase your value by turning away and looking out a window when somebody wants you. . . . I want you. . . . I say *now* and I mean *now,* then and not until then will I call downstairs and tell the hotel cashier that I'm sending a young man down with some traveler's checks to cash for me. . . ." "Aren't you ashamed a little?" asks Chance. "Of course I am," says the Princess. "Aren't you?" "More than a little," answers Chance. Ordering him to draw the curtains, get a little sweet music on the radio and come to her on the bed, the Princess asks him to make her believe they're a pair of young lovers without shame.

Scene II

Reclining on a chaise longue, dressed in a voluminous rust-colored taffeta negligee, the Princess, under Chance's watchful eye, signs checks. "All right," she says, "one more from the front of the book as a token of some satisfaction. I said some, not complete." However, she refuses to let him leave to cash them until she has made up, and is ready to face the day and her face.

Looking out at St. Cloud, Chance says he was born here. Encouraged to tell his life story (if he can hold her interest, says the Princess, she'll wire her studio that she's still alive and on her way to the coast with a young man cut out to be a great star), Chance launches into his youth in St. Cloud.

His great good looks earned him a special place in the town's snob set, but for him that wasn't enough. His ambitions to do great things landed him in the chorus of *Oklahoma,* and his picture in *Life.* His one true talent landed him in New York's best Social Register beds. Always, however, at the point where he might get something back that would solve his own need, the memory of his girl would draw him home. The town would buzz with excitement on his arrival.

At the time of Korea, Chance chose the Navy. Scared that by the time he got out he'd be near thirty, with the peak of his success past, with his hair thinning and his youth gone forever, he began to have palpitations and nightmares. On leave, he'd get drunk and wake up in strange places and finally, haunted by the thought of a stray bullet annihilating him, he completely cracked up. Given a medical discharge, Chance found that now when he came home the town was polite but not cordial. There were no more newspaper headlines, there was just an item on page five saying that Chance Wayne, the son of Mrs. Emily Wayne of North Front Street, had received an honorable discharge from the Navy as the result of illness and was home to recover. "That was when Heavenly became more important to me than anything else." "So . . . I'm being used," says the Princess, adding: "Why not? Even a dead race horse is used to make glue. Is she pretty?"

To Chance the world is divided between those who have had great pleasure in love and those who haven't, and he doesn't mean just ordinary pleasure or the kind that you can buy. With Heavenly, he had such pleasure that few people can look back on in their lives. "No questions," says the Princess; "go on with your story."

As the Princess continues to touch up her face here and there, Chance recounts how he returned after each disappointment or failure, and how each time Heavenly healed him. The Princess can't understand why he didn't marry her. Chance had forgotten to say that Heavenly's father, Boss Finley, had prevented their marrying. But the last time he came home, and Heavenly told him to meet her at Diamond Rock, she never came near him. After waiting a long, long time, Chance saw her circle around the rock in a boat, all the time crying out things like: "Chance, go away. Don't come back to St. Cloud—Chance, you're a liar—Chance, I'm sick of your lies! My father's right about you!—Chance, you're no good any more—Chance, stay away from St. Cloud." The last time around the sand bar she shouted nothing, just waved goodbye and turned the boat back to shore. Chance feels that the end of his story is up to the Princess. He outlines the plan he has for her: first he will show Heavenly his contract, then the Princess and he will leave. They'll only go as far as New Orleans, where the Princess, revealing her true identity to the press, will stage a contest to discover a pair of young people to star as unknowns in a picture she will produce to show her faith in Youth. Since the final decision will rest with the Princess, Heavenly and he will win it. And then, off they'll go together into the West Coast sun.

Left out of the scenario, the Princess is lukewarm to the project. However, she gets up, goes to the phone and informs the cashier that Chance is coming down with some traveler's checks. Chance's next demand is for her white Cadillac. He wants to be seen all over town. Considerably softened, the Princess says that she would really like to help him find himself. "I passed the screen test," crows Chance. Her arms outstretched, declaring her love, the Princess asks him to kiss her. Ducking out of her reach, Chance outlines his program for tonight. He will display himself in the Cadillac and wave his contract under the noses of unbelievers. In the morning, the Princess will have her car and what remains of the money. "Where will you be?" asks the Princess. "With my girl," cries Chance, "or nowhere."

Crying that she's not a phony, that she wants to be his friend, the Princess is rebuffed. "Go back to sleep," says Chance. "As far as I know you're not a bad person, but you just got into bad company on this occasion."

ACT II

On his terrace, talking to Scudder about Heavenly, Boss Finley knows by the photograph taken of her in the nude (and circulated by the developing studio) that Chance had had her when she was a little girl of fifteen. "That was when I first warned the son of a bitch to git and stay out of St. Cloud. But he's back in St. Cloud now—" As Scudder advises Finley to call off his appearance at tonight's rally and go instead for a short cruise with Heavenly, Finley orders his servant Charles to fetch her.

Refusing to spare himself, Boss knows he'll have a coronary one of these days—but not because Chance Wayne had the gall to come back to St. Cloud. Shouting for his son, Tom Junior, Boss wants to know if Chance has checked out yet, and if the manager is a talker or can keep his mouth shut. Scudder says that he impressed the manager with the importance of discretion. "Discreetly, like you handled that operation you done on my daughter," says Boss; "so discreetly that a hillbilly heckler is shouting me questions about it wherever I speak."

Tom Junior reports that Chance finds it impossible for Alexandra Del Lago to travel. "Okay," says Boss to Scudder, "you're the doctor, remove her to a hospital. Call an ambulance and haul her out of the Royal Palms Hotel." As soon as she's removed, they can remove Chance Wayne. As Scudder protests, Finley says then it's up to him to figure out a way, but he won't have Chance passing another night in St. Cloud. Scudder doesn't care to be involved in this. "Okay," says Tom, "don't be involved in it. There's a pretty fair doctor that lost his license because of helping a girl out of trouble and he won't be so goddam finicky about doing this absolutely just thing." Not questioning the moral justification of what Tom proposes, Scudder yet, as chief of staff of the great hospital put up by Boss Finley, cannot afford to become involved. And although he is the source of all this violence, Boss Finley wants to have nothing to do with it.

A blast of a horn announces that Chance has driven right up to their driveway. "Is Chance insane?" cries Tom Junior. "Is a criminal degenerate sane or insane is a question," says Scudder, "that lots of law-courts haven't been able to settle." "Take it to the Supreme Court," advises Boss; "they'll hand you down a decision on that question. They'll tell you a handsome young criminal degenerate like Chance Wayne is the mental and moral equal of any white man in the country."

Chance apparently had been trying to speak to Aunt Nonnie, who scuttled away like a frightened rabbit. Arriving on the terrace, she says nervously that she has just left a message at the hotel for Chance to get out of town right away. "He's gonna get out," says Tom Junior, "but not in that fish-tail Caddy." Begging them not to use violence, Aunt Nonnie promises to get Chance out of St. Cloud herself. "Tom, you know Heavenly says it wasn't Chance that—She says it wasn't Chance—" Breaking in to say that Nonnie is as gullible as her dead sister, as his wife, Boss Finley tells her she has a whole lot to answer for.

Boss—Yes, you sure have, Nonnie. You favored Chance Wayne, encouraged, aided and abetted him in his corruption of Heavenly over a long, long time. You go get her. You sure do have a lot to answer for. You got a helluva lot to answer for.

Nonnie—I remember when Chance was the finest, nicest, sweetest boy in St. Cloud, and he stayed that way till you, till you—

Boss—Go get her, go get her!

Accusing everyone he shelters and provides for of pulling him down, Boss now accuses Tom Junior of degeneracy. "I got more newspaper coverage in the last six months than—" protests Tom. "Once for drunk drivin', once for a stag party you thrown in Capital City that cost me five thousand dollars to hush up!" "You are so unjust," says Tom. "And everyone knows," continues Boss, "you had to be drove through school like a blaze-face mule pullin' a plow up hill: flunked out of college with grades that only a moron would have an excuse for—" "I got readmitted to college," says Tom. "At my insistence," counters his father. "By fake examinations, answers provided beforehand, stuck in your fancy pockets. And your promiscuity. Why, these 'Youth for Tom Finley' clubs are practically nothin' but gangs of juvenile delinquents, wearin' badges with my name and photograph on them."

Slashing back, Tom asks his father about his own well-known promiscuity and in particular about Miss Lucy. Playing dead, Boss says: "Who's Miss Lucy?" But he comes to life when Tom says that Miss Lucy, kept by Boss in a fifty-dollar-a-day suite at the Royal Palms, wrote on the ladies' room mirror that "Boss Finley is too old to cut the mustard." Furious, Boss says he will check on it—and Tom Junior should mind his own goddamn business. "A man with a mission, which he holds sacred, and on the strength of which he rises to high public office crucified in this way," intones Boss, "publicly, by his own offspring!"

Left alone with Heavenly, Boss first talks sweet; then, when she won't respond, gets tough. She has become an issue, a subject of talk, of scandal, which can defeat the mission that— "Don't give me your 'Voice of God' speech, Papa," says Heavenly. "There was a time when you could have saved me, by letting me marry a boy that was still young and clean, but instead you drove him away, drove him out of St. Cloud, and tried to force me to marry a fifty-year-old moneybag that you wanted something out of . . . And then another, another, all of them ones that you wanted something out of. I'd gone, so Chance went away. Tried to compete, make himself big as these big-shots you wanted me for a bond with. He went. He tried. The right doors wouldn't open, and so he went in the wrong ones, and—Papa, you married for love, why wouldn't you let me do it, while I was alive, inside, and the boy still clean, still decent?" With mounting hysteria Heavenly brings in Miss Lucy, and then asks to leave. Changing his tactics again, Boss Finley, all sweetness and light, bribes her with clothes and jewels and furs. When Heavenly starts to laugh and scream hysterically, Finley grabs her, tells about the heckler who is always taunting him about her operation. Sorry that her operation has been such a source of embarrassment for *him,* Heavenly announces her decision to enter a convent. That really riles Boss: in a Protestant state, no daughter of his is going into any convent.

The telephone has been ringing: the manservant always says that Miss Heavenly is not at home. Which brings Boss Finley to his threat: If she won't appear at his side on the platform tonight, dressed in virgin white, "as a shining example of white Southern youth in danger," there will be consequences that she won't like. As Chance phones again, and again the servant says that Miss Heavenly is not at home, Boss Finley comes right out with it: "I'm going to remove him, he's going to be removed from Saint Cloud. How do you want him to leave, in that white Cadillac he's riding around in, or in the scow that totes the garbage out to the dumping place in the Gulf?" A lot of people around here, he reminds her, approve of taking violent action against corrupters—"and all of them that want to adulterate the pure white blood of the South." As the manservant and Heavenly exchange looks, Boss Finley launches into his "Voice of God" speech. Having had his say, he picks up his cane, a gift box, and goes to pay his respects to Miss Lucy.

Scene II

In the cocktail lounge of the Royal Palms Hotel, Miss Lucy, all dressed up for Boss Finley's banquet, complains bitterly to the bartender of how she was seated miles from the dais with a couple of upstate legislators. While in a complaining mood she tells off Stuff, the bartender, for talking too much: what happened today was the direct consequence of his big mouth. The boss brought her a present of a large Easter egg today, says Miss Lucy, and what's more, in the egg was a large jewel box. "I open the jewel box," she continues, "an' start to remove the great big diamond clip in it. I just got my fingers on it, and start to remove it and the old son of a bitch slams the lid of the box on my fingers. One fingernail is still blue. And the boss says to me: 'Now go downstairs to the cocktail lounge and go in the ladies' room and describe this diamond clip with lipstick on the ladies' room mirror down there.'" And putting the jewel box back in his pocket, Boss Finley had slammed out of her room.

Unmoved by this recital, Stuff goes out to set up tables. A coatless hillbilly walks hesitantly into the bar. Sharp-eyed as well as sharp-tongued, Miss Lucy guesses at once that this is the heckler who has been attacking Boss Finley. Delighted to annoy the Boss in any way that she can, Miss Lucy provides the heckler with a jacket and tie that Stuff had hung up behind the bar. Then, handing him a newspaper to hide behind until the Boss starts speaking on a national television hook-up, Miss Lucy settles the heckler on the terrace. Startled by such unexpected kindness as compared to his usual reception at the hands of Finley's roughs, the heckler thanks Miss Lucy. "I thank you, too," she says, "and I wish you more luck than you're likely to have."

Hopped up and loud, Chance drifts into the bar—while in the distance a page boy calls out his name—and at once rubs the bartender the wrong way. Hoping once more to be able to talk to Chance without being seen by others, Aunt Nonnie peeks in, but can't remain inconspicuous for even the brief moment it would take to warn him. At the top of his lungs, Chance orders champagne for her. Begging him to come out on the terrace with her, Aunt Nonnie says: "I've got just one thing to tell you, Chance: get out of St. Cloud." "Why does everybody treat me like a low criminal in the town I was born in?" answers Chance. Aunt Nonnie bids him ask his conscience.

AUNT NONNIE—I'm not going to talk about it. I just can't talk about it. . . . Your head and your tongue run wild. You can't be trusted. We have to live in Saint Cloud. . . . Oh, Chance, why have you changed like you've changed? Why do you live on nothing but wild dreams now, and have no address where anybody can reach you in time to—reach you?

CHANCE—Wild dreams! Yes. Isn't life a wild dream? I never heard a better description of it. (*Takes a pill and a swallow from flask.*)

NONNIE—What did you just take, Chance? You took something out of your pocket and washed it down with liquor.

CHANCE—Yes, I took a wild dream and—washed it down with another wild dream, Aunt Nonnie, that's my life now. . . .

Refusing to face the present, Chance regales Nonnie instead with memories of his first hours with Heavenly, which she, who had been their chaperon, remembers only too well. If, instead of spinning dreams and spilling lies, he had come back and admitted his failure, Aunt Nonnie thinks things might have been better. Now she just cringes as Chance waves his contract in front of her and shouts about the national contest that his patroness, Princess "Kos," is going to run and which he and Heavenly will win. Aunt Nonnie begs him to lower his voice. Wanting people to hear him, Chance talks louder and louder. Warned of his danger, Chance cries: "I go back to Heavenly, or I don't. I live or die. There's nothing in between for me." "What you want to go back to is your clean, unabashed youth, and you can't," says Aunt Nonnie. With a final warning to leave St. Cloud at once, Aunt Nonnie slips away.

The page continues to call for Chance in the distance, as more and more of the St. Cloud crowd come into the bar. In spite of his former acquaintances' real distaste and obvious snubs, Chance takes over the room. His only warm greeting comes from that kindred soul, Miss Lucy. Appreciative as always of a good-looking man, she does remark on the change in Chance's appearance; and gossipy as always she asks about his job as beach-boy in Palm Beach.

STUFF—Rubbing oil into big fat millionaires.
CHANCE—What joker thought up that one?
SCOTTY—You ought to get their names and sue them for slander.
CHANCE—I long ago gave up tracking down sources of rumors about me. Of course, it's flattering, it's gratifying to know that you're still being talked about in your old home town, even if what they say is completely fantastic. Hahaha.

Again Miss Lucy finds some change in him that she can't figure out. One of the men asks Chance if he knew that Boss Finley was holding a "Youth for Tom Finley" rally here tonight, to state his position on that emasculation business that's stirred up such a mess in the state. Chance knows nothing about it, but says at once that he doubts that story. "You doubt they cut that nigger?" asks one of the men. "Oh, no, that I don't doubt," answers Chance; "you know what that is, don't you? Sex-envy is what that is, and the revenge for sex-envy, which is a widespread disease that I have run into personally too often for me to doubt its existence or any manifestation—" As the crowd backs away from him, Chance becomes increasingly noisy. Miss Lucy warns him about this. "Not loud enough, Miss Lucy," cries Chance. "No. What I meant that I doubt is that Heavenly Finley, that only I know in Saint Cloud, would stoop to stand on a platform next to her father while he explains and excuses on TV this random emasculation of a young nigra caught on a street after midnight. . . ."

By now, the entire watchful bar crowd comments on Chance's washing down another pill with vodka, and Miss Lucy understands why Chance is changed. She quickly asks him about the famous old movie star he is traveling with. Chance grandly refuses to reveal the name of the vice-president and major stockholder of the studio that has just signed him, but Miss Lucy notices that he is literally in a sweat. She adds her warnings to all the others. Leaning against a door, one of the men asks Chance just why he did come back? Baited from all sides, Chance loudly proclaims that he's come back to visit his mother's grave, choose a monument for it, and take Heavenly away to share his success, glory and happiness. Asked if he has his contract, Chance says it just so happens that he has it on him. No one is interested. Making a last bid for their attention, Chance becomes personal and tactless. There is increasing animosity in the room.

Alone at the table with Chance, Miss Lucy announces her firm intention of seeing him safely onto the New Orleans helicopter. Before she can persuade Chance to accept her help, there is a diversion. Reeling behind a page boy, her dress undone, her manner maudlin, the Princess staggers up to Chance. There is a wave of laughter throughout the bar. Recognizing her former picture idol and hurrying to her side to adjust her dress, Miss Lucy offers to take her upstairs. Altogether ignoring Miss Lucy, the Princess throws herself at Chance's feet.

Somehow recognizing through the fog that Chance's comeback has been the failure hers was, touched by his sense of defeat and aware that for the first time she feels pity for someone beside herself, the Princess thinks now that she can stop being a monster with Chance's help. This morning she saw his kindness: "I saw true kindness in you that you have almost destroyed, but that's still there a little. . . ." As the crowd listens to everything she says, the Princess asserts that Chance is no kind of monster. "You're just—lost in the beanstalk country, the ogre's country at the top of the beanstalk, the country of the flesh-hungry, blood-thirsty ogre—" On cue, sirens and the noise of crowds herald Boss Finley's arrival.

Heavenly, dressed all in white, tries to break away from her father in order to warn Chance, but she is recaptured by Finley, and led away. "Here she is, boys," cries Finley, "ain't she Heavenly?" Running down their quarry, the hotel manager and Tom Junior urge Chance to come down from the terrace. When Chance refuses, Tom says to the manager: "Tell him I'll talk to him in the washroom on the mezzanine floor." "I don't hold conversations in washrooms," says Chance. As Tom and his cronies move on, Chance's taunts follow him. An angry Tom has to be restrained. The Princess, for her part, tries to keep Chance from going down to speak to the Boss's son. "Excuse yourself from the lady," says Tom, "and come on down here. Don't be scared to. I just want to talk to you quietly. Just talk. Quiet talk." Coming down, Chance accepts Tom Junior's offered cigarette.

CHANCE—Just tell me what happened to her.

TOM—Keep your ruttin' voice down.

CHANCE—I know I've done many wrong things in my life, many more than I can name or number, but I swear I never hurt Heavenly in my life.

TOM—You mean to say my sister was had by somebody else—diseased by somebody else the last time you were in Saint Cloud? I know it's possible, it's barely possible that you didn't know what you done to my little sister the last time you come to Saint Cloud. You remember that time, when you came home broke? My sister had to pick up your tabs in restaurants and bars, and had to cover bad checks you wrote on banks where you had no accounts. Until you met this rich-bitch Minnie, the Texas one with the yacht, and started spending week-ends on her yacht, and coming back Mondays with money from Minnie to go on with my sister. I mean, you'd sleep with Minnie, that slept with any goddamn gigolo bastard she could pick up on Bourbon Street or the docks, and then you would go on sleeping again with my sister. And sometime, during that time, you got something besides your gigolo fee from Minnie and passed it onto my sister, my little sister that had hardly even heard of a thing like that, and didn't know what it was till it had gone on too long and—

CHANCE—I left town before I found out I—

TOM—You found out! Did you tell my little sister?

CHANCE—I thought if something was wrong she'd write me or call me—

TOM—How could she write you or call you? There're no addresses, no phone numbers in gutters. I'm itching to kill you—here, on this spot! . . . My little sister, Heavenly, didn't know about the diseases and operations of whores, till she had to be cleaned and cured—I mean spayed like a dawg by Dr. George Scudder's knife. That's right—by the knife! . . . and tonight—if you stay here tonight, if you're here after this rally, you're gonna get the knife too. You know? The knife? That's all. Now go on back to the lady. I'm going back to my father.

As Chance staggers to a terrace chair, the Princess, convinced that she alone can hold him back from destruction, urges him to call the car, have them bring down the luggage, and leave with her along the Old Spanish Trail. "Keep your grabbing hands off me," answers Chance.

Boss Finley, flanked by Heavenly and Tom Junior, forms the head of a procession and marches up the stairs to the ballroom. As the prayers that open the rally are loudly repeated in the distance, the heckler tells Miss Lucy he's going to try it again. With the bar television set turned on, Boss Finley can be seen and heard. His loyal booster, Stuff, yells encouragements at the screen; Miss Lucy would like to have Finley shut up and turned off; and Chance, observing him with some horror, still dreams of taking Heavenly with him.

Conferring on himself the honor of being the colored man's best friend in the South, Boss Finley weasles his way through trying to explain the emotions that prompted "the operation performed on the unfortunate colored gentleman caught prowling the midnight streets of our Capital City." The heckler answers from the TV screen: "Hey, Boss Finley. How about your daughter's operation? How about the operation your daughter had done on her at the Thomas J. Finley Hospital here in St. Cloud? Did she put on black in mourning for her appendix?" As pandemonium reigns, Heavenly wavers at her father's side and he goes on with his oily speech.

Chased down the steps by Finley's bully boys, the escaping heckler is cornered in the bar and beaten to a pulp. Chance looks on, aghast.

ACT III

Upstairs in her room again, wanting to leave this infernal hole as soon as possible, the Princess has a maid at work packing for her while she phones frantically for a chauffeur. At the door of her room, Tom Junior and his henchmen start the process of separating the Princess from Chance. At Tom's bidding, the assistant manager calls out that the Princess' check-out time was three-thirty; it's now past midnight and she can no longer hold the room.

Not one to be bullied, the Princess refuses to deal with the assistant manager—nor even the manager—of any hotel. She talks only to owners. Brushing this aside, Tom Junior orders a search of her room and bathroom. When Chance is not to be found, Tom, ordering his men out, addresses the Princess: "I'm gonna git you a driver, Miss Del Lago—I'll git you a state trooper, half a dozen state troopers if I can't get no driver, OK? Sometime you come back to our town 'n' see us, hear? We'll lay out a red carpet for you, OK? G'night, Miss Del Lago."

As the men disappear, Chance runs to be let in the room.

PRINCESS—Some men were here looking for you. They told me I wasn't welcome in this hotel and this town because I had come here with a criminal degenerate. I asked them to get me a driver so I can go.

CHANCE—I'm your driver. I'm still your driver, Princess.

PRINCESS—You couldn't drive through the palm garden.

CHANCE—I'll be all right in a minute.

PRINCESS—It takes more than a minute. Chance, will you listen to me? Can you listen to me? I listened to you this morning, with understanding and pity, I did, I listened with pity to your story this morning. I felt something in my heart for you which I thought I couldn't feel. I remembered young men who were what you are or what you're hoping to be. I saw them all clearly, all clearly, eyes, voices, smiles, bodies, clearly. But their names wouldn't come back to me. I couldn't get their names back without digging into old programs of plays that I starred in at twenty in which they said, "Madam, the Count's waiting for you. . . ."

She recalls one in particular that she saw in Monte Carlo not too long ago. He followed an old woman around like a blind lap dog, and shortly afterward committed suicide.

Ignoring all this, Chance pulls away from her and goes to the phone. Desperately making one last pitch for his dream, he calls the Hollywood columnist, Sally Powers. First protesting, the Princess tries to take the phone from him. Suddenly resigned, feeling that Chance might as well do this dreadful thing for her, the Princess even gives him Sally's private number. The minute this is done, the Princess feels that in some strange fashion Chance exists only to make this awful call. "It's only this call I care for," muses the Princess. "I seem to be standing in light with everything else dimmed out. He's in the dimmed out background as if he'd never left the obscurity he was born in—"

Chance gets Sally Powers on the phone, and, rallying fast, the Princess hears the startling news of her comeback. Chance tries to have her intercede for him and Heavenly, but ignoring his demand that Sally should announce the young stars of tomorrow, the Princess wallows in the news that she herself was an enormous success. Kicking Chance out of her way, hitting him off with the telephone, the Princess finally asks if she may call back later; she is now too overwhelmed. As she hangs up the phone, Chance grabs it and tries frantically to get Sally back.

PRINCESS—Broken box-office records. The greatest comeback in the history of the industry, that's what she calls it.

CHANCE—You didn't mention me to her.

PRINCESS—I can't appear, not yet. I'll need a week in a clinic, then a week or ten days at the Morning Star Ranch at Vegas. I'd better get Ackermann down there for a series of shots before I go on to the Coast. . . .

CHANCE—Come back here, call her again.

PRINCESS—I'll leave the car in New Orleans and go on by plane to, to, to—Tucson. I'd better get Strauss working on publicity for me. I'd better be sure my tracks are covered up well these last few weeks in—hell!

With her nightmare over, Alexandra Del Lago will no longer be used. She tells off Chance: "You've gone past something you couldn't afford to go past; your time, your youth, you've passed it. It's all you had, and you've had it." Whirling on her, Chance tells her to look in the mirror. She sees only Alexandra Del Lago, artist and star. Told to look at himself, Chance none too confidently sees only Chance Wayne.

To the Princess, this is the face of so many of the young, beautiful men crowned too early, and only in the beginning, with laurel. Chance is a pitiful monster; the Princess acknowledges that she too is one, but with a difference: out of the passion and torment of her existence, she has created a thing of almost heroic proportions that she can unveil. "But you?" says the Princess. "You've come back to the town you were born in to a girl that won't see you because you put such rot in her body she had to be gutted and hung on a butcher's hook, like a chicken dressed for Sunday. . . . Yes, and her brother was one of my callers, threatens the same thing for you: castration, if you stay here." "That can't be done to me twice," answers Chance. "You did that to me this morning, here on this bed, where I had the honor, where I had the great honor—" After a long pause, the Princess, standing over him, replies: "Age does the same thing to a woman."

Gathering up her fur stole and her jewel box, she asks whether Chance is coming or staying. "Staying," he answers. Her mind on the future, figuring all the angles, the Princess urges Chance to accompany her—they've got to go on together. If something should happen to him here, her name would be dragged in.

Realizing that he couldn't go past his youth and yet has done so, Chance no longer has a destination. "You're still young," says the Princess. "Princess," says Chance, "the age of some people can only be calculated by the level of—level of rot—in them, and by that measure I'm ancient." By that measure, the Princess assures him, she is as dead as old Egypt. For Chance, however, *Time* has always been the opposition—who could beat it, defeat it ever? "Gnaws away," he says, "like a rat gnaws off its own foot caught in a trap, and then, with its foot gnawed off and the rat set free, couldn't run, couldn't go, bled and died. . . ."

Outside the door, Tom Junior calls that he has a driver for Miss Del Lago. Once more the Princess tries to persuade Chance to come with her, but when he shakes his head, she gives up. Accepting a state trooper as escort, the Princess departs.

The dividing tactic having finally worked, Tom Junior whistles for his followers. As the men close in, Chance, resigned to his fate, no longer trying to escape, says to the world at large: "I don't ask for your pity, but just for your understanding—not even that—no. Just for your recognition of me in you, and the enemy, time, in us all."

A RAISIN IN THE SUN

A Play in Three Acts

By Lorraine Hansberry

[LORRAINE HANSBERRY *was born in Chicago, Illinois, 28 years ago, and studied painting at the Chicago Art Institute and the University of Wisconsin. She came to New York in 1950 and worked at various jobs while she continued to write. She is the first Negro woman ever to have a play on Broadway, not to mention its winning an award (the Drama Critics Circle Award). "A Raisin in the Sun" was, moreover, her first produced play of any kind.*]

For the cast listing, see page 328.

IN a South Side Chicago apartment, where Lena Younger has lived for many years, everything has been scrubbed, washed, sat on—or used too long and too often. "All pretenses but living itself have long since vanished from the very atmosphere of this room . . ."

One section of the living room has yielded to a kitchen area. The sole natural light that Lena's family enjoys comes feebly through a single small window in the kitchen area. At one side of the living room there is a door to the bedroom that Lena shares with her daughter Beneatha; on the opposite side of the living room is a bedroom for her son Walter Lee and his wife Ruth. Their young son, Travis, has to sleep on the living room couch.

After turning off her alarm clock, Ruth comes out of the bedroom to shake Travis awake. "Come on now, boy," she cries, "it's seven-thirty . . . I say hurry up, Travis! You ain't the only person in the world got to use a bathroom!" Doing his level best to go back to sleep, Travis finally gives in, gets up blindly, somehow finds his towel and clothes, and staggers out into the hall to the bathroom that the Younger family has to share with other tenants.

"A Raisin in the Sun": By Lorraine Hansberry. © Copyright 1958, as an unpublished work, by Lorraine Hansberry and © Copyright 1959 by Lorraine Hansberry. Reprinted by permission of Random House, Inc. See CAUTION notice on copyright page. All inquiries should be addressed to the publisher: Random House, Inc., 457 Madison Avenue, New York 22, N. Y.

Going on with her early morning chores, Ruth calls out repeatedly that it is past seven-thirty and Walter had better get up. "All right," she says in exasperation, "you just go ahead and lay there and next thing you know Travis be finished and Mr. Johnson'll be in there and you'll be fussing and cussing round here like a madman! And be late too—!"

At the kitchen sink, Ruth moistens her still pretty face and runs her fingers through her disheveled hair, then ties on an apron over her housecoat. Still half asleep, Walter appears in the doorway. Hearing that he has to wait for Travis to get out of the bathroom, he complains: "Well, what was you doing all that yelling for if I can't even get in there yet?" His mind clearing, Walter immediately thinks of money and of the check that's coming.

Not wishing to hear Walter's talk about money the last thing at night and the first thing in the morning, Ruth starts to beat some eggs. Then she asks him what kind of eggs he wants. "Not scrambled," says Walter.

Killing time till Travis gets out of the bathroom, Walter glances listlessly at the Chicago *Tribune*. His patience almost exhausted, he yowls that Travis will just have to start getting up earlier. Ruth says sharply that Travis, who is kept awake by Walter and his loudmouthed friends till all hours, will not be getting up earlier. And what's more, she doesn't care for Walter's smoking before breakfast.

WALTER (*at the window*)—Just look at 'em down there . . . Running and racing to work . . . (*He turns and faces his wife and watches her a moment.*) You look young this morning, Baby.

RUTH (*indifferently*)—Yeah?

WALTER—Just for a second, stirring them eggs. It's gone now—just for a second it was—you looked real young again. (Then dryly.) It's gone now—you look like yourself again.

RUTH—Man, if you don't shut up and leave me alone . . .

WALTER (*looking out to the street again*)—First thing a man ought to learn in life is not to make love to no colored woman first thing in the morning Y'all some evil people at eight o'clock in the morning.

On Travis's return to the apartment, Walter grabs his things and makes a dash into the hall. A handsome, sturdy little boy, Travis sits down to the breakfast his mother places in front of him, but his thoughts, like his father's, are on money: "Check coming tomorrow, huh?" says Travis gleefully. "Get your mind off money and eat your breakfast," orders Ruth. Instead, Travis says he has to have fifty cents for school. Ruth has no fifty cents for him. Travis won't drop the subject: he brings his teacher into it—*she* says he has to have it. He wonders if his Grandma would have it, and he next thinks of getting the money from his father. Told to hush and eat, Travis hushes for only a moment. He now proposes to carry groceries after school. When Ruth clamps down on this too, he becomes angry and sullen.

Ruth tells Travis to make his bed. Obeying stiffly, he takes his bedding from the couch to his parents' bedroom, returning immediately. Cap on head, schoolbooks under arm, he announces: "I'm gone." He can't get by Ruth's inspection. He must comb his hair that looks, according to Ruth, like chickens slept in it. "I'm gone," Travis says again. "Get your carfare and milk money and not a single penny for no caps," directs Ruth, "you hear me?" By now Travis is really sullen but still polite. "Yes'm," he says, and outrage stands out all over him.

Looking at her son, Ruth's voice takes on a mocking tone: "Oh, Mama makes me so mad sometimes I don't know what to do. . . . I wouldn't kiss that woman goodbye for nothing in this world this morning!" Laughing, holding out her arms to her son, Ruth embraces him. Under her teasing, Travis melts and, regaining his cockiness, makes a final pitch to carry groceries.

Coming back all dressed for breakfast, Walter backs up Travis. "Well, let him go," he orders Ruth. "I have to," says Travis, "she won't gimme fifty cents . . ." "Why not?" Walter asks. " 'Cause," says Ruth, "we don't have it."

Asking how she can tell the boy such a thing, Walter digs down in his pocket for the fifty cents. Presenting it to Travis with a flourish, Walter stares defiantly at Ruth. Then, with an additional flourish, he comes up with fifty cents more. "Buy yourself some fruit today," improvises Walter, "or take a taxicab to school or something!" With a "Whoopee," Travis throws himself all over his father, who doesn't dare to look at Ruth. "That's my boy," says Walter proudly as Travis departs for school.

As soon as they are alone, Walter gets back to his money-making schemes. This time he does his persuasive best to enlist Ruth's help. "A man needs for a woman to back him up," he says. Sure that, over their morning coffee, his mother would listen to Ruth, Walter explains what it is all about. He, Willy and Bobo need an initial investment of thirty thousand dollars to buy a liquor store. Ten thousand each. " 'Course," Walter adds, "there's a couple of hundred you got to pay so's you don't spend your life just waiting for them clowns to let your license get approved—" Ruth smells graft.

WALTER—Don't call it that. . . . See there, that just goes to show you what women understand about the world. Baby, don't *nothing* happen for you in this world 'less you pay *somebody* off!
RUTH—Walter, leave me alone! Eat your eggs, they gonna be cold.
WALTER—That's it. There you are. Man say to his woman: I got me a dream. His woman say: Eat your eggs. Man say: I got to take hold of this here world, Baby! And a woman will say: Eat your eggs and go to work. Man say: I got to change my life, I'm choking to death, Baby! And his woman say—(*in utter anguish as he brings his fists down on his thighs*)—your eggs is getting cold!—
RUTH (*softly*)—Walter, that ain't none of our money.
WALTER—This morning, I was lookin' in the mirror and thinking about it . . . I'm thirty-five years old; I been married eleven years and I got a boy who sleeps in the living room—(*very, very quietly*) —and all I got to give him is stories about how rich white people live . . .
RUTH—Eat your eggs, Walter.
WALTER—DAMN MY EGGS . . . DAMN ALL THE EGGS THAT EVER WAS!
RUTH—Then go to work.

To Walter, this is just what is wrong with the colored women of this world—they don't understand about building up their menfolk. . . . Ruth allows how there are colored men who do things. "No thanks to the colored woman," says Walter. "Well, being a colored woman I guess I can't help myself none," answers Ruth, and getting out the ironing board, starts sprinkling the clothes and rolling them into tight balls. "We one group of men tied to a race of women with small minds," concludes Walter.

Pajama'd Beneatha, who's missed her chance at the bathroom, collapses into a living room chair and instantly Walter focuses attention on her. In the same tone, and in the same words that he must have used many times before, Walter asks Beneatha about her plans for medical school. "Have we figured out yet," he asks, "just exactly how much medical school is going to cost?" Ignoring Walter, Beneatha makes another stab at gaining the bathroom. Banging on the bathroom door, she yells: "Come out of there, please!" then retreats to the living room.

Walter ignores Ruth's plea to leave his sister alone. "You know the check is coming tomorrow," he says. Beneatha turns on him sharply: "That money belongs to Mama, Walter, and it's for her to decide how she wants to use it. I don't care if she wants to buy a house or a rocket ship or just nail it up somewhere and look at it—it's hers. Not ours—*hers.*" Accusing Beneatha of acting noble while all the time she's taking money from her mother, and not minding the sacrifices of the whole family, Walter refuses to tone down what he has to say. At last he bursts out with: "Who the hell told you you had to be a doctor? If you so crazy 'bout messing round with sick people . . . then go be a nurse like other women —or just get married and be quiet." "Well," says Beneatha, "you finally got it said . . . It took you three years but you finally got it said. Walter, give it up; leave me alone . . . it's Mama's money."

Ruth begs Walter to go to work. Feeling that no one in the house understands him, he growls: "The world's most backward race of people and that's a fact."

BENEATHA (*turning slowly in her chair*)—And then there are all these prophets who would lead us out of the wilderness—(WALTER *slams out of the house*)—into the swamps!

RUTH—Bennie, why you always gotta be pickin' on your brother? Can't you be a little sweeter sometimes? (*Door opens;* WALTER *walks in.*)

WALTER (*to* RUTH)—I need some money for carfare.

RUTH (*warm, teasing*)—Fifty cents? (*Goes to her bag.*) Here, take a taxi.

Mama now enters. Strong, full-bodied and white-haired, she is "a woman who has adjusted to many things in life and overcome many more: a beautiful woman."

Tying a bandana about her head for the day's cleaning, she goes first to the kitchen window, brings in a little plant, feels the dirt, then puts it back on the ledge. "My children and they tempers," says Mama. "Lord, if this little old plant don't get more sun than it's been getting it ain't never going to see Spring again . . ." Noticing how peaked Ruth looks, Mama asks her to leave some of the ironing for her. Seeing the way Travis left the couch, Mama says: "Lord have mercy. Look at that poor bed. Bless his heart—he tries, don't he?" But Ruth knows Travis doesn't try because

Grandma will come along right behind him to fix everything. Ruth says Lena spoils him.

MAMA—Well—he's a little boy. Ain't supposed to know 'bout housekeeping. My baby, that's what he is. What you fix for his breakfast this morning?
RUTH (*angrily*)—I feed my son, Lena!
MAMA—I ain't meddling . . . I just noticed all last week he had cold cereal, and when it starts getting this chilly in the fall a child ought to have some hot grits or something when he goes out in the cold—
RUTH (*furious*)—I gave him hot oats—is that all right?
MAMA—I ain't meddling. (*Pauses from working on the bed.*) Put a lot of nice butter on it?

Mama switches the talk to what all the fussing was about this morning. She knows it was Walter worrying himself sick about money. As Beneatha finally gets her chance at the bathroom, Ruth —as Walter had begged that she would—approaches Mama; tells her that Walter has his heart set on that store. Admitting that she is no more sold on investing in the liquor store than she ever was, Ruth says: "Something is happening between Walter and me. I don't know what it is—but he needs something—something I can't give him any more. He needs this chance, Lena." Mama doesn't dismiss the idea right off, but having thought about it, she concludes: "Well—whether they drinks it or not ain't none of my business. But whether I go into the business selling it to 'em is, and I don't want that on my ledger this late in life."
Looking intently at Ruth and observing her unsteadiness, Mama asks what is the matter. "I'm tired," Ruth says. "Then you better stay home from work today," answers Mama. Ruth insists she must go; they need the money. All this money talk seems foolish to Mama with a big check arriving the next morning. But, says Ruth, that is Mama's money alone—it has nothing to do with her. "Ten thousand dollars," Mama murmurs.
Suddenly gay, Ruth suggests that Mama take a trip to Europe or South America. She should just pack, go away, and enjoy herself. Mama tries to imagine what she'd look like, wandering around Europe by herself. "Shoot—" says Ruth, "these here rich white women do it all the time. They don't think nothing of packing up they suitcases and piling on one of them big steamships and— swoosh!—they gone, child." "Something always told me," says Mama, "I wasn't no rich white woman."

Although Mama hasn't decided what she will do with the money, she does know that nothing will make her touch the part that is Beneatha's school fund. But with a sideways glance at Ruth, Mama says: "Been thinking that we maybe could meet the notes on a little old two-story somewhere with a yard where Travis could play in the summertime, if we use part of the insurance for a down payment and everybody kind of pitch in. I could maybe take on a little day work again, few days a week—" Anxious to encourage Mama without seeming to, Ruth says: "Lord knows, we've put enough rent into this here rat-trap to pay for four houses by now—" Her thoughts going back to when Big Walter brought her here as a bride, Mama says that they had only intended to stay for a year while they put aside enough money to buy a little house. She remembers well the house in Morgan Park that they had their eye on. She remembers how she had dreamt she would fix it up, and how she would make a garden in the back, but they had never been able to swing it. "Life can be a barrel of disappointments sometimes," says Ruth.

Remembering how Big Walter would come home from work all exhausted and depressed, Mama says she thinks that his grief over the loss of their baby Claude drove him to work himself to death: "Like he was fighting his own war with this here world that took his baby from him!" "He sure was a fine man, all right," says Ruth. "I always liked Mr. Younger."

MAMA—Crazy 'bout his children! God knows there was plenty wrong with Walter Younger—hard-headed, mean, kind of wild with women—plenty wrong with him. But he sure loved his children. Always wanted them to have something. That's where Brother gets all these notions, I reckon. Big Walter used to say, he'd get right wet in the eyes sometimes, lean his head back with the water standing in his eyes and say, "Seem like God didn't see fit to give the black man nothing but dreams—but He did give us children to make them dreams worth while." He could talk like that, don't you know.

RUTH—Yes, he sure could. He was a good man, Mr. Younger.

MAMA—Yes, a fine man—just couldn't never catch up with his dreams, that's all.

When Beneatha comes back dressed for school, her language is as fresh as her looks. Mama and Ruth will not tolerate her profanity, but they are rather amused by her announcement that she is starting guitar lessons this afternoon. Unable to imagine why Beneatha has decided to play the guitar, Mama wonders if she doesn't know what to do with herself. She recalls the play-acting group of last year; the horseback riding club that meant a fifty-five dollar habit, now lying unused in the closet. "Why you got to flit so from one thing to another, baby?" she asks. Adding Beneatha's unused camera equipment to the previous list, Mama repeats her question. "I don't flit!" cries Beneatha; "I—I experiment with different forms of expression . . ." "Like riding horses?" teases Ruth. "People have to express themselves one way or another," Beneatha says. "What is it you want to express?" *"Me!"* snaps Beneatha.

Changing the subject, Mama asks whom Beneatha is going out with Saturday night. Although it's George Murchison again, clearly she's not looking forward to it. Beneatha finds George too shallow to be of interest. Looking up from her ironing, Ruth exclaims: "Shallow—what do you mean he's shallow? He's *rich.*" "Hush, Ruth," says Mama. "I know he's rich," answers Beneatha. "He knows he's rich, too."

Ruth can't get over this attitude: "You mean you wouldn't marry George Murchison if he asked you some day? That pretty, rich thing? Honey, I knew you was odd—" Asserting that she is going to be a doctor, and that she isn't worried about whom she is going to marry—*if* she ever gets married—Beneatha manages to stir up more excitement.

MAMA—'Course you going to be a doctor, honey, God willing.
BENEATHA—God hasn't got a thing to do with it.
MAMA—Beneatha, that just wasn't necessary.
BENEATHA—Well—neither is God. I get sick of hearing about God.
MAMA—Beneatha!
BENEATHA—I mean it! I'm just tired of hearing about God all the time. What has He got to do with anything? Does He pay tuition?
MAMA—You 'bout to get your fresh little jaw slapped!
RUTH—That's just what she needs!
BENEATHA—Why? Why can't I say what I want around here like everybody else?
MAMA—It don't sound nice for a young girl to say things like that—you wasn't brought up that way. Me and your father went to trouble to get you and Brother to church every Sunday.
BENEATHA—Mama, you don't understand. It's all a matter of ideas and God is just one idea I don't accept. It's not important. I am not going out and be immoral or commit crimes because I don't

believe in God. I don't even think about it. It's just that I get tired of Him getting credit for all the things the human race achieves through its own stubborn effort. There simply is no blasted God—there is only man and it is he who makes miracles!

Rising slowly, Mama crosses to Beneatha, slaps her powerfully across the face, and then orders her to repeat after her: "In my mother's house there is still God!" Coming to heel, Beneatha does as she is told. "There are some ideas we ain't going to have in this house. Not long as I am at the head of this family." "Yes Ma'am," says Beneatha.

As Mama leaves the room, Ruth tells Beneatha gently that what she did was childish, so that she was treated as a child. "I see," answers Beneatha, "I also see that everybody thinks it all right for Mama to be a tyrant." Grabbing her books, she stalks out.

Disturbed by her strained relations with Walter, who only thinks of money, and with Beneatha, whose ideas are incomprehensible, Mama looks for comfort to Ruth. "Now . . . you taking it all too seriously," soothes Ruth. "You just got strong-willed children and it takes a strong woman like you to keep 'em in hand." Going to her little plant, sprinkling it with water, Mama concedes: "They spirited all right, my children. Got to admit they got spirit . . . Bennie and Walter. Like this little old plant that ain't never had enough sunshine or nothing—and look at it . . ." But when Mama turns around to look at Ruth, Ruth has quietly fainted away.

Scene II

It is the next morning and a thorough housecleaning is in progress. Beneatha, with a spray gun, tracks down tough South Side roaches as Mama washes down walls. The males and Ruth are not drafted for this work. Travis, as lookout for the postman, is stationed in front of the house; Ruth is out, too, on business of her own; and Walter, talking to Willy Harris on the telephone, says he will be right over for the papers, and rushes out.

Amid all this activity, Beneatha receives a telephone call from a Nigerian admirer. At first, aware of her mother's feelings, she tries to keep him from coming over while the apartment is in disorder. Then hearing that he has a present for her, she lets out a "What the hell" and an invitation to come right up. Mama is horrified that Beneatha can be so lacking in pride, but her daughter answers: "Asagai doesn't care how houses look, Mama—he's an intellectual."

It is not this, so much as Asagai's name, that bothers Mama. She keeps Beneatha repeating it.

BENEATHA—Asagai, Joseph AH-SAH-GUY . . . He's from Nigeria.
MAMA—Oh, that's the little country that was founded by slaves way back . . .
BENEATHA—No, Mama—that's Liberia.
MAMA—I don't think I never met no African before.
BENEATHA—Well, do me a favor and don't ask him a whole lot of ignorant questions about Africans. I mean do they wear clothes and all that—
MAMA—Well, now, I guess if you think we so ignorant 'round here maybe you shouldn't bring your friends here—
BENEATHA—It's just that people ask such crazy things. All anyone seems to know about when it comes to Africa is Tarzan—
MAMA (*indignantly*)—Why should I know anything about Africa?
BENEATHA—Why do you give money at church for the missionary work?
MAMA—Well, that's to help save people.
BENEATHA—You mean save them from *heathenism*.—
MAMA (*innocently*)—Yes.
BENEATHA—I'm afraid they need more salvation from the British and the French.

Ruth returns home with the news that she's pregnant. Not giving her much of a welcome, and wanting to know whether Ruth had planned this child, Beneatha asks if it is going to live on the roof. Then, horrified at what she has just said, Beneatha tries to take it all back. Mama at the same time is suspicious that Ruth has gone to a woman doctor instead of to old Dr. Jones. Distraught and dejected, Ruth breaks into sobs, just as Asagai rings the doorbell.
Mama takes Ruth into the bedroom and Beneatha goes to the door. Noticing her preoccupation, Asagai asks whether something is wrong. "Yes," says Beneatha, "we've all got acute ghetto-itis." It is obvious, though, that Beneatha is genuinely pleased to see Asagai. "Why?" he asks. "You were quite glad when I went away. What happened?" "You went away," answers Beneatha. "Before, you wanted to be serious before there was time." "How much time must there be before one knows what one feels?" he asks.
Sparring and stalling, Beneatha opens Asagai's present of Nigerian robes and records. With Asagai's help, she wraps the material about her and preens in front of a mirror. "You wear it very well,"

says Asagai, "very well . . . mutilated hair and all." Properly stung, Beneatha argues defensively that her hair is so hard to manage when it is—well—raw. She refuses to let Asagai call it "mutilation." Laughing at her seriousness, Asagai remembers the first time they met when he thought her the most serious little thing he'd ever seen. "Mr. Asagai," he mimics, "I want very much to talk to you about Africa. You see, Mr. Asagai, I am looking for my identity." He roars with laughter, but Beneatha is profoundly disturbed. Still teasing, Asagai takes her face in his hands: "Well . . . it is true that this is not so much a profile of a Hollywood queen as perhaps a Queen of the Nile—but what does it matter? Assimilation is so popular in your country." "I am not an assimilationist!" Beneatha cries passionately.

Though she is very much impressed with being given Asagai's family robes, she is still a long way from acting the passive female. She refuses to accept Asagai's contention that there need be only one kind of feeling between man and woman—a feeling he has, right now, for her. "For a woman," says Asagai, "it should be enough."

BENEATHA—I know . . . because that's what it says in all the novels that men write. But it isn't. Go ahead and laugh—but I'm not interested in being someone's little episode in America or—(*with feminine vengeance*)—one of them! (ASAGAI *bursts into laughter again.*) That's funny as hell, huh?

ASAGAI—It's just that every American girl I have known has said that to me. White—black—in this you are all the same. And the same speech, too!

BENEATHA (*angrily*)—Yuk, yuk, yuk!

ASAGAI—It's how you can be sure that the world's most liberated women are not liberated at all. You all talk about it too much!

Mama returns to the room. Exuding social charm, liking Asagai's looks and manner, she hopes he understands that their house doesn't always look like this. "You must come again," she says. "I would love to hear all about—" she's not sure of the name—"your country. I think it's so sad the way our American Negroes doesn't know nothing about Africa 'cept Tarzan and all that. And all that money they pour into these churches when they ought to be helping you people over there drive out them French and Englishmen done taken away your land." Feeling rather superior after this performance, Mama accepts Asagai's startled acknowledgement of her unexpected sympathy, and then becomes her usual kindly self. "I bet," she ventures, "you don't half look after yourself, being away from your mama.

I spec' you better come 'round here from time to time and get yourself some decent home-cooked meals . . ." Touched, Asagai is truly grateful.

Taking his leave, addressing Beneatha as *Alayo*, Asagai says he will call on Monday. Beneatha understands that name no better than Mama does. Persuaded to translate this Yoruba nickname, Asagai says that it means "One For Whom Bread Is Not Enough." Now it is Beneatha who is grateful.

After the door closes behind him, Mama says: "Lord, that's a pretty thing just went out here! Yes—I guess I see why we done commence to get so interested in Africa 'round here. Missionaries, my aunt Jenny!"

There is no doubt about it: Beneatha is now entering her African phase. Finding her wiggling and peering at herself in front of the mirror, Travis wonders if she's cracking up. Suddenly after some more squinting and pulling at her hair, Beneatha picks up her raincoat and heads for the door. "Where you going?" Mama calls out. "To become," says Beneatha, "a Queen of the Nile."

With the ring of the doorbell, the moment they all have been waiting for has arrived. There is general excitement when Travis dashes back with the check. But Mama, thinking of her husband whose insurance this was, feels that if it weren't for all of them, she'd be inclined to give the money away. "Now what kind of talk is that?" says Ruth. "Mr. Younger would be just plain mad if he could hear you talking foolish like that." Agreeing that they have plenty to do with the money, Mama turns her attention to Ruth: angrily she wants to know why Ruth went to see "that woman." Once again, before she can get to the heart of the matter, Walter barges in. Grabbing a look at the check, then frantically drawing some papers from his pocket, he begs for his mother's attention. Instead, Mama urges him to have a private talk with his wife.

WALTER—WILL SOMEBODY PLEASE LISTEN TO ME TODAY!

MAMA (*quietly*)—I don't 'low yellin' in this house, Walter Lee, and you know it—and there ain't going to be no investing in no liquor stores. I don't aim to have to speak on that again.

WALTER—Oh—so you don't aim to have to speak on that again? So you have decided . . . (*Crumpling papers.*) Well, you tell that to my boy tonight when you put him to sleep on the living room couch. . . . Yeah—and tell it to my wife, Mama, tomorrow when she has to go out of here to look after somebody else's kids. And tell it to *me*, Mama, every time we need a new pair of curtains and

I have to watch *you* go out and work in somebody's kitchen. Yeah, you tell me then! . . . All I wanted was to make a future for myself in this world . . . All I wanted . . . was to stand in front of my son someday like my father never got a chance to do for me—and tell him that he will have a chance to be somebody in this world."

Starting to leave the room, Walter brushes aside Ruth's plea to go with him. With quiet authority, Mama asks Walter to talk civilly to his wife, but he lashes out instead. When Ruth goes to the bedroom and slams the door behind her, Mama orders Walter to sit down and listen.

Mama has noticed for some time the wild look in Walter's eye, and she warns him that it is a dangerous thing for a man "to go outside his home to look for peace." His frustrations pouring out of him, Walter says his restlessness has nothing to do with another woman: it comes from a job that's no job at all. It's his "yes-sirring" and "no-sirring" and opening car doors all day. Sometimes the future looms up for him like a blank space full of *nothing*. Listening to her son, Mama asks how he can talk so much about money. "Because it's life, Mama," cries Walter passionately. "Oh," she says quietly. "So now it's life. Money is life. Once upon a time freedom used to be life—now it's money." "No," says Walter, "it was always money, Mama. We just didn't know about it." "No," says Mama, "something has changed. You something new, boy. In my time we was worried about not being lynched and getting to the North if we could and how to stay alive and still have a pinch of dignity too. . . . Now here come you and Beneatha—talkin' 'bout things we ain't never even thought about hardly, me and your daddy. You ain't satisfied or proud of nothing we done. I mean that you had a home; that we kept you out of trouble till you was grown; that you don't have to ride to work on the back of nobody's streetcar. You my children—but how different we done become."

Breaking the upsetting news to Walter about the baby Ruth is expecting, Mama adds something: Ruth is thinking of getting rid of it. "No—no—Ruth wouldn't do that," says Walter. "When the world gets ugly enough," Mama answers, "a woman will do anything for her family . . . *that part that's already living*." As Walter repeats that Ruth would never do that, Ruth comes to the bedroom door. She assures Walter that she not only would do such a thing, but has already made a down payment of five dollars.

Mama is waiting to hear Walter act like his father's son. "Your wife says she going to destroy your child," says Mama, "and I'm waiting to hear you talk like him and say we a people who give children life, not who destroys them. . . ." Walter, however, is incapable of saying anything. Accusing him of being a disgrace to his father's memory, Mama demands her hat: she's going out.

ACT II

Later that day, as Ruth irons, Africa stirs in the room. Having had enough of that "assimilationist junk," Beneatha, dressed in tribal regalia, is on a Nigerian kick.

Weaving back and forth as she listens to a simple Nigerian melody on the phonograph, she makes Ruth jump with her shouts of "OCOMOGOSIAY!" Home, and high from the hot-spots, Walter joins Beneatha. Clenching his fists, he screams: "YEAH . . . AND ETHIOPIA STRETCH FORTH HER HANDS AGAIN!" "Yes," sighs Ruth, "and Africa sure is claiming her own tonight."

With Nigerian drums for accompaniment, and the whole room for a forest, Walter says: "In my heart of hearts, I am much warrior!" Without even looking up from her ironing, Ruth replies: "In your heart of hearts you are much drunkard." With Beneatha encouraging him and joining him in his mighty shouts of "OCOMOGOSIAY!", Walter hunts lion throughout the room, and then from the top of the table, addresses his "black brothers." The only one to hear the doorbell, Ruth opens the door to George Murchison.

BENEATHA—OCOMOGOSIAY!

WALTER—Do you hear the singing of the women, singing the war songs of our fathers to the babies in the great houses . . . singing the sweet war songs—OH, DO YOU HEAR, BLACK BROTHERS!

BENEATHA (*completely gone*)—We hear you, Flaming Spear—

WALTER—Telling us to prepare for the greatness of the time— (*To* GEORGE.) Black Brother—! (*He extends his hand for the fraternal clasp.*)

GEORGE—BLACK Brother, Hell!

Walter, off the table, down to earth, and suddenly sick, races for the bathroom. "He had a little to drink," says Ruth; "I don't know what *her* excuse is." Examining Beneatha, George says: "Look, honey, we're going to theatre, we're not going to be in it . . . so go change, huh?" Instead, Beneatha starts a diatribe against assimilationist Negroes. "Will somebody please tell me," asks Ruth, "what assimila-whoever means?"

GEORGE—Oh, it's just a college girl's way of calling people Uncle Toms—but that isn't what it means at all.

RUTH—Well, what does it mean?

BENEATHA (*cutting* GEORGE *off*)—It means someone who is willing to give up—his own culture—and submerge himself completely in the dominant and in this case—*oppressive* culture!

GEORGE—Oh, dear, dear, dear! Here we go! A lecture on the African past! On our Great West African Heritage! In one second we will hear all about the great Ashanti empires; the great Songhay civilizations; and the great sculpture of Benin—and then some poetry in the Bantu—and the whole monologue will end with the word *heritage!* . . . Let's face it, baby, your heritage is nothing but a bunch of raggedyassed spirituals and some grass huts!

Beneatha's outraged rebuttal can be heard only from behind the bedroom door where Ruth has finally pushed her.

Determined to show George what the family is really like, Ruth settles him on the couch and engages him with hostesslike clichés. Walter, coming back into the room, brings his own ideas of entertainment. Circling around George, he examines him from head to toe: "Why," asks Walter, "all you college boys wear them faggoty-looking white shoes?" George ignores this; Ruth apologizes. Foraging in the icebox, Walter finds himself a can of beer. Then, beer in hand, straddling a chair so that he is almost nose to nose with George, Walter launches into big-business advice that George should pass on to his rich father. Brushed aside over this, an offended Walter directs his next remarks against busy little college boys. At last, with considerable distaste, George says that Walter is all whacked up with bitterness. Saying that he is a volcano, a giant surrounded by ants, Walter cries nobody is with him—not even his mother.

Changed into clothes of twentieth-century Chicago, Beneatha goes off to the theatre with George, while Ruth tries to get Walter to sit down and talk to her. Saying he only can talk to people who care about the things he has on his mind, he won't listen to her. "I guess," says Ruth wearily, "that means people like Willy Harris." Walter agrees. "Why don't y'all just hurry up and go into the banking business and stop talking about it?" cries Ruth.

WALTER—Why? You want to know why? 'Cause we all tied up in a race of people that don't know how to do nothing but moan, pray and have babies!

Ruth—Oh, Walter . . . Honey, why can't you stop fighting me?
Walter—Who's fighting you? Who even cares about you—?

When Mama arrives home, out of breath from climbing stairs, Walter shouts: Where has she been all day! Taking her time, Mama slowly breaks the news that she has bought a house. Walter explodes, but Ruth is suddenly radiant. "Praise God!" she says repeatedly. Mama says they'll be moving the first of the month.

Not wanting to make the house sound fancier than it is, Mama says that it is made good and solid, and has a room for Travis and the new baby, and a yard in back. The address is 406 Clybourne Street, Clybourne Park. "Clybourne Park?" cries Ruth. "Mama, there ain't no colored people living in Clybourne Park." "So," exclaims Walter, "that's the peace and comfort you went out and bought for us today!" "Son—I just tried to find the nicest place for the least amount of money for my family," answers Mama.

With her need to get away from this rat-trap, Ruth is rather cheerfully prepared to take the mixture of good and trouble ahead. When, however, Mama pleads with Walter for his approval, he turns his back on her. "What you need me to say you done right for?" he says. "*You* the head of this family. You run our lives like you want to. It was your money and you did what you wanted with it. So what you need for me to say it was all right for? So you butchered up a dream of mine—you—who always talking 'bout your children's dreams . . ." "Walter Lee—" Mama says, but he closes the door behind him.

Scene II

On a Friday night a few weeks later, Beneatha once again has condescended to have a date with George Murchison, and once again he has got nowhere. He complains that he is mighty tired taking her out only to have to hear her discuss the nature of quiet desperation and to speak her thoughts. "Then, why read books?" snaps Beneatha. "Why go to school?" With assumed patience, George points out: "It's simple. You read books—to learn facts—to get grades—to pass the courses—to get a degree. That's all—it has nothing to do with thoughts!" "Good night, George," she dismisses him. George passes Mama on the way out.

Tired from a day's work and all the stairs, Mama still listens patiently to Beneatha's complaints about *her* evening. Beneatha finds George a fool. Mama says sympathetically: "Well—I guess you better not waste your time with no fools." For this sudden understanding, Beneatha thanks Mama warmly.

But Mama has bigger problems. Walter, who has been on the town for a good three days, is now in danger of losing his job. He has become increasingly unruly and uncommunicative. Knowing drastic action is needed, Mama takes Walter aside.

MAMA—I've helped to do it to you, haven't I, son? Walter, I been wrong.
WALTER—Naw—you ain't never been wrong about nothing, Mama.
MAMA—Listen to me, now. I say I been wrong, son. That I been doing to you what the rest of the world been doing to you. Walter—what you ain't never understood is that I ain't got nothing, don't own nothing, ain't never really wanted nothing that wasn't for you. There ain't nothing as precious to me . . . there ain't nothing worth holding on to, money, dreams, nothing else—if it means—if it means it's going to destroy my boy— (*She puts her papers in front of him, and he watches her without speaking or moving.*) I paid the man thirty-five hundred dollars down on the house. That leaves sixty-five hundred dollars. Monday morning I want you to take this money and take three thousand dollars and put it in a savings account for Beneatha's medical schooling. The rest you put in a checking account—with your name on it. And from now on any penny that come out of it or that go in it is for you to look after. For you to decide. It ain't much, but it's all I got in the world and I'm putting it in your hands. I'm telling you to be the head of this family from now on like you supposed to be.

WALTER—You trust me like that, Mama.
MAMA—I ain't never stop trusting you. Like I ain't never stop loving you. (*She goes out and* WALTER *sits looking at the money. Finally, in a decisive gesture, he gets up, takes the money and goes out in a hurry.*)

SCENE III

A week later—moving day—the temper of the whole family has changed noticeably, but the change in Walter is magical. Gay, young and loving to Ruth as he used to be, Walter sweeps her into a dance.

Watching them burlesque the Warwick social dance of their youth, Beneatha comments: "Talk about—olddd-fashionedddd-Negroes!"

WALTER (*stopping momentarily*)—What kind of Negroes?
BENEATHA—Old-fashioned.

WALTER (*as he dances with* RUTH)—You know when all the professional New Negroes have their convention, *that*—(*Pointing to his sister*)—is going to be the chairman of the committee on unending agitation. (*He goes on dancing; then stops.*) Race, race, race ... Girl, I do believe you are the first person in the history of the entire human race to successfully brainwash your own self. (BENEATHA *breaks up and he goes on dancing. He stops again.*)—Damn, even the N DOUBLE A C P takes a holiday ... I can just see that chick some day looking down at some poor cat on an operating table before she starts to slice him, saying ... Now what did you say your views on Civil Rights were ... ?

The doorbell, revealing a middle-aged white visitor, stops the dancing and joking. Invited to come in and to put down his brief case and hat, he introduces himself as Karl Lindner from the Clybourne Park Improvement Association.

Refusing coffee or a drink, Lindner in his gentle, labored, roundabout way, gets down to business. As he describes his Association as a kind of Welcoming Committee, Beneatha is several skeptical steps ahead of him, and of the rest of her family. However, when Lindner says that his organization deplores the incidents that have happened elsewhere in the city when colored people have moved into white neighborhoods and that his group feels that most of the trouble in this world comes from people failing to sit down and talk to each other, Ruth is pleased, and Beneatha and Walter suddenly show genuine interest. This lasts only briefly. What Mr. Lindner really has to say boils down to a hard offer to buy back their house at a financial gain to the Youngers. Telling Lindner off, Walter asks him to leave. In the face of all this hostility Lindner, reaching for his brief case, says: "I don't understand why you people are reacting this way. What do you think you are going to gain by moving into a neighborhood where you aren't wanted and where some elements—well—people can get awful worked up when they feel that their whole way of life and everything they've ever worked for is threatened?" Trying to slip his card to Walter, Lindner beats a hasty retreat.

When Mama comes in with Travis, she is greeted with devilish glee. They tell her about the Clybourne Park Welcoming Committee that just can't wait to see her face.

BENEATHA (*taking card from table, hands it to* MAMA)—In case.
MAMA (*throws it on the floor*)—Father give us strength. Did he threaten us?

BENEATHA—Oh—Mama—they don't do it like that. He talked Brotherhood. He said everybody ought to learn how to sit down and hate each other with good Christian fellowship.

MAMA (*sadly*)—Lord protect us . . .

RUTH—You should hear the money those folks raised to buy the house from us. All we paid and then some.

BENEATHA—What they think we going to do—eat 'em?

RUTH—No, honey, marry 'em.

MAMA—Lord, Lord, Lord . . .

RUTH—Well, that's the way the crackers crumble. Joke.

BENEATHA—Mama, what are you doing?

MAMA—Fixing my plant so it won't get hurt none on the way . . .

BENEATHA—Mama, you going to take *that* to the new house?

MAMA—Uh huh—

BENEATHA—That raggedy-looking old thing?

MAMA (*stopping and looking at her*)—It expresses *me*.

A love feast is brewing. Everyone apparently has chipped in for a surprise for Mama. With enormous affection, Walter presents her with a house gift: gardening tools for their own Mrs. Miniver. The joy from this has hardly died down, when Travis presents his own gift. Travis's idea was to give his grandmother a huge, startlingly elaborate gardening hat. The grown-ups, except Mama, collapse with laughter. "I'm sorry, Mama," chortles Walter, "you look like you ready to go out and chop cotton sure enough!" But hugging Travis, Mama says it's the prettiest hat she ever owned.

Another visitor ends all joy in the house. Breaking the calamitous news that Willy Harris has absconded with the money Walter invested in the liquor store, he takes his sad leave.

Left to the agonized confession that he has squandered every cent entrusted to his care, including that for Beneatha's medical schooling, Walter faces the horror of the family, and the biblical wrath of his mother.

ACT III

An hour later, choosing to pay a cheery call on Beneatha, Asagai is puzzled at her deep gloom. Explaining that Walter had thrown all their insurance money away by investing it with a man whom even Travis wouldn't have trusted, Beneatha confesses to feeling like a cipher . . . a nothing. She had always wanted to be a doctor to cure and mend people. In her present state, she no longer cares.

A realistic man who can face the dangerous facts of his own

A RAISIN IN THE SUN

revolutionary future, Asagai refuses to consider Walter's deed anything more than childish and stupid. He refuses, moreover, to condone Beneatha's defeatist attitude. Proposing that she stop moaning and groaning and come home to Africa with him, Asagai seals his proposal with a long, passionate embrace. Now all mixed up, Beneatha begs for time to think. "All right," says Asagai, "I shall leave you. . . . Just sit a while and think. Never be afraid to sit a while and think. How often I have looked at you and said, 'Ah—so this is what the New World hath finally wrought . . .'"

Sitting alone, Beneatha sees Walter enter from his bedroom. As he starts rummaging through things on the bureau, she hisses at him: "Yes—just look at what the New World hath wrought! . . . Just look! There he is! *Monsieur le petit bourgeois noir*—himself! There he is—Symbol of a Rising Class! Entrepreneur! Titan of the system!" Ignoring Beneatha, searching frantically for something, Walter comes up with the card he was looking for and slams out of the house.

Walter's banging causes Ruth to worry what he will do next. Mama, vague and lost, tries to pull herself and her family together. She suggests that they start unpacking and call the moving men not to come. Begging desperately that Mama not give up the house, Ruth promises to work twenty hours a day if necessary, in all the kitchens of Chicago. But Mama says that she sees things differently now: "Sometimes you just got to know when to give up some things . . . and hold on to what you got."

All attention is riveted on Walter the minute he steps in the door. He's back, he says, from making a call to the *Man* . . . "Like the guys in the streets say—The Man. Captain Boss—Mistuh Charley . . . Old Captain Please—Mr. Bossman . . ." "Lindner!" realizes Beneatha. Answering sharply that she's right, Walter reports that Lindner is coming over to do business with them. Walter has it all figured out: Life is divided between the takers and the tooken; and Walter is grateful to Willy Harris for teaching him. "What did you call that man for, Walter Lee?" demands Ruth.

WALTER—Called him to tell him to come on over to the show. Gone to put on a show for the man. Just what he wants to see. You see, Mama: the man came before today and he told us that them people out there where you want us to move—well, they so upset they willing to pay us not to move out there. (*He laughs again.*) And—and, oh, Mama—you would of been proud of the way me and Ruth and Bennie acted. We told him to get out . . .

Lord have mercy! We told the man to get out. Oh, we was some proud folks this afternoon, yeah. (*He lights a cigarette.*) We were still full of that old-time stuff . . .

RUTH—You talking 'bout taking them people's money to keep us from moving in that house?

WALTER—I ain't just talking 'bout it, Baby—I'm telling you that's what's going to happen.

BENEATHA—Oh God! Where is the bottom!

WALTER—See—that's the old stuff. You and that boy that was here today. You all want everybody to carry a flag and a spear and sing some marching songs, huh? You wanna spend your life looking into things and trying to find the right and the wrong part, huh? Yeah. You know what's going to happen to that boy some day—he'll find himself sitting in a dungeon, locked in forever—and the takers will have the key! Forget it, baby! There ain't no causes—there ain't nothing but taking in this world and he who takes most is smartest—and it don't make a damn bit of difference *how*.

MAMA—You making something inside me cry, son. Some awful pain inside me.

WALTER—Don't cry, Mama. Understand. That white man is going to walk in that door able to write checks for more money than we ever had. It's important to him and I'm going to help him . . . I'm going to put on the show, Mama.

MAMA—Son—I come from five generations of people who was slaves and sharecroppers—but ain't nobody in my family never let nobody pay 'em no money that was a way of telling us we wasn't fit to walk the earth. We ain't never been that poor. (*Raising her eyes and looking at him.*) We ain't never been that dead inside.

BENEATHA—Well, we are dead now. All the talk about dreams and sunlight that goes on in this house. All dead.

Preparing to put on an Uncle Tom show for Lindner, Walter, under the eyes of his horrified family, demonstrates that he's even ready to play it on his knees. . . . "Yassuh! Great White Father," concludes Walter, "just gi' ussen de money fo' God's sake and we's ain't gwine come out de and dirty up you' white folks neighborhood . . ." He goes into the bedroom. "That is not a man," snarls Beneatha, "that is nothing but a toothless rat."

Turning on Beneatha, Mama asks her if she's feeling as if she were better than Walter today. "Yeah. What you tell him a minute ago? That he wasn't a man. Yeah? You give him up for me?

You done wrote his epitaph too—like the rest of the world? Who give you that privilege?"

BENEATHA—Will you be on my side for once? You saw what he just did, Mama! You saw him—down on his knees. Wasn't it you who taught me to despise any man who would do that. Do what he's going to do.

But, says Mama, she and her daddy also taught Beneatha to love him. For Beneatha, there's nothing left to love. Mama assures her that there is always something left to love and if she hasn't learnt that she hasn't learnt anything. "It's when he's at his lowest and can't believe in hisself cause the world done whipped him so. When you starts measuring somebody—measure him right, child. . . ."

The moving men draw up downstairs just as Lindner arrives at the apartment door. Ruth wants Travis out of hearing, but Mama insists that he stay right here. "And," Mama directs Walter, "you make him understand what you doing. You teach him good. Like Willy Harris taught you. You show where our five generations done come to. Go ahead, son."

As Travis grins up at his father, Walter throws his arm about Travis's shoulder.

Lindner was delighted to have heard from Walter. Coming prepared with all the necessary papers and pens, he becomes increasingly confused by Walter's speech. Gropingly, hesitatingly, looking at his shoes rather than at Lindner, Walter says that he and his family are plain people. He himself has worked as a chauffeur, while his wife and mother have done domestic work in people's kitchens. Walter recalls slowly that his father, who was a laborer most of his life, once almost beat a man to death because this man called him a bad name or something. Then suddenly straightening up, Walter says firmly: "Well, what I mean is that we come from people who had a lot of pride. I mean—we are very proud people. And that's my sister over there and she's going to be a doctor—and we are very proud—

LINDNER—Well, I am sure that is very nice, but—

WALTER—What I am telling you is that we called you over here to tell you that we are very proud and that this is—this is my son who makes the sixth generation of our family in this country and that we have all thought about your offer and we have decided to move into our house because my father earned it for us. We don't want to make no trouble for nobody or fight no causes—but we will try to be good neighbors. That's all we got to say. (*He looks the man in the eyes.*) We don't want your money.

LINDNER—I take it then that you have decided to occupy.

BENEATHA—That's what the man said.

LINDNER (*to* MAMA *in her reverie*)—Then I would like to appeal to you, Mrs. Younger. You are older and wiser and understand things better, I am sure. . . .

MAMA (*rising*)—I am afraid you don't understand. My son said we was going to move and there ain't nothing left for me to say. (*Shaking her head.*) You know how these young folks is nowadays, mister. Can't do a thing with 'em. Goodbye.

Picking up his papers, hoping they know what they are doing, Lindner departs. And as he leaves, life returns to the family and with it excitement and activity. "Well, for God's sake," cries Ruth, "LET'S GET THE HELL OUT OF HERE!"

Taking over, Mama orders Ruth to put Travis's good jacket on him, and Walter to fix his tie and shirt.

As Mama gives further orders to the moving men, Beneatha chooses this hectic complicated moment to tell of Asagai's proposal. Mama gives a distracted "Yes, baby." But as they carry their belongings out into the hall, Walter starts in on Beneatha for such silly ideas. He advises her to think of a man with loot, and over Beneatha's angry yells he further advises her to think of George Murchison. Beneatha shouts back that George Murchison can fly a kite.

Fixing her hat and stalling a bit, Mama says quietly to Ruth: "He finally come to manhood today, didn't he? Kind of like a rainbow after the rain—" Bursting with pride, Ruth agrees. Waving Ruth ahead of her, Mama says she'll be down directly. And then, alone for a final look at the home she shared with Big Walter, Mama stifles a cry. Heading for the door, Mama remembers her plant, grabs it, and departs.

KATAKI

("The Enemy")

A Play in Two Acts

BY SHIMON WINCELBERG

[SHIMON WINCELBERG *was born in Germany 34 years ago and came to the United States, as a refugee from the Nazis, at the age of 14. He did combat intelligence in World War II, and his interest in the Japanese began through his teaching Japanese citizens about America. His professional career has included the writing of short stories and articles for a number of magazines along with work in the movies and television. In this last field he wrote "The Sea Is Boiling Hot," which became the basis for "Kataki." In collaboration with his wife he has recently finished a novel, "The Anxious Seat."*]

For the cast listing, see page 332.

AN almost solid mass of jungle rims the beach of a volcanic Central Pacific Island. There, in the tropical dawn, an eighteen-year-old American soldier lies enmeshed in the shroud lines of his parachute. Waking slowly, he finds the enemy standing over him.

Terror making his words almost inaudible, the boy says it wouldn't do any good to torture him. With a knife at the American's throat, the Japanese—whose name is Kimura—issues an explosive command. The American tries to get to his feet, but only manages as far as his knees. He offers his name, rank, serial number, all that he's permitted to tell. Fumbling for his dogtags, he shows them to the Japanese, who tears them off, glances at them and tosses them indifferently into the sand.

"Look, I—I didn't come to fight with you people," says Alvin, the young American. "I'm in the *Air* Corps." He points to the sky. "I'm just here by accident . . . from a plane . . . bomber . . . it was burning, I *had* to get *out*. . . ."

"Kataki": By Shimon Wincelberg. Copyright © 1959 by Shimon Wincelberg. Included by permission of the author. Stock and amateur rights controlled by the author: c/o Paul Kohner, Inc., 9169 Sunset Boulevard, Hollywood 46, Calif.; and c/o Jay Garon-Brooke Associates, Inc., 224 East 33rd Street, New York 16, N. Y.

Ordering him to open his mouth, threatening him with his knife when he doesn't immediately obey, the Japanese yanks his jaws apart. Terrified anew when the Japanese shuts his mouth, Alvin mutters: "Sure, you guys'd kill a man for the gold in his teeth." Giving another sergeant-like shout, the Japanese indicates Alvin's survival kit. Offered it, he knocks it out of the American's hand and studies the contents on the ground at his leisure. Pocketing such recognizable items as cigarettes and chewing gum, he rejects the waterproof-wrapped articles, not knowing what they are. Picking up a signaling mirror, Kimura looks at himself, then throws it back into the sand. He picks up a whistle which he also throws away. In the meantime Alvin has been getting out of his parachute harness. When Kimura notices the wrist watch on his arm and demands it, Alvin instinctively tries to keep it. After a stinging slap in the face, he yields this, too. As the Japanese slips it coolly onto his own arm, it is obvious that he considers Alvin just a corpse.

"*Tewo agero!*" barks the Japanese, demonstrating that this is an order to rise, put up one's hands and turn around. Nervously disclaiming any desire to fight this war all by himself, the American asserts that it's all right by him if he's taken prisoner. He's not even above mentioning his youth and the fact that he's just out of high school. "*Nani o itterunda?*" says Kimura, ignoring what he calls chatter. "Sure, *you* people think it's a disgrace to be a prisoner . . ." says Alvin. "Sooner blow yourself up, so long as you can take a couple of us with you. Treacherous bastards." This last is in a low tone. With a shout and a backhand blow, Kimura reminds him to keep his arms up.

While Alvin wonders where the rest of the Japanese are, Kimura goes through his loot. He plays Alvin's harmonica for a moment, then returns it. Relaxing with a cigarette that he has carefully divided in half, Kimura says: "American shigaretto." He smokes with unaccustomed pleasure.

Under Kimura's watchful eye Alvin collects the scattered contents of his survival kit. Then taking a long, awed look at the endless ocean, he asks the Japanese with gestures if he saw his plane crash. Though Kimura gives a negative shake of his head, it is not clear whether he has understood. Alvin bitterly considers the possibility that the plane got back safe, while he, like the first rat off a sinking ship, felt compelled to jump.

Conscious of the deep silence that envelops them, the American suddenly knows that he and the Japanese are all alone. Observing Kimura's primitive hut partly hidden from the beach, Alvin rather rudely goes and examines it, then turns around with a grin of understanding. With more gestures, Alvin tries to find out how long he's been here and how he got here—whether by plane or by troopship. "Torpedoed?"

KIMURA *nods, then tells, with gestures, how his troopship was sunk by an American submarine, and how he and another soldier swam and swam until they managed to reach this island.*
ALVIN—Guess you were lucky the sharks didn't get you, huh?
KIMURA *points to a large stone near the edge of the jungle with some crude markings on it in Japanese.* ALVIN *goes over and examines it with a mixture of curiosity and shock.*
ALVIN—Was that . . . your buddy? (*Worriedly.*) What happened? He get sick? Or 'd you have a fight?
KIMURA *relates, with gestures, how he and the other soldier quarreled over the matter of hoisting a rescue-signal in these American-controlled waters. How he tried to knock such disgraceful thoughts out of the other soldier's head. And how the other man, in despair, at last committed suicide. All of which fills* ALVIN *with visible dread. He darts a glance of raw suspicion and fear at* KIMURA, *who is staring impassively at the grave.*
ALVIN—He killed *himself?* Why the hell should anybody want to do that? You sure you didn't . . . help him a little? Guess nobody'll ever know, huh? You could bury me like that, and nobody'd ever know. (*Softly.*) What a way to wind up. A head full of sand, and nobody'd ever find your grave—except the ants. (*Low, to himself; with a frightened, sideward glance.*) Get as much mercy from a wild animal . . . (*A new thought.*) How come you didn't kill me before? (*His tone is not provocative; it is sincerely puzzled.*) Don't tell me you guys wouldn't kill a man in cold blood. In a pig's eye you wouldn't. What about in the Philippines? What you did to prisoners, to women and children? The Army even made a movie out of it, to show us why we're fighting this war. . . . Little bitty Chinese kids, sittin' on the ground, crying, because their folks were killed in a bombing. Don't you people have any human feelings, for chrissakes? (*Getting no responses, he settles upon another grievance; in an undertone.*) Three *times* they made us sit through that goddamn picture.

Reminded again that he is an American soldier, Alvin moves his hand automatically to his empty holster and demands to know if the Japanese has his .45. *"Pisutoru?"* answers Kimura, pantomiming the firing of a pistol. Looking all around on the ground, Kimura shows that he has no idea where it is. Realizing that he's lost government property, Alvin excuses himself to himself: "How the hell're you supposed to remember everything, when half the plane's burning away?" Then after angrily slapping his holster, he reconsiders: "Well . . . maybe it's just as well, huh? I can't shoot you, you can't shoot me, huh?"

Having just been told why Kimura's friend died, Alvin thoughtlessly tears a strip from his parachute and starts climbing a tree to plant a rescue flag. *"Yose! Bakana koto o suruna!"* yells Kimura and snatches the flag from Alvin's hand. Arguing that he was only putting the flag up for himself, Alvin says that no one's forcing the Japanese to go home. The knife once more at his throat, Alvin says: "You don't want them nasty Americans to find us, that it? Sure . . . they might send you home alive after the war. That'd be terrible. Your own family'd bounce you out on your ear, because you didn't die for the Emperor. Boy, if there's one thing I don't understand, it's a fanatic. Well, my folks wouldn't kick *me* out, you bet. They wouldn't care what the hell I did, just so long's I get home alive. . . ." *"Nani o itterunda?"* says Kimura. With new-found aggressiveness, Alvin tells the uncomprehending Japanese what a shifty-looking, typically treacherous member of his race he is. Full of braggadocio, he swears that this Jap will have no chance to pull a Pearl Harbor on him. But his pugnaciousness gives way to hunger.

ALVIN—Dammit, *I'm* hungry. . . . You got anything to eat? (*He stares at the jungle with sudden interest.*) What do you *live* on? (*A wry grin.*) You gotta feed your prisoner or you'll get in trouble with the Red Cross. (*Mock serious.*) You get in wrong with the Red Cross, boy, you'll know what trouble *is*. No more stationery, no more Hershey bars, no more brushless shave cream. (*Abruptly.*) Food! Uh . . . *Tabemono?*

KIMURA (*nodding*)—*Ah . . . Tabemono . . . Haraga hetteru noka?* ("Ah . . . Food . . . You are hungry?") *He pantomimes a growling stomach.* ALVIN *nods gratefully.* KIMURA *reaches into his smoking stone hearth, brings out a hot yamlike vegetable and throws it at* ALVIN's *feet. Then, as though disdainful of* ALVIN's *ability to do any harm, he momentarily turns his back. It takes* ALVIN *only a second to decide. His hand darts out for the knife in* KIMURA's *belt. But the Japanese is on his guard. A judo-grip flings* ALVIN *spectacularly to the ground, where he lies shaken and panting.*)

When Kimura, instead of knifing him, gives him a contemptuous kick, Alvin can hardly believe that he's been spared. But he quickly grabs the vegetable and wolfs it down. Then he says shamefacedly:

KATAKI 259

Ben Piazza and Sessue Hayakawa in "Kataki"

"Well, you can't blame a man for trying. . . . Don't tell me you wouldn't have done the same thing. . . ."

Having had the man's food, Alvin at least has the grace to thank him for sparing his life. Extending his hand with the hope that there are no hard feelings, he is aggrieved when the Japanese coldly ignores it. Shrugging the matter off, Alvin strolls away. At the

Japanese's repeated warning, *"Bakana koto o suruna!"* Alvin merely cracks: "Well, I'm not so crazy about *you,* either." They stare at each other with intense hostility.

Scene II

That afternoon, in the stunning heat, Kimura lies motionless in his hut while Alvin busies himself building some kind of shelter out of his parachute. Then discovering the signaling mirror, Alvin tries to pull a fast one on the supposedly sleeping figure. Pretending to go for a swim, he goes down to the edge of the ocean to flash signals. Caught once more and forced to hand over the mirror, Alvin is bitter. Watching Kimura fling it into the water, he cries: "Now that was smart! What are you afraid of, for chrissakes? What do you think the Americans'd do to you—make you take a bath? . . . Sure, you'll lose your 'honor.' Big deal. I'll give you some of mine. . . . No charge. . . . Always more where that came from. You know, if we didn't have honor and spoons, we'd have to eat soup with our hands . . . You know that? You didn't know that? . . . I'll tell you one thing. You'll be treated a lot better than what you guys did to your prisoners. What about Bataan—that Death March? I'll bet you never *heard* of *that.*" About to turn away, he is halted by a fresh grievance: "How'm I gonna shave now?"

Trying to seem as casual and friendly as possible, the American approaches Kimura's hut. Showing him some berries that he's picked, he says: "Wish I remembered what they told us . . . if the birds don't eat 'em . . . that means they're good or they're poison?" Displaying the berries with a hand-to-mouth gesture, he asks for the Japanese's help. After a moment's hesitation, the Japanese shakes his head sharply and orders: *"Ikan."* He gestures for Alvin to throw them away.

ALVIN—I don't get it. Just now. That was about the third chance you had to get rid of me. Now let's get organized . . . I mean, if you want to make peace, it's okay with *me.* I'm not hard to get along with. (*Shrugs.*) Ask anybody. (*He ducks his head, is about to enter the hut, when the Japanese, with a sharp exclamation, points to his shoes.*)

KIMURA—*Oi, oi!* (ALVIN *stops, takes them off, good-naturedly shaking his head.*)

ALVIN—Pretty fancy, aren't we? You and my girl friend's mother —you would have made a perfect pair. Dust covers on all the furniture. "Alvin, dear, if I have to tell you one more time not to put your feet on the couch . . ." She don't care what I do with her daughter, as long as I don't hurt the stinking furniture. (*Shoeless, he enters, squats down, looks about admiringly at the neatness of walls, roof, floor-mat, all woven out of coconut leaves.*) They don't have furniture in your country, do they? What do you do when you have company—eat off the floor?

KIMURA *keeps one hand cautiously over the knife in his sash.*

ALVIN—You make all this yourself? (*Amused.*) They taught us all that crap too. You know, how to live off the jungle, in ten easy lessons. . . . At survival training, at Hickam Field. (*Shrugs, smiling.*) I probably slept through half of them. . . . I mean, you never really expected to use it, so why look on the dark side? There's enough gloom in the world, my Dad used to say. (*A sudden grin.*) About the only thing that sunk in was to keep away from these native broads, because half of them are probably all syphed up, and if their brother catches you, you might have to marry them, in case you don't have enough trouble.

Kimura offers Alvin a halved coconut filled with some kind of mush. Pleased, thanking him, Alvin accepts the bowl but hesitates how to proceed. Handed a pair of chopsticks, he uses them clumsily but manages to get most of the food in his mouth. Alvin says that whatever it is he is eating is pretty good stuff, but then he'll eat anything. Having a Mom who is the world's worst cook, he is "one G.I. who isn't fighting this war for Mom's Apple Pie."

Pointing at himself, the Japanese says suddenly: *"Kimura!"* After he impatiently stabs a finger at his chest and repeats *"Kimura!"* Alvin understands. Pointing at his name stenciled on his shirt, Alvin says: "You know my name? You can call me Alvin. I don't care, everybody else does . . . Al-vin."

With extreme awkwardness they shake hands. His eyes falling on a bamboo-framed photograph of a woman, Kimura withdraws not only his hand but himself.

ALVIN—That your wife? Probably your wife, huh? She looks too old to be a girl friend. . . . That thing she's wearing . . . that what they call a kimona?

KIMURA *politely corrects his pronunciation.*

ALVIN—I promised my girl—uh, this girl I . . . used to go around with, back home—I promised I'd send her one from Tokyo—(*wryly*)—if I lived that long. (*With a sudden shock, he slaps himself on the forehead, and even the Japanese looks startled.*) Holy smokes! You know what I am? I'm "Missing in Action." . . . Wait'll she gets the news . . . Betty Jean will have a fit. She'll lie down in the middle of Main Street and have *kittens*. (*Now the dam has burst.*) It'll be a miracle if she's still waiting when I get home . . . *if* I get home. (*Bitterly.*) She'll have ten kids by the time I get home. . . . Hell, why should she wait for me? What *I* ever do for her? Take her to movies in Dad's car . . . buy her a soda . . . then, you know, go park some place and . . . (*his face and voice suddenly soften.*) She'd say, "Please, Alvin. Don't make me feel cheap." I could have *married* her. She was *willing!* Boy, was she *willing!* You know I was a pretty popular kid, back in Michigan. . . . Hell, it was *her* idea, more than mine. (*Shakes his head; his expression softens; he sighs.*) I was a sucker . . . I should have married her when I had the chance. At least I'd have—something to remember. . . . (*A sudden thought; fiercely.*) If we were married, she'd be my *wife,* she'd *have* to wait for me. (*He glances at the picture.*) What about *your* wife? How do you know what she's doing right now? If you let us be rescued, at least you could write to her. . . . You know . . . through the Red Cross. At least you could tell her you're still alive. (*A comradely grin.*) You could tell her she better start behavin', or you'll take a stick to her when you get home.

KIMURA, *with a grave expression, points at the photo, joins his hands to form a roof over his head.*

ALVIN—Go ahead, I used to be *good* at charades.

KIMURA, *with sound and gesture, now tells of a bomber which flew over, dropped a bomb, destroyed the house, killed the wife. It is clear that he is deeply shaken by the recital, yet his cheeks and teeth retain definite traces of a polite smile, in shocking contrast to his pained moist eyes.*

ALVIN—Gee . . . I'm sorry . . . I didn't know. A bomb fell on the house she was in?

Moved and sympathetic though he is, Alvin can't help commenting angrily on Kimura's smile. "Are you nuts or something?" he says. Putting down the coconut shell, he rises and is about to leave when he sees that Kimura, glaring, holds one hand tensely over the grip of the knife. Then bursting forth in a torrent of bitterness, Kimura seems to be directly accusing Alvin. Unnerved, Alvin watches and listens. Glaring at Alvin, Kimura orders him sharply to get out. Alvin tries to be conciliatory and reasonable and to convince Kimura that he has yet to kill a person. "Hell, *this* was only my second mission . . . I never even got to fire my gun." Another outburst from Kimura causes him to yell: "Well, what about all the people *you* killed? Probably women, too. What about *them?*" As the Japanese is still in the grip of a hard internal struggle, Alvin says lamely: "Well, thanks for the chow."

Sitting down outside to put on his shoes, Alvin is really bewildered. "I thought he wanted to be *friendly.* . . . I was willing . . . Nobody can say I didn't try to meet him halfway." But picking up a jagged rock that catches his eye, he decides: "Last time I'll ever trust a Jap." As Kimura suddenly looks in his direction, Alvin hides the rock behind him.

Scene III

That night, having long tried to remain awake, Alvin drops off to sleep. He is immediately awakened by the sound of Kimura's primitive flute approaching from the beach. Feeling menaced, Alvin says: "Sure . . . wait'll I'm fast asleep . . . then—" He draws a finger across his throat, with the appropriate sound.

Ducking around a tree, his arms raised to strike, he appears behind Kimura. The flute's sound deterring him, he lets Kimura escape unharmed.

When Kimura has doused his flickering light and gone to sleep, Alvin stealthily approaches the hut. Standing over Kimura's mat, he bangs the rock down, only to discover to his horror that Kimura is watching him from a distance.

With deadly determination, and with this time no nonsense, Kimura raises his knife. Dropping the rock, giving an animallike cry, Alvin leaps out of reach and plunges into the jungle. Kimura goes after him. They tear and claw their way through the thick, midnight overgrowth, giving out shouts of rage, pain and exhaustion. At one point Kimura corners Alvin, but Alvin manages to clutch Kimura's knife-arm. In this nightmarish struggle, Kimura's leg is badly cut. Alvin, escaping, plunges on, only to find himself caught in a swamp. Sinking, holding out his hand, he cries for help. Kimura simply stands by, watching him. Pleading, Alvin tries to justify himself. Then just as suddenly, he becomes resigned to death. He withdraws his hand and says: "Guess I . . . ought to beg your forgiveness . . . even if you don't know . . . a word I'm talking about." Ready to die, Alvin mumbles: "The Lord is my shepherd, I shall not want. . . ." When he reaches "Thou preparest a table for me in the face of my enemies—" he has difficulty remembering the rest. Kimura at this point offers him his hand.

"Saa, tsukamare . . . mo ii yamero you!" Turning his head, it takes Alvin a moment to realize Kimura wants to save him. ". . . in the face of my enemy," Alvin repeats softly.

Pulled free, he sinks exhausted to his knees. Then forcing himself to look up at the Japanese, he quickly lowers his head and covers his face with his hands.

Scene IV

At sunrise, it is Kimura's turn to need help. His lower leg, gashed the night before, is already infected. Stoically enduring the pain, he takes ashes from his cigarette and rubs them into the ugly wound. He prays before the ceremonial shelf in his hut. He accepts food from Alvin's hands. But finally, giving in to the pain, he points to his leg and asks Alvin if he can't do something about it.

Immediately concerned, and shamefaced for being the cause of it, Alvin examines the wound. He tries to take Kimura's mind off it; he wishes someone would come and pick them up. "Don't you wish somebody'd come and pick us up?" he asks. Starting to take off his T-shirt, and pointing at the top of the palm tree, he offers to put it up—*if* Kimura wishes it. "It's up to you," he says. "I wouldn't do it if you don't want me to. . . . Heck, you saved my life last night— I'm not gonna cross you up." Kimura refuses firmly. He wants no signal flag. "Okay, buddy," sighs Alvin, "if that's what you want. . . . It's your funeral. . . ." Slipping the shirt back on, looking out over the ocean, he figures: "Guess there ain't a doctor within a thousand miles."

ALVIN—Hurts, huh? Only you guys're not supposed to let on. . . . That's the old "Bushido," huh?

KIMURA *reacts to the familiar word.* ALVIN *sagely nods, reaches for a much-folded clipping in his wallet.*

ALVIN—My kid brother sent me this clipping from a magazine article. "What Makes Your Enemy Tick?" (*Grins.*) He's kind of concerned about me, ever since he read that the American soldier doesn't know what the hell he's fighting for, except souvenirs. (*Sardonically.*) He's only twelve, but he's *fascinated* by the war. Follows it like it was the National League. All the names, dates, batting averages . . . He's a real fan. (*Amused.*) If he ever fell into enemy hands, we'd all have to quit. . . . (*Unfolds clipping.*) Here. . . . Like this is the "Bushido" attitude, supposed to be, when you're fighting with swords:

"I let you cut my skin.
But I cut your flesh.
I let you cut my flesh.
But I cut your bone."

Rough! . . . See, that's why I thought I'd better get *you,* I mean, before you got *me.*

KIMURA *gets up, limps over to his hut.* ALVIN *tries to help him.* KIMURA *shakes off his hand.*

ALVIN (*with simple, sincere interest*)—How come you people're always so fanatical? Is that part of your religion? I don't want to criticize anybody's *religion,* but . . .

KIMURA *moans with pain.*

ALVIN (*concerned*)—Want me to try and do something? Maybe heat the knife and sterilize the wound? (*A little sad.*) But you wouldn't trust me with that knife, would you? Well, I can't exactly say I blame you. . . .

Alvin doesn't know what to do. Romantic South Sea Islands and Dorothy Lamour are fine until you get a toothache. When Kimura arches in a spasm of pain, Alvin finally says: "Look, I've got something to put on there. But suppose I need it for myself later on? I mean I'd share it with you but it's only enough for one." Nevertheless he runs to his kit and returns with his matches and little white envelope.

Having read the instructions, he squeamishly sets about uncovering the wound. He washes it with water he finds in a bowl, then putting aside his wet handkerchief, picks up the envelope and holds it under the other man's face.

"Know what this is?" says Alvin. "Sulfa. Supposed to be a *miracle* drug. This doctor, in one of those mickey-mouse lectures, he said, 'Lose your pants, but don't lose *this.* Because in the tropical climate any little scratch, once you get it infected, boy, with gangrene and all that . . . next thing you know, you're peddling pencils out of a tin cup, with a handcar for legs. . . .' We used to have a veteran like that in our neighborhood, from the other war. . . . Used to scare the living hell out of me, as a kid. I always said if they ever tried to get *me* in the Army, there'd be two guys missing. Me, and the guy who was chasing me. But I guess when you're eighteen you don't really believe *anything* bad can happen to *you.* . . ."

Kimura slowly withdraws his knife from his belt, reverses it and hands it to Alvin. Very businesslike, Alvin wipes the knife against his sleeve, then strikes a match to sterilize the blade. Talking compulsively under Kimura's grim, almost contemptuous gaze, Alvin makes the incision. The pain drives Kimura to talking about it. Watching him tensely, Alvin tries to force himself to understand. "Isn't it silly people talking a million different languages? They don't even get along when they *understand* each other." He pulls the knife out, hastily pours the sulfa powder into the open wound and bandages it. "I guess people just have to fight, they can't help it. . . . Just like when you're kids. One day, deadly enemies. . . . Next day, greatest of pals again. You grow up, and it's still the same. I can't figure it out, can *you?*"

The bandage completed, Alvin slumps forward. Then grinning with relief, he clowns and holds forth his hand for payment. In dead seriousness Kimura slips off Alvin's wrist watch, which Alvin had long ago forgotten, and returns it to him. When Alvin wipes the knife and hands it back to Kimura, the circle is almost completed. Weighing the knife in his hand for a moment, Kimura gives Alvin a searching look, then rises painfully. Plunging the knife into a tree trunk, he challenges Alvin to live up to this act of faith.

ACT II

Two weeks later, Kimura's leg is still causing him considerable discomfort. Deeply concerned, Alvin does what he can to cheer him up, but he is increasingly discouraged about his own situation. With so much time to think, Alvin has grown guilty over his treatment of his girl, Betty Jean.

Showing her picture to Kimura, who is almost comically appreciative of her looks, Alvin waxes maudlin. He says that he's not even fit to touch her picture. He now thinks back to his last Honolulu leave and decides that his going to a brothel was nothing less than wicked. He thinks that maybe that's what he's being punished for. Leaping to his feet, he cries hoarsely: "I tell you, I go crazy just . . . Boy, I can see me six months from now . . . I'll be up in that tree, beating my chest." He suddenly lets out a Tarzan yell that makes the Japanese flinch. "Well," says Alvin, "nobody's gonna take her away from me. Because I *love* her." Abruptly he says he'll get out of here even if he has to kill Kimura. He continues in this vein until he notices the desolate expression on Kimura's face. At once conciliatory, Alvin says: "Oh, it's nothing against you personally. But what the hell's the good of a person if you can't talk to him? . . . I'd just as soon have a dog, or a cat, at least I wouldn't have to have eyes in the back of my head. . . . After all, we're still *enemies,* aren't we? We probably shouldn't even be talkin' to each other like this, sitting here, shooting the breeze, instead of fighting the War. . . . Anybody ever found us, we'd probably *both* get court-martialed for high treason, for goofin' off." He smiles at the thought, but is instantly irritated at the Japanese's lack of response.

ALVIN—Man, you certainly make a concerted effort to hold up *your* end of the conversation. I could write a book about you. I'd just leave all the pages blank. (*A weary sigh.*) Maybe I ought to teach you English . . . or you teach me Japanese . . . or something. Might as well improve our silly minds, as long as we're here. I know a couple of words. *Arigato.* That means "Thank you."

KIMURA, *smiling, corrects his pronunciation.*

ALVIN—*To wo ake-nasai!* Open the door! *Toko suru!* Surrender! (*The unconscious harshness of* ALVIN's *tone is momentarily reflected on the Japanese's face. But he suddenly smiles.*)

KIMURA (*with mock belligerence*)—Dzee Aye, so-rendah! To herr wiz Rozevert! (*It takes* ALVIN *a moment to understand what is being said. Then he breaks into a wry grin.*)

ALVIN—I know some people back home who feel that way. It's really terrible. Some of my dad's own friends, always talking about "Old Moose Jaw" and "The Great White Father." (*Frowns.*) How come they teach you to insult our President? Is that supposed to lower our morale or something? (*He chuckles and* KIMURA *amiably joins in.*)

Alvin really wishes he could talk Japanese so that they could have two-way conversations. By a process of elimination, he finds out that Kimura comes from Kyushu, that he is a moviegoer and an admirer of Gary Cooper. Here Kimura pantomimes firing a six-shooter.

Genuinely puzzled, Alvin says: "You seem to be such nice people and then you go and bomb Pearl Harbor." Recognizing this word, Kimura pantomimes that bombing is a terrible murderous thing no matter who does it.

Alvin now hopes that Kimura is a non-com, or private, because he hates officers like poison—some even worse than the Japs.

Picking up a stick, Alvin starts batting pebbles into the ocean. "Baseboru!" cries Kimura. "What?" says Alvin. "Baseboru," Kimura answers proudly. "Hot dog. Gah dam Yenki . . . (with pantomime) Abraham Rincorn. . . . Okay, Joe." Still laughing, he burlesques an American so devoid of culture that he chews gum in public. "Rousy," crows Kimura.

Continuing in this playful spirit, Alvin and Kimura run through their bags of tricks for each other. That, however, is quickly done. The list of the games that they can play is quickly exhausted too. Again depressed, Alvin turns away. "I want to go home," he says.

Trying to recapture the earlier mood, striking a mock pose of a Samurai, Kimura performs a vaudeville parody of a Kabuki dance. At the end, having made a ceremonial bow, he comes at Alvin with a stick held like a saber, crying: "American you die!" Startled but willing, Alvin joins the fray. Put through some of the paces of "Kendo" swordsmanship, responding happily to Kimura's menacing outcries, Alvin cries: "Okay, now. . . . By the numbers . . . Charge!" At last, laughing and out of breath, they both sink to the ground.

Alvin commends Kimura not only for having a sense of humor, but also for being a good listener. Here he quotes what he learnt in his YMCA course in leadership training. He thinks smugly of the job that's waiting for him in his father's business and of his father, who now appears to him the epitome of righteousness, though to other ears he might suggest an outright fundamentalist. Alvin is all for teaching Kimura a number of things to make him a better Christian, but without a dictionary he finds it impossible.

His anguish and guilt over Betty Jean return.

ALVIN—I should have married her. . . . In fact . . . I *owe* it to her! . . . She's only seventeen. . . . I'm the only fellow she ever went out with. . . . She certainly wasn't exactly . . . *experienced*. . . . I don't even know how it all happened . . . except . . . I guess we were both a little high . . . and the strap of her dress kept slipping, and I kept pretending like I only wanted to fix it. (*A heavy sigh.*) I didn't take care or nothing. I was never so surprised in my life. . . . That was the first time she ever said "I love you." I tried to say it, but I just couldn't. . . . And then she started crying all over the place . . . kept wanting to know if I'd lost all respect for her. . . . What's respect got to do with it, will you tell me? (*Glumly.*) I didn't go home that night. Next thing I knew I was on a Greyhound bus going to Detroit, and when it got light I went into a recruiting office and joined up. . . . (*Shakes his head.*) Boy, girls are crazy! She used to write me twice a day. "Dearest darling." (*Contritely.*) I guess after what happened she was waiting for me to, you know, say that I . . . love her. (*Loud.*) I really wanted to. I still do. But I . . . (*Shrugging.*) I just didn't know how to put it without sounding like a sap. (*Aggrieved.*) Only because of that lousy censorship. I mean, I just didn't like the idea of my stupid lieutenant reading stuff like that. He didn't think too much of me as it was. . . . (*A little choked.*) That's when she practically stopped writing to me. (*Violently.*) By the time I get out of here, there'll be just one letter waiting for me. "Dear John."

Pointing to Alvin's picture of Betty Jean, Kimura says how fortunate he is; pointing to the picture in his hut, he gestures resignedly. Alvin is sympathetic, but at the same time shrugs: "Well, that's the way it goes, huh? I don't want to sound mean, but you know, 'People who live in glass houses . . .'" He pantomimes rocking an infant. "Bambinos?" Nodding, telling of his three children, Kimura speaks particularly about the youngest. He has great difficulty holding back his tears. Alvin realizes how lucky he is that he lives in unbombed America.

Suddenly, far overhead, two planes tangle in a dogfight. Hearing the guns at a great distance, a galvanized Alvin roots them on with everything he's got: "Come on, Yank! Come on, boy, hit him, hit him, hit him! Again. Get that Jap bastard, sonofabitch-bastard! Get him in the guts! Again! Get him! Yo!"

Only when it's over and the American plane is the survivor is Alvin aware of his tactlessness. With a pained look Kimura retires to his hut. Alvin, ashamed, says half-heartedly: "Come on, Kimura. Don't be a sore loser. . . . *Somebody's* gotta lose. . . ."

The sound of the plane grows louder again. Rushing to the water, Alvin—urging Kimura to do the same—waves frantically. Instead Kimura rushes to camouflage Alvin's white tent with green boughs. Alvin yells and begs the pilot to look his way. He starts to light a signal fire, but Kimura quickly stamps it out.

ALVIN (*shouting, with growing rage*)—Don't you want to see your kids again? You lousy rice-eating gook, what kind of a stinking *father* are you? (*He makes a sudden leap for the knife in the tree. And finds himself face to face with* KIMURA. *Each man's hand is within inches of the knife, but neither is willing to make the first move. The plane, this time for good, fades out of the sky.* ALVIN'S *tension suddenly deflates into utter despair.*) Well, you've fixed it now, buddy. . . . We're both gonna die here. . . . Might as well start diggin' our graves, give us something to do. . . . (*His voice breaks.*) First one to die is gonna be the *lucky* one. (*He glances once more, despairingly, at the sky.*)

KIMURA *points, with a well-intentioned cry of warning, at the matches being crushed in* ALVIN'S *trembling fist.* ALVIN, *misunderstanding the warning, flings the lot of them disgustedly at* KIMURA'S *feet.*

ALVIN—All right. All right. . . . I *promised* I wouldn't and I won't. (*He stumbles off in a state of blackest depression.*) All right. . . . (*Yelling.*) ALL RIGHT! (*He throws himself face down on the sand, his shoulders heaving with sobs.*)

KIMURA *approaches him, indecisively extends one hand as though to comfort him. Then seeing it is no use, he sadly withdraws.*

Scene II

Two days have passed in which Alvin has run the gamut from exaggerated hope to bottomless despair. Kimura is calmly planting his rock garden while Alvin, in the pitiless sun, tries to improve on his tent. Slapping away at mosquitoes, he is sure he will get a good case of malaria. "A whole week without atabrine," he says glumly. "I'll bet to the Air Corps I'm officially dead. . . . Boy, that's the U. S. Army Air Corps for you. . . . A man could be dying by inches here, they still wouldn't send up a plane until everybody'd passed latrine inspection." He glares bitterly at the sky. "I'm never gonna see home again. I'm gonna catch some disease here and die like a dog. Or else I'm gonna grow a beard and go off my nut. Just like what's his name . . . that killed the albatross . . . the Ancient Mariner. They put it around his neck and then everybody drops dead, and he slips his trolley and starts hanging around weddings, bothering the guests, prophesying all kinds of bad luck. He was just lucky somebody didn't bust him in the nose."

Alvin bluntly refuses Kimura's invitation to help him with his garden, and out of boredom rather than malice, kicks rocks out of place. Kimura controls his temper, but when Alvin kicks some more he grabs a pointed stick, aims it at Alvin and means business. Alvin stops.

Despairing of ever being found, Alvin thinks passingly of suicide, but as quickly changes the subject. Smiling at Alvin's mention of "Hari-Kari," Kimura seriously pantomimes the entire ritual. Then saying with a grin that he has a much better way, Kimura proceeds to bring a hand grenade out of his hut. Agitated, trying to get as far as possible from this new menace, Alvin puzzles Kimura. Saying that it's nothing to die, Kimura demonstrates how he would hold the grenade against his belly to kill himself. The show over, Kimura returns the grenade to its safe place in his hut, which Alvin carefully notes.

Forcing himself, out of boredom, to hibernate, Alvin goes to sleep. As he sleeps, Kimura gets up and goes to the tree for the knife. After taking a step in Alvin's direction, Kimura turns and goes into the jungle, from which suddenly arises a ghastly cry.

Awakened in a state of terror and finding the hut empty, Alvin calls for Kimura. Apologizing for his behavior, he asks if he should come after him. Discovering that the knife is also missing, Alvin becomes suspicious. Wasting no time, he gets hold of Kimura's hand grenade and hides behind a dune, ready for action.

When Kimura returns, holding a dead monkey in one hand and a bow and arrow in the other, and discovers that Alvin has disappeared, he too is on his guard. Circling around, he holds his primitive bow and arrow taut before him. Only when Alvin rises from behind the dunes does he relax the bowstring.

Disgusted at the sight of the dead monkey, Alvin is suddenly sure that it was killed with his .45. Shown the bow and arrow, he grumbles: "Oh, I know you're sincere and all that. I guess treachery is just second nature to you people." As Kimura cheerfully skins his monkey preparing to cook it, Alvin finds it hard not to be sick. "Why, you're no better than a cannibal!" he cries.

Turning away, he heads aimlessly for the shore. Suddenly he looks up and sees something out at sea. Almost paralyzed with excitement, he glances furtively at Kimura to be sure he is unaware of what is happening.

Going to Kimura, squatting down beside him, Alvin does his best to distract him from looking at the ocean. He puzzles Kimura with his suggestions of a hike toward the mountain or an English lesson.

ALVIN—See if you can say "Peter Piper picked a peck of pickled peppers." Or say "Afflicted by the fickle finger of fate." (*Glumly.*) That's us, boy. (*Sighs.*) See if you can say . . . *"Friend."* (*Pantomimes "hands up."*) "Kimura . . . friend."

KIMURA *violently rejects this.*

ALVIN (*more desperately*)—No. . . . You don't get it. . . . Look . . . Alvin—Kimura—*Friend.* (*He puts out his hand.* KIMURA, *after a moment of hesitation, takes it.*)

KIMURA—Frendu.

ALVIN—Why don't you relax, lie down for a while? You must be exhausted chasing that little monkey. (*Softly.*) Kimura?

KIMURA (*frowns*)—Wan da?

ALVIN—Kimura? Will you try to . . . understand me for a minute? How come you're so afraid of being captured? I mean, your country is going to lose the war anyway. What's the disgrace, if you're losing anyway?

KIMURA *indicates he wishes he could understand.*

ALVIN—Boy, I certainly would give myself up . . . if the situation was hopeless. I'm no hero . . . I just want to live. . . . So do you. You're no different. You just won't admit it. That's all. (KIMURA *makes no response.*) Listen, you don't know how good those P.W.'s have it. You'd be like a guest of Uncle Sam. . . . Movies every week, ice cream on Sunday, turkey for Christmas. . . . Listen, I was at a base once in South Carolina where they had German prisoners. I'm telling you, those Krauts had it better than we did. When you told them to get on the ball, they'd laugh at you. . . . What could you do . . . shoot them? (*He tries to smile, but fails.*) How do we even know the war's still *on?* They might send you right home, to . . . Kyushu.

KIMURA—Kyushu?

ALVIN—That's right. You'd get to see your kids again. Little . . . what's her name? Tommy . . .

KIMURA—Tomiko?

ALVIN—Sure. You want to see her, don't you? Well, all you have to do is . . . (*shyly puts up his hands*) . . . surrender . . . to the Americans?

KIMURA *looks at him, shocked, then violently shakes his head, tells him no, absolutely not.*

ALVIN (*with tears of frustration*)—You're just stubborn, that's all. You won't face facts.

KIMURA *tells him fiercely it is the duty of every Japanese to fight until victory or death.*

ALVIN—Now what the hell is *that* supposed to mean? You people are so *damn* hard to figure out, nobody ever knows *what* you're gonna do. . . . That's how the whole war started in the first place.

With a gesture of hopelessness, Alvin goes to his tent to stuff a few possessions in his pocket. Returning to Kimura, he foists American money on the bewildered man. "You never know . . . might come in handy sometime. Some of the guards, they might go easy on you. . . . You'll be all right. . . . And maybe after the war I could come and . . . look you up sometime. . . . I'll bet I'd get along with your kids . . . I could teach 'em how to tie knots, and how to give Indian signals . . ."

Kimura for the first time is aware of the landing craft. With a look of unbearable reproach, he says the Americans are coming. He rushes back to his hut only to find his grenade missing. Bursting out at Alvin, he leaps for the knife, but Alvin is there ahead of him.

As a machine gun rips the tree above his head, Alvin hollers: "Hey! will you *stop* it!" The next minute Kimura has his hand over Alvin's mouth. Struggling desperately for possession of the knife, Alvin kicks Kimura's game leg and gets it. His hand raised, he is about to stab Kimura, when he sees that the Japanese not only accepts but wants the blow. As Alvin finds that he cannot go through with it, the fight goes out of both of them.

Kimura indicates that he wants the knife only for himself. At first Alvin refuses. He suggests that Kimura disappear into the hills. He promises not to tell where he is. Kimura feels it is better to die. Eventually as the squad comes closer, Alvin, seeing Kimura proud and withdrawn, closes his eyes and plunges the knife into the ground between them. Kimura instantly snatches it up and assumes the hari-kari position. Alvin peels off his T-shirt and waves it cautiously over the dune. The firing ceases.

About to duck over the dune, Alvin turns to Kimura, looks at him pleadingly: "Friend?" Kimura looks through him stonily from some great distance, but for one final moment his expression melts. "Friend," he nods.

Crying softly, "Don't shoot," Alvin disappears over the dune as Kimura poises the knife. "Friend," says Alvin in the distance, as the knife enters Kimura's body.

A GRAPHIC GLANCE

Patricia Bosworth, Patricia Smith, Albert Salmi, Peggy Conklin, Leon Ames, John D. Seymour and Abby Lewis in "Howie"

France Nuyen and William Shatner in "The World of Suzie Wong"

Hermione Gingold, Farley Granger, Polly Bergen and James Mitchell in "First Impressions"

Gwen Verdon cavorts in "Redhead"

Families on the summer theatre circuit: Jessica Tandy and Hume Cronyn in "Triple Play"; James Mason, Pamela Kellino and their daughter Portland in "Mid-Summer"

Tom Ewell in "Patate"

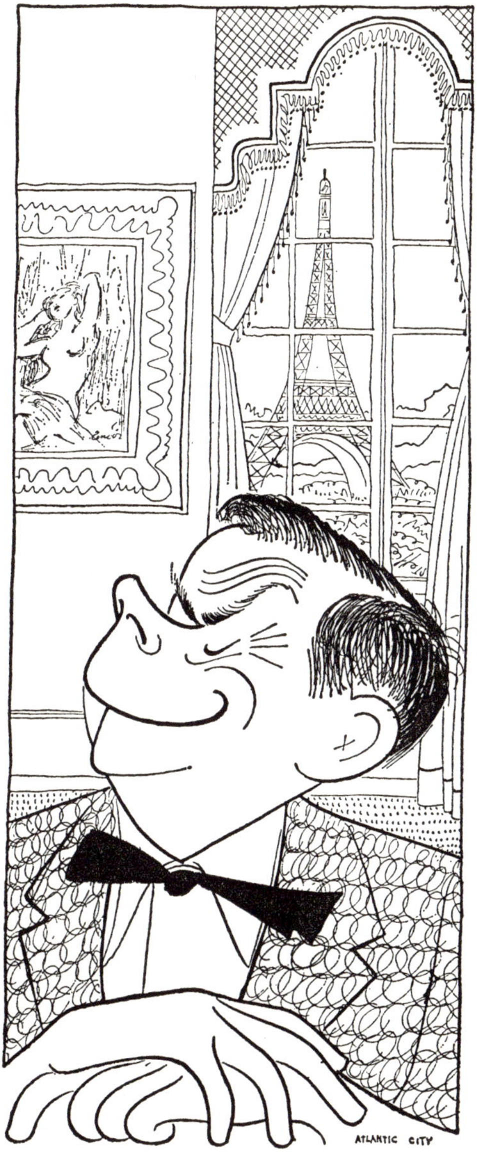
ATLANTIC CITY

In the "Ice Follies of '59": Jo Ann Dawdy; Will and Dova; Glenn and Colleen; Richard Dwyer and Lesley Goodwin

Marlene Dietrich

Asia, Paul Ford, Ralph Young, Susan Johnson, Danny Meehan and Julienne Marie in "Whoop-Up"

Marc Breaux, George Reeder, Swen Swenson, Dolores Gray and Andy Griffith in "Destry Rides Again"

Three imposing authoresses: Frances Parkinson Keyes, Taylor Caldwell and Edna Ferber

Leonard Bernstein—a man of many talents

Judy Garland in her revue at the Metropolitan Opera House

PLAYS PRODUCED IN NEW YORK

PLAYS PRODUCED IN NEW YORK

June 1, 1958—May 31, 1959

(Plays marked "Continued" were still running on June 1, 1959)

AUNTIE MAME

(24 performances)

Comedy in two acts by Jerome Lawrence and Robert E. Lee, based on the novel by Patrick Dennis. Revived by the New York City Center of Music and Drama, Inc., by arrangement with Bowden, Barr & Bullock, with Sylvia Drulie, at the New York City Center, August 11, 1958.

Cast of characters—

Norah Muldoon	Betty Sinclair
Patrick Dennis, as a boy	Guy Russell
Ito	Yoshi Naka
Vera Charles	Shannon Dean
Osbert	Eugene Van Hekle
Ralph Devine	John Granger
M. Lindsay Woolsey	Phil Arthur
Auntie Mame	Sylvia Sidney
Mr. Waldo, a paperhanger	Roy Johnson
Mr. Babcock	Leo Lucker
Al Linden, the stage manager	Edward Fuller
A Theatre Manager	James Pritchett
A Maid	Teresa Savior
A Butler	Paul Savior
Customers	Teresa Savior, Laura Lee
A Customer's Son	Robin Essen
Mr. Loomis, a floor-walker	Eugene Van Hekle
Beauregard Jackson Pickett-Burnside	Mark O'Daniels
Cousin Jeff	James Pritchett
Cousin Fan	Ruth Kelton
Sally Cato MacDougal	Winifred Ainslee
Emoroy MacDougal	Robin Essen
Mother Burnside	Joan Davenport
Fred, a groom	Paul Savior
Sam, another groom	John Granger
Dr. Shurr, a vet	Roy Johnson
Patrick Dennis, a young man	William Berrian
Agnes Gooch	Sudie Bond
Brian O'Bannion	Philip Bosco
Gloria Upson	Francesca Trantum
Doris Upson	Ruth Holden
Claude Upson	T. J. Halligan
Pegeen Ryan	Laura Lee
Michael Dennis	Guy Russell

And a great many friends of Auntie Mame.

The action of the play takes place in Auntie Mame's Beekman Place apartment and various other locales in which she becomes involved during a period of years from 1928-1946.

Staged by Charles Bowden (based on original staging by Morton Da

Costa); settings by Oliver Smith; lighting by Peggy Clark; costumes by Noel Taylor; Miss Sidney's gowns by Travis Banton of Marusia; incidental music by Saul Schechtman; production stage manager, Joe Kapfer; stage managers, Ben Stroback and Jeffery Longe; press representative, Martin Shwartz.

(Closed August 30, 1958)

HOWIE

(5 performances)

Comedy in three acts by Phoebe Ephron. Produced by the Playwrights' Company, James M. Slevin and John Gerstad at the Forty-sixth Street Theatre, September 17, 1958.

Cast of characters—

Edith Simms	Peggy Conklin
Walter Simms	Leon Ames
Sally Simms	Patricia Bosworth
Barbara Dickerson	Patricia Smith
Howie Dickerson	Albert Salmi
Jimmie Keefe	Nicholas Pryor
Martha Robinson	Abby Lewis
Joe Robinson	John D. Seymour
Sylvia	Maggie Grindell
Victor	Robert Paschall
Martin	Stephen Gray
Joseph McNish	Conrad Fowkes
Announcer	Charles McDaniel
Wendy	Barbara Wilkin
The Professor	Gene Saks
Bill Pfeiffer	John Fiedler

Time: the present. Place: the living room of Edith and Walter Simms, somewhere in Long Island. Act I.—Scene 1—An evening late in spring. Scene 2—Later that same night; about ten o'clock. Act II.—Scene 1—Several weeks later; an evening in early summer. Scene 2—The same night; a little after eight o'clock. Act III.—About an hour later.

Staged by John Gerstad; settings and lighting by Frederick Fox; costumes by Patton Campbell; production stage manager, Charles Durand; stage manager, Robert Paschall; press representative, William Fields.

(Closed September 20, 1958)

HANDFUL OF FIRE

(5 performances)

Play in three acts by N. Richard Nash. Produced by David Susskind and the Playwrights' Company at the Martin Beck Theatre, October 1, 1958.

Cast of characters—

Mariachis	Jesus de Jerez, Tomas E. Infante, Alex Hassilev
Rodolfo	Robert Nieves
Bullfighter	Neil Laurence

THE BEST PLAYS OF 1958–1959

Tamale Vendor	Jorge Gonzales
Padre	Angel Rigau
Tourist Wife	Jeanne Barr
Tourist Husband	Jake Sitters
A Woman	Scottie MacGregor
Rodolfo's Mother	Thelma Pelish
Pepe	Roddy McDowall
Alonso	Leonardo Cimino
Matias	Louis Guss
Ruben	William Edmonson
Policemen	Irving Winter, Dario Barri
Manuel	James Daly
Vargas	Gene Gross
Sylvi	Kay Medford
Maria	Joan Copeland
Carmelita	Myriam Acevedo
Young Man	Mark Rydell

The play is set in a Mexican border town. It is summer and the time is now.

Staged by Robert Lewis; settings and lighting by Jo Mielziner; costumes by Lucinda Ballard; production stage manager, Jose Vega; stage manager, Charles Forsythe; press representative, Arthur Cantor.

(Closed October 4, 1958)

A TOUCH OF THE POET

(268 performances)
(Continued)

Play in four acts by Eugene O'Neill. Produced by the Producers Theatre (Robert Whitehead production) at the Helen Hayes Theatre, October 2, 1958.

Cast of characters—

Mickey Maloy	Tom Clancy
Jamie Cregan	Curt Conway
Sara Melody	Kim Stanley
Nora Melody	Helen Hayes
Cornelius Melody	Eric Portman
Dan Roche	John Call
Paddy O'Dowd	Art Smith
Patch Riley	Farrell Pelly
Deborah (Mrs. Henry Harford)	Betty Field
Nicholas Gadsby	Luis Van Rooten

The action takes place in the dining room of Melody's Tavern, in a village a few miles from Boston, on July 27, 1828. Act I.—Morning, 9:00 A.M. Act II.—A half-hour later. Act III.—Evening, 8:00 P.M. Act IV.—Midnight.

Staged by Harold Clurman; designed by Ben Edwards; production stage manager, Joseph Brownstone; press representative, Barry Hyams.

DRINK TO ME ONLY

(77 performances)

Comedy in three acts by Abram S. Ginnes and Ira Wallach. Produced by George Ross, in association with John Robert Lloyd, at the Fifty-fourth Street Theatre (Adelphi), October 8, 1958.

294 THE BEST PLAYS OF 1958–1959

Cast of characters—

Stanley Farrington	John McGiver
Gregory Wendell	Royal Beal
James Porterman	Paul Hartman
Vicky Remsen	Georgann Johnson
Miles Pringle	Tom Poston
Bailiff	John Allen
Judge	Truman Smith
Harvey L. Gruber, Prosecuting Attorney	Lou Polan
Joyce Porterman	Undine Forrest
Dr. Peter Ullman	Jack Gilford
Princess Alexandria	Sherry Britton
Mrs. George Havermeyer	Leona Powers
Sandy Wendell	Diana Millay
Clinton Wheelock	Cameron Prud'homme
Jurors	Leona Noric, Mary Stanton, Frank Ford, Don Penny

Time: the present. Act I.—Scene 1—The Courtroom, New York. Scene 2—The Board Room in the law firm of Wheelock, Wendell and Farrington; Sunday afternoon. Scene 3—Living room in Gregory Wendell's New York apartment; that evening. Act II.—Gregory Wendell's apartment; later that night. Act III.—Scene 1—The Courtroom; next morning. Scene 2—Gregory Wendell's apartment; soon after.

Staged by George Abbott; designed and lighted by John Robert Lloyd; costumes by Julia Sze; production stage manager, Bert Wood; stage manager, John Allen; press representative, Madi Blitzstein.

(Closed December 13, 1958)

GOLDILOCKS

(161 performances)

Musical in two acts, with book by Walter and Jean Kerr; music by Leroy Anderson; lyrics by Joan Ford, Walter and Jean Kerr. Produced by the Producers Theatre (Robert Whitehead) at the Lunt-Fontanne Theatre, October 11, 1958.

Cast of characters—

Maggie Harris	Elaine Stritch
George Randolph Brown	Russell Nype
Max Grady	Don Ameche
Lois Lee	Pat Stanley
Pete	Nathaniel Frey
Andy	Richard Armbruster
Max's Assistants	Gene Varrone, Sam Greene
J. C.	Martin Wolfson
Bessie	Margaret Hamilton
Deputies	Del Anderson, Beau Tilden
Chauffeur	Samye Van

Singers: Jane Carlyle, Jeanne Grant, Josanne Lavalle, Sadie McCollum, Rita Noble, Suzanne Stahl, Richard Armbruster, Del Anderson, John Carter, Sam Greene, Ben Parrish, Rufus Smith, Gene Varrone.

Dancers: Patricia Birsh, Lynne Broadbent, Judith Chazin, Bunty Kelley, Margaret Lithander, Imelda de Martin, Carolyn Morris, Ilona Murai, Patti Nestor, Evelyn Taylor, Diana Turner, Kelly Brown, Donald Barton, Michael Fesco, Loren Hightower, George Jack, Ronnie Landry, David Nillo, Paul Olson, Peter Saul, Ron Stratton

Act I.—Scene 1—Onstage, New York City, 1913. Scene 2—Maggie's dressing room; immediately following. Scene 3—Max's lot; next morning. Scene 4—Outside Max's lot; that evening. Scene 5—Max's lot; four days later. Scene 6—The Fat Cat Roof Garden; later that night. Scene 7—Huckleberry Island; several days later. Act II.—

Scene 1—A rest home on the mainland; two days later. Scene 2—Bessie's barn, up the Hudson; that afternoon. Scene 3—Ballroom, George's town house; that evening. Scene 4—Egypt-on-the-Hudson; next morning.

Staged by Walter Kerr; choreography by Agnes de Mille; settings by Peter Larkin; lighting by Feder; costumes by Castillo; musical director, Lehman Engel; orchestrations by Leroy Anderson and Philip J. Lang; dance music arranged by Laurence Rosenthal; production stage manager, James Gelb; stage manager, Frederic de Wilde; press representative, Barry Hyams.

Musical numbers—

ACT I

"Lazy Moon" .... Company
"Give the Little Lady" .... Elaine Stritch and Company
"Save a Kiss" .... Elaine Stritch and Russell Nype
"No One'll Ever Love You" .... Elaine Stritch and Don Ameche
"If I Can't Take It with Me" .... Nathaniel Frey and Company
"Who's Been Sitting in My Chair?" .... Elaine Stritch
Dance .... Elaine Stritch and Donald Barton
"There Never Was a Woman" .... Don Ameche
"The Pussy Foot" .... Pat Stanley and Company
Huckleberry Island Ballet .... Company

ACT II

"Lady in Waiting" .... Pat Stanley and Russell Nype
Dance .... Pat Stanley, Kelly Brown, Evelyn Taylor and Company
"The Beast in You" .... Elaine Stritch
"Shall I Take My Heart and Go?" .... Russell Nype
"Bad Companions" .... Nathaniel Frey, Margaret Hamilton, Richard Armbruster, Gene Varrone
"I Can't Be in Love" .... Don Ameche
"I Never Know When" .... Elaine Stritch
"The Town House Maxixe" Dance .... Pat Stanley, David Nillo and Company
"Two Years in the Making" ..... Nathaniel Frey, Margaret Hamilton and Singers
"Heart of Stone" (Pyramid Dance) ...... Ilona Murai and Company

(Closed February 28, 1959)

THEATRE NATIONAL POPULAIRE

(23 performances)

Repertory of five plays, presented in French. Produced by S. Hurok under the auspices of the Government of the French Republic.

Repertoire—

Lorenzaccio, drama by Alfred de Musset. Staged by Gerard Philipe; settings by Leon Gischia; music by Maurice Jarre. Premiere: October 14, 1958.

Le Triomphe de l'Amour, comedy by Marivaux. Staged by Jean Vilar; settings and costumes by Leon Gischia; music by Maurice Jarre. Premiere: October 16, 1958.

Marie Tudor, drama by Victor Hugo. Staged by Jean Vilar; settings and costumes by Leon Gischia; music by Maurice Jarre. Premiere: October 21, 1958.

Don Juan, comedy by Moliere. Staged by Jean Vilar; costumes by Leon Gischia; music by Maurice Jarre. Premiere: October 28, 1958.

Le Cid, tragi-comedy by Pierre Corneille. Staged by Jean Vilar; costumes by Leon Gischia; with musical themes from the 17th century. Premiere: October 30, 1958.

THE BEST PLAYS OF 1958-1959

Repertory Company—

Simone Bouchateau	Roger Mollien
Zanie Campan	Jean-Paul Moulinot
Maria Casares	Philippe Noiret
Monique Chaumette	Michel Petit
Catherine Le Couey	Gerard Philipe
Lucienne Le Marchand	Jean-Fraçois Remi
Genevieve Page	Pierre Reynal
Lucien Arnaud	Georges Riquier
Roger Coggio	Andre Schlesser
Coussonneau	Jacques Seiler
Jean-Pierre Darras	Daniel Sorano
Jean Deschamps	Jean Topart
Pierre Garin	Georges Wilson
Yves Gasc	

Director, Jean Vilar; general administrator, Jean Rouvet; director of music, Maurice Jarre; director of lighting, Pierre Saveron; director of scenic construction, Jacques Le Marquet; scenic construction, Andre Bataille; production stage manager, Gene Perlowin; press representative, Martin Feinstein.

(Closed November 2, 1958)

THE WORLD OF SUZIE WONG

(263 performances)
(Continued)

Play in two acts by Paul Osborn, based on the novel by Richard Mason. Produced by David Merrick, Seven Arts Productions, Inc., and Mansfield Productions at the Broadhurst Theatre, October 14, 1958.

Cast of characters—

Robert Lomax	William Shatner
Suzie Wong	France Nuyen
Chinese Officer	Clifford Arashi
Chinese Policeman	David Hill
Ah Tong	Stephen C. Cheng
Waiter	Viraj Amonsin
British Sailor	David Kitchen
Typhoo	Sirat
Gwenny	Takayo
Wednesday Lulu	Flavia Hsu Kingman
Minnie Ho	Mary Mon Toy
Fifi	Vie Von Thom
George O'Neill	Noel Leslie
Kay Fletcher	Sarah Marshall
Ben Jeffcoat	Ron Randell
Drunken Sailor	Warren Robertson
A Bystander	Viraj Amonsin
Lily	Ellen Davalos

Vendors and Coolies: John Mamo, Ichisuki Ishikawa, Tsunao Sato.
Flowers of the Bar: Meiyu Chang, Ellen Davalos, Linda Ho, Jin Jin Mai, Tinya Lang Yun.
Children: Sufei T'ang, Hokon T'ang.
Sailors: William Becker, Jorge Benhur, Kurt Bieber, Bill Harden, Derrick Dobb, Tracey Everitt, Ed Garrabrandt, Karl Held, Bill Jason, Jerry Logas, Marc Marno, Ted Morell, Richard Nieves, Paul Smith, Neil Vipond.
Tourists: Kathleen Widdoes, Fred Starbuck.

The action of the play takes place in Hong Kong. The time is the present. Act I.—Scene 1—A Chinese ferry. Scene 2—A street in Hong Kong; a few hours later. Scene 3—A room at the Nam Kok. Scene 4—The bar at the Nam Kok. Scene 5—Robert's room, a month later. Act II.—Scene 1—A street in front of the Nam Kok; two weeks later. Scene 2—Robert's room. Scene 3—A street in front of the Nam Kok; three weeks later. Scene 4—Robert's room. Scene 5—A street in Hong Kong. Scene 6—Robert's room.

Staged by Joshua Logan; settings and lighting by Jo Mielziner; costumes by Dorothy Jeakins; production stage manager, Neil Hartley; stage manager, John Drew Devereaux; press representatives, Frank Goodman and Seymour Krawitz.

THE GIRLS IN 509

(117 performances)

Comedy in two acts by Howard Teichmann. Produced by Alfred de Liagre, Jr. at the Belasco Theatre, October 15, 1958.

Cast of characters—

Mimsy	Imogene Coca
Aunt Hettie	Peggy Wood
Old Jim	Fred Stewart
Ryan, of the Daily News	Les Damon
Pusey	King Donovan
Miss Freud	Laurinda Barrett
Winthrop Allen	Robert Emhardt
Summers, of the Herald Tribune	Will Hussung
Johnson, of the Journal-American	William Bush
Rosenthal, of the N. Y. Post	Sam Schwartz
Francis X. Nella	Robert Emhardt
Aubrey McKittridge	James Millhollin

The entire action of the play occurs in a not-now fashionable hotel in New York City. The time is the present. Act I.—Scene 1—Noon, April 2nd. Scene 2—A few minutes later. Act II.—Scene 1—One minute later. Scene 2—Morning, April 3rd. Scene 3—Evening.

Staged by Bretaigne Windust; setting and lighting by Donald Oenslager; costumes by Lucinda Ballard; production stage manager, William Chambers; stage manager, Arthur Marlowe; press representative, Ben Washer.

(Closed January 24, 1959)

THE FAMILY REUNION

(32 performances)

Play in two acts by T. S. Eliot. Produced by Theatre Incorporated (T. Edward Hambleton and Norris Houghton) at the Phoenix Theatre, October 20, 1958.

Cast of characters—

Amy, Dowager Lady Monchensey	Florence Reed
Ivy, her sister	Dorothy Sands
Violet, another sister	Margaretta Warwick
Agatha, her youngest sister	Lillian Gish
Col. the Honorable Gerald Piper	Nicholas Joy

```
Hon. Charles Piper .................................Eric Berry
Mary, a cousin ....................................Sylvia Short
Denman, a parlourmaid .........................Christine Thomas
Harry, Lord Monchensey ..........................Fritz Weaver
Downing, his servant and chauffeur ...............Robert Geiringer
Dr. Warburton ....................................Conrad Bain
Sergeant Winchell ............................Meredith Dallas
```

The scene is laid in a country house in the North of England.
Act I.—The drawing room, after tea; an afternoon in late March.
Act II.—The drawing room, after dinner.

Staged by Stuart Vaughan; setting by Norris Houghton; costumes and lighting by Will Steven Armstrong; music composed by David Amram; production stage manager, Robert Woods; stage manager, John Robertson; press representatives, Ben Kornzweig and Karl Bernstein.

(Closed November 16, 1958)

ONCE MORE, WITH FEELING

(255 performances)
(Continued)

Comedy in three acts by Harry Kurnitz. Produced by Martin Gabel and Henry Margolis at the National Theatre, October 21, 1958.

Cast of characters—

```
Chester Stamm .................................Paul E. Richards
Gendels .......................................Leon Belasco
Victor Fabian .................................Joseph Cotten
Maxwell Archer ................................Walter Matthau
Luigi Bardini .................................Rex Williams
Mr. Wilbur ....................................Ralph Bunker
Dolly Fabian ..................................Arlene Francis
Richard Hilliard ..............................Frank Milan
Interviewer ...................................Dan Frazer
```

The time is the present. Act I.—Scene 1—The dressing room off the stage in a concert hall in Sioux City, Iowa. Scene 2—The living room of Victor Fabian's hotel suite in Chicago; several weeks later. Act II.—Scene 1—The living room; the next afternoon. Scene 2—The living room; later that night. Act III.—Fabian's dressing room backstage at the Civic Auditorium; Saturday night.

Staged by George Axelrod; settings and lighting by George Jenkins; men's clothes by Michael Travis; costumes for Miss Francis by Scaasi; production stage manager, David Kanter; stage manager, Paul Leaf; press representatives, Richard Maney and Martin Shwartz.

THE PLEASURE OF HIS COMPANY

(254 performances)
(Continued)

Comedy in two acts by Samuel Taylor, with Cornelia Otis Skinner. Produced by Frederick Brisson and the Playwrights' Company at the Longacre Theatre, October 22, 1958.

Cast of characters—

Toy	Jerry Fujikawa
Biddeford Poole	Cyril Ritchard
Jessica Poole	Dolores Hart
Katharine Dougherty	Cornelius Otis Skinner
Jim Dougherty	Walter Abel
Mackenzie Savage	Charlie Ruggles
Roger Henderson	George Peppard

The action of the play takes place in the living room of a house high on a hill in San Francisco, overlooking the Golden Gate. Act I.—A Monday morning in June. Act II.—Scene 1—Wednesday night. Scene 2—The following afternoon. Scene 3—An hour later.

Staged by Cyril Ritchard; production designed and lighted by Donald Oenslager; costumes by Edith Head; production stage manager, Fred Hebert; stage manager, Gerald O'Brien; press representative, William Fields.

See page 78.

MAKE A MILLION

(252 performances)
(Continued)

Comedy in three acts by Norman Barasch and Carroll Moore. Produced by Joel Spector and Sylvia Harris at the Playhouse Theatre, October 23, 1958.

Cast of characters—

Betty Phillips	Joy Harmon
George Winters	Charles Welch
Mrs. Winters	Barbara Barkley
Claire Manning	Neva Patterson
Sid Gray	Sam Levene
Bernie Leeds	Bill Hickey
Howard Conklin	Don Marye
Harold Fairbanks	Ty Perry
Julie Martin	Ann Wedgeworth
Mr. Mergenthaler	Ralph Dunn
General Potter	Don Wilson
Lieutenant Friedlander	Edgar Hess
Ferris	Richard Blair
King	Conrad Janis
Reeves	Dennis Richards
Bradford	Ed Crowley
Juliano	Guy Perone
Henry Whipple	Hoke Howell
Reardon	Ed Crowley

The entire action of the play takes place in the office of Sid Gray, television producer. Act I.—Scene 1—Monday morning. Scene 2—Wednesday morning. Act II.—One hour later. Act III.—The following morning.

Staged by Jerome Chodorov; setting and lighting by Paul Morrison; costumes by Ann Roth; production stage manager, Bruce Laffey; stage manager, Edgar Hess; press representatives, David Lipsky and Phillip Bloom.

PATATE

(7 performances)

Comedy in three acts by Marcel Achard, adapted by Irwin Shaw. Produced by Gilbert Miller at Henry Miller's Theatre, October 28, 1958.

Cast of characters—
```
Leon Rollo .........................................Tom Ewell
Edith Rollo .....................................Haila Stoddard
Butler .........................................George Turner
Veronique Taillade ............................Murial Williams
Noel Taillade ....................................Lee Bowman
Alexa Rollo .......................................Susan Oliver
```
Act I.—The Taillade living room in Paris; morning. Act II.—The Rollo living room; that evening. Act III.—The same; immediately following.

Staged by Jed Horner; settings by Raymond Sovey; costumes supervised by Kathryn Miller; production stage manager, Richard Bender; stage manager, Eugene Stuckmann; press representatives, Richard Maney and Martin Shwartz.

(Closed November 1, 1958)

THE MARRIAGE-GO-ROUND

(239 performances)
(Continued)

Play in two acts by Leslie Stevens. Produced by Paul Gregory at the Plymouth Theatre, October 29, 1958.

Cast of characters—
```
Paul Delville, Professor of Cultural Anthropology ....Charles Boyer
Content Lowell, Dean of Women
   (Mrs. Paul Delville) ........................Claudette Colbert
Katrin Sveg .......................................Julie Newmar
Ross Barnett ......................................Edmon Ryan
```
The time is the present. The place: the Institute of Advanced Studies (Humanities), in a traditional college town up the river from New York.

Staged by Joseph Anthony; settings and lighting by Donald Oenslager; Miss Colbert's dresses by Lanvin-Castillo; stage manager, Bill Ross; press representatives, Karl Bernstein and Ben Kornzweig.

THE MAN IN THE DOG SUIT

(36 performances)

Comedy in three acts by Albert Beich and William H. Wright, based on a novel by Edwin Corle. Produced by the Producers Theatre at the Coronet Theatre, October 30, 1958.

Cast of characters—

Martha Walling	Jessica Tandy
Oliver Walling	Hume Cronyn
Letty Gaxton	Nancy Cushman
Henry Gaxton	John McGovern
George Stoddard	John Griggs
Eileen Stoddard	Carmen Matthews
Mrs. Louisa Stoddard	Kathleen Comegys
Stewart Stoddard	Clinton Sundberg
Anthony Roberti	Tom Carlin
Mr. Beal	Arthur Hughes

The action takes place in the Wallings' living room in an American suburb. The time is the present. Act I.—Scene 1—Saturday morning, 2:00 A.M. Scene 2—Tuesday evening. Act II.—Scene 1—Wednesday afternoon. Scene 2—Thursday night. Act III.—Friday afternoon.

Staged by Ralph Nelson; setting and lighting by Donald Oenslager; costumes by Anna Hill Johnstone; associate producer, Lewis Allen; production stage manager, Paul A. Foley; stage manager, Marjorie Winfield; press representatives, Harvey B. Sabinson and David Powers.

(Closed November 29, 1958)

EPITAPH FOR GEORGE DILLON

(23 performances)

Play in three acts by John Osborne and Anthony Creighton. Produced by David Merrick and Joshua Logan, by arrangement with the English Stage Company, at the John Golden Theatre, November 4, 1958.

Cast of characters—

Josie Elliot	Wendy Craig
Ruth Gray	Eileen Herlie
Mrs. Elliot	Alison Leggatt
Norah Elliot	Avril Elgar
Percy Elliot	Frank Finlay
George Dillon	Robert Stephens
Geoffrey Colwyn Stuart	James Valentine
Mr. Webb	David Vaughan
Barney Evans	Felix Deebank

The action of the play takes place in the home of the Elliot family just outside London. Act I.—Spring. Act II.—Summer. Act III.—Autumn. Act IV.—Winter.

Staged by William Gaskill; scenery by Stephen Doncaster; scenery and lighting supervised by Ralph Alswang; costumes supervised by Helene Pons; production stage manager, Leonard Patrick; press representative, Harvey B. Sabinson.

(Closed November 22, 1958)

Epitaph for George Dillon was revived later in the season by Norman Twain and Bernard Miller at Henry Miller's Theatre, January 12, 1959, for 48 performances.

MARIA GOLOVIN

(5 performances)

Musical drama in three acts by Gian Carlo Menotti. Produced by David Merrick and the National Broadcasting Co., in association with Byron Goldman, at the Martin Beck Theatre, November 5, 1958.

Cast of characters—

Donato	Richard Cross
Agata	Ruth Kobart
The Mother	Patricia Neway
Dr. Zuckertanz	Norman Kelly
Maria Golovin	Franca Duval
Trottolo	Lorenzo Muti
The Prisoner	William Chapman
Servant	John Kuhn

The entire action takes place at Donato's villa near a frontier in a European country. The time is a few years after a recent war. Act I.—Scene 1—A living room in the villa; early spring. Scene 2—The same; a month later. Act II.—Scene 1—The terrace of the villa; late afternoon, midsummer. Scene 2—The same; that night. Act III.—Scene 1—The living room; afternoon, early fall. Scene 2—The same; in the evening, a week later. Scene 3—The same; a few hours later.

Staged by Mr. Menotti; production supervised by Samuel Chotzinoff; orchestra conducted by Herbert Grossman; production coordinator, Louis B. Ames; scenery by Rouben Ter-Arutunian; lighting by Charles Elson; costumes supervised by Helene Pons; production stage manager, Richard Evans; press representative, Harvey B. Sabinson.

(Closed November 8, 1958)

COMES A DAY

(28 performances)

Play in three acts by Speed Lamkin. Produced by Cheryl Crawford and Alan Pakula at the Ambassador Theatre, November 6, 1958.

Cast of characters—

C. D. Lawton	Brandon de Wilde
Joe Glover	Michael J. Pollard
Caroline Lawton	Diana van der Vlis
Isabel Lawton	Judith Anderson
Katherine Eubanks	Ruth Hammond
Tydings Glen	George C. Scott
Lewis	Joseph Barr
Charley Lawton	Arthur O'Connell
Mrs. McCarthy	Lorna Thayer
Jim Culpepper	Larry Hagman
Gordie Eubanks	Charles White
Lorraine	Eileen Ryan
Bud	John Dutra

The scene is the Lawtons' house in a medium-sized American city. The time is the present. Act I.—Scene 1—A late afternoon in May.

Scene 2—Later that night. Act II.—Scene 1—An evening several weeks later. Scene 2—The next day. Act III.—Scene 1—The following morning. Scene 2—That evening.

Staged by Robert Mulligan; setting and lighting by Sam Leve; costumes by Noel Taylor; production stage manager, Joseph Papp; press representatives, Ben Washer and Tom Trenkle.

(Closed November 29, 1958)

LA PLUME DE MA TANTE

(231 performances)

(Continued)

A revue in two acts, written, devised and directed by Robert Dhery. The Jack Hylton production produced by David Merrick and Joseph Kipness at the Royale Theatre, November 11, 1958.

Principals—

Robert Dhery	Nicole Parent
Colette Brosset	Pamela Austin
Pierre Olaf	Michael Kent
Jacques Legras	Henri Pennec
Roger Caccia	Michel Modo
Jean Lefevre	Yvonne Constant
Ross Parker	Genevieve Coulombel

Staged by Alec Shanks; music and arrangements by Gerard Calvi; choreography by Colette Brosset; English lyrics by Ross Parker; musical direction by Gershon Kingsley; scenery supervised and lighting by Charles Elson; orchestration by Gerard Calvi, Billy Ternent and Ronnie Monro; curtain designed by Vertes; production stage manager, Neil Hartley; stage manager, Harold Stone; press representatives, Frank Goodman and Seymour Krawitz.

Sketches and musical numbers—

ACT I

Introduction .... Robert Dhery
"Speakerine" .... Colette Brosset
"Amsterdam" .... Jean Lefevre
"Mobile Squad"
   The Pride of the Force .... Jacques Legras, Pierre Olaf
                                       Michael Modo, Henri Pennec
"Rider to the Sea" .... Michael Kent
"Le Bal Chez Madame de Mortemouille" (Designed by Dignimont)
   Madame de Mortemouille .... Pamela Austin
   The Major Domo .... Michael Kent
   General Grosfut .... Ross Parker
   The Attache .... Henri Pennec
   The Maitre d'Hotel .... Roger Caccia
   The Spahi .... Michel Modo
   Johnny Walker .... Jean Lefevre
   Master Percy Smith .... Pierre Olaf
   Mr. Spratts .... Jacques Legras
   Miss Innocent .... Mary Reynolds
   Mademoiselle Colette .... Colette Brosset
   Monsieur Robert .... Robert Dhery
"Husbands Beware!"
   The Wife .... Yvonne Constant
   The Lover .... Pierre Olaf
   The Elevator Attendant .... Henri Pennec
   The Husband .... Ross Parker

"Light Soprano" (Designed by Erte) ....Pamela Austin
"In a Small Cafe" (Designed by Lilla De Nobili)
  The Waiter ....Robert Dhery
  The Late Diner ....Ross Parker
"Ballet Classique" (Designed by Erte) with the entire Corps de Ballet
  The Spirit of the Night ....Coka Brossecola
  The Prince ....Pierre Olaf
  The Princess ....Genevieve Coulombel
  The Witch Girl ....Nicole Parent
"Song of the Swing" (Designed by Alec Shanks)
  Veronique ....Pamela Austin
  Florestan ....Michael Kent
"Precision" ....The Royal Croquettes
"Courting Time" (Designed by Erte)
  The Father ....Ross Parker
  The Mother ....Roger Caccia
  Their Daughter ....Brigitte Peynaud
  Her Lover ....Pierre Olaf
  The Explorer ....Michel Modo
  The Gendarme ....Jacques Legras
"Femmes Fatales" (Dresses designed by Jacques Esterel)
  Les Femmes ....Nicole Parent, Jill Hougham, Yvonne Constant,
    Mary Reynolds, Brigitte Peynaud, Colette Brosset
"On the Beach"..........Roger Caccia, Jacques Legras, Jean Lefevre,
    Ross Parker, Genevieve Zanetti, Anna Stroppini
"Queen of the Strip-Tease" ....Colette Brosset
"Freres Jacques" ....Pierre Olaf, Jacques Legras, Roger Caccia,
    Michel Modo, Ross Parker

ACT II

"Hommage Musical" (Designed by Henri Pennec) .....Robert Dhery
    and his Festival Ensemble
  Guest Artistes ....The Ladies Athenian Choir
"Domingo Blazes and his Latin-American Orchestra"
"In an Indian Temple"
  Temple Girls ....The Dugudu Dancers
  The High Priestess ....Yvonne Constant
"This Other Eden"
  Eve ....Colette Brosset
  Adam ....Robert Dhery
  The Serpent ....Jacques Legras
"Men at Work"
  The Workmen ....Jean Lefevre, Henri Pennec
"Administration" (Designed by Lilla De Nobili)
  Filing Clerks ....Roger Caccia, Jacques Legras
  The Secretary ....Yvonne Constant
  The Boss ....Ross Parker
"In the Tuileries Gardens" (Designed by Dignimont)
  The Tie Vendor ....Jean Lefevre
  The Cure ....Henri Pennec
  The Bystander ....Michel Modo
  The Lovers ....Nadine Gorbatcheff, Yvonne Constant
  The Bird Lover ....Mary Reynolds
  Agent de Police ....Michael Kent
  The Schoolmistress ....Pamela Austin
  Her Pupils ....Genevieve Coulombel, Anna Stroppini, Francoise
    Dally, Jill Hougham, Brigitte Peynaud, Claude Perrin
  Pickpockets ....Roger Caccia, Jacques Legras
  Clowns ....Pierre Olaf, Colette Brosset
"Take-Off"
  Air Hostess ....Yvonne Constant
  The Passenger ....Roger Caccia
"Ballet Moderne"
  The Dancers ....Genevieve Coulombel, Francoise Dally,
    Nicole Parent, Mary Reynolds
  The Musicians ....Stan Krell (drums), Ernie Mauro (clarinet),
    Milt Kraus (piano), Aaron Juvelier (bass)
"The Ventriloquist" ....Jean Lefevre
"Trapped" (Designed by Dignimont)
  The Victims ....Jacques Legras, Robert Dhery
  A Butcher ....Ross Parker

A Policeman .... Henri Pennec
A Passer-by .... Mary Reynolds
"Acrobatie" .... Colette Brosset
"Le Finale de Paris" .... The Entire Company
                                    and the Entire Corps de Ballet
    (Designed by Erte)

THE SHADOW OF A GUNMAN

(52 performances)

Play in two acts by Sean O'Casey. Revived by Cheryl Crawford and Joel Schenker, by arrangement with the Actors' Studio, Inc., at the Bijou Theatre, November 20, 1958.

Cast of characters—
    Donal Davoren .... William Smithers
    Seumas Shields .... Gerald O'Loughlin
    Maguire .... Bruce Dern
    Mr. Mulligan .... Daniel Reed
    Minnie Powell .... Susan Strasberg
    Tommy Owens .... Stefan Gierasch
    Mrs. Henderson .... Zamah Cunningham
    Mr. Gallogher .... Arthur Malet
    Mrs. Grigson .... Katherine Squire
    Adolphus Grigson .... George Mathews
    Auxiliary .... James Greene
    Passers-by .... Jack Allen, Tammy Allen,
                                    Hilda Brawner, Tom Wheatley
    The time of the play is May, 1920. The place is Dublin. Act I.—A room in a tenement in Hilljoy Square, Dublin. Act II.—The same; some hours later.
    Staged by Jack Garfein; settings by Peter Larkin; lighting by Tharon Musser; costumes by Ruth Morley; stage manager, Irving Buchman; press representative, Arthur Cantor.

(Closed January 3, 1959)

EDWIN BOOTH

(24 performances)

Play in three acts by Milton Geiger. Produced by Jose Ferrer and the Playwrights' Company at the Forty-sixth Street Theatre, November 24, 1958.

Cast of characters—
    William Winter .... Lorne Greene
    Junius Brutus Booth, the elder .... Ian Keith
    Edwin Booth (the boy) .... Stephen Franken
    Junius Brutus Booth, the younger ... Sydney Smith
    Edwin Booth .... Jose Ferrer
    Asia Booth .... Marion Ross
    John Wilkes Booth .... Richard Waring
    Mary Devlin .... Lois Smith
    Edwina Booth .... Anne Helm
    The action of the play occurs in America, London, Elsinore, Dunsi-

nane, Bosworth Field, Venice, Mantua, Verona, Rome, and the mind of Edwin Booth. The time of the action is from 1851 to 1893.

Staged by Mr. Ferrer; setting and lighting by Zvi Geyra; costumes by Edith Head; music by Paul Bowles; production stage manager, Bernard Gersten; stage manager, Thomas Toner; press representative, William Fields.

(Closed December 13, 1958)

CUE FOR PASSION

(39 performances)

Play in five scenes by Elmer Rice. Produced by the Playwrights Company and Franchot Productions at Henry Miller's Theatre, November 25, 1958.

Cast of characters—

Lucy Gessler	Joanna Brown
Grace Nicholson	Diana Wynyard
Mattie Haines	Anna Revere
Carl Nicholson	Lloyd Gough
Tony Burgess	John Kerr
Lloyd Hilton	Robert Lansing
Hugh Gessler	Russell Gaige

The scene of the play is the living room of a country-house in Southern California. The time is the present. Scene 1—Late Friday afternoon. Scene 2—Saturday morning. Scene 3—Saturday night. Scene 4—Sunday night. Scene 5—Monday morning.

Staged by Mr. Rice; production designed and lighted by George Jenkins; costumes by Dorothy Jeakins; production stage manager, Scott Jackson; stage manager, Carlton Colyer; press representative, William Fields.

(Closed December 27, 1958)

FLOWER DRUM SONG

(208 performances)

(Continued)

Musical in two acts, based on the novel by C. Y. Lee; book by Oscar Hammerstein II and Joseph Fields; lyrics by Oscar Hammerstein II; music by Richard Rodgers. Produced by Rodgers & Hammerstein, in association with Joseph Fields, at the St. James Theatre, December 1, 1958.

Cast of characters—

Madam Liang	Juanita Hall
Liu Ma	Rose Quong
Wang San	Patrick Adiarte
Wang Ta	Ed Kenney
Wang Chi Yang	Keye Luke

Sammy Fong	Larry Blyden
Dr. Li	Conrad Yama
Mei Li	Miyoshi Umeki
Linda Low	Pat Suzuki
Mr. Lung, the tailor	Harry Shaw Lowe
Mr. Huan	Jon Lee
Helen Chao	Arabella Hong
Professor Cheng	Peter Chan
Frankie Wing	Jack Soo
Headwaiter	George Young
Night Club Singer	Anita Ellis
Dr. Lu Fong	Chao Li
Madam Fong	Eileen Nakamura

Dancing ensemble: Fumi Akimoto, Paula Chin, Helen Funai, Pat Griffith, Mary Huie, Marion Jim, Betty Kawamura, Baayork Lee, Wonci Lui, Jo Anne Miya, Denise Quan, Vicki Racimo, Shawnee Smith, Maureen Tiongco, Mabel Wing, Yuriko, Jose Ahumada, Victor Duntiere, George Li, David Lober, Robert Lorca, George Minami, David Toguri, George Young.

Children: Linda and Yvonne Ribuca; Susan Lynn Kikuchi, Luis Robert Hernandez.

The action takes place in San Francisco's Chinatown. The time is the present. Act I.—Scene 1—The living room in the house of Master Wang Chi Yang. Scene 2—A hill overlooking San Francisco Bay. Scene 3—The Wang living room. Scene 4—Wang Chi Yang's bedroom. Scene 5—The garden of the Wang house. Scene 6—Linda's dressing room in the Celestial Bar. Scene 7—The Celestial Bar. Act II.—Scene 1—Helen Chao's room. Scene 2—The Wang living room. Scene 3—Sammy Fong's penthouse apartment. Scene 4—The Three Family Association. Scene 5—Sammy Fong's penthouse apartment. Scene 6—Grant Avenue, San Francisco's Chinatown. Scene 7—The Three Family Association.

Staged by Gene Kelly; scenic production by Oliver Smith; choreography by Carol Haney; costumes designed by Irene Sharaff; lighting by Peggy Clark; orchestrations by Robert Russell Bennett; musical director, Salvatore Dell'Isola; dance arrangements by Luther Henderson, Jr.; general stage manager, James Hammerstein; stage managers, Ted Hammerstein and Fred Hearn; press representative, Michel Mok.

Musical numbers—

ACT I

"You Are Beautiful"	Wang Ta and Madam Liang
"A Hundred Million Miracles"	Mei Li, Dr. Li, Wang Chi Yang, Madam Liang, Liu Ma
"I Enjoy Being a Girl"	Linda and Dancers
"I Am Going to Like It Here"	Mei Li
"Like a God"	Wang Ta
"Chop Suey"	Madam Liang, Wang San and Ensemble
"Don't Marry Me"	Sammy Fong and Mei Li
"Grant Avenue"	Linda and Ensemble
"Love, Look Away"	Helen Chao
"Fan Tan Fannie"	Night Club Singer and Girls
"Gliding Through My Memoree"	Frankie and Girls
Finale: "Grant Avenue"	Entire Company

ACT II

Ballet	Wang Ta, Mei Li (Yuriko), Linda Low (Jo Anne Miya) and Dancers
Reprise: "Love, Look Away"	Helen Chao
"The Other Generation"	Madam Liang and Wang Chi Yang
"Sunday"	Linda and Sammy Fong
Reprise: "The Other Generation"	Wang San and Children
Wedding Parade	Mei Li and Dancers
Finale	Entire Company

THE NIGHT CIRCUS

(7 performances)

Play in three acts by Michael V. Gazzo. Produced by Jay Julien at the John Golden Theatre, December 2, 1958.

Cast of characters—
```
A Waiter ...................................... Michael St. John
Owner-Bartender ............................... Al Lewis
The Businessman ............................... Arthur Storch
Jade .......................................... Albert Morgenstern
A Lady of the Evening ......................... Patricia Roe
David Davidson ................................ John Harkins
Nellie Milwaukee .............................. Arlene Golonka
Daphne Bau .................................... Janice Rule
The Father .................................... Shepperd Strudwick
Charlie P. S. 19 .............................. Albert Paulson
Eddie P. S. 19 ................................ Richard McMurray
Joy ........................................... Ben Gazzara
A Policeman ................................... Hazen Gifford
A Customer .................................... Peter Collins
The Rock ...................................... Bartell LaRue
A Young Girl .................................. Judith Loomis
```
Act I.—Scene 1—The Jolly Roger Bar in New York City; early evening. Scene 2—The same; the next afternoon. Act II.—Scene 1—The apartment; the following morning. Scene 2—The Jolly Roger Bar; that night. Act III.—Scene 1—The apartment; evening, several days later. Scene 2—The Jolly Roger Bar; a week later, very late at night.

Staged by Frank Corsaro; settings by David Hays; lighting by Lee Watson; costumes by Patricia Zipprodt; production stage manager, Edward Julien; stage manager, Robert Hacha; press representatives, Karl Bernstein and Ben Kornzweig.

(Closed December 6, 1958)

THE DISENCHANTED

(189 performances)

Play in three acts by Budd Schulberg and Harvey Breit, based on the novel by Mr. Schulberg. Produced by William Darrid and Eleanore Saidenberg at the Coronet Theatre, December 3, 1958.

Cast of characters—
```
Shep Stearns .................................. George Grizzard
Victor Milgrim ................................ Whitfield Connor
Manley Halliday ............................... Jason Robards, Jr.
Jere Halliday ................................. Rosemary Harris
Soldiers ...................... Richard Kneeland, Michael del Medico,
                  Moultrie Patten, Larry Ward, Ned Wertimer
Girls ......... Merle Albertson, Nina Clair, Nancy Kovack, Sybil White
Burt Seixas ................................... Jason Robards, Sr.
Freddie ....................................... Bernard Kates
Georgette ..................................... Salome Jens
Wister LaSalle ................................ Jon Cypher
Boris Shlepnikov .............................. Michael del Medico
```

THE BEST PLAYS OF 1958–1959

Party Guests .... Merle Albertson, Nina Clair, Richard Kneeland, Nancy Kovack, Moultrie Patten, Larry Ward, Ned Wertimer, Sybil White
Dean Llewellyn .... John Leslie
Mrs. Llewellyn .... Eleanor Phelps
Prof. Connelly .... Salem Ludwig
Mrs. Connelly .... Dorothea Biddle
Mr. Ridgefield .... Ned Wertimer

Act I.—A winter's evening, 1939; a beach shack near Malibu Beach. Old business: Armistice Night, 1918; a soldiers' canteen, Paris. Old business: a Paris garret, 1920. Act II.—Mid-afternoon, a few days later; Waldorf-Astoria, New York City. Old business: a mansion in Beverly Hills, December, 1929. Act III.—Late afternoon, the following day; attic room in Webster College Inn. Old business: a beach cottage in La Jolla, California, January, 1930.

Staged by David Pressman; settings by Ben Edwards; lighting by Jean Rosenthal; costumes by Ann Roth; production stage manager, Morty Halpern; stage manager, Julian Barry; press representative, Arthur Cantor.

(Closed May 16, 1959)

THE COLD WIND AND THE WARM

(120 performances)

Play in three acts by S. N. Behrman, suggested by his "New Yorker" series and book "The Worcester Account." Produced by the Producers Theatre (Robert Whitehead production) at the Morosco Theatre, December 8, 1958.

Cast of characters—

Tobey .... Timmy Everett
Willie .... Eli Wallach
Jim Nightingale .... Vincent Gardenia
Ida .... Maureen Stapleton
Ren .... Jada Rowland
Myra .... Carol Grace
Aaron .... Peter Trytler
Rappaport .... Sig Arno
Mr. Sacher .... Morris Carnovsky
Dan .... Sidney Armus
Leah .... Suzanne Pleshette
Norbert Mandel .... Sanford Meisner

Act I.—Worcester, Massachusetts; summer, 1908, early evening. Act II.—Scene 1—Sunday afternoon, one and a half years later. Scene 2—Late afternoon the next day. Scene 3—A month later. Scene 4—Several days later. Act III.—New York City, five years later. Scene 1—Tobey's and Willie's room. Ida's living room. Scene 2—Next evening. Scene 3—Immediately following. Scene 4—Some time later, Worcester.

Staged by Harold Clurman; settings by Boris Aronson; costumes by Motley; lighting by Feder; production stage manager, James Gelb; stage manager, Walter Neal; press representative, Barry Hyams.

(Closed March 21, 1959)

THE OLD VIC COMPANY

(40 performances)

Repertory of three dramas by William Shakespeare: "Twelfth Night" (premiere December 9, 1958), "Hamlet" (premiere December 16, 1958) and "Henry V" (premiere December 25, 1958). Produced, under the management of S. Hurok, by the Old Vic Trust Ltd. and the Arts Council of Great Britain at the Broadway Theatre.

TWELFTH NIGHT

Cast of characters—

Orsino, Duke of Illyria	John Humphry
Curio	Thomas Johnston
Valentine	Peter Cellier
Viola	Barbara Jefford
A Sea Captain, friend to Viola	David Gardner
Sir Toby Belch, uncle to Olivia	Joss Ackland
Maria, gentlewoman to Olivia	Judi Dench
Sir Andrew Aguecheek	John Neville
Feste, clown to Olivia	Dudley Jones
Olivia	Jane Downs
Malvolio	Richard Wordsworth
Sebastian, brother to Viola	Gerald Harper
Antonio, a sea captain, friend to Sebastian	Oliver Neville
Fabian, servant to Olivia	James Culliford
Page to Olivia	Simon Fraser
Officers	Harold Innocent, James Mellor
A Priest	John Gay

Ladies, musicians, sailors: Peggy Butt, Ursula Jenkins, Michael Culver, Peter Hodgson, Dyson Lovell, James Mellor, Crispian Woodgate.

Staged by Michael Benthall; decor and costumes by Desmond Heeley; music arranged by Gordon Jacob; musical director, Arthur Lief; stage managers, Peter Smith and Maurice Stewart; press representative, Martin Feinstein.

HAMLET

Cast of characters—

Horatio	David Dodimead
Guards	Roy Patrick, James Mellor, Joss Ackland
Claudius	Oliver Neville
Laertes	John Humphry
Polonius	Joseph O'Conor
Hamlet	John Neville
Gertrude	Margaret Courtenay
Ophelia	Barbara Jefford
Ghost	Richard Wordsworth
Rosencrantz	Peter Cellier
Guildenstern	Gerald Harper
Player King	Richard Wordsworth
Players	James Culliford, Barbara Leigh-Hunt, Robert Algar
Fortinbras	David Gardner
Captain	Robert Algar
Lady	Jane Downs
Servant	Michael Culver
Sailors	Harold Innocent, Douglas Harris
First Gravedigger	Dudley Jones

Second Gravedigger ....Thomas Johnston
Priest ....Harold Innocent
Osric ....Job Stewart
Ladies, Courtiers, Players, Soldiers, Sailors: Peggy Butt, Jennie Goossens, Ursula Jenkins, Robert Algar, John Bonney, James Culliford, Simon Fraser, David Gardner, John Gay, Timothy Harley, Douglas Harris, Peter Hodgson, Harold Innocent, Thomas Johnston, Dyson Lovell, Crispian Woodgate, William Young.

Staged by Michael Benthall; decor and costumes by Audrey Cruddas; musical accompaniment, Gordon Jacob; musical director, Arthur Lief; dueling direction, Bernard Hepton.

HENRY V

Cast of characters—

Chorus	Joseph O'Conor
King Henry V	Laurence Harvey
Duke of Exeter	Oliver Neville
Earl of Westmoreland	John Bonney
Archbishop of Canterbury	Joss Ackland
Bishop of Ely	Robert Algar
Rambures	Roy Patrick
Bardolph	James Culliford
Nym	Job Stewart
Pistol	Richard Wordsworth
Mistress Quickly	Margaret Courtenay
Boy	Timothy Harley
Katherine	Judi Dench
Alice	Jane Downs
Charles VI	David Dodimead
Lewis	Peter Cellier
Constable of France	Robert Algar
Montjoy	John Humphry
Duke of Orleans	Joss Ackland
Fluellen	Dudley Jones
Gower	David Gardner
Duke of Gloucester	Thomas Johnston
Duke of Bedford	Michael Culver
Sir Thomas Erpingham	John Gay
Williams	Gerald Harper
Duke of Salisbury	William Young
Earl of Warwick	Douglas Harris
Isabel	Margaret Courtenay
Duke of Burgundy	Joss Ackland

Citizens, lords, ladies, pages, soldiers, etc.: James Culliford, Simon Fraser, John Gay, Timothy Harley, Peter Hodgson, James Mellor, Job Stewart, Crispian Woodgate, Peggy Butt, Jennie Goossens, Barbara Leigh-Hunt, Ursula Jenkins.

Staged by Michael Benthall; decor and costumes by Audrey Cruddas; music composed by Frederick Marshall; musical director, Arthur Lief.

(Closed January 10, 1959)

THE POWER AND THE GLORY

(71 performances)

Play in eight scenes by Denis Cannan and Pierre Bost, adapted from the novel by Graham Greene. Produced by Theatre Incorporated (T. Edward Hambleton and Norris Houghton, Managing Directors) at the Phoenix Theatre, December 10, 1958.

Cast of characters—

Tench	Eric Berry
The Chief of Police	Dana Elcar
Diaz	David C. Jones
A Priest	Fritz Weaver
The Lieutenant	Robert Geiringer
A Boy	Marc Sullivan
Maria	Betty Miller
Brigida	Ina Beth Cummins
Francisco	John Astin
Miguel	John Brachita
Villagers	Virginia Donaldson, William Hindman, Marian Paone, Tom Bosley
Private Mendoza	Maurice Kamhi
Mestizo	Jerry Stiller
The Governor's Cousin	Meredith Dallas
The Corporal	Elliott Sullivan
The Spinster	Patricia Falkenhain
A Drunken Prisoner	David C. Jones
Prisoners	John Astin, Tom Bosley, Marian Paone, William Hindman
Lopez	Leonardo Cimino
The Warder	Arthur Watson
Obregon	Albert Quinton
The Schoolmaster	Jack Cannon
A Villager	Virginia Donaldson
Alvarez	Elliott Sullivan
Obregon's Wife	Jane White
Ramon	Harrison Hart
Lola	Patrice Payne
Jose Luis	William Hindman
An Indian	Tom Bosley
A Peasant Woman	Betty Henritze
A Stranger	James Patterson

Townspeople, police, prisoners: Daniel Ades, Roger C. Carmel, Roberto Domingues, Ricki Franklin, Paulette Girard, George Goritz, Taylor Graves, Jesse Jacobs, Ann Raim, Hector Torres, Howard Witt, David Zirlin.

The entire action takes place in Southern Mexico, during the anticlerical period of the early 1930s. The time is the recent past. Scene 1—A dentist's office in the capital city. Scene 2—A hut in a nearby village; one month later. Scene 3—A street in the capital city; two days later. Scene 4—A hotel bedroom in the capital city; immediately following. Scene 5—A street in the capital city; immediately following. Scene 6—The jail in the capital city; immediately following. Scene 7—A cafe in a village in a neighboring state; four days later. Scene 8—The dentist's office; two days later.

Staged by Stuart Vaughan; settings and costumes by Will Steven Armstrong; lighting by Klaus Holm; music composed by David Amram; production stage manager, Robert Woods; stage manager, John Robertson; press representatives, Ben Kornzweig and Karl Bernstein.

(Closed February 8, 1959)

J. B.

(196 performances)

(Continued)

Play in two acts by Archibald MacLeish. Produced by Alfred de Liagre, Jr. at the ANTA Theatre, December 11, 1958.

THE BEST PLAYS OF 1958-1959

Cast of characters—

First Roustabout	Clifton James
Second Roustabout	James Olson
Nickles	Christopher Plummer
Mr. Zuss	Raymond Massey
Prompter	Ford Rainey
J. B.	Pat Hingle
Sarah	Nan Martin
David	Arnold Merritt
Mary	Ciri Jacobsen
Jonathan	Jeffrey Rowland
Ruth	Candy Moore
Rebecca	Merry Martin
The Girl	Janet Ward
Mrs. Botticelli	Helen Waters
Mrs. Lesure	Fay Sappington
Mrs. Adams	Judith Lowry
Mrs. Murphy	Laura Pierpont
Jolly	Lane Bradbury
Bildad	Bert Conway
Zophar	Ivor Francis
Eliphaz	Andreas Voutsinas

The scene is a traveling circus which has been on the roads of the world for a long time.

Staged by Elia Kazan; production designed by Boris Aronson; costumes by Lucinda Ballard; lighting by Tharon Musser; music by David Amram; associate producer, Joseph I. Levine; production stage manager, Robert Downing; stage manager, Daniel S. Broun; press representative, Ben Washer.

THE GAZEBO

(194 performances)

(Continued)

Comedy in two acts by Alec Coppel, based on a story by Myra and Alec Coppel. Produced by the Playwrights' Company and Frederick Brisson at the Lyceum Theatre, December 12, 1958.

Cast of characters—

Elliott Nash	Walter Slezak
Harlow Edison	Edward Andrews
Mathilda	Jane Rose
Nell Nash	Jayne Meadows
Mrs. Chandler	Ruth Gillette
Mr. Thorpe	Ralph Chambers
The Dook	Michael Clarke-Laurence
Louie	Don Grusso
Jenkins	Leon Janney
Dr. Wyner	Richard Posten
Druker	John Ford
Potts	Pat Patterson

The entire action of the play takes place in the living room of the Elliott Nash home near Roslyn, Long Island, New York. Act I.—Scene 1—Saturday afternoon. Scene 2—Tuesday evening. Scene 3—The following morning. Act II.—Scene 1—Late afternoon, the same day. Scene 2—The following evening. Scene 3—The next morning.

Staged by Jerome Chodorov; production designed and lighted by Jo Mielziner; costumes by Virginia Volland; production stage manager, Fred Hebert; stage manager, E. W. Swackhamer; press representative, William Fields.

WHOOP-UP

(56 performances)

Musical comedy in two acts, based on "Stay Away, Joe" by Dan Cushman; with book by Cy Feuer, Ernest H. Martin and Dan Cushman; lyrics by Norman Gimbel; music by Moose Charlap. Produced by Feuer & Martin at the Sam S. Shubert Theatre, December 22, 1958.

Cast of characters—

Glenda Swenson	Susan Johnson
Jiggs Rock Medicine	Michael Kermoyan
Walt Stephenpierre	Tom Raskin
Dub Winter Owl	Jackie Warner
Bix Winter Owl	Bobby Shields
Louis Champlain	Romo Vincent
Annie Champlain	Sylvia Syms
Mary Champlain	Julienne Marie
Matthew Bearchaser	Tony Gardell
Karl Kellenbach	Paul Ford
Clyde Walschmidt	Wallace Rooney
George Potter	Danny Meehan
Medicine Man	Tony Gardell
Joe Champlain	Ralph Young
Marlene Standing Rattle	Ann Barry
Gran'pere	P. J. Kelly
Billie Mae Littlehorse	Asia
Juke Box Voice	Bobby Shields
Mrs. Kellenbach	Vera Walton
Baptiste Three Bird	Paul Michael
Hotel Proprietor	Robert Lenn
Teenager	Robert Karl
State Trooper	Steve Wiland
Justice of the Peace	Earl Lippy
First Stranger	Edward Becker
Second Stranger	Socrates Birsky

Reservation residents: Mari Arnell, Ann Barry, Edward Becker, Jeanna Belkin, Socrates Birsky, Tim Brown, Sandra Devlin, Eleanor Dian, Tina Faye, Tony Gardell, Martha Granese, H. F. Green, Salvador Juarez, Robert Karl, Robert Lenn, Earl Lippy, Rae McLean, Michelle Newton, Estelle Parsons, Yolanda Poropat, Tom Raskin, Tony Rosa, Marla Stevens, Ben Vargas, Barbara Webb, Steve Wiland.

The entire action takes place on or near a United States Indian reservation in northern Montana. The time is the present.

Staged by Cy Feuer; settings and lighting by Jo Mielziner; choreography by Onna White; costumes by Anna Hill Johnstone; musical and vocal director, Stanley Lebowsky; orchestrations by Philip J. Lang; dance music arranged by Peter Matz; production stage manager, Phil Friedman; stage manager, Lawrence N. Kasha; press representative, Karl Bernstein.

Musical numbers—

ACT I

"Glenda's Place"	Glenda and Indians
"When the Tall Man Talks"	Glenda
"Nobody Throw Those Bull"	Louis and Indians
"Rocky Boy Ceremonial"	Medicine Man and Members of the Tribe
"Love Eyes"	Joe
"Men"	Glenda

"Never Before" .... Mary
"Caress Me, Possess Me Perfume" .... (Juke Box Voice)
"Flattery" .... Joe and Glenda
"The Girl in His Arms" .... (Juke Box)
"The Best of What This Country's Got" .... George

ACT II

"I Wash My Hands" .... Joe, Mary, Rock Medicine and Stephenpierre
"Quarrel-tet" .... Glenda, Joe, Proprietor and Stephenpierre
"Sorry for Myself" .... Annie
" 'Til the Big Fat Moon Falls Down" .... Mary, Billie Mae and Friends
"What I Mean to Say" .... George
"Montana" .... Glenda
"She or Her" .... Joe

(Closed February 7, 1959)

A PARTY WITH BETTY COMDEN AND ADOLPH GREEN

(38 performances)

Miss Comden and Mr. Green performing their own comedy and musical numbers, with Peter Howard at the piano. Produced by the Theatre Guild, by special arrangement and in association with Town Productions, Inc. (as originally presented by JJG Productions under the supervision of Gus Schirmer, Jr.), at the John Golden Theatre, December 23, 1958.

Program—

PART I

The Performers
1. Opening .... music by Andre Previn
2. "The Revuers" (night club act) ..... sketches, lyrics and music by The Revuers

PART II

The Performer—Writers
1. "On the Town" .... music by Leonard Bernstein
2. "Billion Dollar Baby" .... music by Morton Gould
3. "Good News" (film) .... music by Roger Edens
4. "Two on the Aisle" .... music by Jule Styne

PART III

The Writer—Performers
1. "Wonderful Town" .... music by Leonard Bernstein
2. "Peter Pan" .... Music by Jule Styne
3. "A Show" .... music by Saul Chaplin
4. "Say, Darling" .... music by Jule Styne.
5. "Bells Are Ringing" .... music by Jule Styne

Associate producer, Frank Perry; decor and lighting by Marvin Reiss; stage manager, Ken Mays; press representatives, Sol Jacobson and Lewis Harmon.

A Party was revived on April 16, 1959, for 44 performances.

(Closed January 24, 1959)

AGES OF MAN

(40 performances)

Sir John Gielgud reads scenes and sonnets from Shakespeare, based on George Rylands' "Shakespeare Anthology." Produced by Jerry Leider, in association with Tennent Productions Ltd., at the Forty-sixth Street Theatre, December 28, 1958.

Program—

PART I: YOUTH

Childhood—Magic and Faery—Love—Jealousy—Lust
"As You Like It"—"Hamlet" (Act I, Scene 2)—Sonnet 11—"A Midsummer Night's Dream" (Act II, Scene 1)—"The Tempest" (Act III, Scene 2—"Romeo and Juliet" (Act I, Scene 4; and Act V, Scene 1)—"The Merchant of Venice" (Act V, Scene 1)—"Much Ado About Nothing" (Act II, Scene 3)—Sonnet 18—"Romeo and Juliet" (Act I, Scene 5)—Sonnet 116—Sonnet 130—"Romeo and Juliet" (Act II, Scene 6; and Act III, Scene 5)—"The Winter's Tale" (Act I, Scene 2)—Sonnet 129—"Measure for Measure" (Act II, Scene 2).

PART II: MANHOOD

War—Civil Strife—Kingship—Government and Society—Passion and Character
"Othello" (Act I, Scene 4)—"Henry IV" (Part 1, Act I, Scene 3)—"Henry VI" (Part 3, Act II, Scene 5)—"Richard II" (Act III, Scene 3; and Act IV, Scene 1)—"Julius Caesar" (Act I, Scene 2)—Sonnets to Sundry—"Hamlet" (Act II, Scene 2).

PART III: OLD AGE

Sickness—Man Against Himself—Old Age—Death—Time
Sonnet 138—Sonnet 73—"Macbeth" (Act II)—"Henry IV" (Part 2, Act III, Scene 2)—"Richard III" (Act I, Scene 4)—"Richard II" (Act II, Scene 1)—"Measure for Measure" (Act III, Scene 1)—"Julius Caesar" (Act II, Scene 2)—"Hamlet" (Act II, Scene 2; Act III, Scene 1; and Act V, Scene 2)—Sonnet 29—"Romeo and Juliet" (Act V, Scene 3)—"King Lear" (Act V, Scene 3)—"The Tempest" (Act IV, Scene 1; Act V, Scene 1; and Epilogue)—"Much Ado About Nothing" (Act V, Scene 3).

Associate producers, Bret Adams and Sanford Leigh; lighting by Ben Edwards; stage manager, David Haber; press representatives, Harvey B. Sabinson, David Powers and Ted Goldsmith.

(Closed January 31, 1959)

THIRD BEST SPORT

(79 performances)

Comedy in three acts by Eleanor and Leo Bayer. Produced by the Theatre Guild at the Ambassador Theatre, December 30, 1958.

Cast of characters—

Bellboy	Spofford Beadle
Helen Sayre	Celeste Holm
Douglas Sayre	Andrew Duggan
Chuck Robbins	James Karen
Arthur Underhill	Howard Wierum

```
Amy Underhill .................................... Jane Hoffman
Marge Robbins ................................. Parker McCormick
John Wagner ..................................... Judson Laire
Dr. Jonas Lockwood ............................. William Prince
Myra McHenry ..................................... Irene Cowan
Spencer McHenry ................................. Joseph Boland
```

The action is contemporary and takes place in the living room of a hotel suite in Palm Beach, Florida. Act I.—Scene 1—11:00 A.M., a day in March. Scene 2—Later that afternoon. Act II.—Scene 1—The next morning. Scene 2—That evening. Act III.—Later that evening.

Staged by Michael Howard; setting by Marvin Reiss; costumes by Michael Travis; associate producer, Henry T. Weinstein; Miss Holm's clothes by Robert Mackintosh; stage manager, Karl Nielsen; press representatives, Dick Weaver and Ned Armstrong.

(Closed March 7, 1959)

EPITAPH FOR GEORGE DILLON

(48 performances)

Play in three acts by John Osborne and Anthony Creighton. Revived by Norman Twain and Bernard Miller, by arrangement with the English Stage Company, at Henry Miller's Theatre, January 12, 1959.

Cast of characters—
```
Josie Elliot ......................................... Wendy Craig
Ruth Gray .......................................... Eileen Herlie
Mrs. Elliot ......................................... Alison Leggatt
Norah Elliot ....................................... Barbara Stanton
Percy Elliot ....................................... George Turner
George Dillon ..................................... Robert Stephens
Geoffrey Colwyn-Stuart ........................... James Valentine
Mr. Webb .......................................... David Vaughan
Barney Evans ...................................... Guy Spaull
```

Staged by William Gaskell; scenery by Stephen Doncaster; scenery and lighting supervised by Ralph Alswang; costumes supervised by Helene Pons; stage manager, Cameron MacCardell; press representatives, Karl Bernstein and Ben Kornzweig.

Epitaph for George Dillon was first produced by David Merrick and Joshua Logan at the John Golden Theatre, November 4, 1958, for 23 performances (see page 301).

(Closed February 21, 1959)

RASHOMON

(143 performances)

(Continued)

Play in two acts by Fay and Michael Kanin, based on stories by Ryunosuke Akutagawa. Produced by David Susskind and Hardy Smith at the Music Box Theatre, January 27, 1959.

Cast of characters—

Priest	Michael Shillo
Woodcutter	Akim Tamiroff
Wigmaker	Oscar Homolka
Deputy	Jack Bittner
Bandit	Rod Steiger
Husband	Noel Willman
Wife	Claire Bloom
Mother	Ruth White
Medium	Elsa Freed

The action takes place in Kyoto, Japan, about a thousand years ago—at a corner of the Rashomon Gate, at a police court and in a nearby forest.

Staged by Peter Glenville; settings and costumes by Oliver Messel; lighting by Jo Mielziner; music by Laurence Rosenthal; associate producer, Michael Abbott; swordplay instructor, Torao Mori; production stage manager, Jose Vega; stage manager, Robert Paschall; press representative, Arthur Cantor.

TALL STORY

(108 performances)

Comedy in three acts by Howard Lindsay and Russel Crouse, suggested by the novel "The Homecoming Game" by Howard Nemerov. Produced by Emmett Rogers and Robert Weiner at the Belasco Theatre, January 29, 1959.

Cast of characters—

Herb	Jeff Harris
Connie	Nancy Baker
Don	Richard Franchot
Walter	Wayne Tippit
Hazel	Janet Fox
Agnes	Sally Jessup
Nancy	Joyce Bulifant
Mary	Sherry LaFolette
Eddie	Kevin Carpenter
Joe	Donald Dawson
Charles Osman, professor of physics	Marc Connelly
Leon Solomon, professor of ethics	Hans Conreid
Myra Solomon, his wife	Marian Winters
Wesley Davis, county prosecutor	Jamie Smith
June Ryder	Nina Wilcox
Ray Blent	Robert Elston
Sandy Hardy	Mason Adams
Mike Giardineri	Ralph Stantley
Baker	Tom Williams
Grant	Charles K. Robinson, Jr.
Fred Jensen	Hazen Gifford
Frieda Jensen	Patricia Finch
Dick Stevens	Edmund Williams
Albert Solomon	Ray Merritt
Myers	Bob Lynn, Jr.
Simpson	Wayne Tippit
Wyman	Jeff Harris
Harmon Nagel, president of Custer College	Robert Wright
Collins	John Astin
Clark	Rex Everhart

The story takes place at Custer College, a co-educational institution in the Middle West. Act I.—Scene 1—Mike's College Cafe; a Monday evening in March. Scene 2—Coach Hardy's office off the gymnasium; Friday afternoon. Scene 3—Professor Solomon's living room; the same afternoon. Act II.—Scene 1—Professor Osman's living room; the same afternoon. Scene 2—Professor Solomon's living room; later that afternoon. Scene 3—Professor Osman's living room; early that evening. Act III.—Scene 1—President Nagel's office; the same evening. Scene 2—Coach Hardy's office; later that evening. Scene 3—Professor Solomon's living room; after midnight.

Staged by Herman Shumlin; sets and lighting by George Jenkins; costumes by Noel Taylor; songs by Joe Hornsby, Ben G. Allen and Jerry Teifer (arranged by Edward Thomas); production stage manager, Mike Thoma; stage manager, Richard Franchot; press representatives, Sol Jacobson, Lewis Harmon and Abner Klipstein.

(Closed May 2, 1959)

REQUIEM FOR A NUN

(43 performances)

Play in three acts by Ruth Ford and William Faulkner, adapted from the novel by Mr. Faulkner. Produced by the Theatre Guild and Myers & Fleischmann at the John Golden Theatre, January 30, 1959.

Cast of characters—

Nancy Mannigoe .... Bertice Reading
Mrs. Gowan Stevens (née Temple Drake) .... Ruth Ford
Gowan Stevens .... Scott McKay
Gavin Stevens .... Zachary Scott
Governor .... House Jameson
Pete .... Christian Flanders
Mr. Tubbs .... John Dorman

The action of the play takes place in the present time in Mississippi —before and after the trial of Nancy Mannigoe for murder. Act I.— Scene 1—Courtroom. Scene 2—Gowan Stevens' living room; half an hour later. Scene 3—The same; four months later. Act II.—Scene 1—Office of the Governor of the State; early next morning. Scene 2—Gowan Stevens' living room; a year before. Scene 3—Office of the Governor of the State. Act III.—The jail; the next day.

Staged by Tony Richardson; London production designed by Motley; American production supervised and lighted by Marvin Reiss; stage manager, John Cornell; press representative, Nat Dorfman.

See page 189.

(Closed March 7, 1959)

REDHEAD

(132 performances)

(Continued)

Musical comedy in two acts, with book by Herbert and Dorothy Fields, Sidney Sheldon and David Shaw; music by Albert Hague; lyrics by Dorothy Fields. Produced by Robert Fryer and Lawrence Carr at the Forty-sixth Street Theatre, February 5, 1959.

THE BEST PLAYS OF 1958-1959

Cast of characters—

Ruth LaRue	Pat Ferrier
Maude Simpson	Cynthia Latham
Sarah Simpson	Doris Rich
May	Joy Nichols
Tilly	Pat Ferrier
Essie Whimple	Gwen Verdon
Inspector White	Ralph Sumpter
Howard Cavanaugh	William Le Massena
George Poppett	Leonard Stone
Tom Baxter	Richard Kiley
Alfy, stage doorman	Lee Krieger
Sir Charles Willingham	Patrick Horgan
The Tenor	Bob Dixon
Inez, the blonde	Bette Graham
Jailer	Buzz Miller

Singers: Mame Dennis, Joan Fagan, Lydia Fredericks, Bette Graham, Dee Harless, Janie Janvier, Kelley Stephens, Bob Dixon, Clifford Fearl, John Lankston, Larry Mitchell, Stan Page, Shev Rodgers.

Dancers: Margery Beddow, Shirley de Burgh, Pat Ferrier, Reby Howells, Patti Karr, Elaine King, Liane Plane, Dean Taliaferro, John Aristides, Kevin Carlisle, David Gold, Harvey Hohnecker, Kazimir Kokich, Dale Moreda, Noel Parenti, Alton Ruff.

Act I.—Prologue—A theatre dressing room. Scene 1—Outside the Simpson Sisters' Waxworks. Scene 2—The interior of the Waxworks. Scene 3—Essie's workshop. Scene 4—A street. Scene 5—Stage of the Odeon Theatre. Scene 6—Corridor, backstage. Scene 7—Tom's apartment. Scene 8—Outside the museum. Scene 9—Backstage of the Odeon Theatre. Scene 10—Stage of the Odeon Theatre. Act II.—Scene 1—Tom's apartment. Scene 2—A street. Scene 3—The Green Dragon Pub. Scene 4—The jail cell. Scene 5—Corridor, backstage. Scene 6—The Museum.

Entire production staged and choreographed by Bob Fosse; designed by Rouben Ter-Arutunian; lighting by Jean Rosenthal; orchestrations by Philip J. Lang and Robert Russell Bennett; musical direction and vocal arrangements by Jay Blackton; dance music arranged by Roger Adams; associate choreographer, Donald McKayle; production manager, Robert Linden; stage manager, Ross Bowman; press representative, Arthur Cantor.

Musical numbers—

ACT I

"The Simpson Sisters"	Singers and Dancers
"The Right Finger of My Left Hand"	Gwen Verdon
"Just for Once"	Gwen Verdon, Richard Kiley and Leonard Stone
"Merely Marvelous"	Gwen Verdon
"The Uncle Sam Rag"	Leonard Stone, Singers and Dancers
"Erbie Fitch's Twitch"	Gwen Verdon
"She's Not Enough Woman for Me"	Richard Kiley, Leonard Stone
"Behave Yourself"	Gwen Verdon, Cynthia Latham, Doris Rich and Richard Kiley
"Look Who's in Love"	Gwen Verdon and Richard Kiley
"My Girl Is Just Enough Woman for Me"	Richard Kiley and Passersby
"Essie's Vision"	Gwen Verdon and her Dream People
"Two Faces in the Dark"	Gwen Verdon, Bob Dixon Singers and Dancers

ACT II

"I'm Back in Circulation"	Richard Kiley
"We Loves Ya, Jimey"	Gwen Verdon, Joy Nichols, Pat Ferrier and Clientele of the Green Dragon
"Pick-Pocket Tango"	Gwen Verdon and Buzz Miller
"Look Who's in Love" (Reprise)	Richard Kiley
"I'll Try"	Gwen Verdon and Richard Kiley
Finale	Gwen Verdon, Richard Kiley and Company

THE RIVALRY

(81 performances)

Play in two acts by Norman Corwin. Produced by Cheryl Crawford and Joel Schenker at the Bijou Theatre, February 7, 1959.

Cast of characters—

Adele Douglas	Nancy Kelly
Stephen A. Douglas	Martin Gabel
Abraham Lincoln	Richard Boone
Townspeople	Woodrow Parfrey, Jim Campbell, Ailsa Dawson

Musicians: Maurice Peress, Frank Vaccaro, Jerry Silverman, Spencer Sinatra, Jules Greenberg.

The action takes place in Washington, D. C., and various cities and towns of Illinois, starting in the summer of 1958. An epilogue follows Act II.

Staged by Norman Corwin; settings by David Hays; costumes by Motley; lighting by Tharon Musser; music composed by David Amram; stage manager, Irving Buchman; press representative, Arthur Cantor.

(Closed April 18, 1959)

THE LEGEND OF LIZZIE

(2 performances)

Play in two acts by Reginald Lawrence. Produced by Hartney Arthur and Nat Stevens at the Fifty-fourth Street Theatre (Adelphi), February 9, 1959.

Cast of characters—

District Attorney Sewell	Douglass Montgomery
Lizzie Borden	Anne Meacham
Emma Borden	Mary Mace
Reverend Phipps	Lee Richardson
Bridget O'Hanlon	Joyce Ballou
Mrs. Steers	Miriam Phillips
Minnie Jameson	Elsa Raven
Officer Mead	Rod Colbin
Cooper (Assistant District Attorney)	William Daniels
Defense Attorney Johnson	Alfred Hinckley
Matron Keenan	Frances Hammond
Judge	Jock MacGregor
County Clerk	Lance Cunard
Jury Foreman	Richard Durham
Clara Buchanan	Geraldine Rehrig
Officer Long	Brendan Fay
Marshal Haynes	Lou Polan
Uncle Morse	Frank Tweddell
Abby Borden	Muriel Kirkland
Andrew Borden	Frank M. Thomas
Court Stenographer	Edward Printz
Dr. Stone	Grant Code
Henry Appleton	Stephen Joyce
Stranger	M. Throne

322   THE BEST PLAYS OF 1958-1959

Children: Danny DePace, Penny Grayam, Jody Lane, John Nutting.
Townspeople: Barbara Lester, Ruth Marion.
The time is late last century; the place, in and around the town of Fall River, Massachusetts.

Staged by Hartney Arthur; production designed by Ballou; lighting by Lee Watson; music by Willard Straight; production stage manager, Bernard Gersten; stage manager, Leon Gersten; press representatives, Howard Atlee and Anne Woll.

(Closed February 10, 1959)

THE MOST HAPPY FELLA

(16 performances)

Musical in two acts, with music, lyrics and libretto by Frank Loesser. Revived by the New York City Center Light Opera Company (Jean Dalrymple, Director) at the New York City Center, February 10, 1959.

Cast of characters—

The Cashier	Lee Cass
Cleo	Libi Staiger
Rosabella	Paula Stewart
The Waitresses	Jessica Albright, Betty Jenkins, Gloria Kaye, Kitty Malone, Sherry McCutchen, Sybil Scotford
The Postman	Lee Cass
Tony	Norman Atkins
Marie	Muriel Birkhead
Max	Win Mayo
Herman	Jack De Lon
Clem	James Schlader
Jake	Ken Adams
Al	Roy Lazarus
Joe	Art Lund
Giuseppe	Kenneth Lane
Pasquale	Bruce MacKay
Ciccio	Michael Davis
Country Girl, City Boy	Jessica Albright, Garold Gardner
The Doctor	Keith Kaldenberg
The Priest	Fred Conway
Tessie	Bernadette Peters
Gussie	Johnny Borden
Train Conductor	Win Mayo
Neighbors	Mary Sue Berry, Gloria Kaye, Barbara Saxby, John Dorrin, Roy Lazarus, George Zima
Neighbor Ladies	Thea Brandon, Terry DeLiva, Maggie Task
Brakeman	Sheldon Ossosky
Bus Driver	Jordan Howard

All the neighbors and all the neighbors' neighbors: Lorrie Bentley, Mary Sue Berry, Jan Canada, Terry DeLiva, Mary Ann Heitzig, Barbara Saxby, Jeanne Schlegel, Shelia Swenson, Maggie Task, Ken Adams, Fred Conway, Michael Davis, John Dorrin, Jordan Howard, Del Horstmann, Robert Ethridge, Roy Lazarus, Jack McMinn, Win Mayo, Jack McCann, James Schlader, Jessica Albright, Betty Jenkins, Gloria Kaye, Kitty Malone, Sherry McCutchen, Sybil Scotford, Garold Gardner, Bob LaCrosse, Sheldon Ossosky, Michael Scrittorale, James Senn, George Zima.

Entire production directed and supervised by Dania Krupska; original choreography by Dania Krupska restaged by Arthur F. Partington; musical direction, Abba Bogin; setting and lighting by Jo Mielziner; costumes by Ruth Morley; art director, Watson Barratt; production stage manager, Chet O'Brien; stage manager, Bert Wood; press representative, Tom Trenkle.

The Most Happy Fella was first produced by Kermit Bloomgarden and Lynn Loesser at the Imperial Theatre, May 3, 1956, for 676 performances.

(Closed February 22, 1959)

A MAJORITY OF ONE

(120 performances)

(Continued)

Comedy in three acts by Leonard Spigelgass. Produced by the Theatre Guild and Dore Schary at the Sam S. Shubert Theatre, February 16, 1959.

Cast of characters—

Mrs. Rubin	Mae Questel
Mrs. Jacoby	Gertrude Berg
Alice Black	Ina Balin
Jerome Black	Michael Tolan
Lady Passenger	Selma Halpern
Koichi Asano	Cedric Hardwicke
Eddie	Marc Marno
House Boy	Arsenio Trinidad
Ayako Asano	Kanna Ishii
Tateshi	Tsuruko Kobayashi
Noketi	Sahomi Tachibana
Servant Girl	Yasuko Adachi
Chauffeur	Arsenio Trinidad
Captain Norcross	Barnard Hughes

Act I.—Scene 1—Mrs. Jacoby's apartment in Brooklyn; a late afternoon in May. Scenes 2, 3 and 4—Promenade deck of the S.S. Leonard Wood, during the two-week voyage to Japan. Act II.—Scene 1—The Blacks' home in Tokyo; August. Scene 2—Mr. Asano's home in Tokyo; a half hour later. Act III.—Scene 1—The Blacks' home; two hours later. Scene 2—Mrs. Jacoby's home in Brooklyn; two months later.

Staged by Dore Schary; production designed and lighted by Donald Oenslager; costumes by Motley; associate producer, Philip Langner; production stage manager, Elliot Martin; stage manager, David Ford; press representative, Nat Dorfman.

THE BEAUX' STRATAGEM

(16 performances)

Comedy in two acts by George Farquhar. Revived by Theatre Incorporated (T. Edward Hambleton and Norris Houghton, Managing Directors) at the Phoenix Theatre, February 24, 1959.

Cast of characters—

Bonniface	Robert Geiringer
Cherry, his daughter	Barbara Barrie
Thomas Aimwell	Robert Blackburn
Francis Archer	David King-Wood
Mrs. Sullen	June Havoc
Dorinda	Patricia Falkenhain
Squire Sullen	Eric Berry
Scrub	Tom Bosley
Gibbet, a highwayman	Meredith Dallas
A Country Woman	Betty Miller
Lady Bountiful	Sylvia Short
Bagshot	Albert Quinton
Hounslow	Jesse Jacobs
Sir Charles Freeman	David C. Jones
Footmen	James Patterson, Jerry W. Hardin

The action takes place in Litchfield, Staffordshire, England; the Inn and the nearby house and garden of Lady Bountiful.

Staged by Stuart Vaughan; settings and costumes by Will Steven Armstrong; lighting by Tharon Musser; songs and music composed by David Amram; production stage manager, Robert Woods; stage manager, John Robertson; press representatives, Ben Kornzweig and Karl Bernstein.

(Closed March 8, 1959)

SAY, DARLING

(16 performances)

Comedy in three acts by Richard Bissell, Abe Burrows and Marian Bissell, based on the novel by Richard Bissell; with songs by Betty Comden, Adolph Green and Jule Styne. Revived by the New York City Center Light Opera Company (Jean Dalrymple, Director) at the New York City Center, February 25, 1959.

Cast of characters—

Mr. Schneider	Gordon B. Clarke
Frankie Jordan	Betsy von Furstenberg
Jack Jordan	Orson Bean
Photographer	Stephen Franken
Pilot Roy Peters	Robert Herrman
Ted Snow	Robert Morse
June, the secretary	Kelly Leigh
Schatzie Harris	Jack Waldron
Richard Hackett	Alexander Clark
Irene Lovelle	Mindy Carson
Rudy Lorraine	David Atkinson
Charlie Williams	James Karr
Maurice, a pianist	Brooks Morton
Arlene McKee	Janyce Wagner
Jennifer Stevenson	Jean Mattox
Earl Jorgeson	Elliott Gould
Cheryl Merrill	Paula Wayne
Accompanist	Joe Richter
Sammy Miles	Buddy Ferrard
Rex Dexter	Mitchell Gregg
Boris Reshevsky	Matt Mattox
Waiter	Stephen Franken
Morty Krebs	Edward Hunt

Others: Marcella Dodge, Kelly Leigh, Paula Lloyd, Jean Mattox, Janyce Wagner, Elliott Gould, George Martin, Calvin von Reinhold, Eddie Weston, Andrew Bagni, Joseph Castka, Tommy Lucas, Ted Flowerman.

Staged by David Clive; designed by Oliver Smith; costumes by Alvin Colt; lighting by Peggy Clark; dances by Matt Mattox; musical director, Colin Romoff; production stage manager, Bill Field; stage manager, Henry Velez; press representative, Tom Trenkle.

Say, Darling was first produced by Jule Styne and Lester Osterman at the ANTA Theatre, April 3, 1958, for 332 performances.

(Closed March 8, 1959)

GOD AND KATE MURPHY

(12 performances)

Play in two acts by Kieran Tunney and John Synge. Produced by Carroll and Harris Masterson and Charles R. Wood at the Fifty-fourth Street Theatre (Adelphi), February 26, 1959.

Cast of characters—

```
Shelagh O'Connor ............................... Lois Nettleton
Carrie Donovan ................................ Maureen Delany
Sean Murphy ....................................... Mike Kellin
Patrick Molloy ................................... John McGiver
Kate Murphy ....................................... Fay Compton
Rory Murphy ..................................... Larry Hagman
Mrs. Cronin ....................................... Nancy Lester
Mrs. Donehue ..................................... Nancy Fields
The Singer ..................................... Pauline Flanagan
```

The locale is the South of Ireland: Kate Murphy's public house in a small town about twenty miles from the city of Cork. Act I.—Scene 1—An early morning in late summer. Scene 2—Early afternoon the following day. Scene 3—Eight hours later. Act II.—Scene 1—An afternoon eighteen months later. Scene 2—Closing time that night.

Staged by Burgess Meredith; setting and lighting by Ben Edwards; costumes by Betty Coe Armstrong; associate producer, Irl Mowery; production stage manager, Edward Padula; press representatives, Nat Dorfman and Irvin Dorfman.

(Closed March 7, 1959)

LOOK AFTER LULU

(39 performances)

Comedy in three acts by Noel Coward, based on "Occupe-toi d'Amelie" by Georges Feydeau. Produced by the Playwrights' Company and Gilbert Miller, Lance Hamilton and Charles Russell, at Henry Miller's Theatre, March 3, 1959.

Cast of characters—

Lulu d'Arville, a cocotte	Tammy Grimes
Philippe de Croze, Lulu's lover	George Baker
Friends of Philippe { Bomba	Rory Harrity
Valery	Craig Huebing
Emile	Bill Berger
Friends of Lulu { Gaby	Barbara Loden
Yvonne	Sasha von Scherler
Paulette	Grace Gaynor
Adonis, a footman	Paul Smith
Gigot, Lulu's father, a retired policeman	Eric Christmas
Claire, the Duchess of Clausonnes	Polly Rowles
Marcel Blanchard	Roddy McDowall
General Koschnadieff	Ellis Rabb
Herr van Putzeboum	Jack Gilford
Two Boys from the Florist's	David Faulkner, David Thurman
The Prince of Salestria	Kurt Kasznar
Rose, a maid	Reva Rose
Oudatte, a clerk at the Town Hall	Earl Montgomery
Cornette, another clerk	John Alderman
The Mayor of the District	Arthur Malet
A Photographer	William Griffis
Aunt Gabrielle	Philippa Bevans
A Little Girl	Ina Cummins
An Inspector of Police	David Hurst

Act I.—The salon of Lulu's apartment in Paris, 1908. Act II.—Marcel's bedroom. Act III.—Scene 1—A room at the Town Hall. Scene 2—Lulu's bedroom.

Staged by Cyril Ritchard; scenery and costumes by Cecil Beaton; lighting by Raymond Sovey; production stage manager, Keene Curtis; stage manager, William Dodds; press representative, William Fields.

(Closed April 4, 1959)

JUNO

(16 performances)

Musical in two acts, based on Sean O'Casey's play, "Juno and the Paycock"; with book by Joseph Stein; music and lyrics by Marc Blitzstein. Produced by the Playwrights' Company, Oliver Smith and Oliver Rea at the Winter Garden, March 9, 1959.

Cast of characters—

Mary Boyle	Monte Amundsen
Johnny Boyle	Tommy Rall
Juno Boyle	Shirley Booth
Jerry Devine	Loren Driscoll
Mrs. Madigan	Jean Stapleton
Mrs. Brady	Nancy Andrews
Mrs. Coyne	Sada Thompson
Miss Quinn	Beulah Garrick
Charlie Bentham	Earl Hammond
Foley	Arthur Rubin
Sullivan	Rico Froehlich
Michael Brady	Robert Rue
Paddy Coyne	Julian Patrick
"Captain" Jack Boyle	Melvyn Douglas
"Joxer" Daly	Jack MacGowran
Molly	Gemze de Lappe
"Needle" Nugent	Liam Lenihan
I. R. A. Men	Tom Clancy, Jack Murray
Mrs. Tancred	Clarice Blackburn

Mrs. Dwyer ....Betty Low
I. R. A. Singer ....Robert Hoyem
Furniture Removal Men ....George Ritner, Frank Carroll
Policeman ....Rico Froehlich
　　Singers: Anne Fielding, Cleo Fry, Pat Huddleston, Gail Johnston, Barbara Lockard, Pat Ruhl, Diana Sennett, Joanne Spiller, Frank Carroll, Ted Forlow, Rico Froehlich, Robert Hoyem, Jack Murray, Julian Patrick, George Ritner, Robert Rue, James Tushar.
　　Dancers: Sharon Enoch, Mickey Gunnersen, Pat Heyes, Rosemary Jourdan, Annabelle Lyon, Marjorie Wittmer, Jenny Workman, Chuck Bennett, Ted Forlow, Curtis Hood, Scott Hunter, Eugene Kelton, James Maher, Eurique Martinez, Howard Parker, Jim Ryan, Glen Tetley.
　　The action takes place in Dublin, 1921. Act I.—Prologue—The street in front of the Boyle home; early evening in summer. Scene 1—The Boyle home. Scene 2—Another street. Scene 3—The street and Foley's bar. Scene 4—A park square. Scene 5—The Boyle home. Scene 6—Another street. Scene 7—A square in the city. Scene 8—A park square; evening, a few days later. Scene 9—The street. Act II.—Scene 1—The Boyle home; evening, a few days later. Scene 2—The yard behind the house. Scene 3—A street. Scene 4—The Boyle home. Scene 5—A park square. Scene 6—The Boyle home. Scene 7—The street and Foley's bar.
　　Staged by Jose Ferrer; dances and musical numbers staged by Agnes de Mille; scenery designed by Oliver Smith; costumes by Irene Sharaff; lighting by Peggy Clark; music direction, Robert Emmett Dolan; orchestrations by Robert Russell Bennett, Marc Blitzstein, Hershy Kay; associate producer, Lyn Austin; production stage manager, Peter Zeisler; stage manager, Randall Brooks; press representative, William Fields.

Musical numbers—
ACT I
"We're Alive" ....Ensemble
"I Wish It So" ....Mary
"Song of the Ma" ....Juno
"We Can Be Proud" ...Foley, Sullivan, Michael Brady, Paddy Coyne
"Daarlin' Man" ....Boyle, Joxer and Ensemble
"One Kind Word" ....Jerry
"Old Sayin's" ....Juno, Boyle
"What Is the Stars?" ....Boyle, Joxer
"Old Sayin's" (Reprise) ....Juno, Boyle
"You Poor Thing" ....Mrs. Madigan, Mrs. Brady,
　　　　　　　　　　　　　　　　　　Mrs. Coyne, Miss Quinn
Ballet: "Dublin Night" ....Johnny, Molly and Ensemble
"My True Heart" ....Mary, Bentham
"On a Day like This": Finale, Act I .....Juno, Boyle and Ensemble
Jig ....Howard Parker and Eugene Kelton
Slip Jig ....Glen Tetley
Shillelagh Dance ....Curtis Hood, Enrique Martinez,
　　　　　　　　　　　　　　　　　Chuck Bennett, Scott Hunter
Jig ....Juno, Boyle and Ensemble

ACT II
"Bird upon the Tree" ....Juno, Mary
The Party
　(a) "Music in the House" ....Boyle and Ensemble
　(b) "It's Not Irish"
　　　[Gramophone] ....Arthur Rubin
　　　[Quartet] ....Foley, Sullivan, Michael Brady, Boyle
　(c) "The Liffy Waltz" ....Ensemble
"Hymn" ....I.R.A. Singer
"Johnny" ....Johnny, Molly
"You Poor Thing" (Reprise) ....Mrs. Madigan, Mrs. Brady,
　　　　　　　　　　　　　　　　　　Mrs. Coyne, Miss Quinn
"For Love" ....Mary
"One Kind Word" (Reprise) ....Jerry
"Where?" ....Juno
Finale, Act II ....Juno, Mary, Boyle, Joxer

(Closed March 21, 1959)

SWEET BIRD OF YOUTH

(95 performances)

(Continued)

Play in three acts by Tennessee Williams. Produced by Cheryl Crawford at the Martin Beck Theatre, March 10, 1959.

Cast of characters—

Chance Wayne	Paul Newman
The Princess Kosmonopolis	Geraldine Page
Fly	Milton J. Williams
Maid	Patricia Ripley
George Scudder	Logan Ramsey
Hatcher	John Napier
Boss Finley	Sidney Blackmer
Tom Junior	Rip Torn
Aunt Nonnie	Martine Bartlett
Heavenly Finley	Diana Hyland
Charles	Earl Sydnor
Stuff	Bruce Dern
Miss Lucy	Madeleine Sherwood
The Heckler	Charles Tyner
Violet	Monica May
Edna	Hilda Brawner
Scotty	Charles McDaniel
Bud	James Jeter
Men in Bar	Duke Farley, Ron Harper, Kenneth Blake
Page	Glenn Stensel

Time: modern—an Easter Sunday from late morning till late night. Act I.—Scene 1—A bedroom in the Royal Palms Hotel, somewhere on the Gulf Coast. Scene 2—The same, later. Act II.—Scene 1—The terrace of Boss Finley's house in St. Cloud. Scene 2—The cocktail lounge and Palm Garden of the Royal Palms Hotel. Act III.—The bedroom again.

Staged by Elia Kazan; settings and lighting by Jo Mielziner; music by Paul Bowles; costumes by Anna Hill Johnstone; production stage manager, David Pardoll; stage managers, Guy Thomajan, Bernard Pollock; press representatives, Sol Jacobson and Lewis Harmon.

See page 209.

A RAISIN IN THE SUN

(94 performances)

(Continued)

Play in three acts by Lorraine Hansberry. Produced by Philip Rose and David J. Cogan at the Ethel Barrymore Theatre, March 11, 1959.

Cast of characters—

Ruth Younger	Ruby Dee
Travis Younger	Glynn Turman
Walter Lee Younger (Brother)	Sidney Poitier
Beneatha Younger	Diana Sands

THE BEST PLAYS OF 1958-1959

Lena Younger (Mother)	Claudia McNeil
Joseph Asagai	Ivan Dixon
George Murchison	Louis Gossett
Bobo	Lonne Elder III
Karl Lindner	John Fiedler
Moving Men	Ed Hall, Douglas Turner

The action of the play is set in Chicago's South Side, sometime between World War II and the present. Act I.—Scene 1—Friday morning. Scene 2—The following morning. Act II.—Scene 1—Later, the same day. Scene 2—Friday night, a few weeks later. Scene 3—Moving day, one week later. Act III.—An hour later.

Staged by Lloyd Richards; setting and lighting by Ralph Alswang; costumes by Virginia Volland; production stage manager, Leonard Auerbach; stage manager, Mervyn Williams; press representatives, James D. Proctor and Merle Debuskey.

See page 232.

LUTE SONG

(14 performances)

Musical in two acts based on the Chinese play, "Pi-Pa-Ki." With book by Sidney Howard and Will Irwin; music by Raymond Scott; lyrics by Bernard Hanighen. Revived by the New York City Center Light Opera Company (Jean Dalrymple, Director) at the New York City Center, March 12, 1959.

Cast of characters—

The Manager } The Honorable Tschang }	Clarence Derwent
First Propertyman	Andre Gregory
Second Propertyman	Epy Baca
Tsai-Yong, the husband	Shai-K-Ophir
Tsai, the father	Tonio Selwart
Madame Tsai, the mother	Estelle Winwood
Tchao-Ou-Niang, the wife	Dolly Haas
Prince Nieou, the Imperial Preceptor	Philip Bourneuf
Princess Nieou-Chi, his daughter	Leueen MacGrath
Si-Tchun, a lady in waiting	Rain Winslow
Waiting Women	Maxine Taylor, Margaret Sheehan
Hand Maiden	Shizu Moriya
Chi-Mao-Chiu Players	Isabel Farrell, Trudi Gasparinetti, Sigrid Geiger, Barbara Monte
Youen-Kong, the steward	Joseph Daubenas
A Marriage Broker	Diane de Brett
Sweeper of Heaven and Earth	Asia
The Imperial Chamberlain	Donald Symington
The Food Commissioner	Gene Galvin
First Clerk	Anthony Edwards
Second Clerk	Epy Baca
First Applicant	John Darren
Second Applicant	Donald Hotton
Street Beggar	Mark Fleischman
Crippled Beggar	Michael de Marco
Blind Beggar	Alan Kirk
Imperial Guards	Anthony Edwards, Carl Clark
Imperial Attendants	Bob Daley, Michael Fesco, Arnott Mader, Sheldon Ossosky
The Genie	Donald Symington
The White Tiger	Asia
The Ape	Dean Crane

THE BEST PLAYS OF 1958-1959

```
Phoenix Birds .................................Asia, Dean Crane
Li-Wang .......................................Ted van Griethuysen
Priest of Amida Buddha ......................Tom Emlyn Williams
A Bonze .......................................Gene Galvin
Two Lesser Bonzes .....................Andre Gregory, Epy Baca
A Rich Man ...................................Wesley Owen
The Lion ...........................Dean Crane, Dick Colacino
Ribbon Spinner ................................Asia
Children .........................Olivia Johnson, Gloria Kaye,
                                    Coco Ramirez, Tina Ramirez
Palace Guards .....................Walter Adams, Peter Deign,
                                Paul Eden, John Pero, Vic Vallaro
Secretary .....................................Epy Baca
```
  Travelers on the North Road, beggars, guards, attendants, gods and others: Isabel Farrell, Trudi Gasparinetti, Sigrid Geiger, Olivia Johnson, Gloria Kaye, Barbara Monte, Shizu Moriya, Coco Ramirez, Tina Ramirez, Margaret Sheehan, Maxine Taylor, Walter Adams, Carl Clark, Dick Colacino, Bob Daley, Peter Deign, Michael de Marco, John Darren, Paul Eden, Anthony Edwards, Michael Fesco, Mark Fleischman, Andre Gregory, Donald Hotton, Alan Kirk, Arnott Mader, Sheldon Ossosky, Wesley Owen, John Pero, Vic Vallaro, Ted Van Griethuysen.

  Staged by John Paul; choreography by Yeichi Nimura; scenery, costumes and lighting by Robert Edmond Jones; musical director, Sylvan Levin; art director, Watson Barratt; costume supervisor, Ruth Morley; production stage manager, Chet O'Brien; stage manager, John Sieg; press representative, Tom Trenkle.

Lute Song was first produced by Michael Myerberg at the Plymouth Theatre, February 6, 1946, for 142 performances.

(Closed March 22, 1959)

MASQUERADE

(1 performance)

Play in three acts by Sigmund Miller. Produced by Richard W. Krakeur, in association with Louis d'Almeida, at the John Golden Theatre, March 16, 1959.

Cast of characters—
```
Isabel Chamberlin ............................Glenda Farrell
Ralph Grenville ..............................Mark Richman
Amy Grenville ................................Cloris Leachman
Mrs. Emily Hilburt ...........................Anne Ives
Jess Grenville ...............................Gene Lyons
Oliver Casey .................................Donald Cook
Charles Morrell ..............................Jack Cannon
```
  The action of the play takes place in the Grenville home in Shorewood, Connecticut. Act I.—Early autumn, late afternoon. Act II.—The following night, 8:00 P.M. Act III.—One hour later.
  Staged by Warren Enters; setting and lighting by Paul Morrison; costumes designed by Robert Mackintosh; production stage manager, Herman Shapiro; stage manager, William Callan; press representatives, Karl Bernstein and Ben Kornzweig.

(Closed March 16, 1959)

FIRST IMPRESSIONS

(92 performances)

Musical in two acts, based on Jane Austen's "Pride and Prejudice" and the play by Helen Jerome; with book by Abe Burrows; music and lyrics by Robert Goldman, Glenn Paxton and George Weiss. Produced by George Gilbert and Edward Specter Productions, Inc. at the Alvin Theatre, March 19, 1959.

Cast of characters—

Mr. Bennet	Laurie Main
Mary Bennet	Lois Bewley
Mrs. Bennet	Hermione Gingold
Lydia Bennet	Lynn Ross
Kitty Bennet	Lauri Peters
Jane Bennet	Phyllis Newman
Maid	Beverley Jane Welch
Elizabeth Bennet	Polly Bergen
Lady Lucas	Sibyl Bowan
Charlotte Lucas	Ellen Hanley
Caroline Bingley	Marti Stevens
Charles Bingley	Donald Madden
Fitzwilliam Darcy	Farley Granger
Coachmen	Garrett Lewis, John Starkweather
Captain Wickham	James Mitchell
Lieutenant Denny	Bill Carter
Lieutenant Rockingham	Stuart Hodes
Sir William Lucas	Richard Bengal
Butler	Norman Fredericks
Mr. Stubbs	Casper Roos
Williams	Jay Stern
Collins	Christopher Hewett
Butler at Rosings	John Starkweather
Lady Catherine de Bourgh	Mary Finney
Lady Anne	Martha Mathes

Dancers: Arlene Avril, Janise Gardner, Sally Gura, Harriet Leigh, Martha Mathes, Dorothy Jeanne Mattis, Wendy Nickerson, Alvin Beam, Jim Corbett, Stuart Fleming, Richard Gain, Stuart Hodes, Garrett Lewis, John Starkweather.

Singers: Adrienne Angel, Suzie Baker, Marian Haraldson, Jeannine Masterson, Louise Pearl, Beverley Jane Welch, Stuart Damon, Norman Fredericks, Warren Hays, Casper Roos, Tony Rossi, Jay Stern.

The year is 1813; the scene is England. Act I.—Scene 1—Longbourn: home of the Bennets in Hertfordshire. Scene 2—A road in Meryton. Scene 3—The assembly at Meryton. Scene 4—Longbourn. Scene 5—Netherfield Hall. Scene 6—Longbourn. Scene 7—The garden at Netherfield Hall. Scene 8—The lawn at Netherfield Hall. Scene 9—Longbourn. Act II.—Scene 1—A church in Kent. Scene 2—Rosings: home of Lady Catherine de Bourgh in Kent. Scene 3—A street in Meryton. Scenes 4 & 5—Longbourn. Scene 6—Netherfield Hall.

Staged by Abe Burrows; choreography by Jonathan Lucas; production designed by Peter Larkin; costumes by Alvin Colt; musical direction by Frederick Dvonch; orchestrations by Don Walker; lighting by Charles Elson; production stage manager, Phil Friedman; stage manager, Fred Smith; press representative, John L. Toohey.

Musical numbers—

ACT I

"Five Daughters"	Mrs. Bennet
"I'm Me"	Elizabeth and Sisters

"Have You Heard the News?" .... Mrs. Bennet and Townspeople
The Assembly Dance .... Townspeople and Officers
"A Perfect Evening" .... Darcy and Elizabeth
"As Long as There's a Mother" .... Mrs. Bennet and Daughters
"Love Will Find Out the Way" .... Elizabeth
"Gentlemen Don't Fall Wildly in Love" .... Darcy
"This Really Isn't Me" .... Elizabeth

ACT II

"Wasn't It a Simply Lovely Wedding?" ...... Elizabeth, Mrs. Bennet, Charlotte, Collins and Ensemble
"A House in Town" .... Mrs. Bennet
"The Heart Has Won the Game" .... Darcy
"I'm Me" (Reprise) .... Elizabeth
Dance .... Wickham, Lydia and Officers
"Let's Fetch the Carriage" .... Elizabeth and Mrs. Bennet
"The Heart Has Won the Game" (Reprise) .... Darcy and Elizabeth

(Closed May 30, 1959)

A DESERT INCIDENT

(7 performances)

Play in three acts by Pearl S. Buck. Produced by Tad Danielewski, in association with Morris Feld, at the John Golden Theatre, March 24, 1959.

Cast of characters—

Professor Ashley	Cameron Prud'homme
Pokey	Chailendra Jones
Angela Ashley	Mary Susan Locke
Robbie Horton	Ronnie Tourso
Mrs. Elinor Ashley	Sylvia Daneel
Rose Endicott	Lynne Forrester
Lewis Endicott	John Heldabrand
General Horton	Walter Klavun
Dr. Basil Ashley	Shepperd Strudwick
Sir Mark Grahame	Paul Roebling
Edwin Barkley	Charles Gerald
Tom Thunder	Philip Kenneally
Mrs. Horton	Dorothy Blackburn

Scene: a house in the desert. Act I.—Afternoon. Act II.—Scene 1—Evening; a week later. Scene 2—Late afternoon; the next day. Act III.—The next morning.

Staged by Tad Danielewski; scenery and lighting by Howard Bay; costumes by Ann Roth; music by Peter Howard; musical arrangements by Mickey Leonard; stage manager, Karl Nielsen; press representatives, Nat Dorfman Associates.

(Closed March 28, 1959)

KATAKI

(20 performances)

Play in two acts by Shimon Wincelberg. Produced by Jay Garon and Bob Sokoler at the Ambassador Theatre, April 9, 1959.

Cast of characters—

```
Alvin ........................................... Ben Piazza
Kimura ........................................ Sessue Hayakawa
```
The action of the play takes place on a small island in the Pacific during the latter part of World War II. Act I.—Scene 1—Sunrise. Scene 2—That afternoon. Scene 3—Later that night. Scene 4—The following morning. Act II.—Scene 1—One week later; morning. Scene 2—Two days later; late afternoon.

Staged by Alan Schneider; scenery by Peter Dohanos; lighting by Paul Morrison; music composed by David Amram; costumes by Anne Graham; associate producer, Richard Randall; stage manager, Bill Callan; press representative, Madi Blitzstein.

See page 255.

(Closed April 25, 1959)

TRIPLE PLAY

(37 performances)

A program of three short plays and a monologue, by Tennessee Williams, Anton Chekhov and Sean O'Casey. Produced by the Theatre Guild and Dore Schary at the Playhouse Theatre, April 15, 1959.

PART ONE
PORTRAIT OF A MADONNA by Tennessee Williams

Cast of characters—

```
Miss Lucretia Collins ........................... Jessica Tandy
The Porter ..................................... George Mathews
Elevator Boy ................................... Biff McGuire
The Doctor ..................................... Hume Cronyn
The Nurse ..................................... Margot Stevenson
Mr. Abrams .................................... John Randolph
```
The play takes place in the living room of a moderately priced apartment. The time is the present.

PART TWO
SOME COMMENTS ON THE HARMFUL EFFECTS OF
TOBACCO by Anton Chekhov

"Professor" Ivan Ivanovitch Nyukhin .... Hume Cronyn
Time: early 1900s.

A POUND ON DEMAND by Sean O'Casey

Cast of characters—

```
A Girl in Charge ............................... Margot Stevenson
Jerry .......................................... Hume Cronyn
Sammy ......................................... Biff McGuire
The Public ..................................... Jessica Tandy
A Policeman .................................... George Mathews
```
The play takes place in a Dublin district post office, just after World War I. It is late afternoon.

PART THREE
BEDTIME STORY by Sean O'Casey

Cast of characters—

```
John Jo Mulligan ............................... Hume Cronyn
Angela Nightingale ............................. Jessica Tandy
```

Daniel Halibut ....Biff McGuire
   The action takes place in a bachelor-flat in Dublin in 1925. The time is 3:15 A.M.
   Staged by Hume Cronyn; costumes by Anna Hill Johnstone; setting and lighting by David Hays; associate producer, Henry T. Weinstein; production stage manager, Paul A. Foley; stage manager, Marjorie Winfield; press representatives, Harvey B. Savinson and David Powers.

(Closed May 16, 1959)

DESTRY RIDES AGAIN

(44 performances)

(Continued)

Musical in two acts, based on the story by Max Brand; with music and lyrics by Harold Rome; book by Leonard Gershe. Produced by David Merrick, in association with Max Brown, at the Imperial Theatre, April 23, 1959.

Cast of characters—

Prologue	Don Crabtree, David London, Lanier Davis, Nolan Van Way
Bartender	Ray Mason
Frenchy	Dolores Gray
Wash	Jack Prince
Sheriff Keogh	Oran Osburn
Kent's Gang { Gyp Watson	Marc Breaux
Bugs Watson	Swen Swenson
Rockwell	George Reeder
Mayor Slade	Don McHenry
Claggett	Don Crabtree
Kent	Scott Brady
Chloe	Libi Staiger
Rose Lovejoy	Elizabeth Watts
Jack Tyndall	Nolan Van Way
Destry	Andy Griffith
Stage Driver	Chad Block
Ming Li	Reiko Sato
Mrs. Claggett	May Muth
Bailey	Ray Mason
Clara	Rosetta Le Noire
Dimples	Sharon Shore

   Rose Lovejoy Girls: Lynne Broadbent, Joan Broderick, Shelah Hackett, Reiko Sato, Sharon Shore, Carol Stevens.
   Frenchy's Girls: Shelly Chaplan, Lillian D'Honau, Maureen Hopkins, Betty Jenkins, Jillana, Andrina Miller, Shirley Nelson, Adriane Rogers, Carol Warner.
   Cowboys: Jack Beaber, Chad Block, Mel Davidson, Al Lanti, Ken Malone, Frank Pietri, John Ray, Larry Roquemore, Merritt Thompson.
   Townspeople: Maria Graziano, Betty Kent, Shelia Mathews, May Muth, Don Crabtree, Lanier Davis, Ralph Farnworth, David London, Ray Mason, Oran Osburn, Nolan Van Way.
   The action takes place in the western town of Bottleneck. The time is just before the turn of the century. Act I.—Scene 1—The Last Chance Saloon. Scene 2—The same. Scene 3—A street. Scene 4—A corral. Scene 5—Frenchy's house. Scene 6—Paradise Alley. Scene 7—A road in Bottleneck. Scene 8—The Last Chance Saloon. Act II.—Scene 1—Outside the jailhouse. Scene 2—Frenchy's house. Scene 3—The Sheriff's office. Scene 4—The Last Chance Saloon.
   Entire production directed and choreographed by Michael Kidd;

production designed by Oliver Smith; costumes by Alvin Colt; lighting by Jean Rosenthal; musical direction and vocal arrangements by Lehman Engel; orchestrations by Philip J. Lang; dance music arranged by Genevieve Pitot; hair styles by Ernest Adler; stage manager, Leonard Patrick; press representative, Harvey B. Sabinson.

Musical numbers—

ACT I

"Bottleneck" .... Patrons of the Last Chance Saloon
"Ladies" .... Frenchy and Girls
"Hoop-de-Dingle" .... Wash and Patrons of the Saloon
"Tomorrow Morning" .... Destry
"Ballad of the Gun" .... Destry and Wash
"The Social" .... Townspeople, Gyp, Bugs and Rockwell
"I Know Your Kind" .... Frenchy
"I Hate Him" .... Frenchy
"Paradise Alley" .... Cowboys and the Rose Lovejoy Girls
"Anyone Would Love You" .... Destry and Frenchy
"Once Knew a Fella" .... Destry, Wash and Friends
"Every Once in a While" .... Gyp, Bugs, Rockwell, Cowboys and Saloon Girls
"Fair Warning" .... Frenchy

ACT II

"Are You Ready, Gyp Watson?" .... Friends of Gyp Watson
"Not Guilty" .... The Jury
"Only Time Will Tell" .... Destry
"Respectability" .... Rose Lovejoy and Girls
"That Ring on the Finger" .... Frenchy and Girls
"Once Knew a Fella" (Reprise) .... Destry and Frenchy
"I Say Hello" .... Frenchy

ONCE UPON A MATTRESS

(26 performances)
(Continued)

Musical in two acts, with book by Jay Thompson, Marshall Barer and Dean Fuller; music by Mary Rodgers; lyrics by Marshall Barer. Produced by T. Edward Hambleton, Norris Houghton, and William and Jean Eckart at the Phoenix Theatre, May 11, 1959.

Cast of characters—

Minstrel .... Harry Snow
Prince .... Jim Maher
Princess .... Chris Karner
Queen .... Gloria Stevens
Wizard .... Robert Weil
Princess Number Twelve .... Mary Stanton
Lady Rowena .... Dorothy Aull
Lady Merrill .... Patsi King
Prince Dauntless .... Joe Bova
The Queen .... Jane White
Lady Lucille .... Luce Ennis
Lady Larken .... Anne Jones
Sir Studley .... Jerry Newby
The King .... Jack Gilford
Jester .... Matt Mattox
Sir Harry .... Allen Case
Princess Winnifred .... Carol Burnett
Sir Harold .... David Neuman
Lady Beatrice .... Gloria Stevens

THE BEST PLAYS OF 1958–1959

Sir Luce	Tom Mixon
Lady Mabelle	Chris Karner
The Nightingale of Samarkand	Ginny Perlowin
Lady Dorothy	Dorothy D'Honau
Sir Christopher	Christopher Edwards
Lord Howard	Howard Parker
Lady Dora	Dorothy Frank
Sir Daniel	Dan Resin
Sir Steven	Jim Stevenson
Lord Patrick	Julian Patrick

Act I.—Prologue. Scene 1—Throne room. Scene 2—The yellow gallery. Scene 3—Courtyard. Scene 4—A corridor. Scene 5—Winnifred's dressing chamber. Scene 6—The grey gallery. Scene 7—On the Greensward. Scene 8—The yellow gallery. Scene 9—Great hall. Act II.—Scene 1—Castle. Scene 2—Winnifred's dressing chamber. Scene 4—Wizard's chamber. Scene 3—A corridor. Scene 4—Wizard's chamber. Scene 5—The grey gallery. Scene 6—The bed chamber. Scene 7—A corridor. Scene 8—Breakfast hall.

Staged by George Abbott; dances and musical numbers staged by Joe Layton; scenery and costumes by William and Jean Eckart; lighting by Tharon Musser; musical direction by Hal Hastings; orchestrations by Hershy Kay, Arthur Beck and Carroll Huxley; dance music arranged by Roger Adams; stage managers, John Allen and George Quick; press representatives, Karl Bernstein and Ben Kornzweig.

Musical numbers—

ACT I

"Many Moons Ago"	Minstrel and Court
"An Opening for a Princess"	Prince Dauntless, Lady Larken, Knights and Ladies
"In a Little While"	Lady Larken and Sir Harry
"In a Little While" (Reprise)	Lady Larken and Sir Harry
"Shy"	Winnifred, Sir Studley, Knights and Ladies
"The Minstrel, The Jester and I"	King, Minstrel and Jester
"Sensitivity"	Queen and Wizard
"Swamps of Home"	Winnifred, Dauntless and Ladies
"Normandy"	Minstrel, Jester, King and Lady Larken
"Spanish Panic"	Jester, Lady Dora, Lady Beatrice, Queen, Winnifred, Dauntless, Knights and Ladies
"Song of Love"	Dauntless, Winnifred, Knights and Ladies

ACT II

"Quiet"	Jester, Knights and Ladies
"Happily Ever After"	Winnifred
"Man to Man Talk"	King and Dauntless
"Very Soft Shoes"	Jester, Knights and Ladies
"Yesterday I Loved You"	Sir Harry and Lady Larken
"Lullaby"	The Nightingale of Samarkand
Finale	Entire Court

THE NERVOUS SET

(23 performances)

Musical in two acts, based on the novel by Jay Landesman; with book by Jay Landesman and Theodore J. Flicker; music by Tommy Wolf; lyrics by Fran Landesman. Produced by Robert Lantz at Henry Miller's Theatre, May 12, 1959.

Cast of characters—

Bummy Carwell	Larry Hagman
Brad	Richard Hayes
Danny	Thomas Aldredge

Jan	Tani Seitz
Yogi	Del Close
A Customer	Barry Primus
Landlady	Florence Gassner
Joan	Arlene Corwin
Sari Shaw	Janice Meshkoff
Danny's Girl	Elvira Pallas
Max the Millionaire	Gerald Hiken
Henry Calhoun	David Sallade
Katherine Sloan-Wittiker	Florence Gassner
Irving	Don Heller
Tony	Lee Lindsey
Rejected Boy	Zale Kessler

Act I.—Scene 1—Sunday afternoon in late summer; Washington Square Park, New York City. Scene 2—The following spring; Brad and Jan's apartment on Perry Street. Scene 3—That week-end; Jan's parents' home, Fairfield County, Connecticut. Scene 4—The same evening; the bottom of an unfilled pool. Scene 5—Later; inside the house again. Scene 6—The next week-end; Bummy Carwell's apartment on Avenue A. Act II.—Scene 1—A few days later; Brad and Jan's apartment. Scene 2—Later the same day; the Melancholy Pigeon. Scene 3—That evening; Katherine Sloan-Wittiker's apartment on Sutton Place. Scene 4—Later at Brad and Jan's apartment.

Staged by Theodore J. Flicker; settings and lighting by Paul Morrison; costumes by Theoni Vachlioti Aldredge; music arrangements and direction by Mr. Wolf; stage manager, Allan Mankoff; press representative, Dorothy Ross.

Musical numbers—
1. "Man, We're Beat"
2. "New York"
3. "What's to Lose"
4. "Stars Have Blown My Way"
5. "Fun Life"
6. "How Do You Like Your Love"
7. "Party Song"
8. "If I Could Put You in a Song"
9. "Night People"
10. "I've Got a Lot to Learn about Life"
11. "Rejection"
12. "The Ballad of the Sad Young Men"
13. "A Country Gentleman"
14. "Max the Millionaire"
15. "Laugh, I Thought I'd Die"
16. "Travel the Road of Life"

(Closed May 30, 1959)

GYPSY

(12 performances)
(Continued)

Musical in two acts, suggested by the memoirs of Gypsy Rose Lee; with book by Arthur Laurents; music by Jule Styne; lyrics by Stephen Sondheim. Produced by David Merrick and Leland Hayward at the Broadway Theatre, May 21, 1959.

Cast of characters—

Uncle Jocko	Mort Marshall
George	Willy Sumner
Arnold (and his guitar)	John Borden
Balloon Girl	Jody Lane

```
Baby Louise .......................................... Karen Moore
Baby June ...................................... Jacqueline Mayro
Rose ............................................. Ethel Merman
Pop ................................................ Erv Harmon
Newsboys ......................... Bobby Brownell, Gene Castle,
                                   Steve Curry, Billy Harris
Weber ............................................... Joe Silver
Herbie ............................................ Jack Klugman
Louise ........................................... Sandra Church
June ............................................ Lane Bradbury
Tulsa ............................................. Paul Wallace
Yonkers ......................................... David Winters
Angie ............................................. Ian Tucker
L.A. ............................................ Michael Parks
Kringelein ........................................ Loney Lewis
Mr. Goldstone .................................... Mort Marshall
Farm Boys ...... Marvin Arnold, Ricky Coll, Don Emmons, Michael
                 Parks, Ian Tucker, Paul Wallace, David Winters
Miss Cratchitt .................................... Peg Murray
Hollywood Blondes
    Agnes ....................................... Marilyn Cooper
    Marjorie May ................................. Patsy Bruder
    Dolores ..................................... Marilyn D'Honau
    Thelma ....................................... Merle Letowt
    Edna ......................................... Joan Petlack
    Gail ..................................... Imelda de Martin
Pastey ........................................ Richard Porter
Tessie Tura .................................. Maria Karnilova
Mazeppa ............................................ Faith Dane
Cigar .............................................. Loney Lewis
Electra ........................................... Chotzi Foley
Showgirls .................... Kathryn Albertson, Gloria Kristy,
                    Denise McLaglen, Barbara London, Theda
                    Nelson, Carroll Jo Towers, Marie Wallace
Maid ........................................... Marsha Rivers
Phil ................................................ Joe Silver
Bougeron-Cochon .................................. George Zima
Cow ........................... Willy Sumner & George Zima
```

The action of the play covers a period from the early twenties to the early thirties, and takes place in various cities throughout the country.

Staged and choreographed by Jerome Robbins; settings and lighting by Jo Mielziner; costumes by Raoul Pene du Bois; musical direction by Milton Rosenstock; orchestrations by Sid Ramin with Robert Ginzler; dance music arranged by John Kander; stage manager, Lo Hardin; press representatives, Frank Goodman and Seymour Krawitz.

Musical numbers—

ACT I

```
"May We Entertain You" ............ Baby June and Baby Louise
"Some People" ............................................ Rose
Traveling
"Small World" .................................. Rose and Herbie
Baby June and Her Newsboys
"Mr. Goldstone, I Love You" ................ Rose and Ensemble
"Little Lamb" ........................................... Louise
Dainty June and Her Farmboys
"You'll Never Get Away From Me" .............. Rose and Herbie
"If Momma Was Married" ...................... Louise and June
"All I Need Is the Girl" ....................... Tulsa and Louise
"Everything's Coming up Roses" ........................... Rose
```

ACT II

```
"Madame Rose's Toreadorables" .......... Louise and Toreadorables
"Together, Wherever We Go" .......... Rose, Louise and Herbie
"You Gotta Have a Gimmick" ....... Tessie, Mazeppa and Electra
"Small World" (Reprise) ................................. Rose
"Let Me Entertain You" .................... Louise and Company
"Rose's Turn" ........................................... Rose
```

FACTS AND FIGURES

VARIETY'S TABULATION OF FINANCIAL HITS AND FLOPS

HITS

J. B.
La Plume de Ma Tante
A Majority of One
The Marriage-Go-Round
Once More, with Feeling
Party with Betty Comden and Adolph Green
The Pleasure of His Company
A Raisin in the Sun
Shakespeare's Ages of Man
Sweet Bird of Youth
Tall Story
A Touch of the Poet
The World of Suzie Wong

STATUS NOT YET DETERMINED

Destry Rides Again
Flower Drum Song
The Gazebo
Gypsy
Make a Million
Rashomon
Redhead

FAILURES

The Cold Wind and the Warm
Comes a Day
Cue for Passion
A Desert Incident
The Disenchanted
Drink to Me Only
Edwin Booth
Epitaph for George Dillon
First Impressions
The Girls in 509
God and Kate Murphy
Goldilocks
Handful of Fire
Howie
Juno
Kataki
The Legend of Lizzie
Look After Lulu
The Man in the Dog Suit
Maria Golovin
Masquerade
The Nervous Set
The Night Circus
Patate
Requiem for a Nun
The Rivalry
The Shadow of a Gunman
Third Best Sport
Triple Play
Whoop-Up

SPECIAL, MISCELLANEOUS (UNRATED)

Auntie Mame
Lute Song
The Most Happy Fella

Old Vic
Say, Darling
Theatre National Populaire

CLOSED DURING TRYOUT TOUR

At the Grand
Crazy October
Enrico
Gay Felons
Listen to the Mocking Bird

Not in the Book
Poker Game
Starward Ark
Swim in the Sea

Holdovers from the 1957-1958 Season, Since Clarified

HITS

Jamaica
Sunrise at Campobello

The Visit

FAILURES

Blue Denim
Jane Eyre
Oh Captain
Say, Darling

Time Remembered
Who Was That Lady I Saw You With?

STATISTICAL SUMMARY

(Last Season Plays Which Ended Runs After June 1, 1958)

Plays	Number Performances	Closing Date
Jane Eyre	52	June 14, 1958
Time Remembered	248	June 28, 1958
Auntie Mame	639	June 28, 1958
Li'l Abner	693	July 12, 1958
Oh Captain!	192	July 19, 1958
Blue Denim	166	July 19, 1958
Who Was That Lady I Saw You With?	208	August 30, 1958
Romanoff and Juliet	389	September 13, 1958
Look Back in Anger	407	September 20, 1958
The Visit	189	November 29, 1958
The Dark at the Top of the Stairs	468	January 17, 1959
Say, Darling	332	January 17, 1959
Bells Are Ringing	924	March 7, 1959
Look Homeward, Angel	564	April 4, 1959
Jamaica	555	April 11, 1959
Sunrise at Campobello	556	May 30, 1959

LONG RUNS ON BROADWAY

To June 1, 1959

(Plays marked with asterisk were still playing June 1, 1959)

Plays	Number Performances
Life with Father	3,224
Tobacco Road	3,182
Abie's Irish Rose	2,327
Oklahoma!	2,248
South Pacific	1,925
Harvey	1,775
Born Yesterday	1,642
The Voice of the Turtle	1,557
Arsenic and Old Lace	1,444
Hellzapoppin	1,404
* My Fair Lady	1,339
Angel Street	1,295
Lightnin'	1,291
The King and I	1,246
Guys and Dolls	1,200
Mister Roberts	1,157
Annie Get Your Gun	1,147
The Seven Year Itch	1,141
Pins and Needles	1,108
Kiss Me, Kate	1,070
Pajama Game	1,063
The Teahouse of the August Moon	1,027
Damn Yankees	1,019
Anna Lucasta	957
Kiss and Tell	957
The Moon Is Blue	924
Bells Are Ringing	924
Can-Can	892
Carousel	890
Hats Off to Ice	889
Fanny	888
Follow the Girls	882
The Bat	867
My Sister Eileen	865
White Cargo	864
Song of Norway	860
A Streetcar Named Desire	855
Comedy in Music	849
You Can't Take It with You	837
Three Men on a Horse	835
Inherit the Wind	806
No Time for Sergeants	796
Where's Charley?	792
The Ladder	789
State of the Union	765
The First Year	760
Death of a Salesman	742
Sons o' Fun	742
The Man Who Came to Dinner	739
Call Me Mister	734
High Button Shoes	727
Finian's Rainbow	725
Claudia	722
The Gold Diggers	720
The Diary of Anne Frank	717
I Remember Mama	714
Tea and Sympathy	712
Junior Miss	710
Seventh Heaven	704
* West Side Story	700
Cat on a Hot Tin Roof	694
Li'l Abner	693
Peg o' My Heart	692
The Children's Hour	691
Dead End	687

THE BEST PLAYS OF 1958-1959

Plays	Number Performances	Plays	Number Performances
The Lion and the Mouse	686	The Show-Off	571
Dear Ruth	683	Sally	570
East Is West	680	One Touch of Venus	567
The Most Happy Fella	676	Happy Birthday	564
The Doughgirls	671	Look Homeward, Angel	564
Irene	670	The Glass Menagerie	561
Boy Meets Girl	669	Wonderful Town	559
Blithe Spirit	657	Rose Marie	557
The Women	657	Strictly Dishonorable	557
A Trip to Chinatown	657	Sunrise at Campobello	556
Bloomer Girl	654	Jamaica	555
The Fifth Season	654	Ziegfeld Follies	553
Rain	648	Floradora	553
Witness for the Prosecution	645	Dial "M" for Murder	552
		Good News	551
Call Me Madam	644	Let's Face It	547
Janie	642	Within the Law	541
The Green Pastures	640	The Music Master	540
Auntie Mame	639	Pal Joey	540
The Fourposter	632	What a Life	538
Is Zat So?	618	The Red Mill	531
Anniversary Waltz	615	The Solid Gold Cadillac	526
The Happy Time	614	The Boomerang	522
Separate Rooms	613	Rosalinda	521
Affairs of State	610	Chauve Souris	520
Star and Garter	609	Blackbirds	518
The Student Prince	608	Sunny	517
* The Music Man	604	Victoria Regina	517
Broadway	603	The Vagabond King	511
Adonis	603	The New Moon	509
Street Scene	601	Shuffle Along	504
Kiki	600	Up in Central Park	504
Wish You Were Here	598	Carmen Jones	503
A Society Circus	596	The Member of the Wedding	501
Blossom Time	592		
The Two Mrs. Carrolls	585	Personal Appearance	501
Kismet	583	Panama Hattie	501
Detective Story	581	Bird in Hand	500
Brigadoon	581	Sailor, Beware!	500
Brother Rat	577	Room Service	500
Show Boat	572	Tomorrow the World	500
* Two for the Seesaw	572		

NEW YORK DRAMA CRITICS CIRCLE AWARDS

At their annual meeting, the New York Drama Critics Circle chose Lorraine Hansberry's *A Raisin in the Sun* as the best play of the season. As the best foreign play, it chose Friedrich Duerrenmatt's *The Visit*, and as the best musical, the revue *La Plume de Ma Tante*.

Circle awards have been—

1935-36—Winterset, by Maxwell Anderson
1936-37—High Tor, by Maxwell Anderson
1937-38—Of Mice and Men, by John Steinbeck
1938-39—No award.
1939-40—The Time of Your Life, by William Saroyan
1940-41—Watch on the Rhine, by Lillian Hellman
1941-42—No award.
1942-43—The Patriots, by Sidney Kingsley
1943-44—No award.
1944-45—The Glass Menagerie, by Tennessee Williams
1945-46—No award.
1946-47—All My Sons, by Arthur Miller
1947-48—A Streetcar Named Desire, by Tennessee Williams
1948-49—Death of a Salesman, by Arthur Miller
1949-50—The Member of the Wedding, by Carson McCullers
1950-51—Darkness at Noon, by Sidney Kingsley
1951-52—I Am a Camera, by John van Druten
1952-53—Picnic, by William Inge
1953-54—The Teahouse of the August Moon, by John Patrick
1954-55—Cat on a Hot Tin Roof, by Tennessee Williams
1955-56—The Diary of Anne Frank, by Frances Goodrich and Albert Hackett
1956-57—Long Day's Journey into Night, by Eugene O'Neill
1957-58—Look Homeward, Angel, by Ketti Frings
1958-59—A Raisin in the Sun, by Lorraine Hansberry

PULITZER PRIZE WINNERS

The Pulitzer Prize went to Archibald MacLeish's *J. B.* Pulitzer awards have been—

1917-18—Why Marry?, by Jesse Lynch Williams
1918-19—No award.
1919-20—Beyond the Horizon, by Eugene O'Neill
1920-21—Miss Lulu Bett, by Zona Gale
1921-22—Anna Christie, by Eugene O'Neill
1922-23—Icebound, by Owen Davis
1923-24—Hell-bent for Heaven, by Hatcher Hughes
1924-25—They Knew What They Wanted, by Sidney Howard
1925-26—Craig's Wife, by George Kelly
1926-27—In Abraham's Bosom, by Paul Green
1927-28—Strange Interlude, by Eugene O'Neill
1928-29—Street Scene, by Elmer Rice
1929-30—The Green Pastures, by Marc Connelly
1930-31—Alison's House, by Susan Glaspell
1931-32—Of Thee I Sing, by George S. Kaufman, Morrie Ryskind, Ira and George Gershwin
1932-33—Both Your Houses, by Maxwell Anderson
1933-34—Men in White, by Sidney Kingsley
1934-35—The Old Maid, by Zoë Akins
1935-36—Idiot's Delight, by Robert E. Sherwood
1936-37—You Can't Take It with You, by Moss Hart and George S. Kaufman
1937-38—Our Town, by Thornton Wilder
1938-39—Abe Lincoln in Illinois, by Robert E. Sherwood
1939-40—The Time of Your Life, by William Saroyan
1940-41—There Shall Be No Night, by Robert E. Sherwood
1941-42—No award.
1942-43—The Skin of Our Teeth, by Thornton Wilder
1943-44—No award.
1944-45—Harvey, by Mary Coyle Chase
1945-46—State of the Union, by Howard Lindsay and Russel Crouse
1946-47—No award.
1947-48—A Streetcar Named Desire, by Tennessee Williams

1948-49—Death of a Salesman, by Arthur Miller
1949-50—South Pacific, by Richard Rodgers, Oscar Hammerstein II and Joshua Logan
1950-51—No award.
1951-52—The Shrike, by Joseph Kramm
1952-53—Picnic, by William Inge
1953-54—The Teahouse of the August Moon, by John Patrick
1954-55—Cat on a Hot Tin Roof, by Tennessee Williams
1955-56—The Diary of Anne Frank, by Frances Goodrich and Albert Hackett
1956-57—Long Day's Journey into Night, by Eugene O'Neill
1957-58—Look Homeward, Angel, by Ketti Frings
1958-59—J. B., by Archibald MacLeish

BOOKS ON THE THEATRE
1958-1959

Agate, James (Editor). *The English Dramatic Critics (1660-1932)*. Hill & Wang. $1.45 (paperback).

Anouilh, Jean. *Five Plays (Ardèle, Restless Heart, Time Remembered, Mademoiselle Colombe, The Lark)*. (Variously translated.) Hill & Wang. $3.95.

Aristophanes. *Ladies' Day (Thesmophoriazusae)*. (Translated by Dudley Fitts.) Harcourt, Brace. $4.00.

Arnott, Peter D. *Introduction to the Greek Theatre*. St. Martin's Press. $5.00.

Atkinson, Brooks (Editor). *Four Great Comedies of the Restoration and 18th Century*. Bantam. $0.50 (paperback).

Behrman, S. N. *The Cold Wind and the Warm*. Random House. $2.95.

Bentley, Eric (Editor). *The Classic Theatre: Volume I—Six Italian Plays*. (Machiavelli, Beolco, Goldoni and Gozzi.) Anchor. $1.25 (paperback).

Bentley, Eric (Editor). *The Classic Theatre: Volume II—Five German Plays*. (Goethe, Schiller and Kleist.) Anchor. $1.45 (paperback).

Blum, Daniel. *Theatre World: 1957-58*. Chilton. $6.00.

Bowen, Croswell, and O'Neill, Shane. *The Curse of the Misbegotten: A Tale of the House of O'Neill*. McGraw-Hill. $5.00.

Bowers, Faubion. *Broadway U.S.S.R.* Nelson. $5.00.

Bowers, Faubion. *Japanese Theatre*. Hill & Wang. $2.25 (paperback).

Camus, Albert. *Caligula and Three Other Plays (The Misunderstanding, State of Siege, The Just Assassins)*. (Translated by Stuart Gilbert.) Knopf. $5.00.

Chambers, Sir Edmund. *Shakespeare: A Survey.* Hill & Wang. $1.45 (paperback).

Chapman, John (Editor). *Broadway's Best.* Doubleday. $4.50.

Chekhov, Anton. *The Brute and Other Forces.* (Edited by Eric Bentley and Theodore Hoffman.) Evergreen. $1.45 (paperback).

Churchill, R. C. *Shakespeare and His Betters.* University of Indiana Press. $5.00.

Clurman, Harold. *Lies Like Truth:* Theatre Reviews and Essays. Macmillan. $6.00.

Cocteau, Jean. *The Hand of a Stranger.* Horizon. $3.95.

Cordell, Richard, and Matson, Lowell. *The Off-Broadway Theatre: Seven Plays* (*Purple Dust, Ardèle, Dragon's Mouth, Ulysses in Nighttown, Career, The Girl on the Via Flaminia, Héloïse*). Random House. $5.00.

Costigan, James. Two Television Plays: *Little Moon of Alban* and *A Wind from the South.* Simon & Schuster. $3.50.

Dennis, Nigel. *Two Plays and a Preface* (*Cards of Identity, The Making of Moo*). Vanguard. $3.95.

Ernst, Earle. *The Kabuki Theatre.* Grove. $2.45 (paperback).

Ewen, David. *Complete Book of the American Musical Theater.* Holt. $7.50.

Falk, Doris V. *Eugene O'Neill and the Tragic Tension.* Rutgers University Press. $4.50.

Faulkner, William, and Ford, Ruth. *Requiem for a Nun.* Random House. $2.95.

Fay, Gerard. *The Abbey Theatre.* Macmillan. $4.50.

Fernandez, Ramon. *Molière: The Man Seen Through the Plays.* Hill & Wang. $3.75.

Genet, Jean. *The Balcony.* Evergreen. $1.75 (paperback).

Gibson, William. *The Seesaw Log.* Knopf. $3.95.

Giraudoux, Jean. *Four Plays* (*Ondine, The Madwoman of Chaillot, The Enchanted, The Apollo of Bellac*). (Translated by Maurice Valency.) Hill & Wang. $1.75 (paperback).

Greene, David H., and Stephens, Edward M. *J. M. Synge, 1871-1909*. Macmillan. $6.95.

Hewitt, Bernard. *Theatre U.S.A.: 1668-1957*. McGraw-Hill. $9.95.

Howard, Leslie Ruth. *A Quite Remarkable Father:* The Biography of Leslie Howard. Harcourt, Brace. $4.75.

Ibsen, Henrik. *The Last Plays (Little Eyolf, When We Dead Awaken, John Gabriel Borkman)*. (Translated by William Archer.) Hill & Wang. $1.45 (paperback).

Inge, William. *Four Plays (Come Back, Little Sheba, Picnic, Bus Stop, The Dark at the Top of the Stairs)*. Random House. $5.00.

Jablonski, Edward, and Stewart, Lawrence D. *The Gershwin Years*. (Introduction by Carl Van Vechten.) Doubleday. $6.95.

Kerr, Walter and Jean. *Goldilocks*. Doubleday. $2.75.

Kökeritz, Helge. *Shakespeare's Names: A Pronouncing Dictionary*. Yale University Press. $2.00.

Kronenberger, Louis (Editor). *The Best Plays of 1957-1958*. Dodd, Mead. $6.00.

Kurnitz, Harry. *Once More, with Feeling*. Random House. $2.95.

Lattimore, Richard. *The Poetry of Greek Drama*. Johns Hopkins. $3.50.

Levin, Harry. *The Question of Hamlet*. Oxford University Press. $3.75.

Levin, Meyer. *Compulsion*. Simon & Schuster. $3.50.

Lewis, Robert. *Method—or Madness?* Samuel French. $3.00.

Lindsay, Howard, and Crouse, Russel. *Tall Story*. Random House. $2.95.

Marcel, Gabriel. *Three Plays (A Man of God, Ariadne, The Funeral Pyre)*. Hill & Wang. $3.75.

Matthews, John F. (Editor). *Shaw's Dramatic Criticism (1895-98)*. Hill & Wang. $1.45 (paperback).

Mayorga, Margaret. *Best Short Plays, 1957-1958.* Beacon Press. $5.95.

McCullers, Carson. *The Square Root of Wonderful.* Houghton Mifflin. $3.00.

Nagler, A. M. *Shakespeare's Stage.* Yale University Press. $2.00.

Nicoll, Allardyce (Editor). *Shakespeare Survey 12.* Cambridge University Press. $4.00.

O'Neill, Eugene. *Hughie.* Yale University Press. $3.00.

Oppenheimer, George. *The Passionate Playgoer:* A Personal Scrapbook. Viking. $5.95.

Osborne, John, and Creighton, Anthony. *Epitaph for George Dillon.* Criterion. $2.75.

Pirandello, Luigi. *The Mountain Giants and Other Plays.* (Translated by Marta Abba.) Crown. $3.95.

Rodgers, Richard, and Hammerstein, Oscar. *Flower Drum Song.* Farrar, Straus. $3.50.

Schulberg, Budd, and Breit, Harvey. *The Disenchanted.* Random House. $2.95.

Scott, A. C. *An Introduction to the Chinese Theatre.* Theater Arts Books. $2.95.

Selden, Samuel, and Sellman, Hunton D. *Stage Scenery and Lighting.* Appleton-Century-Crofts. $7.50.

Shattuck, Charles H. (Editor). *Bulwer and Macready.* University of Illinois Press. $5.75.

Southern, Richard. *The Medieval Theatre in the Round.* Theatre Arts. $8.50.

Strindberg, August. *The Saga of the Folkungs; Engelbrekt.* (Translated by Walter Johnson.) University of Washington Press. $4.00.

Strindberg, August. *The Vasa Trilogy (Master Olof, Gustav Vaga, Erik XIV).* (Translated by Walter Johnson.) University of Washington Press. $6.00.

Taylor, Samuel (with Cornelia Otis Skinner). *The Pleasure of His Company.* Random House. $2.95.

Van Doren, Mark. *The Last Days of Lincoln.* Hill & Wang. $3.75.

Wickham, Glynne. *Early English Stages:* Vol. I, 1300-1576. Columbia University Press. $7.50.

Young, Stark. *Immortal Shadows.* Hill & Wang. $1.65 (paperback).

PREVIOUS VOLUMES OF BEST PLAYS

Plays chosen to represent the theatre seasons from 1899 to 1958 are as follows:

1899-1909

BARBARA FRIETCHIE, by Clyde Fitch. Life Publishing Co.
THE CLIMBERS, by Clyde Fitch. Macmillan.
IF I WERE KING, by Justin Huntly McCarthy. Samuel French.
THE DARLING OF THE GODS, by David Belasco. Little, Brown.
THE COUNTY CHAIRMAN, by George Ade. Samuel French.
LEAH KLESCHNA, by C. M. S. McLellan. Samuel French.
THE SQUAW MAN, by Edwin Milton Royle.
THE GREAT DIVIDE, by William Vaughn Moody. Samuel French.
THE WITCHING HOUR, by Augustus Thomas. Samuel French.
THE MAN FROM HOME, by Booth Tarkington and Harry Leon Wilson. Samuel French.

1909-1919

THE EASIEST WAY, by Eugene Walter. G. W. Dillingham and Houghton Mifflin.
MRS. BUMPSTEAD-LEIGH, by Harry James Smith. Samuel French.
DISRAELI, by Louis N. Parker. Dodd, Mead.
ROMANCE, by Edward Sheldon. Macmillan.
SEVEN KEYS TO BALDPATE, by George M. Cohan. Published by Bobbs-Merrill as a novel by Earl Derr Biggers; as a play by Samuel French.
ON TRIAL, by Elmer Reizenstein. Samuel French.
THE UNCHASTENED WOMAN, by Louis Kaufman Anspacher. Harcourt, Brace and Howe.
GOOD GRACIOUS ANNABELLE, by Clare Kummer. Samuel French.
WHY MARRY?, by Jesse Lynch Williams. Scribner.
JOHN FERGUSON, by St. John Ervine. Macmillan.

1919-1920

ABRAHAM LINCOLN, by John Drinkwater. Houghton Mifflin.
CLARENCE, by Booth Tarkington. Samuel French.
BEYOND THE HORIZON, by Eugene G. O'Neill. Boni & Liveright.

DÉCLASSÉE, by Zoë Akins. Liveright, Inc.
THE FAMOUS MRS. FAIR, by James Forbes. Samuel French.
THE JEST, by Sem Benelli. (American adaptation by Edward Sheldon.)
JANE CLEGG, by St. John Ervine. Henry Holt.
MAMMA'S AFFAIR, by Rachel Barton Butler. Samuel French.
WEDDING BELLS, by Salisbury Field. Samuel French.
ADAM AND EVA, by George Middleton and Guy Bolton. Samuel French.

1920-1921

DEBURAU, adapted from the French of Sacha Guitry by H. Granville Barker. Putnam.
THE FIRST YEAR, by Frank Craven. Samuel French.
ENTER MADAME, by Gilda Varesi and Dolly Byrne. Putnam.
THE GREEN GODDESS, by William Archer. Knopf.
LILIOM, by Ferenc Molnar. Boni & Liveright.
MARY ROSE, by James M. Barrie. Scribner.
NICE PEOPLE, by Rachel Crothers. Scribner.
THE BAD MAN, by Porter Emerson Browne. Putnam.
THE EMPEROR JONES, by Eugene G. O'Neill. Boni & Liveright.
THE SKIN GAME, by John Galsworthy. Scribner.

1921-1922

ANNA CHRISTIE, by Eugene G. O'Neill. Boni & Liveright.
A BILL OF DIVORCEMENT, by Clemence Dane. Macmillan.
DULCY, by George S. Kaufman and Marc Connelly. Putnam.
HE WHO GETS SLAPPED, adapted from the Russian of Leonid Andreyev by Gregory Zilboorg. Brentano's.
SIX CYLINDER LOVE, by William Anthony McGuire.
THE HERO, by Gilbert Emery.
THE DOVER ROAD, by Alan Alexander Milne. Samuel French.
AMBUSH, by Arthur Richman.
THE CIRCLE, by William Somerset Maugham.
THE NEST, by Paul Geraldy and Grace George.

1922-1923

RAIN, by John Colton and Clemence Randolph. Liveright, Inc.
LOYALTIES, by John Galsworthy. Scribner.
ICEBOUND, by Owen Davis. Little, Brown.
YOU AND I, by Philip Barry. Brentano's.
THE FOOL, by Channing Pollock. Brentano's.

MERTON OF THE MOVIES, by George Kaufman and Marc Connelly, based on the novel of the same name by Harry Leon Wilson.
WHY NOT? by Jesse Lynch Williams. Walter H. Baker Co.
THE OLD SOAK, by Don Marquis. Doubleday, Page.
R.U.R., by Karel Capek. Translated by Paul Selver. Doubleday, Page.
MARY THE 3D, by Rachel Crothers. Brentano's.

1923-1924

THE SWAN, translated from the Hungarian of Ferenc Molnar by Melville Baker. Boni & Liveright.
OUTWARD BOUND, by Sutton Vane. Boni & Liveright.
THE SHOW-OFF, by George Kelly. Little, Brown.
THE CHANGELINGS, by Lee Wilson Dodd. Dutton.
CHICKEN FEED, by Guy Bolton. Samuel French.
SUN-UP, by Lula Vollmer. Brentano's.
BEGGAR ON HORSEBACK, by George Kaufman and Marc Connelly. Boni & Liveright.
TARNISH, by Gilbert Emery. Brentano's.
THE GOOSE HANGS HIGH, by Lewis Beach. Little, Brown.
HELL-BENT FER HEAVEN, by Hatcher Hughes. Harper.

1924-1925

WHAT PRICE GLORY? by Laurence Stallings and Maxwell Anderson. Harcourt, Brace.
THEY KNEW WHAT THEY WANTED, by Sidney Howard. Doubleday, Page.
DESIRE UNDER THE ELMS, by Eugene G. O'Neill. Boni & Liveright.
THE FIREBRAND, by Edwin Justus Mayer. Boni & Liveright.
DANCING MOTHERS, by Edgar Selwyn and Edmund Goulding.
MRS. PARTRIDGE PRESENTS, by Mary Kennedy and Ruth Hawthorne. Samuel French.
THE FALL GUY, by James Gleason and George Abbott. Samuel French.
THE YOUNGEST, by Philip Barry. Samuel French.
MINICK, by Edna Ferber and George S. Kaufman. Doubleday, Page.
WILD BIRDS, by Dan Totheroh. Doubleday, Page.

1925-1926

CRAIG'S WIFE, by George Kelly. Little, Brown.
THE GREAT GOD BROWN, by Eugene G. O'Neill. Boni & Liveright.
THE GREEN HAT, by Michael Arlen.
THE DYBBUK, by S. Ansky, Henry G. Alsberg-Winifred Katzin translation. Boni & Liveright.
THE ENEMY, by Channing Pollock. Brentano's.
THE LAST OF MRS. CHEYNEY, by Frederick Lonsdale. Samuel French.
BRIDE OF THE LAMB, by William Hurlbut. Boni & Liveright.
THE WISDOM TOOTH, by Marc Connelly. George H. Doran.
THE BUTTER AND EGG MAN, by George Kaufman. Boni & Liveright.
YOUNG WOODLEY, by John van Druten. Simon & Schuster.

1926-1927

BROADWAY, by Philip Dunning and George Abbott. George H. Doran.
SATURDAY'S CHILDREN, by Maxwell Anderson. Longmans, Green.
CHICAGO, by Maurine Watkins. Knopf.
THE CONSTANT WIFE, by William Somerset Maugham. George H. Doran.
THE PLAY'S THE THING, by Ferenc Molnar and P. G. Wodehouse. Brentano's.
THE ROAD TO ROME, by Robert Emmet Sherwood. Scribner.
THE SILVER CORD, by Sidney Howard. Scribner.
THE CRADLE SONG, translated from the Spanish of G. Martinez Sierra by John Garrett Underhill. Dutton.
DAISY MAYME, by George Kelly. Little, Brown.
IN ABRAHAM'S BOSOM, by Paul Green. McBride.

1927-1928

STRANGE INTERLUDE, by Eugene G. O'Neill. Boni & Liveright.
THE ROYAL FAMILY, by Edna Ferber and George Kaufman. Doubleday, Doran.
BURLESQUE, by George Manker Watters and Arthur Hopkins. Doubleday, Doran.
COQUETTE, by George Abbott and Ann Bridgers. Longmans, Green.
BEHOLD THE BRIDEGROOM, by George Kelly. Little, Brown.
PORGY, by DuBose Heyward. Doubleday, Doran.
PARIS BOUND, by Philip Barry. Samuel French.
ESCAPE, by John Galsworthy. Scribner.

THE RACKET, by Bartlett Cormack. Samuel French.
THE PLOUGH AND THE STARS, by Sean O'Casey. Macmillan.

1928-1929

STREET SCENE, by Elmer Rice. Samuel French.
JOURNEY'S END, by R. C. Sherriff. Brentano's.
WINGS OVER EUROPE, by Robert Nichols and Maurice Browne. Covici-Friede.
HOLIDAY, by Philip Barry. Samuel French.
THE FRONT PAGE, by Ben Hecht and Charles MacArthur. Covici-Friede.
LET US BE GAY, by Rachel Crothers. Samuel French.
MACHINAL, by Sophie Treadwell.
LITTLE ACCIDENT, by Floyd Dell and Thomas Mitchell.
GYPSY, by Maxwell Anderson.
THE KINGDOM OF GOD, by G. Martinez Sierra; English version by Helen and Harley Granville-Barker. Dutton.

1929-1930

THE GREEN PASTURES, by Marc Connelly (adapted from "Ol' Man Adam and His Chillun," by Roark Bradford). Farrar & Rinehart.
THE CRIMINAL CODE, by Martin Flavin. Horace Liveright.
BERKELEY SQUARE, by John Balderston.
STRICTLY DISHONORABLE, by Preston Sturges. Horace Liveright.
THE FIRST MRS. FRASER, by St. John Ervine. Macmillan.
THE LAST MILE, by John Wexley. Samuel French.
JUNE MOON, by Ring W. Lardner and George S. Kaufman. Scribner.
MICHAEL AND MARY, by A. A. Milne. Chatto & Windus.
DEATH TAKES A HOLIDAY, by Walter Ferris (adapted from the Italian of Alberto Casella). Samuel French.
REBOUND, by Donald Ogden Stewart. Samuel French.

1930-1931

ELIZABETH THE QUEEN, by Maxwell Anderson. Longmans, Green.
TOMORROW AND TOMORROW, by Philip Barry. Samuel French.
ONCE IN A LIFETIME, by George S. Kaufman and Moss Hart. Farrar & Rinehart.
GREEN GROW THE LILACS, by Lynn Riggs. Samuel French.
AS HUSBANDS GO, by Rachel Crothers. Samuel French.

ALISON'S HOUSE, by Susan Glaspell. Samuel French.
FIVE-STAR FINAL, by Louis Weitzenkorn. Samuel French.
OVERTURE, by William Bolitho. Simon & Schuster.
THE BARRETTS OF WIMPOLE STREET, by Rudolf Besier. Little, Brown.
GRAND HOTEL, adapted from the German of Vicki Baum by W. A. Drake.

1931-1932

OF THEE I SING, by George S. Kaufman and Morrie Ryskind; music and lyrics by George and Ira Gershwin. Knopf.
MOURNING BECOMES ELECTRA, by Eugene G. O'Neill. Horace Liveright.
REUNION IN VIENNA, by Robert Emmet Sherwood. Scribner.
THE HOUSE OF CONNELLY, by Paul Green. Samuel French.
THE ANIMAL KINGDOM, by Philip Barry. Samuel French.
THE LEFT BANK, by Elmer Rice. Samuel French.
ANOTHER LANGUAGE, by Rose Franken. Samuel French.
BRIEF MOMENT, by S. N. Behrman. Farrar & Rinehart.
THE DEVIL PASSES, by Benn W. Levy. Martin Secker.
CYNARA, by H. M. Harwood and R. F. Gore-Browne. Samuel French.

1932-1933

BOTH YOUR HOUSES, by Maxwell Anderson. Samuel French.
DINNER AT EIGHT, by George S. Kaufman and Edna Ferber. Doubleday, Doran.
WHEN LADIES MEET, by Rachel Crothers. Samuel French.
DESIGN FOR LIVING, by Noel Coward. Doubleday, Doran.
BIOGRAPHY, by S. N. Behrman. Farrar & Rinehart.
ALIEN CORN, by Sidney Howard. Scribner.
THE LATE CHRISTOPHER BEAN, adapted from the French of René Fauchois by Sidney Howard. Samuel French.
WE, THE PEOPLE, by Elmer Rice. Coward-McCann.
PIGEONS AND PEOPLE, by George M. Cohan.
ONE SUNDAY AFTERNOON, by James Hagan. Samuel French.

1933-1934

MARY OF SCOTLAND, by Maxwell Anderson. Doubleday, Doran.
MEN IN WHITE, by Sidney Kingsley. Covici-Friede.
DODSWORTH, by Sinclair Lewis and Sidney Howard. Harcourt, Brace.

AH, WILDERNESS, by Eugene O'Neill. Random House.
THEY SHALL NOT DIE, by John Wexley. Knopf.
HER MASTER'S VOICE, by Clare Kummer. Samuel French.
NO MORE LADIES, by A. E. Thomas.
WEDNESDAY'S CHILD, by Leopold Atlas. Samuel French.
THE SHINING HOUR, by Keith Winter. Doubleday, Doran.
THE GREEN BAY TREE, by Mordaunt Shairp. Baker International Play Bureau.

1934-1935

THE CHILDREN'S HOUR, by Lillian Hellman. Knopf.
VALLEY FORGE, by Maxwell Anderson. Anderson House.
THE PETRIFIED FOREST, by Robert Sherwood. Scribner.
THE OLD MAID, by Zoë Akins. Appleton-Century.
ACCENT ON YOUTH, by Samson Raphaelson. Samuel French.
MERRILY WE ROLL ALONG, by George S. Kaufman and Moss Hart. Random House.
AWAKE AND SING, by Clifford Odets. Random House.
THE FARMER TAKES A WIFE, by Frank B. Elser and Marc Connelly.
LOST HORIZONS, by John Hayden.
THE DISTAFF SIDE, by John van Druten. Knopf.

1935-1936

WINTERSET, by Maxwell Anderson. Anderson House.
IDIOT'S DELIGHT, by Robert Emmet Sherwood. Scribner.
END OF SUMMER, by S. N. Behrman. Random House.
FIRST LADY, by Katharine Dayton and George S. Kaufman. Random House.
VICTORIA REGINA, by Laurence Housman. Samuel French.
BOY MEETS GIRL, by Bella and Samuel Spewack. Random House.
DEAD END, by Sidney Kingsley. Random House.
CALL IT A DAY, by Dodie Smith. Samuel French.
ETHAN FROME, by Owen Davis and Donald Davis. Scribner.
PRIDE AND PREJUDICE, by Helen Jerome. Doubleday, Doran.

1936-1937

HIGH TOR, by Maxwell Anderson. Anderson House.
YOU CAN'T TAKE IT WITH YOU, by Moss Hart and George S. Kaufman. Farrar & Rinehart.
JOHNNY JOHNSON, by Paul Green. Samuel French.
DAUGHTERS OF ATREUS, by Robert Turney. Knopf.

THE BEST PLAYS OF 1958–1959 361

STAGE DOOR, by Edna Ferber and George S. Kaufman. Doubleday, Doran.
THE WOMEN, by Clare Boothe. Random House.
ST. HELENA, by R. C. Sherriff and Jeanne de Casalis. Samuel French.
YES, MY DARLING DAUGHTER, by Mark Reed. Samuel French.
EXCURSION, by Victor Wolfson. Random House.
TOVARICH, by Jacques Deval and Robert E. Sherwood. Random House.

1937-1938

OF MICE AND MEN, by John Steinbeck. Covici-Friede.
OUR TOWN, by Thornton Wilder. Coward-McCann.
SHADOW AND SUBSTANCE, by Paul Vincent Carroll. Random House.
ON BORROWED TIME, by Paul Osborn. Knopf.
THE STAR-WAGON, by Maxwell Anderson. Anderson House.
SUSAN AND GOD, by Rachel Crothers. Random House.
PROLOGUE TO GLORY, by E. P. Conkle. Random House.
AMPHITRYON 38, by S. N. Behrman. Random House.
GOLDEN BOY, by Clifford Odets. Random House.
WHAT A LIFE, by Clifford Goldsmith. Dramatists' Play Service.

1938-1939

ABE LINCOLN IN ILLINOIS, by Robert E. Sherwood. Scribner.
THE LITTLE FOXES, by Lillian Hellman. Random House.
ROCKET TO THE MOON, by Clifford Odets. Random House.
THE AMERICAN WAY, by George S. Kaufman and Moss Hart. Random House.
NO TIME FOR COMEDY, by S. N. Behrman. Random House.
THE PHILADELPHIA STORY, by Philip Barry. Coward-McCann.
THE WHITE STEED, by Paul Vincent Carroll. Random House.
HERE COME THE CLOWNS, by Philip Barry. Coward-McCann.
FAMILY PORTRAIT, by Lenore Coffee and William Joyce Cowen. Random House.
KISS THE BOYS GOOD-BYE, by Clare Boothe. Random House.

1939-1940

THERE SHALL BE NO NIGHT, by Robert E. Sherwood. Scribner.
KEY LARGO, by Maxwell Anderson. Anderson House.
THE WORLD WE MAKE, by Sidney Kingsley.
LIFE WITH FATHER, by Howard Lindsay and Russel Crouse. Knopf.

THE MAN WHO CAME TO DINNER, by George S. Kaufman and Moss Hart. Random House.
THE MALE ANIMAL, by James Thurber and Elliott Nugent. Random House, New York, and MacMillan Co., Canada.
THE TIME OF YOUR LIFE, by William Saroyan. Harcourt, Brace.
SKYLARK, by Samson Raphaelson. Random House.
MARGIN FOR ERROR, by Clare Boothe. Random House.
MORNING'S AT SEVEN, by Paul Osborn. Samuel French.

1940-1941

NATIVE SON, by Paul Green and Richard Wright. Harper.
WATCH ON THE RHINE, by Lillian Hellman. Random House.
THE CORN IS GREEN, by Emlyn Williams. Random House.
LADY IN THE DARK, by Moss Hart. Random House.
ARSENIC AND OLD LACE, by Joseph Kesselring. Random House.
MY SISTER EILEEN, by Joseph Fields and Jerome Chodorov. Random House.
FLIGHT TO THE WEST, by Elmer Rice. Coward-McCann.
CLAUDIA, by Rose Franken Meloney. Farrar & Rinehart.
MR. AND MRS. NORTH, by Owen Davis. Samuel French.
GEORGE WASHINGTON SLEPT HERE, by George S. Kaufman and Moss Hart. Random House.

1941-1942

IN TIME TO COME, by Howard Koch. Dramatists' Play Service.
THE MOON IS DOWN, by John Steinbeck. Viking.
BLITHE SPIRIT, by Noel Coward. Doubleday, Doran.
JUNIOR MISS, by Jerome Chodorov and Joseph Fields. Random House.
CANDLE IN THE WIND, by Maxwell Anderson. Anderson House.
LETTERS TO LUCERNE, by Fritz Rotter and Allen Vincent. Samuel French.
JASON, by Samson Raphaelson. Random House.
ANGEL STREET, by Patrick Hamilton. Constable & Co., under the title "Gaslight."
UNCLE HARRY, by Thomas Job. Samuel French.
HOPE FOR A HARVEST, by Sophie Treadwell. Samuel French.

1942-1943

THE PATRIOTS, by Sidney Kingsley. Random House.
THE EVE OF ST. MARK, by Maxwell Anderson. Anderson House.

THE SKIN OF OUR TEETH, by Thornton Wilder. Harper.
WINTER SOLDIERS, by Dan James.
TOMORROW THE WORLD, by James Gow and Arnaud d'Usseau. Scribner.
HARRIET, by Florence Ryerson and Colin Clements. Scribner.
THE DOUGHGIRLS, by Joseph Fields. Random House.
THE DAMASK CHEEK, by John van Druten and Lloyd Morris. Random House.
KISS AND TELL, by F. Hugh Herbert. Coward-McCann.
OKLAHOMA!, by Oscar Hammerstein 2nd and Richard Rodgers. Random House.

1943-1944

WINGED VICTORY, by Moss Hart. Random House.
THE SEARCHING WIND, by Lillian Hellman. Viking.
THE VOICE OF THE TURTLE, by John van Druten. Random House.
DECISION, by Edward Chodorov.
OVER 21, by Ruth Gordon. Random House.
OUTRAGEOUS FORTUNE, by Rose Franken. Samuel French.
JACOBOWSKY AND THE COLONEL, by S. N. Behrman. Random House.
STORM OPERATION, by Maxwell Anderson. Anderson House.
PICK-UP GIRL, by Elsa Shelley.
THE INNOCENT VOYAGE, by Paul Osborn.

1944-1945

A BELL FOR ADANO, by Paul Osborn. Knopf.
I REMEMBER MAMA, by John van Druten. Harcourt, Brace.
THE HASTY HEART, by John Patrick. Random House.
THE GLASS MENAGERIE, by Tennessee Williams. Random House.
HARVEY, by Mary Chase.
THE LATE GEORGE APLEY, by John P. Marquand and George S. Kaufman.
SOLDIER'S WIFE, by Rose Franken. Samuel French.
ANNA LUCASTA, by Philip Yordan. Random House.
FOOLISH NOTION, by Philip Barry.
DEAR RUTH, by Norman Krasna. Random House.

1945-1946

STATE OF THE UNION, by Howard Lindsay and Russel Crouse. Random House.
HOME OF THE BRAVE, by Arthur Laurents. Random House.

DEEP ARE THE ROOTS, by Arnaud d'Usseau and James Gow. Scribner.
THE MAGNIFICENT YANKEE, by Emmet Lavery. Samuel French.
ANTIGONE, by Lewis Galantière (from the French of Jean Anouilh). Random House.
O MISTRESS MINE, by Terence Rattigan. Published and revised by the author.
BORN YESTERDAY, by Garson Kanin. Viking.
DREAM GIRL, by Elmer Rice. Coward-McCann.
THE RUGGED PATH, by Robert E. Sherwood. Scribner.
LUTE SONG, by Will Irwin and Sidney Howard. Published version by Will Irwin and Leopoldine Howard.

1946-1947

ALL MY SONS, by Arthur Miller. Reynal & Hitchcock.
THE ICEMAN COMETH, by Eugene G. O'Neill. Random House.
JOAN OF LORRAINE, by Maxwell Anderson. Published by Maxwell Anderson.
ANOTHER PART OF THE FOREST, by Lillian Hellman. Viking.
YEARS AGO, by Ruth Gordon. Viking.
JOHN LOVES MARY, by Norman Krasna. Copyright by Norman Krasna.
THE FATAL WEAKNESS, by George Kelly. Samuel French.
THE STORY OF MARY SURRATT, by John Patrick. Dramatists' Play Service.
CHRISTOPHER BLAKE, by Moss Hart. Random House.
BRIGADOON, by Alan Jay Lerner and Frederick Loewe. Coward-McCann.

1947-1948

A STREETCAR NAMED DESIRE, by Tennessee Williams. New Directions.
MISTER ROBERTS, by Thomas Heggen and Joshua Logan. Houghton Mifflin.
COMMAND DECISION, by William Wister Haines. Random House.
THE WINSLOW BOY, by Terence Rattigan.
THE HEIRESS, by Ruth and Augustus Goetz.
ALLEGRO, by Richard Rodgers and Oscar Hammerstein 2d. Knopf. Music published by Williamson Music, Inc.
EASTWARD IN EDEN, by Dorothy Gardner. Longmans, Green.
SKIPPER NEXT TO GOD, by Jan de Hartog.

An Inspector Calls, by J. B. Priestley.
Me and Molly, by Gertrude Berg.

1948-1949

Death of a Salesman, by Arthur Miller. Viking.
Anne of the Thousand Days, by Maxwell Anderson. Sloane.
The Madwoman of Chaillot, by Maurice Valency, adapted from the French of Jean Giraudoux. Random House.
Detective Story, by Sidney Kingsley. Random House.
Edward, My Son, by Robert Morley and Noel Langley. Random House, New York, and Samuel French, London.
Life with Mother, by Howard Lindsay and Russel Crouse. Knopf.
Light Up the Sky, by Moss Hart. Random House.
The Silver Whistle, by Robert Edward McEnroe. Dramatists' Play Service.
Two Blind Mice, by Samuel Spewack. Dramatists' Play Service.
Goodbye, My Fancy, by Fay Kanin. Samuel French.

1949-1950

The Cocktail Party, by T. S. Eliot. Harcourt, Brace.
The Member of the Wedding, by Carson McCullers. Houghton Mifflin.
The Innocents, by William Archibald. Coward-McCann.
Lost in the Stars, by Maxwell Anderson and Kurt Weill. Sloane.
Come Back, Little Sheba, by William Inge. Random House.
The Happy Time, by Samuel Taylor. Random House.
The Wisteria Trees, by Joshua Logan. Random House.
I Know My Love, by S. N. Behrman. Random House.
The Enchanted, by Maurice Valency, adapted from a play by Jean Giraudoux. Random House.
Clutterbuck, by Benn W. Levy. Dramatists' Play Service.

1950-1951

Guys and Dolls, by Jo Swerling, Abe Burrows and Frank Loesser.
Darkness at Noon, by Sidney Kingsley and Arthur Koestler. Random House.
Billy Budd, by Louis O. Coxe and Robert Chapman. Princeton University Press.
The Autumn Garden, by Lillian Hellman. Little, Brown & Co.

BELL, BOOK AND CANDLE, by John van Druten. Random House.
THE COUNTRY GIRL, by Clifford Odets. Viking Press.
THE ROSE TATTOO, by Tennessee Williams. New Directions.
SEASON IN THE SUN, by Wolcott Gibbs. Random House.
AFFAIRS OF STATE, by Louis Verneuil.
SECOND THRESHOLD, by Philip Barry. Harper & Bros.

1951-1952

MRS. MCTHING, by Mary Coyle Chase.
THE SHRIKE, by Joseph Kramm. Random House.
I AM A CAMERA, by John van Druten. Random House.
THE FOURPOSTER, by Jan de Hartog.
POINT OF NO RETURN, by Paul Osborn. Random House.
BAREFOOT IN ATHENS, by Maxwell Anderson. Sloane.
VENUS OBSERVED, by Christopher Fry. Oxford.
JANE, by S. N. Behrman and Somerset Maugham. Random House.
GIGI, by Anita Loos and Colette. Random House.
REMAINS TO BE SEEN, by Howard Lindsay and Russel Crouse. Random House.

1952-1953

THE TIME OF THE CUCKOO, by Arthur Laurents. Random House.
BERNARDINE, by Mary Coyle Chase.
DIAL "M" FOR MURDER, by Frederick Knott. Random House.
THE CLIMATE OF EDEN, by Moss Hart. Random House.
THE LOVE OF FOUR COLONELS, by Peter Ustinov.
THE CRUCIBLE, by Arthur Miller. Viking.
THE EMPEROR'S CLOTHES, by George Tabori. Samuel French.
PICNIC, by William Inge. Random House.
WONDERFUL TOWN, by Joseph Fields, Jerome Chodorov, Betty Comden and Adolph Green. Random House.
MY 3 ANGELS, by Sam and Bella Spewack.

1953-1954

THE CAINE MUTINY COURT-MARTIAL, by Herman Wouk. Doubleday & Company, Inc.
IN THE SUMMER HOUSE, by Jane Bowles. Random House.
THE CONFIDENTIAL CLERK, by T. S. Eliot. Harcourt, Brace and Company, Inc.
TAKE A GIANT STEP, by Louis Peterson.
THE TEAHOUSE OF THE AUGUST MOON, by John Patrick. G. P. Putnam's Sons.

THE IMMORALIST, by Ruth and Augustus Goetz. Ruth and Augustus Goetz. Dramatists' Play Service.
TEA AND SYMPATHY, by Robert Anderson. Random House.
THE GIRL ON THE VIA FLAMINIA, by Alfred Hayes.
THE GOLDEN APPLE, by John Latouche and Jerome Moross. Random House.
THE MAGIC AND THE LOSS, by Julian Funt. Samuel French.

1954-1955

THE BOY FRIEND, by Sandy Wilson.
THE LIVING ROOM, by Graham Greene. Viking.
BAD SEED, by Maxwell Anderson. Dodd, Mead.
WITNESS FOR THE PROSECUTION, by Agatha Christie.
THE FLOWERING PEACH, by Clifford Odets.
THE DESPERATE HOURS, by Joseph Hayes. Random House.
THE DARK IS LIGHT ENOUGH, by Christopher Fry. Oxford.
BUS STOP, by William Inge. Random House.
CAT ON A HOT TIN ROOF, by Tennessee Williams. New Directions.
INHERIT THE WIND, by Jerome Lawrence and Robert E. Lee. Random House.

1955-1956

A VIEW FROM THE BRIDGE, by Arthur Miller. Viking.
TIGER AT THE GATES, by Jean Giraudoux, translated by Christopher Fry. Oxford.
THE DIARY OF ANNE FRANK, by Frances Goodrich and Albert Hackett. Random House.
NO TIME FOR SERGEANTS, by Ira Levin. Random House.
THE CHALK GARDEN, by Enid Bagnold. Random House.
THE LARK, by Jean Anouilh, adapted by Lillian Hellman. Random House.
THE MATCHMAKER, by Thornton Wilder. Harper.
THE PONDER HEART, by Joseph Fields and Jerome Chodorov. Random House.
MY FAIR LADY, by Alan Jay Lerner and Frederick Loewe. Coward-McCann.
WAITING FOR GODOT, by Samuel Beckett. Grove.

1956-1957

SEPARATE TABLES, by Terence Rattigan. Random House.
LONG DAY'S JOURNEY INTO NIGHT, by Eugene O'Neill. Yale University Press.
A VERY SPECIAL BABY, by Robert Alan Aurthur. Dramatists Play Service.
CANDIDE, by Lillian Hellman, Richard Wilbur, John Latouche, Dorothy Parker and Leonard Bernstein. Random House.
A CLEARING IN THE WOODS, by Arthur Laurents. Random House.
THE WALTZ OF THE TOREADORS, by Jean Anouilh, translated by Lucienne Hill. Coward-McCann.
THE POTTING SHED, by Graham Greene. Viking.
VISIT TO A SMALL PLANET, by Gore Vidal. Little, Brown.
ORPHEUS DESCENDING, by Tennessee Williams. New Directions.
A MOON FOR THE MISBEGOTTEN, by Eugene O'Neill. Random House.

1957-1958

LOOK BACK IN ANGER, by John Osborne. Criterion Books.
UNDER MILK WOOD, by Dylan Thomas. New Directions.
TIME REMEMBERED, by Jean Anouilh, adapted by Patricia Moyes. Coward-McCann.
THE ROPE DANCERS, by Morton Wishengrad. Crown.
LOOK HOMEWARD, ANGEL, by Ketti Frings. Scribner's.
THE DARK AT THE TOP OF THE STAIRS, by William Inge. Random House.
SUMMER OF THE 17TH DOLL, by Ray Lawler. Random House.
SUNRISE AT CAMPOBELLO, by Dore Schary. Random House.
THE ENTERTAINER, by John Osborne. Criterion Books.
THE VISIT, by Friedrich Duerrenmatt, adapted by Maurice Valency. Random House.

WHERE AND WHEN THEY WERE BORN

(Compiled from the most authentic records available)

Abbott, George	Forestville, N. Y.	1889
Abel, Walter	St. Paul, Minn.	1898
Addy, Wesley	Omaha, Neb.	1912
Adler, Luther	New York City	1903
Aherne, Brian	King's Norton, England	1902
Aldrich, Richard	Boston, Mass.	1902
Anderson, Judith	Australia	1898
Anderson, Maxwell	Atlantic City, Pa.	1888
Anderson, Robert	New York City	1917
Andrews, Julie	London, England	1935
Arthur, Jean	New York City	1905
Ashcroft, Peggy	Croydon, England	1907
Atkinson, Brooks	Melrose, Mass.	1894
Bainter, Fay	Los Angeles, Cal.	1892
Bankhead, Tallulah	Huntsville, Ala.	1902
Barrymore, Ethel	Philadelphia, Pa.	1879
Barton, James	Gloucester, N. J.	1890
Begley, Ed	Hartford, Conn.	1901
Behrman, S. N.	Worcester, Mass.	1893
Bellamy, Ralph	Chicago, Ill.	1904
Bergman, Ingrid	Stockholm, Sweden	1917
Bergner, Elisabeth	Vienna, Austria	1900
Berlin, Irving	Russia	1888
Bernstein, Leonard	Brookline, Mass.	1918
Best, Edna	Hove, England	1900
Blackmer, Sidney	Salisbury, N. C.	1898
Blaine, Vivian	Newark, N. J.	1923
Bolger, Ray	Dorchester, Mass.	1904
Bondi, Beulah	Chicago, Ill.	1892
Booth, Shirley	New York City	1909
Bourneuf, Philip	Boston, Mass.	1912
Boyer, Charles	Figeac, France	1899
Brando, Marlon	Omaha, Neb.	1924

Brent, Romney	Saltillo, Mex.	1902
Brown, Joe E.	Holgate, Ohio	1892
Burke, Billie	Washington, D. C.	1895
Byington, Spring	Colorado Springs, Colo.	1898
Cagney, James	New York City	1904
Cantor, Eddie	New York City	1892
Carnovsky, Morris	St. Louis, Mo.	1898
Carradine, John	New York City	1906
Carroll, Leo G.	Weedon, England	1892
Carroll, Madeleine	West Bromwich, England	1906
Channing, Carol	Seattle, Wash.	1921
Chase, Ilka	New York City	1905
Chatterton, Ruth	New York City	1893
Claire, Ina	Washington, D. C.	1895
Clark, Bobby	Springfield, Ohio	1888
Clift, Montgomery	Omaha, Neb.	1921
Clurman, Harold	New York City	1901
Cobb, Lee	New York City	1911
Coburn, Charles	Macon, Ga.	1877
Collinge, Patricia	Dublin, Ireland	1894
Collins, Russell	New Orleans, La.	1897
Conroy, Frank	London, England	1885
Cook, Donald	Portland, Ore.	1902
Cook, Joe	Evansville, Ind.	1890
Cooper, Gladys	Lewisham, England	1888
Cooper, Melville	Birmingham, England	1896
Corbett, Leonora	London, England	1908
Cornell, Katharine	Berlin, Germany	1898
Coulouris, George	Manchester, England	1906
Coward, Noel	Teddington, England	1899
Crawford, Cheryl	Akron, Ohio	1902
Cromwell, John	Toledo, Ohio	1888
Cronyn, Hume	London, Ontario	1912
Crothers, Rachel	Bloomington, Ill.	1878
Crouse, Russel	Findlay, Ohio	1893
Cummings, Constance	Seattle, Wash.	1911
Dale, Margaret	Philadelphia, Pa.	1880
Dana, Leora	New York City	1923
Daniell, Henry	London, England	1894
Derwent, Clarence	London, England	1884
Douglas, Melvyn	Macon, Ga.	1901

THE BEST PLAYS OF 1958–1959

Dowling, Eddie	Woonsocket, R. I.	1894
Drake, Alfred	New York City	1914
Duncan, Todd	Danville, Ky.	1900
Dunning, Philip	Meriden, Conn.	1890
Durante, Jimmy	New York City	1893
Eldridge, Florence	Brooklyn, N. Y.	1901
Eliot, T. S.	St. Louis, Mo.	1888
Elsom, Isobel	Cambridge, England	1893
Evans, Edith	London, England	1888
Evans, Maurice	Dorchester, England	1901
Evans, Wilbur	Philadelphia, Pa.	1908
Evelyn, Judith	Seneca, S. Dak.	1913
Ewell, Tom	Owensboro, Ky.	1912
Fabray, Nanette	New Orleans, La.	1921
Fay, Frank	San Francisco, Cal.	1897
Ferber, Edna	Kalamazoo, Mich.	1887
Ferrer, José	Puerto Rico	1912
Field, Betty	Boston, Mass.	1918
Field, Virginia	London, England	1917
Fields, Gracie	Rochdale, England	1898
Fitzgerald, Barry	Dublin, Ireland	1888
Fitzgerald, Geraldine	Dublin, Ireland	1914
Flemyng, Robert	Liverpool, England	1912
Fletcher, Bramwell	Bradford, Yorkshire, Eng.	1904
Fonda, Henry	Grand Island, Neb.	1905
Fontanne, Lynn	London, England	1887
Forbes, Brenda	London, England	1909
Foy, Eddie, Jr.	New Rochelle, N. Y.	1907
Francis, Arlene	Boston, Mass.	1908
Fry, Christopher	England	1907
Gahagan, Helen	Boonton, N. J.	1900
Gaxton, William	San Francisco, Cal.	1893
Gazzara, Ben	New York City	1930
Geddes, Barbara Bel	New York City	1922
Geddes, Norman Bel	Adrian, Mich.	1893
George, Grace	New York City	1879
Gershwin, Ira	New York City	1896
Gielgud, Sir John	London, England	1904
Gillmore, Margalo	England	1901
Gilmore, Virginia	El Monte, Cal.	1919

THE BEST PLAYS OF 1958–1959

Gish, Dorothy	Massillon, Ohio	1898
Gish, Lillian	Springfield, Ohio	1896
Gordon, Ruth	Wollaston, Mass.	1896
Green, Martyn	London, England	1899
Greenwood, Joan	London, England	1921
Guinness, Alec	London, England	1914
Guthrie, Tyrone	Tunbridge Wells, England	1900
Gwenn, Edmund	Glamorgan, Wales	1875
Hagen, Uta	Göttingen, Germany	1919
Hammerstein, Oscar, II	New York City	1895
Hardie, Russell	Griffin Mills, N. Y.	1906
Hardwicke, Sir Cedric	Lye, Stourbridge, England	1893
Harris, Julie	Grosse Point, Mich.	1925
Harrison, Rex	Huyton, Lancashire, England	1908
Hart, Moss	New York City	1904
Havoc, June	Seattle, Wash.	1916
Haydon, Julie	Oak Park, Ill.	1910
Hayes, Helen	Washington, D. C.	1900
Hayward, Leland	Nebraska City, Neb.	1902
Heflin, Frances	Oklahoma City, Okla.	1924
Hellman, Lillian	New Orleans, La.	1905
Helmore, Tom	London, England	1912
Helpmann, Robert	South Australia	1911
Henie, Sonja	Oslo, Norway	1913
Hepburn, Audrey	Brussels, Belgium	1929
Hepburn, Katharine	Hartford, Conn.	1909
Herlie, Eileen	Glasgow, Scotland	1920
Hiller, Wendy	Bramhall, England	1912
Holliday, Judy	New York City	1924
Holloway, Stanley	London, England	1890
Holm, Celeste	New York City	1919
Homolka, Oscar	Vienna, Austria	1898
Hull, Henry	Louisville, Ky.	1890
Hunt, Martita	Argentine Republic	1900
Hunter, Kim	Detroit, Mich.	1922
Hussey, Ruth	Providence, R. I.	1917
Ives, Burl	Hunt Township, Ill.	1909
Johnson, Harold J. (Chic)	Chicago, Ill.	1891
Joy, Nicholas	Paris, France	1889

Kanin, Garson	Rochester, N. Y.	1912
Karloff, Boris	Dulwich, England	1887
Kaufman, George S.	Pittsburgh, Pa.	1889
Kaye, Danny	New York City	1914
Kazan, Elia	Constantinople	1909
Keith, Robert	Fowler, Ind.	1898
Kennedy, Arthur	Worcester, Mass.	1914
Kerr, Deborah	Helensburgh, Scotland	1921
Kerr, John	New York City	1931
Killbride, Percy	San Francisco, Cal.	1880
King, Dennis	Coventry, England	1897
Kingsley, Sidney	New York City	1906
Kirkland, Patricia	New York City	1927
Knox, Alexander	Ontario	1907
Kruger, Otto	Toledo, Ohio	1885
Lahr, Bert	New York City	1895
Landis, Jessie Royce	Chicago, Ill.	1904
Laughton, Charles	Scarborough, England	1899
Laurents, Arthur	New York City	1920
LeGallienne, Eva	London, England	1899
Leigh, Vivien	Darjeeling, India	1913
Leighton, Margaret	Barnt Green, England	1922
Lerner, Alan Jay	New York City	1918
Lillie, Beatrice	Toronto, Canada	1898
Lindsay, Howard	Waterford, N. Y.	1899
Linn, Bambi	Brooklyn, N. Y.	1926
Logan, Joshua	Texarkana, Tex.	1908
Lukas, Paul	Budapest, Hungary	1891
Lunt, Alfred	Milwaukee, Wis.	1893
MacGrath, Leueen	London, England	1914
MacMahon, Aline	McKeesport, Pa.	1899
Mamoulian, Rouben	Tiflis, Russia	1898
Mann, Iris	Brooklyn, N. Y.	1939
Marceau, Marcel	Near Strasbourg, France	1923
March, Fredric	Racine, Wis.	1897
Martin, Mary	Weatherford, Texas	1913
Mason, James	Huddersfield, England	1909
Massey, Raymond	Toronto, Canada	1896
Maugham, W. Somerset	England	1874
McClintic, Guthrie	Seattle, Wash.	1893
McCormick, Myron	Albany, Ind.	1907

McCracken, Joan .... Philadelphia, Pa. 1923
McDowall, Roddy .... London, England 1928
McGrath, Paul .... Chicago, Ill. 1900
McGuire, Dorothy .... Omaha, Neb. 1918
McKenna, Siobhan .... Belfast, Ireland 1923
Menotti, Gian-Carlo .... Italy 1912
Meredith, Burgess .... Cleveland, Ohio 1908
Merkel, Una .... Covington, Ky. 1903
Merman, Ethel .... Astoria, L. I. 1909
Middleton, Ray .... Chicago, Ill. 1907
Mielziner, Jo .... Paris, France 1901
Miller, Arthur .... New York City 1915
Miller, Gilbert .... New York City 1884
Mitchell, Thomas .... Elizabeth, N. J. 1892
Moore, Victor .... Hammonton, N. J. 1876
Moorehead, Agnes .... Clinton, Mass. 1906
Morgan, Claudia .... New York City 1912
Morley, Robert .... Semley, England 1908
Moss, Arnold .... Brooklyn, N. Y. 1910
Muni, Paul .... Lemberg, Austria 1895

Nagel, Conrad .... Keokuk, Iowa 1897
Natwick, Mildred .... Baltimore, Md. 1908
Neal, Patricia .... Packard, Ky. 1926
Nesbitt, Cathleen .... Cheshire, England 1889
Nugent, Elliott .... Dover, Ohio 1900

Odets, Clifford .... Philadelphia, Pa. 1906
Oenslager, Donald .... Harrisburg, Pa. 1902
Olivier, Sir Laurence .... Dorking, Surrey, England 1907
Olsen, John Siguard (Ole) ... Peru, Ind. 1892
O'Malley, Rex .... London, England 1906
O'Neal, Frederick .... Brookville, Miss. 1905
Osborn, Paul .... Evansville, Ind. 1901

Page, Geraldine .... Kirksville, Mo. 1925
Palmer, Lilli .... Posen, Austria 1914
Petina, Irra .... Leningrad, Russia 1900
Picon, Molly .... New York City 1898
Porter, Cole .... Peru, Ind. 1892
Portman, Eric .... Yorkshire, England 1903
Price, Vincent .... St. Louis, Mo. 1914

Quayle, Anthony .... Ainsdale, England 1913

Rains, Claude .... London, England 1889
Raitt, John .... Santa Ana, Cal. 1917
Rathbone, Basil .... Johannesburg, Africa 1892
Rattigan, Terence .... London, England 1911
Redgrave, Michael .... Bristol, England 1908
Redman, Joyce .... Newcastle, Ireland 1918
Reed, Florence .... Philadelphia, Pa. 1883
Rennie, James .... Toronto, Canada 1890
Rice, Elmer .... New York City 1892
Richardson, Sir Ralph ...... Cheltenham, England 1902
Ritchard, Cyril .... Sydney, Australia 1898
Rodgers, Richard .... New York City 1902
Royle, Selena .... New York City 1905
Russell, Rosalind .... Waterbury, Conn. 1911

Sarnoff, Dorothy .... Brooklyn, N. Y. 1919
Saroyan, William .... Fresno, Cal. 1908
Schildkraut, Joseph .... Vienna, Austria 1895
Scott, Martha .... Jamesport, Mo. 1914
Segal, Vivienne .... Philadelphia, Pa. 1897
Sherman, Hiram .... Boston, Mass. 1908
Shumlin, Herman .... Atwood, Colo. 1898
Silvers, Phil .... Brooklyn, N. Y. 1911
Simms, Hilda .... Minneapolis, Minn. 1920
Skinner, Cornelia Otis ...... Chicago, Ill. 1902
Slezak, Walter .... Vienna, Austria 1902
Smith, Kent .... Smithfield, Me. 1910
Stanley, Kim .... Tularosa, N. M. 1921
Stapleton, Maureen .... Troy, N. Y. 1926
Starr, Frances .... Oneonta, N. Y. 1886
Stickney, Dorothy .... Dickinson, N. D. 1903
Stone, Carol .... New York City 1917
Stone, Dorothy .... New York City 1905
Stone, Ezra .... New Bedford, Mass. 1918
Stone, Fred .... Denver, Colo. 1873
Straight, Beatrice .... Old Westbury, N. Y. 1918
Sullavan, Margaret .... Norfolk, Va. 1910

Tandy, Jessica .... London, England 1909
Tetzel, Joan .... New York City 1923
Thorndike, Sybil .... Gainsborough, England 1882

Tone, Franchot .... Niagara Falls, N. Y. 1906
Tozere, Frederick .... Brookline, Mass. 1901
Tracy, Lee .... Atlanta, Ga. 1898
Truex, Ernest .... Red Hill, Mo. 1890

van Druten, John .... London, England 1902
Van Patten, Dick .... New York City 1929
Varden, Evelyn .... Venita, Okla. 1893
Verdon, Gwen .... Culver City, Cal. 1926

Walker, June .... New York City 1904
Walker, Nancy .... Philadelphia, Pa. 1922
Wallach, Eli .... Brooklyn, N. Y. 1915
Wanamaker, Sam .... Chicago, Ill. 1919
Waring, Richard .... Buckinghamshire, England ...1912
Waters, Ethel .... Chester, Pa. 1900
Watson, Douglas .... Jackson, Ga. 1921
Watson, Lucile .... Quebec, Canada 1879
Wayne, David .... Travers City, Mich. 1914
Webb, Alan .... York, England 1906
Webb, Clifton .... Indiana 1891
Webster, Margaret .... New York City 1905
Welles, Orson .... Kenosha, Wis. 1915
West, Mae .... Brooklyn, N. Y. 1892
Weston, Ruth .... Boston, Mass. 1911
Widmark, Richard .... Sunrise, Minn. 1914
Wilder, Thornton .... Madison, Wis. 1897
Williams, Emlyn .... Wales 1905
Williams, Rhys .... Wales 1903
Williams, Tennessee .... Columbus, Miss. 1914
Winwood, Estelle .... England 1883
Wood, Peggy .... Brooklyn, N. Y. 1894
Wyatt, Jane .... Campgaw, N. J. 1912
Wynn, Ed .... Philadelphia, Pa. 1886
Wynn, Keenan .... New York City 1917

Yurka, Blanche .... Bohemia 1893

NECROLOGY

June 1, 1958—May 31, 1959

Akins, Zoe, 72, playwright. She was educated at Hosmer Hall in St. Louis. She wrote poems and short stories for "The Mirror" there and at 21 published her first volume of poems. Her first Broadway play was "The Magical City," followed in 1919 by "Papa." The same year she attained great success with "Déclassée," starring Ethel Barrymore. Some 16 plays followed, including "Foot-Loose," "The Varying Shore," "The Texas Nightingale," "The Moon Flower," "First Love" and in 1935 "The Old Maid," which won her the Pulitzer Prize. During all this time she wrote short stories and several screen scenarios. Born Humansville, Ohio; died Los Angeles, Oct. 29, 1958.

Anderson, Maxwell, 70, playwright. The son of a minister, he moved from parsonage to parsonage when young and worked on farms. During his travels he attended some 13 schools. After graduating from the University of North Dakota he went to Stanford University, where he taught English while earning an M.A. In 1918 he joined the staff of "The New Republic," then joined "The New York Evening Globe" as an editorial writer and later the "World." At that time he was one of the founders of the poetry magazine "The Measure." He wrote "White Desert," which Brock Pemberton produced. With Laurence Stallings he wrote "What Price Glory?" which hit the theatrical jackpot in 1924. For 30 years he turned out about one play a season. Some of these were "Night Over Taos," "Key Largo," "The Eve of St. Mark," "Joan of Lorraine," "Anne of the Thousand Days," the musical, "Lost in the Stars" with a score by Kurt Weill. Others were "The Wingless Victory," "Elizabeth the Queen," "The Masque of Kings," "Mary of Scotland," "Valley Forge" and "Storm Operation." He won the Pulitzer Prize in 1933 for "Both Your Houses" and the Drama Critics Circle Award in 1936 for "Winterset" and the following year for "High Tor." In 1938, with Robert Sherwood and other playwrights, he organized the Playwrights' Company. He had a deep dislike for drama critics, calling them the "Jukes family of journalism." At the time of his death he was working on a comedy, "Madonna and Child." Born Atlantic, Pa.; died Stamford, Conn., Feb. 28, 1959.

Bennett, Barbara, age not given, actress. A daughter of Richard Bennett, she made her stage debut at 14 with James Kirkwood in "The Fool." At 16 she was the dancing partner of Maurice Mouvet. This was followed by "The Stork," "The Dancers," "The Dream Girl" and a road tour of "Cyrano" with her father. She made films with Mary Pickford, Buck Jones, Fred Waring and Morton Downey. Her last Broadway appearance was in 1943 in "Victory Belles." Born Palisades, N. J.; died Montreal, Canada, Aug. 8, 1958.

Blore, Eric, 71, actor. He gave up a college education for the insurance business and then appeared in the chorus of "A Girl from Kay's." Later he toured the English provinces and Australia, wrote romantic serials and lyrics of popular songs as well as singing in London Music Halls. He played in London in "All the Winners," "Nuts and Wine" and "Alice Up to Date." In 1923 he came to this country to appear with Irene Bordoni in "Little Miss Bluebeard." Other Broadway appearances followed in "The Ghost Train," "Just Fancy" and "Meet the Prince." He was in "The Gay Divorcee" with Fred Astaire and also appeared in the movie version. He made 26 Hollywood films in two years, among them "Flying Down to Rio" and "Bowery of Bagdad." He was also in "Top Hat," "Fancy Pants," "Love Happy" and others. Born London; died Hollywood, March 1, 1959.

Clark, Charles Dow, 89, actor. He graduated from Tufts University and later was football coach at Mississippi U. and Colby College. His first Broadway appearance was in 1896 in "The Prisoner of Zenda." Thereafter he was in hundreds of plays and movies, making a special mark as Gramp Maple in "The Petrified Forest." Some of his other plays were "Welcome Stranger," "Never Say Die," "The Vanderbilt Cup," "For Valor" and "Big Hearted Herbert." Birthplace not given; died New York, March 26, 1959.

Cohen, Octavus Roy, 67, playwright. After graduating from Clemson College in 1911, he worked as a newspaper reporter before being admitted to the South Carolina bar in 1913. He practiced law for two years before taking seriously to writing. In all he wrote 60 books, 30 motion pictures, many Amos and Andy radio shows, hundreds of short stories and five plays: "The Crimson

Alibi," "The Scourge," "Come Seven," "Shadows" and "Every Saturday Night." He was on the council of the Authors Guild of America. Born Charleston, S. C.; died Los Angeles, Jan. 6, 1959.

Cook, Joe, 69, actor. He made his first appearance on the stage with a traveling show at the age of 12. In 1907 he appeared with his brother as "The Juggling Kids" and thereafter, for many years, was well known in vaudeville. His first appearance in a regular theatre was in New York in "Hitchy Koo of 1919." He made a real hit in the "Earl Carroll Vanities of 1923" and went on to tremendous successes in "Smiling," "Rain or Shine" and "Fine and Dandy." Later in New York he was in "Hold Your Horses" and "On to Buffalo." His imitation of four Hawaiians became a classic. His last New York appearance was in "It Happens on Ice" in 1940, after which he retired because of illness. Born Evansville, Ind.; died Staatsburg, N. Y., May 16, 1959.

Costello, Lou, 52, actor. He went to school in Paterson, N. J. He worked his way to Hollywood, where he met William (Bud) Abbott and they formed their famous comedy team. Their first break came on the Kate Smith radio show. They did "The Streets of Paris" on Broadway and soon afterward were signed by Universal-International for the movies. Their second picture, "Buck Privates," made them stars almost overnight and grossed nearly ten million. The team broke up amicably in 1957. Born Paterson, N. J.; died Beverly Hills, Calif., March 3, 1959.

Crothers, Rachel, 79, playwright. In her day she was America's leading woman playwright. She attended the State Normal School in Bloomington, Ill. She directed almost all of her plays throughout her career. She reached Broadway with "The Three of Us" and followed it with many hits such as "39 East," "Myself Bettina," "Old Lady 31," "A Little Journey," "He and She," "Everyday," "Mary the Third," "Let Us Be Gay," "As Husbands Go," "When Ladies Meet," which won the Megrue Prize in 1933, and "Susan and God," which captured the gold medal of the Theatre Club. She founded the Stage Women's War Relief during World War I and was one of the founders of the American Theatre Wing. She was a member of the Society of American Dramatists and the Authors League of America. Born Bloomington, Ill.; died Danbury, Conn., July 5, 1958.

Davis, Eddie, 58, writer. A taxi driver in the thirties, he attracted the attention of Eddie Cantor, who hired him as a gag writer;

he also worked for Jimmy Durante, Jack Haley, Bob Hope, Milton Berle and others. In association with other writers he wrote the books for such musicals as "Hold On to Your Hats," "Follow the Girls" and "Ankles Aweigh." Born New York; died New York, July 30, 1958.

De Mille, Cecil B., 77, actor, film producer. At 17 he went on the stage appearing in "Lord Chumley," "The Warrens of Virginia," "The Prince Chap" and "Hearts Are Trumps." In 1913 he formed a motion picture company with Jesse Lasky and Sam Goldwyn. Their first picture was "The Squaw Man," in which indoor lighting was first tried out on an actor. Among his films were "The Ten Commandments," "The Crusades," "The Sign of the Cross," "King of Kings," "Cleopatra" and a long list of spectaculars. In 1953 he won an Academy Award for "The Greatest Show on Earth" and thereafter was showered with honors including the Milestone Award of the Producers Guild, the Great Living Americans Award of the United States Chamber of Commerce, the Fame Award of Achievement of the motion picture industry and the Washington Pilgrimage Award of the Religious Heritage of America, Inc. He also received citations from the Salvation Army and, for ten consecutive years, was voted the industry's top producer-director by the Motion Picture Exhibitors. France made him a Knight of the Legion of Honor, The Netherlands inducted him into the Order of Orange Nassau, and Thailand conferred on him the Most Exalted Order of the White Elephant. Born Ashfield, Mass.; died Hollywood, Jan. 21, 1959.

Derwent, Elfrida, in her 80's, actress. She appeared with her brother, Clarence Derwent, in many plays such as "Lady in Danger," "Lady Precious Stream," "Kind Lady" and "Nathan the Wise." In summer stock she was in "Nellie Bly," "Alice Sit-by-the-Fire," "King Nicolo" and others. Born England; died Islip, L. I., N. Y., July 5, 1958.

Donat, Robert, 53, actor. He studied voice and diction under actor James Bernard and later joined Sir Frank Benson's famous Shakespearean company, making his debut at 16 as Lucius in "Julius Caesar." His London debut was later in "Children of Darkness." Still later he was in "Precious Bane." This led to a film career and among his films were "Thirty-Nine Steps," "The Ghost Goes West," "The Winslow Boy" and "Goodbye, Mr. Chips." The latter won him the 1939 Academy Award. Born Manchester, Eng.; died London, June 9, 1958.

Dukes, Ashley, 73, writer. He was a university lecturer in science and turned to the theatre early in the century. Between 1909 and 1925 he was drama critic for several publications. Besides adapting many German and French plays for the British theatre, he was for many years director of the Mercury Theatre in London. In 1938, together with Gilbert Miller, he produced "Murder in the Cathedral" here. His best-known play in this country was "Man with a Load of Mischief" done on Broadway in 1925. In 1950 his translation of Henri Becque's "Parisienne" was produced here and in 1956 his translation of Machiavelli's "Mandragola." Born England; died London, May 4, 1959.

Gibbs, Wolcott, 56, author, dramatic critic. He was a reporter for Long Island newspapers before he went to "The New Yorker" as a copy reader in 1927. Ten years later he took over the "Talk of the Town" section and in 1940 became the magazine's drama critic. He had a hit play, "Season in the Sun," which ran for 367 performances on Broadway. Born New York; died Fire Island, L. I., N. Y., Aug. 16, 1958.

Glaser, Lulu, 84, actress. She was Marie Jansen's understudy in "The Lion Tamer" when she got her chance to sing the lead one night and was an instant hit. A few of her successes include "Miss Dolly Dollars," "Lola from Berlin," "Mlle. Mischief," "Dolly Varden" and "The Aero Club." She retired in 1918 while still at the top. Born Allegheny, Pa.; died Norwalk, Conn., Sept. 5, 1958.

Gleason, James, 72, actor. When only two months old he appeared on the stage as a bundled baby in his mother's arms. By the time he was five he was "starring" in "Stricken Blind" with his parents' touring company. His greatest stage success came in 1925 with "Is Zat So?" of which he was co-author as well as star. He also wrote "The Fall Guy" with George Abbott and "The Shannons of Broadway" with his wife Lucille Webster Gleason. He went to Hollywood and wrote or acted in more than 100 pictures, which included "Down to Earth," "Come Fill the Cup," "What Price Glory?," "Here Comes Mr. Jordan" and his last picture, "The Last Hurrah." Born New York; died Hollywood, April 12, 1959.

Hackett, Raymond, 53, actor. He began his career at the age of four with Lionel Barrymore. His Broadway credits include "Cradle Snatchers," "Nightstick," "Adam Had Two Sons" and "Conquest." On the screen he was seen in "Madame X," "The Trial of Mary Dugan," "On Your Back" and "Seed." Born New York; died Los Angeles, July 7, 1958.

Herndon, Richard G., 85, producer. He attended school abroad and came to New York as a young man. His first production venture was in 1914, when he put on "The Lady in Red." He then turned to arranging tours for such noted foreign artists as Anna Pavlova and Nijinski. By the mid-twenties he concentrated on legitimate plays and produced about 50, among them "The Potters," "Girl Trouble," "You and I," "The Passion Flower" and "Americana" (which introduced Helen Morgan and Charles Butterworth). He formerly owned two Broadway theatres, the Belmont and the Klaw. For five years he worked with the "47 Workshop" at Harvard and sponsored the Harvard Prize play competition. Born Paris; died Philadelphia, July 11, 1958.

Hobart, Doty, 72, playwright. Among his Broadway successes were "Thoroughbred," "Every Thursday" and "Double Dummy." He also wrote scenarios for Mary Pickford and Dorothy and Lillian Gish. Birthplace not given; died New York, Nov. 16, 1958.

Housman, Laurence, 93, author, playwright. By training an artist and illustrator he became an author at the age of 27. For about 35 years of his career he was in conflict with the Lord Chamberlain. More than 30 of his plays were banned mostly because of the law against representing the Holy Family or British monarchs on the stage. His "Victoria Regina" was produced in London after its tremendous Broadway success only after Edward VIII intervened in its behalf shortly before he abdicated in 1936. Among his other plays were "Prunella" and "Jacob." He was the brother of A. E. Housman. Born England; died Somerset, Eng., Feb. 20, 1959.

Ivan, Rosalind, 75, actress. She began her career as a musician, playing her first piano recital in London at the age of ten. Bernard Shaw chose her for "Candida" and John Masefield for Nan in "The Tragedy of Nan." On Broadway she was Queen Margaret to John Barrymore's "Richard III." She was with Ina Claire in "Once Is Enough" and co-starred with Charles Coburn in "The Bourgeois Gentleman." Other plays include "Don't Throw Glass Houses" and "A Night's Lodging." Some of her films were "Three Strangers," "The Suspect," "Johnny Belinda," "The Corn Is Green" and "The Verdict." Born England; died New York, April 6, 1959.

McComb, Kate, 87, actress. She began her stage career at 52 when she replaced the leading woman opposite Augustin Duncan in "Juno and the Paycock." The next 35 years were spent mostly on radio and TV. In the latter medium she was on "One Man's Family" and "We, the People." Her Broadway appearances included "Blood Money," "Magnolia," "Riddle Me This" and

"No Questions Asked." Birthplace not given; died New York, April 15, 1959.

Mallory, Boots, 45, actress. She appeared in George White's "Scandals" and Ziegfeld's "Hot-Cha" on Broadway as well as in such motion pictures as "Handle with Care," "Humanity" and "Hello Sisters." Born New Orleans; died Santa Monica, Calif., Dec. 1, 1958.

Mestel, Jacob, 74, actor, director. He attended Teachers College in Lvov, Poland, and the Academy of Acting and Directing in Vienna. In 1921 he came here and was with Maurice Schwartz at the Yiddish Art Theatre for years. He was co-editor of "Yiddishe Kultur" and of "Lexicon of Yiddish Theatre." As actor and director he toured North and South America with Jacob Ben-Ami and his company. He was on TV and radio in "The Goldbergs" and last appeared on Broadway in "A Hole in the Head." Born Poland; died New York, Aug. 6, 1958.

Murray, Thomas C., 86, playwright. He was associated with the earliest and most distinguished days of the Abbey Theatre. His first play was "The Wheel of Fortune"; two of his best known ones were "Maurice Harte" and "Autumn Fire," both done successfully in London and New York. He was a member of the Irish Censorship of Films Appeal Board, director of the Authors' Guild of Ireland and a member of the Irish Academy of Letters. Born Ireland; died Dublin, March 7, 1959.

Norton, Jack, 69, actor. He started working in cabarets and did a song there with the line "There'll come a night when you'll get tight—then follow the car tracks home." From then on, although a teetotaler himself, he was typed as a stage drunk and after 1934 as a film drunk. Among the 200 films in which he played a lovable souse were "The Farmer's Daughter," "The Spoilers," "The Fleet's In," "Taxi, Mister" and "Stage Confession." Born Brooklyn; died Saranac Lake, N. Y., Oct. 15, 1958.

O'Connor, Una, 78, actress. She studied in convent schools and in Paris and was about to become a teacher when the theatre lured her. She made her debut at the Abbey Theatre, Dublin, in 1911, in "The Shewing-Up of Blanco Posnet" and came to the United States in it later in the year. In 1913 she was first seen in London in "The Magic Glass." Then she appeared in "The Starlight Express," "Paddy the Next Best Thing" and "Plus Fours." She made a hit in London in 1924 in "The Fake" and later at the Hudson in New York. London saw her again in "Macbeth," "The Passing of the Third Floor Back" and "Cavalcade." New York saw her in "The Ryan Girl," "The Linden Tree," "The Enchanted" and "The Starcross Story." Her film career began in 1929 with "Dark Red Roses" and included "David Copperfield," "Cavalcade," "Rose Marie" and "Of Human Bondage." She was also on radio and TV. Born Belfast, Ireland; died New York, Feb. 4, 1959.

Oysher, Moishe, 51, cantor, actor. He made his stage debut with a Jewish troupe in Winnipeg, Manitoba, in 1925. Two years later he toured South America, returning to New York in 1934. He played in light opera on the Jewish stage for many years. For 18 years he was in motion pictures, his last role being in "Singing in the Dark," for which he composed the words and music. He was also a popular recording artist. Born Lipkon, Bessarabia; died New Rochelle, N. Y., Nov. 27, 1958.

Pangborn, Franklin, 59, actor. He had a distinguished career as a serious actor before he became an outstanding success as a comedian. He began his stage career with Mildred Holland in stock, later joining Jessie Bonstelle. He was with Nazimova in "The Marionettes" and with Pauline Frederick in "Joseph and His Brethren." He played Messale in "Ben Hur" on tour. He was one of the screen's better-known comedians in such pictures as "Never Give a Sucker an Even Break" with W. C. Fields, "The Horn Blows at Midnight" with Jack Benny and "George Washington Slept Here." Born Newark, N. J.; died Santa Monica, Calif., July 20, 1958.

Pearson, Molly, 83, actress. She came to the United States with Olga Nethersole in 1906. She was best known for her roles in "Bunty Pulls the Strings," "The Passing of the Third Floor Back" and "Hobson's Choice." Other plays included "Lean Harvest," "Housewarming," "Laburnum Grove" and "Lady Precious Stream." Her last performance was in "Ladies in Retirement." Born Edinburgh, Scotland; died Newton, Conn., Jan. 26, 1959.

Power, Tyrone, 44, actor. At seven he was a supporting player to his father (also Tyrone Power) in a play in the San Gabriel Mission, Calif. He studied with both his father and his actress mother, Patia Power. Katharine Cornell really gave him his Broadway start as general understudy to the three male leads in "Flowers of the Forest" in 1935. A year later he was with Miss Cornell as Benvolio in "Romeo and Juliet" and as Bertrand de Poulengy in "Saint Joan." Then came a contract with 20th-Century Fox and he carried on the tradition of Valentino and Douglas Fairbanks, Sr. He won immediate success with

"Lloyds of London" in 1936. In 1941 he had Valentino's role in a remake of "Blood and Sand." He was in more than 40 films, among them "The Sun Also Rises," "The Eddie Duchin Story," "Abandon Ship," "The Long Gray Line" and "Witness for the Prosecution." In 1950 he played in London in "Mister Roberts" and he was on Broadway in 1953 in "John Brown's Body" and in 1955 in "The Dark Is Light Enough" with Miss Cornell. He played in Dublin in Shaw's "The Devil's Disciple" and returned to Broadway in 1958 in "Back to Methuselah." Born Cincinnati; died Madrid, Spain, Nov. 15, 1958.

Rinehart, Mary Roberts, 82, writer. She was for many years a best-selling novelist and had four plays on Broadway: "The Bat," "Seven Days," "Spanish Love" and "The Breaking Point." The first three she wrote in collaboration with Avery Hopwood. "The Bat" became one of the best-known mystery plays ever written and has been frequently revived. Born Pittsburgh; died New York, Sept. 22, 1958.

Robinson, Bertrand, 70, actor, playwright. He began his career as a bellboy at the Brown Palace Hotel in Denver. With his saved tips he entered a dramatic school in Los Angeles and then went into vaudeville and stock. In a few years he was one of the leading writers of vaudeville sketches. He collaborated with Howard Lindsay on three Broadway productions, "Tommy," "Your Uncle Dudley" and "Oh Promise Me." He played many roles on Broadway and in radio. Born Creston, Iowa; died Bronx, N. Y., Feb. 4, 1959.

Robinson, Dr. Lennox, 72, playwright. His association with Dublin's Abbey Theatre spanned 50 years. From 1907 on, he was manager-producer and, at intervals, director. During periods away from the theatre he worked as secretary to George Bernard Shaw and as organizing librarian of the Carnegie Trust of Ireland. He was for many years general manager of the Irish National Theatre Society. His best-known plays included "The White-Headed Boy," "The Lost Leader," "The Far-Off Hills," "The Big House," "Is Life Worth Living?" and "Drama at Inish." He also gave lecture courses at Amherst College, Carnegie Tech, the Universities of Michigan, Montana and North Carolina and Ohio State. Born near Cork, Ireland; died Dublin, Ireland, Oct. 14, 1958.

Saylor, Oliver, 71, writer. In 1922 he sponsored a visit of the Moscow Art Theatre to this country. From 1924 through 1953 he was business agent of the Association of Theatrical Press Agents and Managers. He was editor and author of The Moscow Art

Theatre Series of Russian Plays, the Eleanora Duse Series of Plays, "Max Reinhardt and His Theatre" and others. He was a member of the American-Russian Institute. Born Huntington, Ind.; died Mamaroneck, N. Y., Oct. 19, 1958.

Siegel, Max, 57, producer. In 1918 he became associated with Sam H. Harris and was for many years his general manager. With Milton Gropper he was co-author of "We Americans," which introduced Paul Muni in 1926. He assisted Irving Thalberg in the production of movies and was associate producer of "A Day at the Races" and other Marx Brothers films. In 1950 he became a writer and associate producer of Max Liebman's "Show of Shows" and other spectaculars on TV. Most recently he was general manager of "Say, Darling." Birthplace not given; died New York, Nov. 16, 1958.

Squire, Ronald, 72, actor. After leaving college he entered journalism and later made his first stage appearance in 1909 in Eastbourne. The following year he was in London in "Nobody's Daughter." In New York he was seen first in "Gamblers All" in 1917. Other plays on Broadway included "The Last of Mrs. Cheyney," "By Candlelight" and "The Sex Fable." Born Tiverton, Eng.; died London, Nov. 18, 1958.

Sterling, Richard, 78, actor. He made his first stage appearance in "An American Citizen" with Nat Goodwin and Maxine Elliott in Boston in 1897. He remained with Mr. Goodwin for several years, then joined Richard Mansfield in "Julius Caesar," "Henry V" and other Shakespearean plays. He also appeared several times with Robert Edison, accompanying him to London in 1907 in "Strongheart." While there, he appeared with Cyril Maude. Other New York appearances include "It Pays to Advertise," "Fair and Warmer," "A Tailor Made Man," "Alien Corn" and "Ah, Wilderness!" He was Dr. Lloyd for seven years in "Life with Father" and was with Katharine Cornell in "That Lady." Born New York; died New York, April 15, 1959.

Stone, Fred, 85, actor. His career spanned more than 50 years. He made his first public appearance as an entertainer at nine, when he won a prize for climbing a greased pole. Later he spent six weeks with a circus troupe. At 13 he went with another circus and there followed a series of circuses and carnivals. At 14 he performed for the first time in a theatre in Kansas City with his brother Eddie. Later he met David Montgomery and they formed the team of Montgomery and Stone, which became famous throughout the country. They were at first in minstrel shows and vaudeville. In 1900 they made their first appearance in a regular musical, "The Girl from Up There." In 1903 they were in "The Wizard of Oz," and as the Scarecrow Mr. Stone overnight became the most talked-of comedian in the land. This production was followed by "The Red Mill," "The Old Town," "The Lady of the Slipper" (with Elsie Janis) and "Chin-Chin." After Montgomery's death in 1917, Mr. Stone made his first appearance as an individual star in "Jack O' Lantern." Then came "Tip-Top," "Stepping Stones" and "Criss-Cross." In 1936 he moved to Hollywood and made infrequent appearances thereafter, one of which was a revival of "Lightnin'." His last appearance was in Hollywood in 1950 in "You Can't Take It with You." Born Longmont, Colo.; died Hollywood, March 6, 1959.

Varden, Evelyn, 73, actress. She made her first appearance as a babe-in-arms in a repertory company headed by her aunts. When she was 15 she appeared in New York in Zelda Sears' "The Nest Egg." Later she played with Otis Skinner and with Edward Everett Horton. She retired for a few years but was persuaded to return to the New York stage by Florence Reed. She was prominent on Broadway in "Russet Mantle," "Prelude to Exile," "Cradle in the Wind" and "Family Portrait." One of her best roles was Mrs. Gibbs in "Our Town." She made some 30-odd motion pictures, among them "Hilda Crane" and "The Bad Seed," in both of which she played her original Broadway roles. She was also prominent in radio and TV. Born Adair, Okla.; died New York, July 11, 1958.

Vincent, Walter, 90, writer, actor, producer. He left college to become a reporter for the Denver "Republican." After playing small parts at the Tabor Grand Opera House, he decided on a theatrical career. He came to New York in 1889 and played Horatio to the Hamlet of Alexander Salvini; he later appeared in "The Two Orphans" and "The Three Guardsmen." Then, with Sidney Wilmer, he wrote two hit shows: "A Stranger in a Strange Land" and "In New England." In 1901 he and Mr. Wilmer started a chain of movie houses. During the following years he produced many plays. Active in The Actors' Fund, he was in 1940 chosen its president. In 1958 he received the Kelcey Allen Award for his work in this organization. Born Lake Geneva, Wis.; died New York, May 10, 1959.

von Twardowski, Hans Heinrich, 60, actor, director. After a long and distinguished career in Germany, he was brought to this country by Warner Brothers and made such pictures as "Private Jones," "Adorable," "Espionage Agent." He directed at the

Pasadena Playhouse and in Brooklyn he staged "Shakespeare's Merchant—1939." He also supported Flora Robson on Broadway in "Anne of England." Born Germany; died New York, Nov. 19, 1958.

Williams, Frances, 57, actress. She started her career at 14 in the chorus of Gus Hill's "Hans and Fritz" and came to New York two years later with an acrobatic troupe, the Yip Yap Hankers. Her first real theatrical chance came with her West Coast appearance in George M. Cohan's "Mary." She made her New York debut in "Big Lake." She was later at the old Civic Repertory in "Three Sisters" and "Martine" and alternated with Eva Le Gallienne there in "Cradle Song." She achieved her greatest success in musical comedy and was in "Artists and Models," "The Cocoanuts" and several George White's "Scandals." Born St. Paul, Minn.; died New York, Jan. 27, 1959.

Woolf, Stanley, 59, producer. He started his career as a song-and-dance man in vaudeville, later organizing the "Stanley Woolf Revue." In the 1930's he became a booking agent and later founded the Stanley Woolf Players to present plays at resort hotels. Birthplace not given; died on board the liner *Homeric*, Feb. 28, 1959.

THE DECADES' TOLL

(Prominent Theatrical Figures Who Have Died in Recent Years)

	Born	Died
Adams, Maude	1872	1953
Anderson, John Murray	1886	1954
Anglin, Margaret	1877	1958
Arliss, George	1869	1946
Bennett, Richard	1873	1944
Bernstein, Henri	1876	1953
Buchanan, Jack	1891	1957
Calhern, Louis	1895	1956
Carroll, Earl	1893	1948
Carte, Rupert D'Oyly	1876	1948
Christians, Mady	1900	1951
Cochran, Charles B.	1872	1951
Collier, Willie	1866	1943
Cowl, Jane	1884	1950
Craven, Frank	1890	1945
Crosman, Henrietta	1865	1944
Davis, Owen	1874	1956
Digges, Dudley	1879	1947
Duncan, Augustin	1872	1954
Errol, Leon	1881	1951
Fields, W. C.	1879	1946
Gaige, Crosby	1883	1949
Garfield, John	1913	1952
Geddes, Norman Bel	1893	1958
Golden, John	1874	1955
Guitry, Sacha	1885	1957
Hampden, Walter	1879	1955
Hart, Lorenz	1895	1943
Hart, William S.	1870	1946
Hooker, Brian	1881	1947
Howard, Willie	1883	1949

	Born	Died
Jolson, Al	1886	1950
Jouvet, Louis	1887	1951
Kane, Whitford	1882	1956
Kern, Jerome D.	1885	1945
Lawrence, Gertrude	1898	1952
Lehar, Franz	1870	1948
Loftus, Cecilia	1876	1943
Lord, Pauline	1890	1950
Mantle, Burns	1873	1948
Marlowe, Julia	1866	1950
Merivale, Philip	1886	1946
Molnar, Ferenc	1878	1952
Moore, Grace	1901	1947
Nathan, George Jean	1882	1958
Nazimova, Alla	1879	1945
Nethersole, Olga	1870	1951
O'Neill, Eugene	1888	1953
Patterson, Joseph Medill	1879	1946
Perry, Antoinette	1888	1946
Pinza, Ezio	1895	1957
Powers, James T.	1862	1943
Reinhardt, Max	1873	1943
Romberg, Sigmund	1887	1951
Scheff, Fritzi	1879	1954
Selwyn, Edgar	1875	1944
Shaw, G. B.	1856	1950
Sheldon, Edward	1886	1946
Sherwood, Robert E.	1896	1955
Shubert, Lee	1875	1953
Tarkington, Booth	1869	1946
Tauber, Richard	1890	1948
Todd, Mike	1909	1958
Tyler, George C.	1867	1946
van Druten, John	1902	1957
Ward, Fannie	1872	1952
Warfield, David	1866	1951
Webster, Ben	1864	1947
Whitty, Dame May	1865	1948
Woods, Al H.	1870	1951
Woollcott, Alexander	1887	1943
Youmans, Vincent	1899	1946

INDEX OF AUTHORS AND PLAYWRIGHTS

Abbott, George, 356, 357, 369, 381
Achard, Marcel, 22, 300
Ade, George, 354
Akins, Zoë, 347, 355, 360, 377
Akutagawa, Ryunosuke, 317
Alsberg, Henry G., 357
Anderson, Maxwell, 55, 346, 347, 356, 357, 358, 359, 360, 361, 362, 363, 364, 365, 366, 367, 369, 377
Anderson, Robert, 367, 369
Andreyev, Leonid, 355
Anouilh, Jean, 349, 364, 367, 368
Ansky, S., 357
Anspacher, Louis Kaufman, 354
Anthony, Rock, 51
Archer, William, 351, 355
Archibald, William, 52, 365
Arden, John, 43, 47-48
Aristophanes, 349
Arlen, Michael, 357
Atlas, Leopold, 360
Auden, W. H., 52
Aurthur, Robert Alan, 368
Austen, Jane, 4, 30, 34, 331

Bagnold, Enid, 367
Baker, Melville, 356
Balderston, John, 358
Banks, Nathaniel, 51
Barasch, Norman, 299
Barbour, Thomas, 51
Barer, Marshall, 335
Barkenstein, Marjorie, 55
Barrie, James M., 355
Barry, Philip, 21, 355, 356, 357, 358, 359, 361, 363, 366
Baum, Vicki, 359
Bayer, Eleanor, 24-25, 316
Bayer, Leo, 24-25, 316
Beach, Lewis, 356
Beckett, Samuel, 46, 367
Becque, Henri, 381
Behan, Brendan, 43, 47, 49, 51
Behrman, S. N., 3, 6, 23-24, 144, 309, 349, 359, 360, 361, 363, 365, 366, 369
Beich, Albert, 8, 300
Belasco, David, 354
Benelli, Sem, 355
Beolco, 349
Berg, Gertrude, 365
Besier, Rudolf, 359
Biggers, Earl Derr, 354
Bishop, Stuart, 53
Bissell, Marian, 324
Bissell, Richard, 324
Blitzstein, Marc, 3, 34-35
Bolitho, William, 359
Bolton, Guy, 355, 356
Boothe, Clare, 361, 362

Bost, Pierre, 311
Bowles, Jane, 366
Bradford, Roark, 358
Brand, Max, 334
Brecht, Bertholt, 54
Breit, Harvey, 3, 10, 121, 308, 352
Bridgers, Ann, 357
Browne, Maurice, 358
Browne, Porter Emerson, 355
Buck, Pearl, 3, 19, 332
Burrows, Abe, 3, 4, 34, 324, 331, 365
Butler, Rachel Barton, 355
Byrne, Dolly, 355

Caldwell, Taylor, 286
Camus, Albert, 349
Cannan, Denis, 47, 311
Capek, Karel, 356
Carroll, Paul Vincent, 361
Casalis, Jeanne de, 361
Casella, Alberto, 358
Chapman, Lonny, 50
Chapman, Robert, 365
Chase, Mary Coyle, 347, 363, 366
Chekhov, Anton, 27, 28, 47, 49, 333, 350
Chodorov, Edward, 363
Christie, Agatha, 367
Clements, Colin, 363
Cocteau, Jean, 350
Coffee, Lenore, 361
Cohan, George M., 354, 359, 388
Cohen, Octavus Roy, 378-379
Colette, 366
Colton, John, 355
Congreve, William, 27
Conkle, E. P., 361
Connelly, Marc, 347, 355, 356, 357, 358, 360
Coppel, Alec, 25, 313
Coppel, Myra, 313
Corle, Edwin, 300
Cormack, Bartlett, 358
Corneille, Pierre, 27, 295
Corwin, Norman, 3, 29, 321
Costigan, James, 350
Coward, Noel, 3, 26, 325, 359, 362, 370
Cowen, William Joyce, 361
Coxe, Louis O., 365
Craven, Frank, 355
Creighton, Anthony, 10, 101, 301, 317, 352
Crothers, Rachel, 355, 356, 358, 359, 361, 370, 379
Crouse, Russel, 25, 318, 347, 351, 361, 363, 365, 366, 370
Cushman, Dan, 314

Dane, Clemence, 355
Davis, Donald, 360

391

INDEX OF AUTHORS AND PLAYWRIGHTS

Davis, Eddie, 379-380
Davis, Owen, 347, 355, 360, 362, 389
Dayton, Katherine, 360
Delaney, Shelagh, 43, 47
Dell, Floyd, 358
Dennis, Nigel, 51, 350
Dennis, Patrick, 291
Dent, Wade, 50
Deval, Jacques, 361
Dey, James, 51
Dhery, Robert, 303
Dodd, Lee Wilson, 356
Drake, W. A., 359
Drinkwater, John, 354
Duerrenmatt, Friedrich, 346, 368
Dukes, Ashley, 380-381
Dunnings, Philip, 357
d'Usseau, Arnaud, 363, 364

Eliot, T. S., 12, 28, 43, 297, 365, 366, 371
Elser, Frank B., 360
Emery, Gilbert, 355, 356
Ephron, Phoebe, 20, 292
Ervine, St. John, 354, 355, 358
Evslin, Bernard, 51

Farquhar, George, 323
Fauchois, René, 359
Faulkner, William, 3, 6, 16-17, 121, 189, 319, 350
Ferber, Edna, 286, 356, 357, 359, 361, 371
Ferris, Walter, 358
Feuer, Cy, 314
Feydeau, Georges, 26, 325
Field, Salisbury, 355
Fields, Dorothy, 319
Fields, Herbert, 319
Fields, Joseph, 306, 362, 363, 366, 367
Fitch, Clyde, 354
Fitts, Dudley, 349
Flavin, Martin, 358
Flicker, Theodore J., 336
Forbes, James, 355
Ford, John, 52
Ford, Ruth, 189, 319, 350
Forsyth, James, 51
Franken, Rose, 359, 363
Frings, Ketti, 346, 348, 368
Fry, Christopher, 366, 367, 371
Fuller, Dean, 335
Funt, Julian, 367

Galantière, Lewis, 364
Gale, Zona, 347
Galsworthy, John, 355, 357
Gardner, Dorothy, 364
Gazzo, Michael V., 8, 308
Geiger, Milton, 12, 305
Genet, Jean, 51, 350
George, Grace, 355
Geraldy, Paul, 355
Gershe, Leonard, 334
Gibbs, Wolcott, 366, 381
Gide, André, 52
Gilbert, Stuart, 349
Ginnes, Abram S., 20, 293
Giraudoux, Jean, 39, 50, 350, 365, 367
Glaspell, Susan, 347, 359
Gleason, James, 356, 381
Gleason, Lucille Webster, 381

Goethe, 349
Goetz, Augustus, 364, 367
Goetz, Ruth, 364, 367
Goldoni, 349
Goldsmith, Clifford, 361
Goodrich, Frances, 346, 348, 367
Gordon, Ruth, 363, 364, 372
Gore-Browne, R. F., 359
Goulding, Edmund, 356
Gow, James, 363, 364
Gozzi, 349
Granville-Barker, Harley, 355, 358
Granville-Barker, Helen, 358
Green, Paul, 50, 347, 357, 359, 360, 362
Greene, Graham, 311, 367, 368
Gressieker, Hermann, 51
Gropper, Milton, 386
Guitry, Sacha, 355

Hackett, Albert, 346, 348, 367
Hagan, James, 359
Haines, William Wister, 364
Hall, Willis, 43, 48
Hamilton, Patrick, 362
Hammerstein, Oscar, 2nd, 306
Hansberry, Lorraine, 15, 232, 328, 346
Hart, Moss, 347, 358, 360, 361, 362, 363, 364, 365, 366, 372
Hartog, Jan de, 364, 366
Harwood, H. M., 359
Hawthorne, Ruth, 356
Hayden, John, 360
Hayes, Alfred, 367
Hayes, Joseph, 367
Hecht, Ben, 358
Heggen, Thomas, 364
Hellman, Lillian, 346, 360, 361, 362, 363, 364, 365, 367, 368, 372
Herbert, F. Hugh, 363
Heyward, DuBose, 357
Hill, Lucienne, 368
Hobart, Doty, 382
Hopkins, Arthur, 357
Hopwood, Avery, 385
Housman, Laurence, 360, 382
Howard, Leopoldine, 364
Howard, Sidney, 54, 329, 347, 356, 357, 359, 364
Howarth, Donald, 43
Hughes, Hatcher, 357, 356
Hugo, Victor, 27, 295
Hurlbut, William, 357

Ibsen, Henrik, 351
Inge, William, 346, 348, 351, 365, 366, 367, 368
Ionesco, 51
Irwin, Will, 329, 364

James, Dan, 363
James, Henry, 52
Jerome, Helen, 331, 360
Job, Thomas, 362
Joyce, James, 55, 121

Kanin, Fay, 4, 17, 19, 317, 365
Kanin, Garson, 364, 373
Kanin, Michael, 4, 17, 19, 317
Katzin, Winifred, 357

INDEX OF AUTHORS AND PLAYWRIGHTS

Kaufman, George S., 347, 355, 356, 357, 358, 359, 360, 361, 362, 363, 373
Kelly, George, 347, 356, 357, 364
Kennedy, Mary, 356
Kerr, Jean, 3, 30, 294, 351
Kerr, Walter, 3, 30, 294, 351
Kesselring, Joseph, 362
Keyes, Frances Parkinson, 286
Kingsley, Sidney, 346, 347, 359, 360, 361, 362, 365, 373
Kleist, Heinrich von, 349
Knott, Frederick, 366
Koch, Howard, 362
Koestler, Arthur, 365
Kops, Bernard, 51
Kramm, Joseph, 348, 366
Krasna, Norman, 363, 364
Kummer, Clare, 354, 360
Kurnitz, Harry, 22, 298, 351

Lamkin, Speed, 8, 302
Landesman, Jay, 336
Langley, Noel, 365
Lardner, Ring W., 358
Latouche, John, 367, 368
Laurents, Arthur, 38, 52, 337, 363, 366, 368
Lavery, Emmet, 364
Lawler, Ray, 368
Lawrence, Jerome, 291, 367
Lawrence, Reginald, 321
Lee, C. Y., 306
Lee, Robert E., 291, 367
Lerner, Alan Jay, 364, 367, 373
Levin, Ira, 367
Levin, Meyer, 351
Levy, Benn W., 359, 365
Lewis, Sinclair, 359
Lindsay, Howard, 25, 318, 347, 351, 361, 363, 365, 366, 373, 385
Logan, Joshua, 348, 364, 365, 373
Lonsdale, Frederick, 46, 357
Loos, Anita, 366

MacArthur, Charles, 358
Machiavelli, 349, 381
MacLeish, Archibald, 3, 12-13, 168, 312, 347, 348
Marcel, Gabriel, 351
Marivaux, 295
Marquand, John P., 363
Marquis, Don, 356
Martin, Ernest H., 314
Martinez Sierra, G., 357, 358
Masefield, John, 382
Mason, Richard, 11, 296
Massey, Valgene, 50
Maugham, William Somerset, 355, 357, 366, 373
Mayer, Edwin Justus, 356
McCarthy, Justin Huntly, 354
McCullers, Carson, 346, 352, 365
McEnroe, Robert Edward, 365
McGuire, William Anthony, 355
McKenzie, Neil, 50
McLellan, C. M. S., 354
Meloney, Rose Franken, 362
Merlin, Frank, 50
Middleton, George, 355

Miller, Arthur, 52, 53, 346, 348, 364, 365, 366, 367, 374
Miller, Sigmund, 330
Milne, Alan Alexander, 355, 358
Mitchell, Thomas, 358, 374
Molière, 27, 295, 350
Molnar, Ferenc, 355, 356, 357, 390
Moody, William Vaughn, 354
Moore, Carroll, 299
Morley, Robert, 365, 374
Moross, Jerome, 367
Morris, Lloyd, 363
Moyes, Patricia, 368
Murray, Thomas C., 383
Musset, Alfred de, 27, 295

Nash, N. Richard, 7, 292
Nemerov, Howard, 318
Nichols, Robert, 358
Nicholson, Kenyon, 144
Nugent, Elliott, 362, 374

O'Casey, Sean, 3, 7, 27, 28, 30, 34, 35, 49, 52, 305, 326, 333, 358
O'Connor, Frank, 50
Odets, Clifford, 360, 361, 366, 367, 374
O'Neill, Eugene, 3, 6-7, 48, 50, 59, 293, 346, 347, 348, 349, 350, 352, 354, 355, 356, 357, 359, 360, 364, 368, 390
Osborn, Paul, 3, 4, 11, 296, 361, 362, 363, 366, 374
Osborne, John, 10, 43-46, 101, 301, 317, 352, 368

Parker, Louis N., 354
Patrick, John, 346, 348, 363, 364, 366
Peterson, Louis, 366
Pirandello, Luigi, 352
Pollock, Channing, 355, 357
Priestley, J. B., 365

Randolph, Clemence, 355
Raphaelson, Samson, 360, 362
Rattigan, Terrence, 364, 368, 375
Reed, Mark, 361
Reizenstein, Elmer, 354
Rice, Elmer, 3, 4, 12, 54, 306, 347, 358, 359, 362, 364, 375
Richman, Arthur, 355
Riggs, Lynn, 358
Rinehart, Mary Roberts, 385
Roberts, Meade, 50
Robinson, Bertrand, 385
Robinson, Dr. Lennox, 385
Rotter, Fritz, 362
Royle, Edwin Milton, 354
Ryerson, Florence, 363
Rylands, George, 316
Ryskind, Morrie, 347, 359

Saroyan, William, 346, 347, 362, 375
Saylor, Oliver, 55, 385-386
Schary, Dore, 368
Schiller, Friedrich, 349
Schulberg, Budd, 3, 10, 121, 308, 352
Scollay, J. Fred, 51
Sears, Zelda, 387
Selver, Paul, 356
Selwyn, Edgar, 356, 390
Shaffer, Peter, 43, 47

INDEX OF AUTHORS AND PLAYWRIGHTS

Shairp, Mordaunt, 360
Shakespeare, William, 4, 12, 27-28, 29, 40, 41, 43, 52, 310, 316, 341, 350, 351, 352, 380, 386
Shaw, David, 319
Shaw, George Bernard, 27, 43, 351, 382, 385, 390
Shaw, Irwin, 22, 300
Sheldon, Edward, 354, 355, 390
Sheldon, Sidney, 319
Shelley, Elsa, 363
Sherriff, R. C., 358, 361
Sherwood, Robert E., 347, 357, 359, 360, 361, 364, 377, 390
Siegel, Max, 386
Skinner, Cornelia Otis, 21, 78, 298, 353, 375
Smith, Dodie, 360
Smith, Harry James, 354
Sophocles, 52
Spewack, Bella, 360, 366
Spewack, Samuel, 360, 365, 366
Spigelgass, Leonard, 26, 323
Stallings, Laurence, 356, 377
Stavis, Barry, 51
Stein, Joseph, 326
Steinbeck, John, 53, 346, 361, 362
Stevens, Leslie, 22, 300
Stewart, Donald Ogden, 358
Sturges, Preston, 358
Swerling, Jo, 365
Swinburne, Algernon, 48
Synge, John, 19, 325, 351

Tabori, George, 366
Tarkington, Booth, 354, 390
Taylor, Samuel, 3, 21, 78, 298, 353, 365
Teichmann, Howard, 21, 297
Thomas, A. E., 360
Thomas, Augustus, 354
Thomas, Dylan, 368
Thompson, Jay, 335
Thurber, James, 362
Totheroh, Dan, 356
Treadwell, Sophie, 358, 362
Tunney, Kieran, 325
Turney, Robert, 360

Underhill, John Garrett, 357
Ustinov, Peter, 40, 366

Valency, Maurice, 350, 365, 368
van Druten, John, 346, 357, 360, 363, 366, 376, 390
Vane, Sutton, 356
Varesi, Gilda, 355
Verneuil, Louis, 366
Vidal, Gore, 368
Vinaver, Stephen, 53
Vincent, Allen, 362
Vincent, Walter, 387
Vollmer, Lula, 356

Wallach, Ira, 20, 293
Walter, Eugene, 354
Watkins, Maurine, 357
Watters, George Manker, 357
Weitzenkorn, Louis, 359
West, Mae, 376
Wexley, John, 358, 360
Wilder, Thornton, 49, 347, 361, 363, 367, 376
Williams, Emlyn, 42, 362, 376
Williams, Jesse Lynch, 347, 354, 356
Williams, Tennessee, 3, 6, 7, 14, 15, 28, 40, 50, 209, 328, 333, 346, 347, 348, 363, 364, 366, 367, 368, 376
Williams, William Carlos, 50
Wilmer, Sidney, 387
Wilson, Harry Leon, 354, 356
Wilson, Sandy, 367
Wincelberg, Shimon, 19, 255, 332
Windham, Donald, 209
Winter, Keith, 360
Wishengrad, Morton, 368
Wodehouse, P. G., 357
Wolfson, Victor, 361
Woollcott, Alexander, 390
Wouk, Herman, 366
Wright, Richard, 362
Wright, William H., 8-9, 300
Wulp, John, 51

Yeats, William Butler, 52
Yordan, Philip, 363

Zilboorg, Gregory, 355

INDEX OF PLAYS AND CASTS

Bold face page numbers refer to pages on which
Cast of **Characters** may be found.

Abe Lincoln in Illinois, 347, 361
Abie's Irish Rose, 344
Abraham Lincoln, 354
Accent on Youth, 360
Adam and Eva, 355
Adam Had Two Sons, 381
Adonis, 345
Aero Club, The, 381

Affairs of State, 345, 366
Ages of Man, 29, 42, 316, 341
Ah, Wilderness, 360, 386
Alice Sit-by-the-Fire, 380
Alice Up to Date, 378
Alien Corn, 359, 386
Alison's House, 347, 359
All My Sons, 346, 364

INDEX OF PLAYS AND CASTS

All the Winners, 378
Allegro, 364
Ambush, 355
American Citizen, An, 386
American Way, The, 361
Americana, 382
Amphitryon, 38, 361
Angel Street, 344, 362
Animal Kingdom, 359
Ankles Aweigh, 380
Anna Christie, 59, 347, 355
Anna Lucasta, 344, 363
Anne of England, 388
Anne of the Thousand Days, 365, **377**
Annie Get Your Gun, 344
Anniversary Waltz, 345
Another Language, 359
Another Part of the Forest, 364
Antigone, 364
Antony and Cleopatra, 52
Apollo of Bellac, The, 350
Ardéle, 349, 350
Aria da Capo, 50
Ariadne, 351
Arsenic and Old Lace, 344, 362
As Husbands Go, 358, 379
Artists and Models, 388
As You Like It, 316
At the Grand, 342
Auntie Mame, 41, 42, **291-292**, 342, 343, 345
Autumn Fire, 383
Autumn Garden, The, 365
Awake and Sing, 360

Back to Methuselah, 385
Bad Man, The, 355
Bad Seed, 367, 387
Bald Soprano, The, 51
Barbara Frietchie, 354
Barefoot in Athens, 366
Barretts of Wimpole Street, 359
Bat, The, 344, 385
Battle of Angels, 209
Beaux' Stratagem, The, **323-324**
Bedside Manners, 144
Bedtime Story, 28, **333-334**
Beggar on Horseback, 356
Behold the Bridegroom, 357
Bell, Book and Candle, 366
Bell for Adano, A, 363
Bells Are Ringing, 343, 344
Ben Hur, 384
Berkeley Square, 358
Bernardine, 366
Beyond the Horizon, 59, 347, 354
Big Hearted Herbert, 378
Big House, The, 385
Big Lake, 388
Bill of Divorcement, A, 355
Billy Budd, 53, 365
Biography, 144, 359
Bird in Hand, 345
Blackbirds, 345
Blithe Spirit, 345, 362
Blood Money, 382
Bloomer Girl, 345
Blossom Time, 345
Blue Denim, 342, **343**
Boomerang, The, 345
Born Yesterday, 344, 364

Both Your Houses, 347, 359, 377
Bourgeois Gentleman, The, 382
Boy Friend, The, 53, 367
Boy Meets Girl, 345, 360
Breaking Point, The, 385
Bride of the Land, 357
Brief Moment, 144, 359
Brigadoon, 345, 364
Broadway, 345, 357
Brother Rat, 345
Buffalo Skinner, The, 50
Bunty Pulls the Strings, 384
Burlesque, 357
Bus Stop, 351, 367
Butter and Egg Man, The, 357
By Candlelight, 386

Caine Mutiny Court-Martial, The, 366
Caligula, 349
Call It a Day, 360
Call Me Madam, 345
Call Me Mister, 344
Camino Real, 7, 209
Can-Can, 344
Candida, 382
Candide, 368
Candle in the Wind, 362
Captain Fury, 78
Cards of Destiny, 101
Cards of Identity, 350
Carmen Jones, 345
Carousel, 344
Cat on a Hot Tin Roof, 209, 344, 346, 348, 367
Cavalcade, 383-384
Cave Dwellers, The, 53
Chalk Garden, The, 367
Changelings, The, 356
Chaparral, 50
Chauve Souris, 345
Chicago, 357
Chicken Feed, 356
Children of Darkness, 380
Children's Hour, The, 344, 360
Chin-Chin, 387
Christopher Blake, 364
Cid, Le, 27, 295
Circle, The, 40, 355
Clarence, 354
Claudia, 344, 362
Clearing in the Woods, A, 52, 368
Climate of Eden, The, 366
Climbers, The, 354
Clutterbuck, 365
Cock-a-Doodle Dandy, 52
Cocktail Party, The, 28, 365
Cocoanuts, The, 388
Cold Wind and the Warm, The, 20, 23-24, 144-167, 309, 341, 349
Come Back, Little Sheba, 351, 365
Come Seven, 379
Comedy in Music, 344
Comes a Day, 8, **302-303**, 341
Command Decision, **364**
Compulsion, 351
Confidential Clerk, The, 366
Conquest, 381
Constant Wife, The, 357
Coquette, 357
Corn Is Green, The, 362
Country Girl, The, 366

INDEX OF PLAYS AND CASTS

Country Wife, The, 53
County Chairman, The, 354
Cradle in the Wind, 387
Cradle Snatchers, 381
Cradle Song, The, 357, **388**
Craig's Wife, 347, 357
Crazy October, 342
Criminal Code, The, 358
Crimson Alibi, The, 378-379
Criss-Cross, 387
Crucible, The, 53, 366
Cue for Passion, 4, 12, **306**, 341
Cynara, 359
Cyrano de Bergerac, 378

Daisy Mayme, 357
Damask Cheek, The, 363
Damn Yankees, 344
Dancers, The, 378
Dancing Mothers, 356
Dark at the Top of the Stairs, The, 41, 42, 343, 351, 368
Dark Is Light Enough, The, 367, 385
Darkness at Noon, 346, 365
Darling of the Gods, The, 354
Daughters of Atreus, 360
Dead End, 344, 360
Dear Ruth, 345, 363
Death of a Salesman, 344, 346, 348, 365
Death of Cuchulain, The, 52
Death of Satan, The, 101
Death Takes a Holiday, 358
Deathwatch, 51
Deburau, 355
Decision, 363
Declassée, 355, 377
Deep Are the Roots, 364
Desert Incident, A, 19-20, **332**, 341
Design for Living, 359
Desire Under the Elms, 356
Desperate Hours, The, 367
Destry Rides Again, 5, 30, 35, 285, **334-335**, 341
Detective Story, 345, 365
Devil Passes, The, 359
Devil's Disciple, The, 385
Dial "M" for Murder, 345, 366
Diary of Anne Frank, The, 344, 346, 348, 367
Dinner at Eight, 359
Disenchanted, The, 10-11, 121-143, **308-309**, 341, 352
Disraeli, 354
Distaff Side, The, 360
Diversions, 53
Dodsworth, 359
Dolly Varden, 381
Don Juan, 27, 101, 295
Don't Throw Glass Houses, 382
Double Dummy, 382
Doughgirls, The, 345, 363
Dover Road, The, 355
Dragon's Mouth, 350
Drama at Inish, 385
Dream Girl (Rice), 364
Dream Girl, The (Young and Atteridge), 378
Drink to Me Only, 20-21, 293-**294**, 341
Dulcy, 355
Dybbuk, The, 357

Earl Carroll Vanities of 1923, 379
Easiest Way, The, 354
East Is West, 345
Eastward in Eden, 364
Edward, My Son, 365
Edwin Booth, 12, **305-306**, 341
Elder Statesman, 43
Electra, 52
Elizabeth the Queen, 358, 377
Emperor Jones, The, 355
Emperor's Clothes, The, 366
Enchanted, The, 350, 365, 384
End Game, 46
End of Summer, 144, 360
Enemy, The, 357
Enemy of the People, An, 52
Enrico, 342
Enter Madame, 355
Entertainer, The, 10, 43, 101, 368
Epitaph for George Dillon, 6, 10, 101-**120**, 301, 317, 341, 352
Escape, 357
Ethan Frome, 360
Eve of St. Mark, The, 362, 377
Evening with Mary Martin, An, 42
Every Saturday Night, 379
Every Thursday, 382
Everyday, 379
Excursion, 361

Fair and Warmer, 386
Fall Guy, The, 356, 381
Family Portrait, 361, 387
Family Reunion, The, 28, **297-298**
Famous Mrs. Fair, The, 355
Fanny, 344
Farmer Takes a Wife, The, 360
Far-Off Hills, The, 385
Fashion, 53
Fatal Weakness, The, 364
Fifth Season, The, 345
Fin de Partie, 46
Fine and Dandy, 379
Finian's Rainbow, 344
Firebrand, The, 356
First Impressions, 34, 278, **331-332**, 341
First Lady, 360
First Love, 377
First Mrs. Fraser, The, 358
First Year, The, 344, 355
Five Finger Exercise, 47
Five-Star Final, 359
Flight to the West, 362
Floradora, 345
Flower Drum Song, 4, 11, 30-31, **32-33**, **306-307**, 341, 352
Flowering Peach, The, 367
Flowers of the Forest, 384
Foenix in Choir, 50
Follow the Girls, 344, 380
Fool, The, 355, 378
Foolish Notion, 363
Foot-Loose, 377
For Valor, 378
Fourposter, The, 345, **366**
Front Page, The, 358
Fun Time, 41, 42
Funeral Pyre, The, 351

Gamblers All, 386
Garden District, 14, 40, 42

INDEX OF PLAYS AND CASTS

Gay Divorcee, The, 378
Gay Felons, 342
Gazebo, The, 25, **313**, 341
George Washington Slept Here, 362
Geranium Hat, The, 51
Ghost Train, The, 378
Gigi, 366
Girl from Kay's, A, 378
Girl from Up There, The, 387
Girl on the Via Flaminia, The, 350, 367
Girl Trouble, 382
Girls in 509, The, 21, 40, 42, **297**, 341
Girls of Summer, 7
Glass Menagerie, The, 40, 209, 345, 346, 363
God and Kate Murphy, 19, **325**, 341
Gold Diggers, The, 344
Golden Apple, 367
Golden Boy, 361
Golden Six, The, 55
Goldilocks, 30, **294-295**, 341, 351
Good Gracious Annabelle, 354
Good News, 345
Good Place to Raise a Boy, A, 50
Goodbye, My Fancy, 365
Goose Hangs High, The, 356
Grand Hotel, 359
Great Divide, The, 354
Great God Brown, The, 357
Great Sebastians, The, 39
Green Bay Tree, The, 360
Green Goddess, The, 355
Green Grow the Lilacs, 358
Green Hat, The, 357
Green Pastures, The, 345, 347, 358
Guests of the Nation, 50
Guys and Dolls, 344, 365
Gypsy (Anderson), 358
Gypsy (musical), 36-37, 38, **337-338**, 341

Hamlet, 4, 10, 12, 27, 40, 41, 51, **310-311**, 316, 351, 387
Hamlet of Stephey Green, The, 51
Handful of Fire, 7, **292-293**, 341
Hans and Fritz, 388
Happy Birthday, 345
Happy Time, The, 345, 365
Harriet, 363
Harvey, 344, 347, 363
Hasty Heart, The, 363
Hatful of Rain, 8
Hats Off to Ice, 344
He and She, 379
He Who Gets Slapped, 355
Hearts Are Trumps, 380
Heartsease, 39
Heiress, The, 364
Hell-bent for Heaven, 347, **356**
Hellzapoppin, 31, 344
Héloïse, 51, 350
Henry IV, 316
Henry V, 27-28, 41, 310, 311, 386
Henry VI, 316
Her Master's Voice, 360
Here Come the Clowns, 361
Hero, The, 355
High Button Shoes, 344
High Tor, 346, 360, 377
Hilda Crane, 387
Hitchy Koo of 1919, 379
Hobson's Choice, 384

Hold On to Your Hats, 380
Hold Your Horses, 379
Hole in the Head, A, 383
Holiday, 358
Home of the Brave, 363
Hope for a Harvest, 362
Hostage, The, 47
Hot-Cha, 383
House of Connelly, The, 359
Housewarming, 384
Howie, 20, 276, **292**, 341

I Am a Camera, 346, 366
I Know My Love, 144, 365
I Remember Mama, 344, 363
I Rise in Flame Cried the Phoenix, 50
Ice Follies of '59, 282
Icebound, 347
Iceman Cometh, The, 6, 53, 364
Idiot's Delight, 347, 360
If I Were King, 354
Immoralist, The, 367
In Abraham's Bosom, 347, 357
In New England, 387
In the Summer House, 366
In Time to Come, 362
Inherit the Wind, 344, 367
Innocent Voyage, The, 363
Innocents, The, 52, 365
Inspector Calls, An, 365
Irene, 345
Is Life Worth Living?, 385
Is Zat So?, 345, 381
It Happens on Ice, 379
It Pays to Advertise, 386
Ivanov, 49, 52, 53

J. B., 12-14, 168-188, 312-**313**, 341, 347, 348
Jack, 51
Jack O' Lantern, 387
Jackknife, 51
Jacob, 382
Jacobowsky and the Colonel, 144, 363
Jamaica, 342, 343, 345
Jane, 144, 366
Jane Clegg, 355
Jane Eyre, 342, 343
Janie, 345
Jason, 362
Jest, The, 355
Joan of Lorraine, 364, 377
John Brown's Body, 385
John Ferguson, 354
John Gabriel Borkman, 351
John Loves Mary, 364
Johnny Johnson, 360
Joseph and His Brethren, 384
Journey's End, 358
June Moon, 358
Junior Miss, 344, 362
Juno, 34-35, **326-327**, 341
Juno and the Paycock, 7, 34, 35, 326, 382
Julius Caesar, 316, 380, 386
Just Assassins, The, 349
Just Fancy, 378

Kataki, 11, 19, 255-273, 332-**333**, 341
Key Largo, 361, 377
Kiki, 345
Kind Lady, 380

398 INDEX OF PLAYS AND CASTS

King and I, The, 30, 344
King Lear, 52, 316
King Nicolo, 380
Kingdom of God, The, 358
Kismet, 345
Kiss and Tell, 344, 363
Kiss Me, Kate, 344
Kiss the Boys Goodbye, 361

Laburnum Grove, 384
Ladder, The, 344
Ladies' Day, 349
Ladies in Retirement, 384
Lady in Danger, 380
Lady in Red, The, 381
Lady in the Dark, 362
Lady of the Slipper, The, 387
Lady Precious Stream, 380, 384
Lady Windermere's Fan, 78
Lark, The, 349, 367
Last Mile, The, 358
Last of Mrs. Cheyney, The, 357, 386
Late Christopher Bean, The, 359
Late George Apley, The, 363
Leah Kleschna, 354
Lean Harvest, 384
Left Bank, The, 359
Legend of Lizzie, The, **321**, 341
Let Them Eat Cake, 46
Let Us Be Gay, 358, 379
Let's Face It, 345
Letters to Lucerne, 362
Life with Father, 344, 361, 386
Life with Mother, 365
Light Up the Sky, 365
Lightnin', 344, 387
Li'l Abner, 41, 42, 343, **344**
Liliom, 355
Linden Tree, The, 384
Lion and the Mouse, The, 345
Lion Tamer, The, 381
Listen to the Mocking Bird, 342
Listen to the Quiet, 51
Little Accident, 358
Little Eyolf, 351
Little Foxes, The, 361
Little Journey, A, 379
Little Miss Bluebeard, 378
Little Moon of Alban, 350
Live like Pigs, 47-48
Living Room, The, 367
Lola from Berlin, 381
Long and the Short and the Tall, The, 48
Long Day's Journey into Night, 4, 6, 48, 59, 346, 348, 368
Look After Lulu, 26-27, 45, **325-326**, 341
Look Back in Anger, 10, 40-41, 42, 43, 53, 101, 343, 368
Look Homeward, Angel, 343, 345, 346, 348, 368
Lord Chumley, 380
Lorenzaccio, 27, 295
Lost Horizons, 360
Lost in the Stars, 365, 377
Lost Leader, The, 385
Love of Four Colonels, The, 366
Loyalties, 355
Lute Song, 54, 55, **329-330**, 342, 364

Macbeth, 316, 383
Machinal, 358

Mademoiselle Colombe, 349
Madonna and Child, 378
Madwoman of Chaillot, The, 350, 365
Magic and the Loss, The, 367
Magic Glass, The, 383
Magical City, The, 377
Magnificent Yankee, The, 364
Magnolia, 382
Maidens and Mistresses at Home at the Zoo, 50
Majority of One, A, 5, 11, 25, 26, **323**, 341
Make a Million, 24, **299**, 341
Making of Moo, The, 51, 101, 350
Male Animal, The, 362
Mamma's Affair, 355
Man from Home, The, 354
Man in the Dog Suit, The, 9-10, **300-301**, 341
Man of God, A, 351
Man Who Came to Dinner, The, 344, 362
Man with a Load of Mischief, 381
Man Who Never Died, The, 51
Mandragola, 381
Many Loves, 50
Margin for Error, 362
Maria Golovin, **302**, 341
Marie Tudor, 27, 295
Marionettes, The, 384
Mark Twain Tonight, 50
Marriage-Go-Round, The, 22, 23, **300**, 341
Martine, 388
Mary, 388
Mary of Scotland, 359, 377
Mary Rose, 355
Mary the 3d, 356, 379
Mask and Gown, 42
Masque of Kings, The, 377
Masquerade, 330, 341
Matchmaker, The, 53, 367
Maurice Harte, 383
Me and Molly, 365
Measure for Measure, 316
Meet the Prince, 378
Member of the Wedding, The, 345, 346, 365
Men in White, 347, 359
Merchant of Venice, The, 316
Merrily We Roll Along, 360
Merton of the Movies, 356
Michael and Mary, 358
Mid-Summer, 280
Midsummer Night's Dream, A, 316
Minick, 356
Miss Dolly Dollars, 381
Miss Lulu Bett, 347
Mister Roberts, 344, 364, 385
Misunderstanding, The, 349
Mlle. Mischief, 381
Moon Flower, The, 377
Moon for the Misbegotten, A, 368
Moon Is Blue, The, 344
Moon Is Down, The, 362
Morning's at Seven, 362
Most Happy Fella, The, **322-323**, 342, 345
Mountain Giants, The, 352
Mourning Becomes Electra, 359
Mr. and Mrs. North, 362
Mrs. Bumpstead-Leigh, 354
Mrs. McThing, 366
Mrs. Partridge Presents, 356

INDEX OF PLAYS AND CASTS

Much Ado About Nothing, 316
Murder in the Cathedral, 381
Music Man, The, 40, 42, 345
Music Master, The, 345
My Fair Lady, 40, 42, 43, 344, 367
My Sister Eileen, 344, 362
My 3 Angels, 366
Myself Bettina, 379

Nathan the Wise, 380
Native Son, 362
Nellie Bly, 380
Nervous Set, The, 38, 336-337, 341
Nest, The, 355
Nest Egg, The, 387
Never Say Die, 378
New Moon, The, 345
Nice People, 355
Night Circus, The, 8, **308**, 341
Night of the Auk, 53
Night Over Taos, 377
Night's Lodging, A, 382
Nightstick, 381
No More Ladies, 360
No Questions Asked, 383
No Time for Comedy, 144, 361
No Time for Sergeants, 344, 367
Nobody's Daughter, 386
Not in the Book, 342
Nuts and Wine, 378

O Mistress Mine, 364
Of Mice and Men, 53, 346, **361**
Of Thee I Sing, 347, 359
Oh Captain!, 342, 343
Oh Promise Me, 385
Oklahoma!, 344, 363
Old Lady, 31, 379
Old Maid, The, 347, 360, 377
Old Soak, The, 356
Old Town, The, 387
Olé, 53
On Borrowed Time, 361
On the Town, 53
On to Buffalo, 379
On Trial, 354
Once in a Lifetime, 358
Once Is Enough, 382
Once More, with Feeling, 22, **298**, 341, 351
Once Upon a Mattress, **335-336**
Ondine, 350
One Sunday Afternoon, 359
One Touch of Venus, 345
Orpheus Descending, 14, 53, 209, 368
Othello, 52, 316
Our Town, 49, 53, 347, 361, 387
Outrageous Fortune, 363
Outward Bound, 356
Over 21, 363
Overture, 359

Paddy the Next Best Thing, 383
Pajama Game, The, 344
Pal Joey, 345
Panama Hattie, 345
Papa, 377
Paris Bound, 357
Parisienne, 381
Party with Betty Comden and Adolph Green, A, 54, 315, 341

Passing of the Third Floor Back, The, 383, 384
Passion Flower, The, 382
Patate, 22-23, 280, **300**, 341
Patriots, The, 346, 362
Peg o' My Heart, 344
Personal Appearance, 345
Petrified Forest, The, 360, 378
Philadelphia Story, The, 361
Philoctetes, 52
Pick-up Girl, 363
Picnic, 346, 348, 351, 366
Pigeons and People, 359
Pins and Needles, 344
Pi-Pa-Ki, 329
Play of Daniel, The, 52
Play's the Thing, The, 357
Pleasure of His Company, The, 20, 21-22, 78-100, **298-299**, 341, 353
Plough and the Stars, The, 358
Plume de Ma Tante, La, 30, 31, 34, **303-305**, 341, 346
Plus Fours, 383
Point of No Return, 366
Poker Game, 342
Ponder Heart, The, 367
Porgy, 357
Portrait of a Madonna, **333**
Potters, The, 382
Potting Shed, The, 53, 368
Pound on Demand, A, **333**
Power and the Glory, The, **311-312**
Precious Bane, 380
Prelude to Exile, 387
Pride and Prejudice, 34, 331, 360
Prince Chap, The, 380
Prisoner of Zenda, The, 378
Prologue to Glory, 361
Prunella, 382
Purple Dust, 350

Quare Fellow, The, 49

R.U.R., 356
Racket, The, 358
Rain, 345, 355
Rain or Shine, 379
Rainmaker, The, 8
Raisin in the Sun, A, 4, 6, 15-16, 40, 42, 232-254, **328-329**, 341, 346
Rashomon, 4, 5, 11, 17-19, **317-318**, 341
Rebound, 358
Reclining Figure, 22
Red Mill, The, 345, 387
Redemptor, The, 51
Redhead, 35, 279, **319-320**, 341
Remains to Be Seen, 366
Requiem for a Nun, 16-17, 189-208, **319**, 341, 350
Restless Heart, 349
Reunion in Vienna, 359
Richard II, 316
Richard III, 316, 382
Riddle Me This, 382
Rivalry, The, 6, 29, **321**, 341
Road to Rome, The, 357
Rocket to the Moon, 361
Romance, 354
Romanoff and Juliet, 40, 42, 343
Romeo and Juliet, 316, 384
Room Service, 345

INDEX OF PLAYS AND CASTS

Rope Dancers, The, 53, 368
Rosalinda, 345
Rose Marie, 345
Rose Tattoo, The, 209, 366
Royal Family, The, 357
Royal Gambit, 51
Rugged Path, The, 364
Russet Mantle, 387
Ryan Girl, The, 384

Sabrina Fair, 78
Sailor, Beware!, 345
St. Helena, 361
Saint Joan, 384
Saintliness of Margery Kempe, The, 51
Salad Days, 53
Sally, 345
Saturday's Children, 357
Say, Darling, 324-325, 342, 343, 386
Scourge, The, 379
Searching Wind, The, 78, 363
Season in the Sun, 366, 381
Season of Choice, 51
Second Man, The, 144
Second Threshold, 366
See the Jaguar, 7
Separate Rooms, 345
Separate Tables, 53, 368
Seven Days, 385
Seven Deadly Sins, The, 54
Seven Keys to Baldpate, 354
Seven Year Itch, The, 344
Seventh Heaven, 344
Sex Fable, The, 386
Shadow and Substance, 361
Shadow of a Gunman, The, 27, **305**, 341
Shadows, 379
Shakespeare's Merchant—1939, **388**
Shannons of Broadway, The, 381
She Shall Have Music, 53
Shewing-Up of Blanco Posnet, The, 383
Shining Hour, The, 360
Show Boat, 345
Show-Off, The, 20, 345, 356
Shrike, The, 348, 366
Shuffle Along, 345
Silver Cord, The, 357
Silver Whistle, The, 365
Six Cylinder Love, 40, 355
Skin Game, The, 355
Skin of Our Teeth, The, 347, 363
Skipper Next to God, 364
Skylark, 362
Smiling, 379
Smokeweaver's Daughter, The, 51
Society Circus, A, 345
Soldier's Wife, 363
Solid Gold Cadillac, The, 345
Some Comments on the Harmful Effects of Tobacco, **333**
Song of Norway, 344
Song of Songs, 50
South Pacific, 344, 348
Spanish Love, 385
Square Root of Wonderful, The, 352
Star and Garter, 345
Squaw Man, The, 354
Stage Door, 361
Starcross Story, The, 384
Starlight Express, The, 383
Star-Wagon, The, 361

Starward Ark, 342
State of Siege, 349
State of the Union, 344, 347, 363
Stepping Stones, 387
Stork, The, 378
Storm Operation, 363, 377
Story of Mary Surrat, The, 364
Strange Interlude, 59, 347, 357
Stranger in a Strange Land, A, 387
Street Scene, 54, 345, 347, 358
Streetcar Named Desire, A, 209, 344, 346, 347, 364
Streets of Paris, The, 379
Stricken Blind, 381
Strictly Dishonorable, 345, 358
Strongheart, 386
Student Prince, The, 345
Summer and Smoke, 53, 209
Summer of the 17th Doll, 368
Sunny, 345
Sunrise at Campobello, 342, 343, 345, 368
Sun-Up, 356
Susan and God, 361, 379
Swan, The, 356
Sweet Bird of Youth, 14-15, 209-231, **328**, 341
Swim in the Sea, 342

Tailor Made Man, A, 386
Take a Giant Step, 366
Tall Story, 25-26, **318-319**, 341, 351
Tarnish, 356
Taste of Honey, A, 47
Tea and Sympathy, 344, 367
Teahouse of the August Moon, The, 344, 346, 348, 366
Tempest, The, 316
Texas Nightingale, The, 377
That Lady, 386
There Shall Be No Night, 347, 361
They Knew What They Wanted, 347, 356
They Shall Not Die, 360
Third Best Sport, The, 24-25, **316-317**, 341
39 East, 379
Thoroughbred, 382
Three Guardsmen, The, 387
Three Men on a Horse, 344
Three of Us, The, 379
Three Sisters, 388
Threepenny Opera, The, 53
Tiger at the Gates, 367
Time of the Cuckoo, The, 52, **366**
Time of Your Life, The, 346, 347, **362**
Time Remembered, 342, 343, 349, 368
Tip-Top, 387
'Tis Pity She's a Whore, 52
Tobacco Road, 344
Tommy, 385
Tomorrow and Tomorrow, 358
Tomorrow the World, 345, 363
Touch of the Poet, A, 6-7, 59-77, **293**, 341
Tovarich, 361
Tragedy of Nan, The, 382
Triomphe de l'Amour, Le, 295
Trip to Bountiful, A, 53
Trip to Chinatown, A, 345
Triple Play, 28, 280, **333-334**, 341
Tunnel of Love, 41, 42
Twelfth Night, 27, 28, 41, 52, **310**
Two Blind Mice, 365
Two for the Seesaw, 40, 42, 345

INDEX OF PLAYS AND CASTS   401

Two Mrs. Carrolls, The, 345
Two Orphans, The, 387

Ulysses in Nighttown, 55, 350
Unchastened Woman, The, 354
Uncle Harry, 362
Under Milk Wood, 368
Up in Central Park, 345

Vagabond King, The, 345
Valley Forge, 360, 377
Vanderbilt Cup, The, 378
Varying Shore, The, 377
Venus Observed, 366
Very Special Baby, A, 368
Victoria Regina, 345, 360, 382
Victory Belles, 378
View from the Bridge, A, 367
Visit, The, 342, 343, 346, 368
Visit to a Small Planet, 368
Voice of the Turtle, The, 344, 363

Waiting for Godot, 53, 367
Waltz of the Toreadors, The, 53, 368
Warm Peninsula, The, 41, 42
Warrens of Virginia, The, 380
Watch on the Rhine, 346, 362
We Americans, 386
We, the People, 359
Wedding Bells, 355
Wednesday's Child, 360
Welcome Stranger, 378
West Side Story, 43, 344
What a Life, 78, 345, 361
What Price Glory?, 356, 377
Wheel of Fortune, The, 383
When Ladies Meet, 359, 379
When We Dead Awaken, 351
Where's Charlie?, 344
White Cargo, 344
White Desert, 377
White Steed, The, 361

White-Headed Boy, The, 385
Who Was That Lady I Saw You With?, 342, 343
Whoop-Up, 31, 284, 314, 341
Who's Your Father?, 47
Why Marry?, 347, 354
Why Not?, 356
Wild Birds, 356
Wind from the South, A, 350
Winesburg, Ohio, 24
Winged Victory, 363
Wingless Victory, The, 377
Wings Over Europe, 358
Winslow Boy, The, 364
Winter Soldiers, 363
Winter's Tale, The, 316
Winterset, 346, 360, 377
Wisdom Tooth, The, 357
Wish You Were Here, 345
Wisteria Trees, The, 365
Witching Hour, The, 354
Within the Law, 345
Witness for the Prosecution, 345, 367
Wizard of Oz, The, 387
Women, The, 345, 361
Wonderful Town, 345, 366
World of Paul Slickey, The, 44-46
World of Suzie Wong, The, 4, 11-12, 277, 296-297, 341
World We Make, The, 361

Years Ago, 364
Yes, My Darling Daughter, 361
You and I, 355, 382
You Can't Take It with You, 344, 347, 360, 387
You Touched Me, 209
Young Woodley, 357
Youngest, The, 356
Your Uncle Dudley, 385

Ziegfeld Follies, 345

INDEX OF PRODUCERS, DIRECTORS, DESIGNERS, STAGE MANAGERS, COMPOSERS, LYRICISTS AND CHOREOGRAPHERS

Abbott, George, 21, 78, 294, 336
Abbott, Michael, 318
Actors' Studio, Inc., 305
Adams, Bret, 316
Adams, Roger, 320, 336
Adler, Ernest, 335
Aldredge, Theoni Vachlioti, 337
Allen, Ben G., 319
Allen, John, 294, 336
Allen, Lewis, 301
Alswang, Ralph, 301, 317, 329
Ames, Louis B., 302
Amram, David, 298, 312, 313, 321, 333
Anderson, Leroy, 30, 294, 295
Anthony, Joseph, 300

Armstrong, Betty Coe, 325
Armstrong, Will Steven, 298, 312
Aronson, Boris, 13, 309, 313
Arthur, Hartney, 321, 322
Arts Council of Great Britain, 310
Auerbach, Leonard, 329
Austin, Lyn, 327
Axelrod, George, 298

Ball, William, 49
Ballard, Lucinda, 293, 297, 313
Ballou, 322
Banton, Travis, 292
Barer, Marshall, 335
Barratt, Watson, 322-323, 330

402 INDEX OF PRODUCERS, DIRECTORS, DESIGNERS

Barry, Julian, 309
Bataille, Andre, 296
Bay, Howard, 332
Beaton, Cecil, 26, 326
Beck, Arthur, 336
Bender, Richard, 300
Bennett, Robert Russell, 307, 320, 327
Benthall, Michael, 310, 311
Berlin, Irving, 369
Bernstein, Leonard, 287, 315, 368, 369
Bilowit, Ira, 53
Blackton, Jay, 320
Blitzstein, Marc, 3, 34-35, 326, 327
Bloomgarden, Kermit, 323
Bogin, Abba, 322
Bowden, Charles, 291
Bowles, Paul, 306, 328
Bowman, Ross, 320
Brisson, Frederick, 298, 313
Brooks, Alfred, 53
Brooks, Randall, 327
Brosset, Colette, 303
Broun, Daniel S., 313
Brown, Max, 334
Brownstone, Joseph, 293
Buchman, Irving, 305, 321
Burrows, Abe, 331

Callan, William, 330, 333
Calvi, Gerard, 303
Campbell, Patton, 292
Carr, Alan, 40
Carr, Lawrence, 319
Carroll, Earl, 389
Carte, Rupert D'Oyly, 389
Chambers, William, 297
Chaplin, Saul, 315
Charlap, Moose, 314
Chodorov, Jerome, 299, 313, 362, 366, 367
Chotzinoff, Samuel, 302
Circle-in-the-Square, 49, 53
Clark, Peggy, 292, 307, 325, 327
Clarke, Harley, 40
Clive, David, 325
Clurman, Harold, 293, 309, 350, 370
Cogan, David J., 328
Colt, Alvin, 325, 331, 335
Colyer, Carlton, 306
Comden, Betty, 3, 28, 54, 315, 324, 366
Cornell, John, 319
Corsaro, Frank, 308
Corwin, Norman, 321
Crawford, Cheryl, 302, 305, 321, 328, 370
Cronyn, Hume, 334
Cruddas, Audrey, 311
Curtis, Keene, 326

DaCosta, Morton, 291-292
d'Almeida, Louis, 330
Dalrymple, Jean, 322, 324, 329
Danielewski, Tad, 332
Darrid, William, 308
Dell'Isola, Salvatore, 307
De Mille, Agnes, 35, 295, 327
De Mille, Cecil B., 380
De Nobili, Lilla, 304
Devereaux, John Drew, 297
de Wilde, Frederic, 295
Dhery, Robert, 303
Dignimont, 303, 304

Dodds, William, 326
Dohanos, Peter, 333
Dolan, Robert Emmett, 327
Doncaster, Stephen, 301, 317
Downing, Robert, 313
Drulie, Sylvia, 291
du Bois, Raoul Pène, 338
Dukes, Ashley, 380-381
Durand, Charles, 292
Dvonch, Frederick, 331

East End Theatre Workshop (London), 47
Eckart, Jean, 335, 336
Eckart, William, 335, 336
Edens, Roger, 315
Edwards, Ben, 293, 309, 316, 325
Elson, Charles, 302, 303, 331
Engel, Lehman, 295, 335
English Stage (Royal Court) Company, 45, 47, 48, 101, 301, 317
Enters, Warren, 330
Equity Library Theatre, 53
Erte, 304, 305
Esterel, Jacques, 304
Evans, Richard, 302

Feder, 309
Feld, Morris, 332
Ferrer, José, 305, 306, 327, 371
Feuer, Cy, 314
Field, Bill, 325
Fields, Dorothy, 319
Fields, Joseph, 306
Flicker, Theodore J., 337
Foley, Paul A., 301, 334
Ford, David, 323
Ford, Joan, 294
Forsythe, Charles, 293
Fosse, Bob, 320
Fox, Frederick, 292
Franchot, Richard, 319
Franchot Productions, 306
Friedman, Phil, 314, 331
Fryer, Robert, 319

Gabel, Martin, 298
Garen, Leo, 51
Garfein, Jack, 305
Garon, Jay, 332
Gaskill, William, 301, 317
Gelb, James, 295, 309
Gershwin, George, 347, 351, 359
Gershwin, Ira, 347, 359, 371
Gerstad, John, 292
Gersten, Bernard, 306, 322
Gersten, Leon, 322
Geyra, Zvi, 306
Gielgud, Sir John, 27, 29, 42, 371
Gilbert, George, 331
Gimbel, Norman, 314
Ginzler, Robert, 338
Gischia, Leon, 295
Glenville, Peter, 19, 318
Goldman, Byron, 302
Goldman, Robert, 331
Gould, Morton, 315
Graham, Anne, 333
Green, Adolph, 3, 28, 54, 315, 324, 366

INDEX OF PRODUCERS, DIRECTORS, DESIGNERS 403

Gregory, Paul, 300
Grossman, Herbert, 302

Haber, David, 316
Hacha, Robert, 308
Hague, Albert, 319
Halpern, Morty, 309
Hambleton, T. Edward, 297, 311, 323, 335
Hamilton, Lance, 325
Hammerstein, James, 307
Hammerstein, Oscar, 2nd, 3, 4, 30-31, 306, 348, 352, 363, 364, 372
Hammerstein, Ted, 307
Haney, Carol, 307
Hanighen, Bernard, 329
Hardin, Lo, 338
Harris, Sam, 40, 386
Harris, Sylvia, 299
Hart, Lorenz, 31, 389
Hartley, Neil, 297, 303
Hastings, Hal, 336
Hays, David, 49, 308, 321, 334
Hayward, Leland, 337
Head, Edith, 299, 306
Hearn, Fred, 307
Hebert, Fred, 299, 313
Heeley, Desmond, 310
Henderson, Luther, Jr., 307
Hepton, Bernard, 311
Herndon, Richard G., 381-382
Hess, Edgar, 299
Holm, Klaus, 312
Horner, Jed, 300
Hornsby, Joe, 319
Houghton, Norris, 297, 298, 311, 323, 335
Howard, Michael, 317
Howard, Peter, 315, 332
Hurok, Sol, 295, 310
Huxley, Carroll, 336
Hylton, Jack, 303

Jackson, Scott, 306
Jacob, Gordon, 310, 311
Jarre, Maurice, 295, 296
Jeakins, Dorothy, 297, 306
Jenkins, George, 298, 306, 319
JJG Productions, 315
Johnstone, Anna Hill, 301, 314, 328, 334
Jones, Robert Edmond, 330
Julien, Edward, 308
Julien, Jay, 308

Kander, John, 338
Kanter, David, 298
Kapfer, Joseph, 292
Kasha, Lawrence N., 314
Kay, Hershy, 327, 336
Kazan, Elia, 13, 171, 313, 328, 373
Kelly, Gene, 307
Kern, Jerome D., 390
Kerr, Jean, 294
Kerr, Walter, 294, 295
Kidd, Michael, 334
Kingsley, Gershon, 303
Kipness, Joseph, 303
Krakeur, Richard W., 330
Krupska, Dania, 322

Laffey, Bruce, 299
Landesman, Fran, 336

Lang, Philip J., 295, 314, 320, 335
Langner, Philip, 323
Lantz, Robert, 336
Lanvin-Castillo, 300
Larkin, Peter, 295, 305, 331
Layton, Joe, 336
Leaf, Paul, 298
Lebowsky, Stanley, 314
Lehar, Franz, 390
Lehr, Wilson, 53
Leider, Jerry, 316
Leigh, Sanford, 316
Le Marquet, Jacques, 296
Leonard, Mickey, 332
Leve, Sam, 303
Levin, Sylvan, 330
Levine, Joseph I., 313
Lewis, Robert, 293
Liagre, Alfred de, Jr., 297, 312
Liebman, Max, 386
Lief, Arthur, 310, 311
Linden, Robert, 320
Lloyd, John Robert, 293, 294
Loesser, Frank, 322, 365
Loesser, Lynn, 323
Loewe, Frederick, 364, 367
Logan, Joshua, 297, 301, 317, 348, 373
Longe, Jeffery, 292
Lucas, Jonathan, 331

MacCardell, Cameron, 317
Mackintosh, Robert, 317, 330
Mamoulian, Rouben, 373
Mankoff, Allan, 337
Mansfield Productions, 296
Margolis, Henry, 298
Marlowe, Arthur, 297
Marshall, Frederick, 311
Martin, Elliot, 323
Martin, Ernest H., 314
Masterson, Carroll, 325
Masterson, Harris, 325
Mattox, Matt, 325
Matz, Peter, 314
Mays, Ken, 315
McKayle, Donald, 320
Menotti, Gian-Carlo, 302, 374
Meredith, Burgess, 55, 325, 374
Merrick, David, 296, 301, 302, 303, 317, 334, 337
Messel, Oliver, 17, 318
Mestel, Jacob, 383
Meyer, Dede, 53
Mielziner, Jo, 17, 293, 297, 313, 314, 318, 322, 328, 338, 374
Miller, Bernard, 301, 317
Miller, Gilbert, 300, 325, 374, 381
Miller, Kathryn, 300
Monro, Ronnie, 303
Moorehead, Agnes, 374
Mori, Torao, 318
Morley, Ruth, 305, 322, 330
Morrison, Paul, 299, 330, 333, 337
Morse, Barry, 53
Motley, 309, 319, 321, 323
Mowery, Irl, 325
Mulligan, Robert, 303
Musser, Tharon, 305, 313, 321, 336
Myerberg, Michael, 330
Myers & Fleischmann, 319

404 INDEX OF PRODUCERS, DIRECTORS, DESIGNERS

National Broadcasting Company, 302
Neal, Walter, 309
Nelson, Ralph, 301
New York City Center Light Opera Company, 322, 324, 329
New York City Center of Music and Drama, Inc., 291
Nielsen, Karl, 317, 332
Nimura, Yeichi, 330

O'Brien, Chet, 323, 330
O'Brien, Gerald, 299
Oenslager, Donald, 297, 299, 300, 301, 323, 374
Old Vic Company, The, 27, 28, 41, 42, 310-311, 342
Osterman, Lester, 325

Padula, Edward, 325
Pakula, Alan, 302
Papp, Joseph, 52, 303
Pardoll, David, 328
Parker, Dorothy, 368
Parker, Ross, 303
Partington, Arthur F., 322
Paschall, Robert, 292, 318
Patrick, Leonard, 301, 335
Paul, John, 330
Paxton, Glenn, 331
Pennec, Henri, 304
Perlowin, Gene, 296
Perry, Frank, 315
Philipe, Gerard, 295
Phoenix Theatre, 28
Pitot, Genevieve, 335
Playwrights' Company, 144, 292, 298, 305, 306, 313, 325, 326, 377
Pollock, Bernard, 328
Pons, Helene, 301, 302, 317
Porter, Cole, 374
Pressman, David, 309
Previn, Andre, 315
Producers Theatre, 293, 294, 300, 309
Psacharopoulos, Nikos, 52

Quick, George, 336
Quintero, José, 49

Ragotzy, Jack, 52
Ramin, Sid, 338
Randall, Richard, 333
Rea, Oliver, 326
Reiss, Marvin, 315, 317, 319
Rice, Elmer, 306
Richards, Lloyd, 329
Richardson, Tony, 319
Ritchard, Cyril, 21, 26, 299, 326, 375
Robertson, John, 298, 312
Robbins, Jerome, 38, 338
Rodgers, Mary, 335
Rodgers, Richard, 3, 4, 30-31, 306, 348, 352, 363, 364, 375
Rogers, Emmett, 318
Romberg, Sigmund, 390
Rome, Harold, 3, 35, 334
Romoff, Colin, 325
Rose, Philip, 328
Rosenstock, Milton, 338
Rosenthal, Jean, 309, 320, 335
Rosenthal, Laurence, 295, 318

Ross, Bill, 300
Ross, George, 293
Roth, Ann, 299, 309, 332
Russell, Charles, 325

Saidenberg, Eleanore, 308
San Francisco Actors Workshop, 53
Saveron, Pierre, 296
Scaasi, 298
Schary, Dore, 323, 333
Schechtman, Saul, 292
Schenker, Joel, 305, 321
Schirmer, Gus, Jr., 315
Schneider, Alan, 333
Scott, Raymond, 54, 329
Selwyn, Archie, 40
Selwyn, Edgar, 40
Seven Arts Productions, Inc., 296
Shanks, Alec, 303, 304
Shapiro, Herman, 330
Sharaff, Irene, 307, 327
Shubert, Lee, 390
Shumlin, Herman, 319, 375
Sieg, John, 330
Siegel, Max, 386
Slevin, James M., 292
Smith, Fred, 331
Smith, Hardy, 317
Smith, Oliver, 292, 307, 325, 326, 327, 335
Smith, Peter, 310
Sokoler, Bob, 332
Sondheim, Stephen, 38, 337
Sovey, Raymond, 300, 326
Specter Productions, Inc., 331
Spector, Joel, 299
Stevens, Nat, 321
Stewart, Maurice, 310
Stone, Harold, 303
Straight, Willard, 322
Strobach, Ben, 292
Stuckmann, Eugene, 300
Styne, Jule, 38, 315, 324, 337
Susskind, David, 292, 317
Swackhamer, E. W., 313
Sze, Julia, 294

Taylor, Noel, 292, 303, 319
Teifer, Jerry, 319
Tennent Productions Ltd., 316
Ter-Arutunian, Rouben, 302, 320
Ternent, Billy, 303
Thalberg, Irving, 386
Theatre Guild, 315, 316, 319, 323, 333
Theatre Incorporated, 297, 311, 323
Théâtre National Populaire, 27, 295-296, 342
Thoma, Mike, 319
Thomajan, Guy, 328
Thomas, Edward, 319
Todd, Michael, 390
Todd, Michael, Jr., 39, 40
Toner, Thomas, 306
Town Productions, Inc., 315
Travis, Michael, 298, 317
Twain, Norman, 301, 317

Vaughan, Stuart, 298, 312
Vega, Jose, 293, 318
Velez, Henry, 325

INDEX OF PRODUCERS, DIRECTORS, DESIGNERS

Vertes, 303
Vilar, Jean, 27, 295, 296
Vincent, Walter, 387
Volland, Virginia, 313, 329
von Twardowski, Hans Heinrich, 387-388

Walker, Don, 331
Watson, Lee, 308, 322
Weill, Kurt, 54, 365, 377
Weiner, Robert, 318
Weinstein, Henry T., 317, 334
Weiss, George, 331
Welles, Orson, 376
Whelen, Christopher, 46
White, George, 383, 388
White, Onna, 314

Whitehead, Robert, 293, 294, 309
Wilbur, Richard, 368
Williams, Mervyn, 329
Windust, Bretaigne, 297
Winfield, Marjorie, 301, 334
Wolf, Tommy, 336, 337
Wood, Bert, 294, 323
Wood, Charles R., 325
Woods, Robert, 298, 312
Woolf, Stanley, 388

Youmans, Vincent, 390

Zeisler, Peter, 327
Ziegfeld, Florenz, 383
Zipprodt, Patricia, 308